D0929665

Colonialism and Cold War

Colonialism and Cold War

THE UNITED STATES AND THE STRUGGLE FOR INDONESIAN INDEPENDENCE, 1945–49

ROBERT J. MCMAHON

Cornell University Press

ITHACA AND LONDON

Cornell University Press gratefully acknowledges a grant from the Andrew W. Mellon Foundation that aided in bringing this book to publication.

First published 1981 by Cornell University Press.
Published in the United Kingdom by Cornell University Press Ltd.,
Ely House, 37 Dover Street, London W1X 4HQ.

International Standard Book Number 0-8014-1388-5
Library of Congress Catalog Card Number 81-66648
Printed in the United States of America
Librarians: Library of Congress cataloging information appears on the last page of the book.

To my parents,
William J. McMahon *and*
Mary Sullivan McMahon

CONTENTS

MAPS

PREFACE

The proceedings were solemn and moving, though surprisingly matter-of-fact for such a historic occasion. Only about three hundred people witnessed the thirty-two-minute ceremony in the marble Burgherzall (Hall of Citizens) in the seventeenth-century royal palace in Amsterdam. The seven Indonesian delegates and the members of the Dutch cabinet, along with other high-ranking Dutch officials and some members of the diplomatic corps, stood at their places along both sides of a red-felt-covered table as Queen Juliana was escorted into the hall by two of her ministers. Dressed in black velvet, with a collar of emeralds glimmering at her neck, she took the seat left vacant for her between Indonesian Prime Minister Mohammed Hatta and Dutch Prime Minister Willem Drees.

A protocol covering the results of the recent round-table conference was read aloud, and the two leaders signed it. Then the queen signed an act of confirmation in which she gave her assent to "the new order of law" between the Netherlands and the Indonesian Republic. "It is a privilege to perform this act of transfer as it stands in history," she declared, "or rather in the face of God, who knows why this march hand-in-hand in freedom was not achieved sooner nor later, and who knows the feelings of generations, but who also watches whether we can use this plan for the progress of mankind. May this now be so."[1]

[1]Quoted in Selden Chapin (ambassador in the Netherlands) to Secretary of State Dean Acheson, December 27, 1949, in *Foreign Relations of the United States*, vol. 7, *The Far East and Australasia*, pt. 1 (Washington, D.C.: U.S. Government Printing Office, 1975), pp. 588–99.

Following her speech, the national anthems of both countries were played; and although a note on the program requested the participants and witnesses to the ceremony not to sing, the sound of voices soon filled the hall. At 10:22 A.M., December 27, 1949, the transfer of sovereignty was completed, formally ending 347 years of Dutch rule over the East Indies.

A simultaneous ceremony in Djakarta, more than 8,000 miles away, was far less restrained. There, in front of the white palace of the Dutch governors, in the city they had called Batavia, Dutch High Commissioner A. H. J. Lovink and Indonesian Deputy Prime Minister Sultan Hamengku Buwono solemnly signed the protocol of transfer. After their speeches, a military band played the Dutch national anthem as the Dutch tricolor was hauled down, and then played the Indonesian national anthem as the flag of Indonesia was hoisted in its place. The sight of the formerly banned red-and-white flag flying majestically over a building that had been the very symbol of the Dutch imperium drove the crowd of 20,000 to a frenzy. The celebration lasted long into the night, with the sounds of Javanese gongs and drums blaring from loudspeakers at the street corners. Seemingly oblivious of the damp heat of a tropical evening, crowds surged throughout the city screaming, "*Merdeka!*" (freedom) and proudly waving homemade red-and-white flags. After four long and often bloody years of conflict, a night of festivity was well earned.

But the real Indonesian celebration did not take place until the next day, when Sukarno, the man who had come to personify the Indonesian independence movement, triumphantly returned to Djakarta. Driven from the capital by the Dutch four years earlier, Sukarno was now coming back to take up residence in the palace of the Dutch governors as the first president of an independent Indonesia. A huge crowd at Kamajoran airport roared as he stepped from his newly painted red-and-white Dakota plane, wearing a simple white naval uniform and a traditional black fez. Along the four-mile route from the airport to the city, crowds snarled traffic in a boisterous and emotional tribute to their president as Sukarno stood in his open maroon Packard, smiling, waving, and warmly responding to the continuous cries of "Merdeka!" The streets were full of exuberant people and the colorful flag of the new republic was everywhere. A crowd of 200,000 filled Koningsplein Square, facing the palace, as Sukarno gave a stirring five-minute speech from the marble steps. He ended his address with the cry "*Sekali merdeka!*" (once free, forever free). One foreign diplomat, waving in the direction of the vast crowds, remarked to a colleague: "Could the Dutch ever have held this, in the face of that?"[2]

Perhaps no process has had a greater influence on the modern era than the dismantling of former colonial empires in Asia and Africa after World War II. Decolonization has few parallels as an agent of historical change. Not only has it irrevocably altered the very political map of the globe, but it has also profoundly affected the international balance of power and challenged the continuation of Western hegemony over the world. "Between 1945 and 1960," observed Geoffrey Barraclough, "no less than forty countries with a population of eight hundred million—more than a quarter of the world's inhabitants—revolted against colonialism and won their independence. Never before in human history had so revolutionary a reversal occurred with such rapidity."[3]

The United States, which emerged as the world's preeminent military and economic power in the postwar period and which prided itself on its anticolonial tradition and heritage, was in a unique position to influence these decolonization struggles. To be sure, Asian and African nationalist leaders were often disappointed by the minimal moral and material support they received from Washington. Still, they looked to the United States as the nation most likely to sympathize with their aspirations and often pointed to it as an inspiration in both its history and its ideals. One area where American diplomacy had a major

[2]Quoted in *Time*, January 9, 1950, p. 20. This account has been drawn also from the following additional sources: *New York Times*, December 27, 1949, p. 18; December 28, 1949, pp. 1, 5; December 29, 1949, p. 12; and January 1, 1950, IV, p. 2; *Newsweek*, January 9, 1950, pp. 30–31; *The Times* (London), December 28, 1949, p. 6, and December 29, 1949, p. 4; *Washington Star*, December 27, 1949, p. 1; Ali Sastroamidjojo, *Milestones on My Journey: The Memoirs of Ali Sastroamidjojo, Indonesian Patriot and Leader*, ed. C. L. M. Penders (St. Lucia: University of Queensland Press, 1979), p. 207.

[3]Geoffrey Barraclough, *An Introduction to Contemporary History* (Baltimore: Penguin, 1967), p. 153.

impact on the decolonization process was the Netherlands East Indies, the sprawling archipelago that since the early seventeenth century had been the jewel of the Dutch colonial empire. Direct American pressure on the Dutch in the spring of 1949, as much as any other single factor, compelled the Netherlands to grant independence to its rich colony, and so paved the way to the historic ceremony in the Burgherzall.

This book examines the role of the United States in the often violent movement toward Indonesian independence. In recent years scholars have shown considerable interest in the confrontation between the United States and revolutionary movements in the so-called Third World, but only rarely have they analyzed the role of American foreign policy in the dénouement of the European imperial order. Yet the interaction between American diplomacy and the rise of numerous independent states in Asia, Africa, and the Middle East is of the utmost historical significance. Only through a careful analysis of the American reaction to the colonial issue—and, conversely, the reaction of the colonized peoples to American diplomacy—can Washington's relations with the Third World be understood in their proper historical context.

The first two chapters provide background material. Chapter 1 surveys the history of Dutch colonial rule in Indonesia and the subsequent rise of nationalism among the peoples of the East Indies. Chapter 2 examines American–East Indian relations before 1945. Since American policy toward the East Indies came to be subsumed under the general problem of colonialism during World War II, this chapter also offers an interpretation of Washington's historical opposition to European imperialism. It demonstrates how idealism and self-interest merged in an American anticolonial tradition—a tradition that influenced and conditioned the U.S. response to nationalism in Indonesia.

The following chapters focus more directly on the American role in the Dutch–Indonesian struggle, beginning with the American reaction to the proclamation of the Republic of Indonesia in August 1945. U.S. diplomacy exerted an important influence on the conflict from its very inception, and these chapters document and interpret the extent of that influence. At first Washington sought to remain neutral and uninvolved, but that policy was tantamount to acquiescence in a return to the status quo ante bellum and it had a profound effect on the early stages of the contest. By 1947 the United States had begun to take a more active interest in the East Indies. As a member of the Good Offices Committee of the United Nations and the UN Commission for Indonesia, the United States played a pivotal role in the mediation of the dispute. Its massive financial assistance to the Netherlands government through the Marshall Plan, moreover, drew the United States even more deeply into the Dutch–Indonesian imbroglio. When the Dutch launched a second military offensive against the republic in December 1948, and were condemned by the international community as well as the American public and Congress, the Truman administration began to reevaluate its policy toward the dispute. Shortly thereafter, the United States threatened to suspend all economic aid to Holland if it did not grant independence to Indonesia. This action proved to be the turning point of the struggle.

Despite its importance, I have tried to avoid an exclusive focus on American policy, which would necessarily distort any study of the decolonization process in the East Indies. Instead, I have attempted to provide the necessary context for an understanding of American policy by examining Indonesian internal developments and the complicated and often tortuous negotiations between the Dutch and the Indonesians, as well as the role of other powers. Great Britain, for example, which occupied the Indies on behalf of the Allies in September 1945, influenced the initial phase of the conflict more than any other power. Consequently, Chapters 3 and 4 closely evaluate British actions, which were crucial for the early establishment of the Republic of Indonesia. These chapters also consider Indonesia as an issue in Anglo–American relations and trace the way in which the United States moved to supplant Britain's influence in the Indies after the withdrawal of British troops in November 1946.

Nonetheless, this work is primarily a study of American diplomacy, and as such it focuses chiefly on American attitudes, policies, and actions. My principal interest is to explain Washington's response to the Indonesian revolution within the context of overall U.S. foreign policy objectives. Consequently, this book does not pretend to be a comprehensive history of the decolonization of the Dutch East Indies, nor does it pretend to offer the final word on the actions and motivations of the other major actors: the Dutch, the British, and the Indonesians themselves.

Although the process of decolonization in Indonesia and elsewhere clearly transcends the immediate issues of postwar diplomacy, including the Cold War, Washington's response to the colonial issue can be understood within that framework. The primary objective of American foreign policy during 1945–49 was the rehabilitation and revitalization of Western Europe. For most American officials, the chief significance of Indonesia, a rich source of raw materials and an integrated part of the Dutch economy, lay in its relationship to that overarching goal. They consequently filtered Indonesian developments through a European prism during those early postwar years. This book, then, attempts to show how other, more dominant interests of American diplomacy, shaped by events outside Indonesia, conditioned American policy toward that area. In short, it seeks to illuminate the fundamental relationship between America's colonial policy and a deepening Cold War.

Two works in particular facilitated my research. George McTurnan Kahin's *Nationalism and Revolution in Indonesia,* published in 1952, provided invaluable material on Indonesian internal developments. His work, along with that of other Indonesian specialists, helped me to appreciate the subtleties and complexities of Indonesian history. Alastair M. Taylor's *Indonesian Independence and the United Nations,* published in 1960, provided a balanced and judicious account of the critical role played by the UN. Though at times I disagree with their judgments, I respect their consistently high standards of scholarship and thank both authors for their very useful insights. The other scholars on whom I have depended are cited in the notes. I am grateful to them all.

I thank the highly competent staffs at the libraries of the University of Connecticut, the University of North Carolina, Cornell University, Yale University, the University of Virginia, and Princeton University. Also helpful and courteous were the archivists at the National Archives (Washington, D.C.), the Library of Congress (Washington, D.C.), the Washington Navy Yard, the Washington National Records Center (Suitland, Md.), the Public Record Office (London), the Franklin D. Roosevelt Library (Hyde Park, N.Y.), the Harry S. Truman Library (Independence, Mo.), the Douglas MacArthur Memorial Archives (Norfolk, Va.), the Hoover Institution on War, Revolution, and Peace (Stanford, Calif.), and the United Nations Library (New York). I especially thank the United Nations Library for kindly allowing me access to formerly classified Security Council records for the period 1947–49.

I thank the University of Connecticut and the Eleanor Roosevelt Institute of the Franklin D. Roosevelt Library for their generous financial support. In addition, I thank Bruce M. Stave, of the University of Connecticut, for helping to provide me with employment at a critical time, thus enabling me to begin this project.

Several former American diplomats who helped to formulate and execute American policy objectives in Indonesia in the 1940s graciously granted me personal interviews. For their cooperation and their innumerable insights and anecdotes I thank James Barco, James Nevins Hyde, Phillip Jessup, Abbot Moffat, Frederick Nolting, Charlton Ogburn, Dean Rusk, and Joseph Scott.

I am deeply indebted to Thomas G. Paterson, of the University of Connecticut, for his assistance and encouragement throughout the course of this project. His warm friendship and the example of his own scholarship helped me immensely. I also thank A. William Hoglund and Edmund Wehrle for reading the manuscript and offering valuable comments. My colleagues at the University of Connecticut were a constant source of friendly encouragement. I thank Matthew Magda, J. Donald Miller, and Thomas Zoumaras in particular for reading several earlier versions of this manuscript, and for patiently and often enthusiastically listening to my ideas. I am especially grateful to my former colleague Aaron David Miller for his excellent advice during the final stages of the manuscript. The professional assistance of Nancy Reilly in typing the manuscript is also warmly acknowledged.

Most of all, I thank my wife, Alison, for reasons only she can truly understand.

Robert J. McMahon

Washington, D.C.

Colonialism and Cold War

1

The Growth of Indonesian Nationalism

The East Indian archipelago is a sprawling chain of some three thousand islands lying between mainland Southeast Asia and the shores of Australia. This territory, ruled since 1949 by an independent government of Indonesia and today the fifth most populous nation in the world, has long been recognized for its great economic and strategic value. In 1948 Stanley K. Hornbeck, one of the State Department's leading Far Eastern experts, called the East Indies "the world's richest island empire . . . a region of political, economic and strategic importance to the whole world."[1] That view has been echoed by U.S. officials throughout the past few decades. "With its 100 million people and its 3,000 mile arc of islands containing the region's richest hoard of natural resources," wrote Richard M. Nixon in 1967, "Indonesia constitutes the greatest prize in the Southeast Asia area."[2] After a brief tour of the islands in 1968, Senator Joseph A. Clark marveled that "potentially, Indonesia is one of the richest nations in the world."[3] Writing only three years later, former American ambassador to Indonesia Howard Palfrey Jones estimated that Indonesia already ranked as the third richest country in the world in terms of natural resources. "It alone," he as-

[1]Stanley K. Hornbeck, "The United States and the Netherlands East Indies, *Annals of the American Academy of Political and Social Science,* 255 (January 1948): 124–25.

[2]Richard M. Nixon, "Asia after Vietnam," *Foreign Affairs,* 45 (October 1967): 111–25.

[3]*Indonesia: Sick Man on the Mend,* a Report to the Senate Committee on Foreign Relations by Senator Joseph A. Clark on a Study Mission to Indonesia, May 2, 1968 (Washington, D.C.: U.S. Government Printing Office), p. 9.

serted, "has the potential to become a major power in Asia. . . . Strategically located, Croesus-rich in resources largely unexploited, except in the case of oil, it is the pivot around which the future of Southeast Asia revolves."[4]

Such unbridled enthusiasm for the wealth and strategic value of Indonesia is hardly a recent development. Indeed, it was the lure of the fabled riches of the Indies, and especially its renowned spice trade, that first brought European merchants to those islands back in the sixteenth and seventeenth centuries.

In order to facilitate economic penetration of the Indies, the Netherlands government granted a monopoly in Far Eastern trade to the East India Company in 1602. Although nominally a private concern, the Dutch company had the complete backing of its government's naval and military power; with this support, it quickly established commercial supremacy over its chief rival, Portugal. Initially the company was attracted to the extensive trade of the Moluccas—the legendary spice islands—but soon it began to focus on the well-established spice trade of the main island of Java as well. With Javanese society politically fragmented during the early seventeenth century, the Dutch found it relatively easy to gain an early foothold there. Through a combination of war and treaties, they were able to establish dominance of the Indonesian seas between 1650 and 1680. As the spice trade declined, the East India Company explored new commercial opportunities. In the early eighteenth century the company began to concentrate on the production of coffee for the European market. This venture proved to be extremely

[4]Howard Palfrey Jones, *Indonesia: The Possible Dream* (New York: Harcourt Brace Jovanovich, 1971), pp. xv, 4. For a sampling of similar statements about the unparalleled wealth of the Indies, see Rupert Emerson, *The Netherlands Indies and the United States* (Boston: World Peace Foundation, 1942), p. 34; Raymond Kennedy, *The Ageless Indies* (New York: John Day, 1942), pp. 169–74; Albert G. Hopkins, "Netherlands Indies: What Holland's Wealthiest Colonial Possession Means to Western Industry," *Foreign Commerce Weekly*, 16 (September 16, 1944): 3; U.S. Economic Survey Team to Indonesia, *Indonesia: Perspective and Proposals for United States Economic Aid, a Report to the President* (New Haven: Yale University Southeast Asia Studies, 1963), pp. 112–13; Malcolm Caldwell, *Indonesia* (London: Oxford University Press, 1968), p. 6; Crocker National Bank, *Indonesia: The Inevitable Miracle* (San Francisco, 1973), pp. 47–49; Allen M. Sievers, *The Mystical World of Indonesia: Culture and Economic Development in Conflict* (Baltimore: Johns Hopkins University Press, 1974), p. 79.

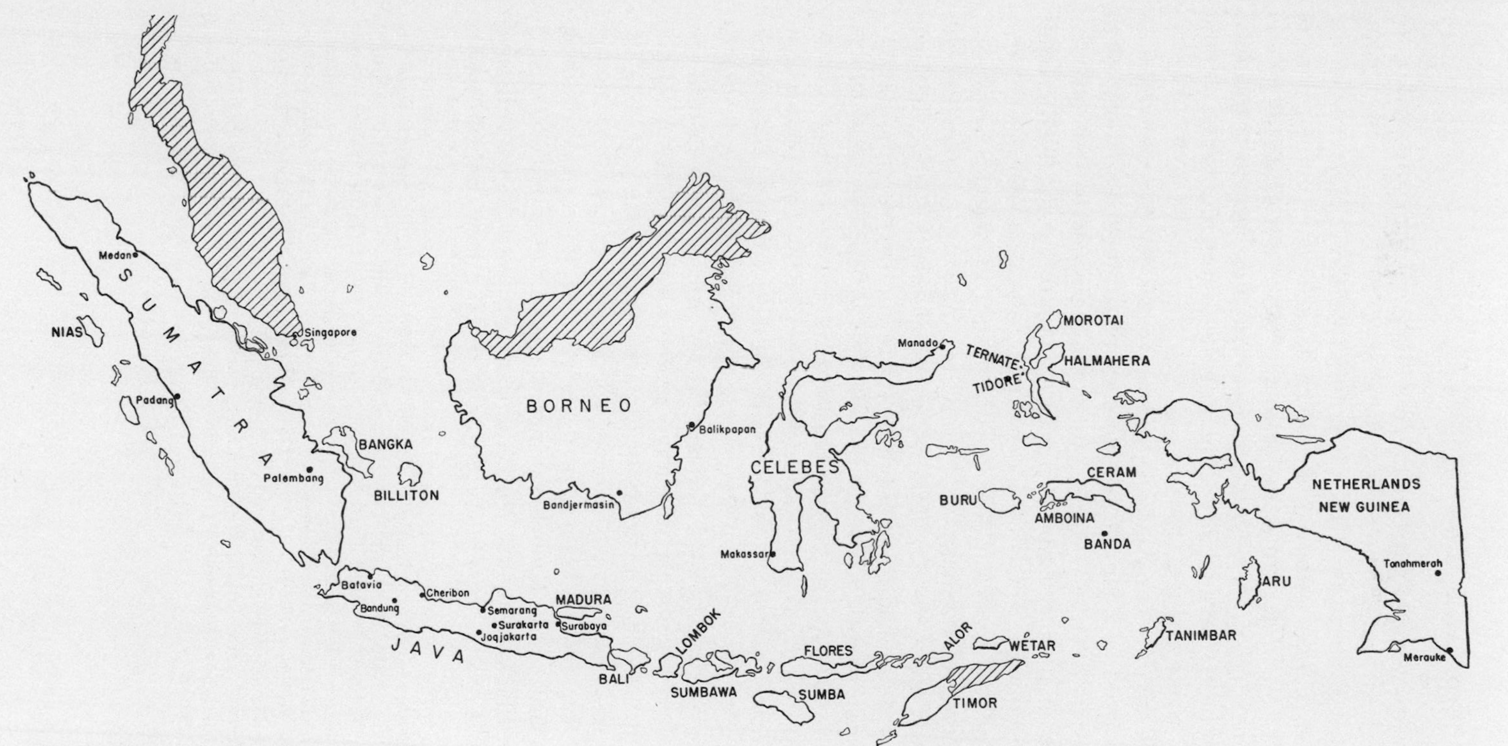

The Netherlands East Indies

lucrative, enhancing considerably the economic value of Java. In order to protect their growing commercial empire, the Dutch gradually expanded their territorial holdings in Java and the outer islands. Although the Dutch did not gain complete control over the Indies until well into the twentieth century, by the beginning of the eighteenth century they already controlled over half of Java while dominating the commercial activity of the rest of the archipelago.[5]

Despite its early successes, in 1798 the East India Company collapsed, a victim of its own corrupt administration and inept financial policies. The area formerly controlled by the company was then placed under the direct control of the Netherlands government. This shift did not lead to any substantial changes in policy, however, for, as one leading historian has noted, "There was no sharp break with the Company's system: indeed, nearly all the old institutions, such as forced labor, deliveries in kind, feudalism, and monopolies in certain crops were maintained. The old idea that colonies existed for the benefit of the mother country was still predominant."[6]

After a brief period of British rule over the East Indies, commencing in 1811, the Dutch regained control of their prized colony in 1816. When Dutch authorities attempted to reestablish their power in Java, however, they encountered determined resistance from certain native aristocrats. Using Islam, the religion of the vast majority of the archipelago's people, as a unifying symbol, Prince Diponegoro declared a "holy war" against the European intruders in 1825. With strong support from the peasantry, the Javanese prince waged an effective and bloody guerrilla war against the Dutch for five years. Only with great difficulty did the Dutch bring the revolt under control by 1830.

[5]George McTurnan Kahin, *Nationalism and Revolution in Indonesia* (Ithaca: Cornell University Press, 1952), pp. 3–4; Robert van Niel, "The Course of Indonesian History," in Ruth T. McVey, ed., *Indonesia* (New Haven: Yale University Southeast Asia Studies, 1963), pp. 279–82; Ailsa Zainu'ddin, *A Short History of Indonesia* (New York: Praeger, 1970), pp. 94–95; Leslie Palmier, *Indonesia* (New York: Walker, 1965), pp. 39–41; George Masselman, *The Cradle of Colonialism* (New Haven: Yale University Press, 1963), pp. 211–13.

[6]Amry Vandenbosch, *The Dutch East Indies: Its Government, Problems, and Politics* (Berkeley: University of California Press, 1941), p. 34. See also Caldwell, *Indonesia*, p. 43.

The casualties were astonishingly high: nearly 15,000 on the Dutch side lost their lives and about 200,000 Javanese were killed. The rebellion was sparked primarily by Dutch encroachment on the traditional prerogatives of native elites, but it also had strongly nationalistic overtones; the broad-based support for Diponegoro's rebellion was indeed an ominous sign to the Dutch rulers. As a result of the war in Java and a series of conflicts in Europe, Dutch finances became severely strained; accordingly, pressure mounted in governmental circles in Holland to draw greater profits out of the Indies.[7] As one Dutch policy maker mused at the time: "All turns on the great question whether we can compete with other countries; if so, Java is a gold mine; if not, it is nothing."[8]

In order to ensure a greater rate of profits for the mother country, the Netherlands installed the infamous cultivation system of agriculture in the Indies in 1830. Geared to producing crops for export—especially coffee, sugar, and indigo—at the lowest possible cost, the cultivation system crudely exploited the labor of the East Indian peasantry. The peasants were required to place a percentage of their land and labor at the government's disposal.[9] The Dutch government, according to one critic of this policy, compelled a peasant "to grow on *his* land what pleases *it*; it punishes him when he sells the crop so produced to anyone else but *it*; and *it* fixes the price it pays him. . . . And since after all, the entire business must yield a profit, this profit can be made in no other way than by paying the Javanese just *enough* to keep him from starving, which would decrease the producing power of the nation."[10] A series of devastating famines between 1843 and 1848 testified to the sheer brutality of the Dutch agricultural program.

[7]Justus M. van der Kroef, "Prince Diponegoro, Progenitor of Indonesian Nationalism," *Far Eastern Quarterly*, 9 (August 1949): 424–50; Zainu'ddin, *Short History of Indonesia*, pp. 127–28; Palmier, *Indonesia*, pp. 65–67.

[8]Quoted in John S. Furnivall, *Netherlands India: A Study of Plural Economy* (New York: Macmillan, 1944), p. 111.

[9]John S. Furnivall, *Colonial Policy and Practice: A Comparative Study of Burma and Netherlands India* (New York: New York University Press, 1956), pp. 220–23; Zainu'ddin, *Short History of Indonesia*, pp. 128–31; Kahin, *Nationalism and Revolution*, pp. 11–13; van Niel, "Course of Indonesian History," pp. 284–85.

[10]Quoted in Zainu'ddin, *Short History of Indonesia*, p. 131.

For the Netherlands, though, the success of the system was self-evident; it could be measured in cold financial terms. By 1877 the cultivation system had paid off all of the East India Company's debts and was bringing a sizable amount of additional revenue into The Hague's home treasury. The East Indies, between 1831 and 1877, earned on the average 18 million guilders a year in profit; in view of a national budget that did not exceed 60 million guilders a year during the same period, the considerable contribution of the colony to the health of the home economy is unmistakable.[11] "It is certain," wrote Dutch governor General J. van den Bosch, "that without the generous contributions of the Indies, the State would have been ruined and we would have been forced to submit ourselves to the mercy of the opposition."[12] "Java," one colonial minister rapturously declared, "poured forth riches upon riches on the homeland as if by a magician's wand."[13]

By the 1860s and 1870s, liberal voices in Holland began to protest against the excesses of the cultivation system, contending that a colony should not be used exclusively for the purpose of enriching the mother country. Their agitation led to some significant reforms, and in 1870 the cultivation system was replaced by a less exploitive system of private enterprise. Toward the end of the century, the pressure within Holland for a more humane colonial policy increased substantially. In 1899 Conrad Th. Van Deventer, a leader of the Dutch Liberal Party, wrote a highly influential pamphlet, *A Debt of Honor*, in which he charged that the Netherlands government had been immorally exploiting the natural wealth of the Indies while completely neglecting the welfare of the native inhabitants of the islands. This point of view gained increasing sympathy in Holland and led to the formation of the so-called Ethical Party. The Ethicals advocated the abolition of unjust taxation and appropriation, a sharp upgrading of social welfare measures for the Indonesians,

[11]B. H. M. Vlekke, *Nusantara: A History of Indonesia*, rev. ed. (Chicago: Quadrangle Books, 1960), pp. 291–92. See also Sievers, *Mystical World*, pp. 112–16.

[12]Quoted in C. L. M. Penders, ed., *Indonesia: Selected Documents on Colonialism and Nationalism, 1830–1942* (St. Lucia: University of Queensland Press, 1977), p. 20.

[13]Quoted in Furnivall, *Netherlands India*, p. 127.

and the gradual preparation of native elites for political positions. In addition, the Ethicals emphasized education, believing that they could help to bring about a closer association between the Dutch and the natives by opening up educational opportunities for Indonesians. By 1902, the main goals of the Ethical Party were adopted as official policy by the Dutch government, with a resultant paternalistic liberalization of Dutch rule in the Indies.[14] As one Dutch politician explained this new philosophy: "We must bring up the child in such a way that it can learn to dispense with our help."[15] But "the child" would not be satisfied with paternalistic reforms; on the contrary, Indonesian nationalists soon began to extend the arguments of the Ethical Party to their logical conclusion—nothing less than complete self-government for the Indonesian people.

The rise of nationalism as a potent force in the East Indies is a phenomenon of the twentieth century. While the beginnings of Indonesian nationalism probably go back as far as the initial period of Dutch penetration of the islands, active and organized resistance to Dutch rule dates from the first two decades of this century. The question logically arises as to why organized nationalist opposition to Dutch hegemony took so long to develop if the system imposed on the natives was as brutalizing and exploitive as most leading authorities have maintained.[16] Part of the explanation for this seeming paradox is that the East India Company and the cultivation system benefited elites within Indonesian society, thus depriving the peasants—clearly the chief victims of Dutch policies—of their natural leaders. On the few occasions when the aristocracy challenged Dutch rule, as in the case of Prince Diponegoro's rebellion, it found strong support within the Indonesian peasantry. For the most part, though, the personal interests of Indonesian elites were well served by Dutch rule; identification with peasant grievances was thus a rare occurrence. Without the aid of the indigenous aris-

[14]Bernhard Dahm, *History of Indonesia in the Twentieth Century* (New York: Praeger, 1971), pp. 12–15; Vlekke, *Nusantara*, pp. 330–31; Furnivall, *Colonial Policy and Practice*, pp. 226–30. For a criticism of the limits of the Ethical policy, see Zainu'ddin, *Short History of Indonesia*, pp. 154–57.

[15]Quoted in Dahm, *History of Indonesia*, p. 14.

[16]See, for example, Kahin, *Nationalism and Revolution*, pp. 7, 11–14; Furnivall, *Netherlands India*, pp. 136–39; Sievers, *Mystical World*, pp. 93–95, 120–22.

tocracy, the peasants were unable to comprehend the complex relationship between the Dutch imperium and the deterioration of their own position within Indonesian society. Peasant frustration was generally channeled not against the Dutch, but against the more visible symbols of oppression—such as the indigenous aristocracy itself. "By virtue of their indirect political rule and indirect economic exploitation," one historian has written, "the Dutch for three centuries were able to avoid collision with the reaction and opposition of the general Indonesian population to the conditions for which in an ultimate sense the Dutch were responsible."[17]

With the abandonment of the cultivation system after 1870, the reality of Dutch rule gradually became more apparent. When the indirectly administered state monopoly was replaced by a more directly administered private enterprise, the Indonesian people had much more direct contact with the Dutch and with Dutch economic power. Indonesian consciousness of Dutch political and economic control was greatly heightened; increasingly, natives learned that there was a direct relationship between Dutch imperialism and their own political and economic grievances. This distress was further aggravated by the increasingly heavy taxes that the Dutch compelled peasants to pay.[18]

The initial stirrings of peasant discontent took the form of both violent and nonviolent protest movements. One of these movements, the Saminist rebellion, began in 1890 and grew into a fairly large-scale peasant revolt. Essentially the Saminists opposed governmental interference in peasant life; they wanted to return to the traditional, communalistic social organizations that had characterized Indonesian society before Dutch rule. The Dutch finally suppressed the movement in 1917, but only through the use of considerable armed force. While revolts of this type were not, strictly speaking, nationalistic—in fact, the Saminists exhibited anarchistic tendencies—they did represent strong feelings of opposition to the Dutch Indies government

[17]Kahin, *Nationalism and Revolution*, p. 41.
[18]Ibid., pp. 42–43; Sievers, *Mystical World*, pp. 122–27.

which awaited only the emergence of an organized nationalist elite to direct them into more clearly nationalistic channels.[19]

Ironically, the Dutch helped to provide the Indonesian peasants with such an educated nationalist elite. As part of the Ethical Party program, the Netherlands government had committed itself to broadening educational opportunities for natives. This commitment was reinforced by an expanding colonial governmental structure that required the services of educated native elites. Moreover, Dutch officials believed that an educational program would turn the Indonesian populace away from a growing Islamic modernist movement that Dutch authorities saw as a challenge to continued Western hegemony in the archipelago. A Western-educated elite, the Dutch believed, would help Indonesians to reject Islam and move toward closer cultural association with the Dutch. "It is to our vital interest," wrote one Dutch colonial minister, "not to wait until unexpected circumstances compel us to give that which we can grant to the Indonesians voluntarily and in the form which seems to us the best."[20]

For a variety of reasons, then, the Dutch inaugurated a program of Western education for a select group of Indonesians during the first two decades of the twentieth century. Many of the natives were to be educated in Europe, most of them in Holland itself. Yet in the long run this educational program proved counterproductive to Dutch interests, because only a small portion of those people educated in the West could find jobs in the East Indies commensurate with their training. The upper ranks of the East Indian civil service, for instance, remained closed to non-Europeans. The great majority of the educated Indonesians thus became increasingly discontented with the structure of a colonial society that blocked their personal advancement. Instead of creating a group of native leaders loyal

[19]Kahin, *Nationalism and Revolution*, pp. 43–44. For a detailed study of these movements, see Sartono Kartodirdjo, *Protest Movements in Rural Java: A Study of Agrarian Unrest in the Nineteenth and Early Twentieth Centuries* (Singapore: Oxford University Press, 1973).

[20]Quoted in Kahin, *Nationalism and Revolution*, p. 48. See also Zainu'ddin, *Short History of Indonesia*, pp. 145–54.

to the regime, then, the Dutch actually created an elite whose interests were at variance with those of the colonial government.[21]

By providing a program of Western education, the Dutch also exposed Indonesian students to ideas that often were used to justify demands for greater self-government and, ultimately, independence. It would have been difficult for an Indonesian student not to draw parallels between the history of Dutch opposition to outside controls and the subjugation of his own people. Mohammed Hatta, who emerged as one of the leaders of the Indonesian nationalist movement, explained this process:

> In the schools of the ruler himself Indonesian students were told about the Dutch freedom fighters and learned to appreciate them. They were also taught that the Netherlands are indebted to those courageous heroes for the independence of their country, then and now. They could not help thinking of their own heroes who only wanted to do what the heroes of the ruler himself had done: liberate their country from the foreign yoke and keep it free from foreign blemishes.[22]

The whole tradition of Western political and social thought seemed to justify the inclination of nationalistic students to oppose Dutch political and economic subjugation. In European schools, Indonesian students were exposed to the writings of Karl Marx; to many of them Marxism seemed to explain the plight of their homeland. Equally intrigued by the works of Vladimir Ilyich Lenin and Nikolai Bukharin, some of these students came to equate capitalism with imperialism and became convinced that true independence would have to be economic as well as political.[23]

[21]Ibid., pp. 46–49; Harry J. Benda, "Indonesia," in *Continuity and Change in Southeast Asia: Collected Journal Articles of Harry J. Benda* (New Haven: Yale University Southeast Asia Studies, 1972), pp. 7–8; Palmier, *Indonesia*, pp. 79–80.

[22]Mohammed Hatta, "National Claims," in *Portrait of a Patriot: Selected Writings by Mohammed Hatta* (The Hague: Mouton, 1972), p. 318.

[23]Kahin, *Nationalism and Revolution*, pp. 49–52; Benda, "Indonesia," p. 5. Hatta, himself educated in Holland, pointed to the importance of Western education in the development of leaders for the Indonesian nationalist movement. See Hatta, "Indonesia Free: Plea before the Court of Justice in The Hague, March 9, 1928," in *Portrait of a Patriot*, pp. 209–11, 214–15.

While the spread of Western ideas was beginning to discredit the notion that colonial people were not capable of governing themselves, the rapid pace of events in Asia at the turn of the century further undermined that notion. The Filipino resistance to Spanish and American rule, the rise of Chinese nationalism under Sun Yat-sen, the activities of the Congress Party in India, the successes of Kemal Ataturk against Western military power, the rapid modernization of Japan, and especially Russia's defeat at the hands of an Asian nation in the Russo-Japanese War—all of these events were sharply etched on the minds of Indonesian nationalists.[24] According to Hatta:

> A shock went through the edifice of Western imperialism when the Land of the Rising Sun defeated the Russian colossus in 1905. This brought about a revision of ideas both in the white as well as the coloured world. The herald of a new day had come! The booming of the cannons of Chushima proclaimed to the world that the divine right of the white man in Asia had ceased to be.[25]

As a leading authority on the rise of Afro-Asian nationalism has noted: "Once the rising colonial elite had shaken off their awe of the almost magical mastery of power produced by the alien rulers, they demanded that an end be put to the gross discrepancy between the ideals of freedom and equality which the West preached and the colonialism which it practiced."[26]

The first organized and articulate expression of Indonesian nationalism, not surprisingly, came from a student group. The Budi Utomo (High Endeavor), founded by two Indonesian medical students in 1908, was the cradle of the Indonesian nationalist movement. The organization aspired both to help the Indonesian peasantry and to create a movement that would embrace the whole archipelago. Within a year it had attracted nearly 10,000 members from the ranks of Indonesian students and civil servants. But Budi Utomo's strength was short-lived; it

[24]Kahin, *Nationalism and Revolution*, p. 50; Benda, "Indonesia," p. 4.

[25]Mohammed Hatta, "The Anti-Colonial Congress in Brussels in the Light of World History," in *Portrait of a Patriot*, pp. 185–99.

[26]Rupert Emerson, *From Empire to Nation: The Rise to Self-Assertion of Asian and African Peoples* (Boston: Beacon Press, 1960), p. 54.

soon began to lose all but its most conservative and aristocratic members to new, more politically conscious organizations.[27]

The Indische Partij (National Indies Party) was the first organization in the East Indies to translate the arguments of the Ethical Party into specific nationalist demands. Founded in 1912 by Douwes Dekker, editor of a leading Indonesian newspaper, the Indische Partij took as its motto "The Indies for those who make their home there." Dekker asserted to Dutch Governor General Alexander Idenburg that the policy of the Ethicals included preparing the colony for self-government and that the ultimate consequence of that policy must be independence. Idenburg, insisting that the Indies would never be independent, declared the party illegal on March 31, 1913. Dekker then appealed to the queen herself in a series of open letters, arguing the case for Indonesian independence. "No, Your Majesty," he implored in one letter, "this is not your country. It is our country, our homeland. One day it will be free, free for ever—we have sworn it!"[28] Despite the eloquence of his plea, the Dutch responded by exiling Dekker and two other leaders to one of the outer islands and suppressed the party.

The third major nationalist organization, Sarekat Islam, became the first to achieve a mass following. Initially formed as a merchants' protective association, Sarekat Islam was reorganized in 1912 along more forthrightly nationalist lines. Riding the crest of a popular Islamic modernist movement, the new organization showed that Islam could be used as a rallying point for native solidarity against Dutch rule. Gradually, however, Sarekat Islam strayed from its original purpose, becoming more of a political group and less of a religious one. By the early 1920s it had lost much of its earlier vitality.[29]

In response to pressure from this burgeoning nationalist movement, the Dutch created the Volksraad (People's Council)

[27]Dahm, *History of Indonesia*, pp. 24–28; Kahin, *Nationalism and Revolution*, pp. 64–65; Zainu'ddin, *Short History of Indonesia*, pp. 174–75; Ali Sastroadmijojo, "Survey of the Indonesian Nationalist Movement," *Asian Horizon*, 2 (Fall 1949):29.

[28]Quoted in Dahm, *History of Indonesia*, p. 36. See also Penders, ed., *Indonesia*, pp. 228–32; Palmier, *Indonesia*, pp. 93–94; van Niel, "Course of Indonesian History," p. 293.

[29]Van Niel, "Course of Indonesian History," pp. 293–95.

in 1916. Its members represented the major population groups in the Indonesian archipelago and its expressed purpose was to advise the colonial government. But the Volksraad was never truly representative, and while it gradually evolved into more than a merely advisory body, it never assumed any real legislative function; rather, it served more as a forum for the airing of political views and economic grievances. Indeed, "it was a case of too little too late."[30] Real power was still vested in the governor general, who was appointed by the Dutch crown, and to whom all the heads of departments were responsible.[31]

While the Dutch were offering the carrot of increased native political participation to moderate nationalists with the Volksraad, they were using the stick of repression against nationalists whose demands were more radical. One such radical group was the Indonesian Communist Party (PKI). Founded in 1920 by Tan Malaka, a Western-educated schoolteacher, the party demanded total independence from Dutch rule. Within a few short years it had attracted nearly 3,000 members. Seriously miscalculating the depth of its popular support, however, the PKI launched a premature rebellion against the colonial government in 1926–27. The poorly planned and executed revolt ended in a crushing defeat for the Communists and a destruction of their organization throughout the Indies. In fact, the power of the Indonesian Communist Party remained broken for the next two decades.[32]

Throughout the 1920s and 1930s, Indonesian nationalist organizations proliferated despite the best efforts of Dutch authorities to quash them. The Indonesian Nationalist Party (PNI), founded in 1927 under the chairmanship of a dynamic young engineer named Sukarno, posed a formidable threat to the colonial regime. Largely as a result of Sukarno's exceptional oratorical skills and charismatic leadership, the PNI quickly became the foremost nationalist party in the Indies. Sukarno, one of the few

[30]Zainu'ddin, *Short History of Indonesia*, p. 197.

[31]Ibid., pp. 197–98; van Niel, "Course of Indonesian History," pp. 292, 296–97; Penders, ed., *Indonesia*, pp. 121–49.

[32]Ruth T. McVey, *The Rise of Indonesian Communism* (Ithaca: Cornell University Press, 1965); Ruth T. McVey and Harry J. Benda, eds., *The Communist Uprisings of 1926–1927 in Indonesia: Key Documents* (Ithaca: Cornell University Modern Indonesia Project, 1960).

1930s. Those Indonesians who dared follow in the steps of their banished leaders were promptly arrested; the increased vigilance of the Dutch secret police made underground activity equally hazardous. On the eve of the Japanese invasion, Dutch repression had thus successfully subdued and controlled the nationalist movement. Governor General B. C. de Jonge, the architect of this repressive policy, complacently predicted that the Dutch would rule the East Indies for at least another three hundred years.[39]

The outbreak of war in the Pacific in 1941 profoundly affected developments in the Netherlands East Indies. Intent on seizing the rich raw materials of the Dutch colony, especially its oil, the Japanese invaded and quickly overran the East Indies in February and March 1942, beginning an occupation that lasted until the Japanese surrender to the Allies in August 1945. This relatively brief period of Japanese rule initiated momentous changes in Indonesian society; most significantly, it proved to be a watershed in the history of the Indonesian nationalist movement.[40]

The surprisingly easy Japanese victory dealt a severe blow to Dutch prestige in the Indies. As a wartime American intelligence report emphasized: "The subsequent retreat and internment of the Dutch and their Allies altered radically the position of the white man in the estimation of the Indonesians."[41] Wel-

[39]Zainu'ddin, *Short History of Indonesia*, p. 204; Harry J. Benda, "The Pattern of Administrative Reforms in the Closing Years of Dutch Rule in Indonesia," *Journal of Asian Studies*, 25 (August 1966):290–91. See also Kahin, *Nationalism and Revolution*, p. 94.

[40]This interpretation of the significance of the Japanese occupation has been generally accepted by scholars. See, for example, Benedict R. O'G. Anderson, *Some Aspects of Indonesian Politics under the Japanese Occupation, 1944–1945* (Ithaca: Cornell University Modern Indonesia Project, 1961), and *Java in a Time of Revolution: Occupation and Resistance, 1944–1946* (Ithaca: Cornell University Press, 1972); George S. Kanahele, "The Japanese Occupation of Indonesia: Prelude to Independence," Ph.D. dissertation, Cornell University, 1967; M. A. Aziz, *Japan's Colonialism and Indonesia* (The Hague: Martinius Nijhoff, 1955); Harry J. Benda, *The Crescent and the Rising Sun: Indonesian Islam under the Japanese Occupation, 1942–1945* (The Hague: W. van Hoeve, 1958); Willard H. Elsbree, *Japan's Role in Southeast Asian Nationalist Movements, 1941–1945* (Cambridge: Harvard University Press, 1953).

[41]U.S. Office of Strategic Services (OSS), "Effects of the Japanese Occupation," Research and Analysis Report no. 3293, 1945, in U.S. Department of State Records, Record Group (RG) 59, National Archives, Washington, D.C. (hereafter cited as DSR).

coming the Dutch humiliation, Indonesian nationalists generally greeted their new overlords as liberators. Tokyo's initial policy in the Indies encouraged such sentiment; the new rulers permitted the display of the Indonesian flag and the singing of the Indonesian national anthem, for instance—activities that had been strictly forbidden by the Dutch. More important, expediency led the new Japanese administration to effect a tremendous rise in socioeconomic status for the educated class of Indonesians. Within six months of the invasion, the Japanese interned practically the entire Dutch population of the Indies, opening up thousands of mid- and upper-level administrative and technical jobs. Since the Japanese had only a limited number of military personnel, Indonesians, out of necessity, filled many of the vacated jobs. This new mobility became a significant factor after the war; now there was a large class in the East Indies whose rapid elevation in status would be threatened by a return to Dutch rule and repressive prewar conditions.[42]

This initial goodwill soon dissipated, however, as the Japanese military began to harness the Indonesian economy to meet Japan's wartime needs. The aims of the Japanese occupation were quite explicit: "to plan for the prompt development and utilization of military resources in the occupied areas and to look to strengthening and augmenting the Empire's war potential."[43] To Indonesians, economic exploitation at the hands of fellow Asians bore a remarkable resemblance to economic exploitation at the hands of the Dutch. Moreover, the arrogance and brutality of many Japanese helped to erode any lingering

[42]Sutan Sjahrir, *Out of Exile* (New York: John Day, 1949), p. 237; Abu Hanifah, *Tales of a Revolution* (Sydney: Angus & Robertson, 1972), p. 119; Elsbree, *Japan's Role*, pp. 96–101; Aziz, *Japan's Colonialism*, p. 149; Genevieve C. Linebarger, "The Aftermath of Japanese Colonialism in Southeast Asia," in Robert Strausz-Hupé and Harry W. Hazard, eds., *The Idea of Colonialism* (New York: Praeger, 1958), p. 208; John R. W. Smail, *Bandung in the Early Revolution, 1945–1946: A Study in the Social History of the Indonesian Revolution* (Ithaca: Cornell University Modern Indonesia Project, 1964), pp. 13–15; Kahin, *Nationalism and Revolution*, p. 133; Saburo Ienaga, *The Pacific War: World War II and the Japanese, 1931–1945* (New York: Pantheon, 1978), pp. 176–77.

[43]Japanese Military Affairs Bureau, Ministry of the Navy, "Statement by the Director upon the Inauguration of the Southern Area Administration Office: Draft," December 7, 1941, in Harry Benda, James K. Irikura, and Koichi Kishi, *Japanese Military Administration in Indonesia: Selected Documents* (New Haven: Yale University Southeast Asia Studies, 1965), p. 13. See also Elsbree, *Japan's Role*, pp. 164–66; Kahin, *Nationalism and Revolution*, p. 104.

belief that the new rulers were indeed liberators. Having lost the support of the Indonesian population, Japan reevaluated its policy. Tokyo reluctantly came to realize that nationalism was a real and powerful force in the archipelago and that some accommodation was needed if the aims of its occupation policy were to succeed.[44] One high-ranking military commander explained the rationale for this new policy:

> If we judge the trend of native sentiments correctly and, while advancing their education, promise in the near future to meet their desires, the extremely sensitive natives will be impressed and although there may be material shortages they will tolerate this and steadily strengthen their cooperation. In effect, they will become Imperial subjects and will form a powerful link in the new order of Greater East Asia during the war, not to mention after the war; thus the founding of a second Japan in a corner of the South Seas will become a certainty.
>
> On the other hand, if we regard the natives as ignorant people and err in the ways of winning their hearts, we shall receive an unexpected counterblow—as the saying goes, "Even a small worm has a large spirit"—and we must then be prepared to partake of the same bitter cup suffered by the former Dutch regime at the time of its collapse.[45]

In order to achieve a rapproachement with the Indonesians, the Japanese turned to those nationalist leaders who commanded widespread support—Sukarno and Hatta. Japanese officials promised concessions to Indonesian nationalism in return for an Indonesian commitment to Tokyo's war effort. Sukarno and Hatta willingly accepted this quid pro quo when Japanese authorities assured them that the Indies would be granted independence in the near future.[46]

This political arrangement between the Japanese rulers and prominent Indonesian nationalist leaders later led both Indonesian and Dutch enemies of Sukarno and Hatta to accuse them of

[44]Kahin, *Nationalism and Revolution*, p. 104; Benda et al., *Japanese Military Administration*, pp. 237–56.

[45]Commander, Osamu Group, "Suggestions on the Future Status of Java," 1943, in Benda et al., *Japanese Military Administration*, pp. 238–39.

[46]Legge, *Sukarno*, pp. 149–53; Dahm, *Sukarno*, pp. 221–24.

collaboration with the Japanese fascists. In fairness, Sukarno and Hatta hardly deserve the pejorative epithet "collaborationist"; they were not dupes of Japanese propaganda, as some charged, but sincere nationalists who seized a unique opportunity to further the nationalist movement.[47] Even Sjahrir, who worked in the anti-Japanese underground and was the bitterest opponent of those who actually did collaborate with the Japanese, recognized that Sukarno and Hatta agreed to do "everything legally possible to give the nationalist struggle a broader legal scope, and at the same time secretly support the revolutionary resistance."[48] The real value of Sukarno's and Hatta's wartime activity was that, while ostensibly rallying Indonesians behind the Japanese effort, they were actually spreading and intensifying nationalist ideas among the populace and simultaneously forcing the Japanese to make concessions that eventually led to self-government. Using all the means of modern communication that the Japanese had placed at their disposal, the Indonesian leaders carried the nationalist message throughout the archipelago, heightening the consciousness of the peasantry and preparing the way for the independence struggle that lay ahead.[49]

[47]The Dutch vigorously tried to portray Sukarno and Hatta as "quislings." See, for example, *Ten Years of Japanese Burrowing in the Netherlands East Indies: Official Report of the Netherlands East Indies Government on Japanese Subversive Activities during the Last Decade* (New York: Netherlands Information Bureau, 1944); Peter S. Gerbrandy, *Indonesia* (London: Hutchinson, 1950), pp. 60, 69–70; Stanley K. Hornbeck (American ambassador to the Netherlands) to Secretary of State James Byrnes, October 1, 1945, 856E.00/10-145, RG 59, DSR; Sir Neville Bland (British ambassador to the Netherlands) to Foreign Office, November 3, 1945, FO 371, F9454/6398/61, Records of the British Foreign Office, Public Record Office, London (hereafter cited as PRO). Willard Hanna accepts this characterization of Sukarno as a collaborationist in his study *Eight Nation-Makers: Southeast Asia's Charismatic Statesmen* (New York: St. Martin's Press, 1964), chap. 1. The Dutch lieutenant governor general of the East Indies, the highly respected Hubertus J. van Mook, categorically rejected this charge in his book *The Stakes of Democracy in Southeast Asia* (New York: Norton, 1950), pp. 150–51. Van Mook's view is corroborated in most of the reliable secondary literature. See, for example, Kahin, *Nationalism and Revolution*; Anderson, *Some Aspects*; Kanahele, "Japanese Occupation"; Elsbree, *Japan's Role*; Dahm, *Sukarno*; Aziz, *Japan's Colonialism*.

[48]Sjahrir, *Out of Exile*, p. 246.

[49]Elsbree, *Japan's Role*, p. 167; Legge, *Sukarno*, pp. 178–80; Kahin, *Nationalism and Revolution*, pp. 104–8; Leslie Palmier, "Sukarno, the Nationalist," *Pacific Affairs*, 30 (March 1957):105.

In March 1945 the Japanese war effort began to falter badly. Concerned with the prospect of an imminent Allied invasion of the islands, Japanese officials made a desperate attempt to rally the Indonesian people behind them by setting up an Investigating Committee for the Preparation of Independence. As Japan's military position continued to deteriorate in the early days of August, they replaced this organization with the Indonesian Independence Preparatory Committee (PPKI) and selected Sukarno as chairman and Hatta as vice-chairman. The stated function of this new committee was to prepare for the transfer of authority from the Japanese military government to it; August 24 was set as the day that the Japanese would officially confer independence on the Indies. Militant youth and underground leaders, however, fearing that Indonesia would appear to be a Japanese-created puppet state, prevailed on Sukarno and Hatta to make their own declaration of independence without waiting for Japanese approval.[50]

On August 17, 1945, years of nationalist struggle culminated in Sukarno and Hatta's proclamation of independence. The declaration read simply: "We, the people of Indonesia, hereby declare Indonesia's independence. Matters concerning the transfer of power and other matters will be executed in an orderly manner and in the shortest possible time." It was signed: "In the name of the Indonesian People, Sukarno-Hatta."[51] The struggle to make a reality of this proclamation would commence shortly.

The Japanese occupation completely transformed Indonesian society. The development of the independence movement was accelerated considerably as a result of the brief Japanese reign. In addition, many of the organizations that the Japanese military rulers had created as means of rallying support for their cause later played prominent roles in the fight for Indonesian independence. The Peta, for example, was an Indonesian military organization that the Japanese formed to resist a possible Allied

[50]Benda et al., *Japanese Military Administration*, pp. 263–79; Anderson, pp. 61–82; Mohammed Hatta, "Legend and Reality Surrounding the Proclamation of the 17th August," in *Portrait of a Patriot*, pp. 518–27; Anthony J. S. Reid, *Indonesian National Revolution, 1945–1950* (Hawthorn, Australia: Longman, 1974), pp. 25–29; Louis Allen, *The End of the War in Asia* (London: Hart-Davis, MacGibbon, 1976), pp. 76–81.

[51]Quoted in Anderson, *Java*, p. 82.

attack on the islands. By the middle of 1945 it numbered 120,000 men; it would become the nucleus of the Indonesian Republic's army. The Japanese also formed various military and paramilitary groups of Indonesian youth, or *pemudas,* which were indoctrinated with powerful anti-Western ideas. These pemuda groups would also play a dominant role in the later Indonesian revolution, especially in its early and most critical stages. In all of these ways, then, the Japanese helped to create conditions in Indonesia which militated against a return to prewar conditions.[52] A report written in 1945 by the U.S. Office of Strategic Services noted emphatically that the "Japanese occupation of the Netherlands East Indies has made impossible the return of the Indies to the *status quo ante bellum.*"[53]

With the Japanese surrender to the Allies, a clash between the newly proclaimed Republic of Indonesia and the recently liberated Kingdom of the Netherlands appeared unavoidable. Throughout their three hundred years of rule the Dutch had become more dependent on a colony than any other European imperial power. As some Dutch imperialists were fond of saying, "Indonesia is the cork on which Netherlands prosperity floats."[54] Now in 1945, with the economy of Holland shattered by a devastating war, Dutch policy makers believed that they would have to rely even more heavily on their rich colony for aid in the massive recovery process. The Netherlands' economic stake in Indonesia was enormous. Its investment alone totaled over $1.4 billion in 1940, earning more than $100 million annually in profits. A study commissioned by The Hague in 1945 concluded that one-sixth of the national wealth of the Netherlands was invested in the East Indies.[55] By way of comparison, the

[52]Kahin, *Nationalism and Revolution*, pp. 109–10, 130–31; Anderson, *Java*, pp. 10–34; Zainu'ddin, *Short History of Indonesia*, pp. 216–17; Guy J. Pauker, "The Role of the Military in Indonesia," in John J. Johnson, ed., *The Role of the Military in Underdeveloped Countries* (Princeton: Princeton University Press, 1962), p. 194; OSS, "Japanese Attempts at Indoctrination of Youth in Occupied Areas," Research and Analysis Report no. 2982S, 1945, DSR.

[53]OSS, "Effects of the Japanese Occupation."

[54]Hatta, "Indonesia Free," p. 210.

[55]J. B. D. Derken and J. Tinbergen, "An Evaluation of the Economic Significance of the Netherlands Indies for the Netherlands," *Monthly of the Netherlands Central Bureau of Statistics*, The Hague, October/December 1945, Box 75, Louis B. Wehle Papers, Franklin D. Roosevelt Library, Hyde Park, N.Y.; memorandum

investment of Royal Dutch Shell in the Indies alone was greater than the combined investment of all American firms in China and Japan.[56] "The Indies," one scholar wrote at the time, "have been the most profitable colonial possession of their size in the world."[57]

Aside from strictly financial considerations, Holland's dependence on Indonesia had an important psychological dimension. With the East Indies, the Netherlands ranked as the world's third or fourth greatest colonial power; without the East Indies, Holland was merely a third-rate European power. "One thing is certainly clear," said one expert, "the Netherlands would be far poorer without the Indies, and any other nation which might possess them correspondingly stronger. It is the Indies which make Holland a world power."[58] The belief that Indonesia made the Netherlands a "great" nation was firmly implanted in the minds of the Dutch. As Peter S. Gerbrandy, the wartime prime minister of Holland, asserted:

> Our overseas interests condition our very existence. . . . The conclusions which have been reached by distinguished economists of every school of thought, those of the Left and those of the Right, [are] that if the bonds which attach the Netherlands to the Indies are severed there will be a permanent reduction in the national income of the Netherlands which will lead to the country's pauperization. Ten million people would have to maintain themselves on their few acres in a corner of Europe.[59]

Conscious of these attitudes, most observers at the time believed that the Dutch would not tolerate the existence of an independent Indonesia.[60] "The bonds between the Netherlands

---

from John C. Weigel (Foreign Economic Administration) to Wehle (chief, Foreign Economic Administration, Netherlands) concerning "activities of the F.E.A. in connection with the Netherlands Empire," May 23, 1947, Foreign Economic Administration Files, Box 44, Wehle Papers.

[56]Christopher Thorne, *The Limits of Foreign Policy: The West, The League, and the Far Eastern Crisis of 1931–1933* (New York: Putnam, 1972), p. 50.

[57]Kennedy, *Ageless Indies*, p. 169.

[58]Arthur S. Keller, "Netherlands India as a Paying Proposition," *Far Eastern Survey*, 1 (January 17, 1940):11–18.

[59]Gerbrandy, *Indonesia*, pp. 26–27.

[60]B. H. M. Vlekke, *The Netherlands and the United States* (Boston: World Peace Foundation, 1945), pp. 47–49; Herbert Feith, *The Decline of Constitutional Democ-*

and the East Indies," Gerbrandy warned, "cannot be severed. The prosperity of both is indivisible."[61]

Indonesian leaders fully expected to arouse implacable hostility from the Dutch. The traditional balance of power in East Asia had been profoundly shaken as a result of the war, however, and within the framework of the new order that was in the process of being created, Dutch policy was not the nationalists' paramount concern. In fact, they recognized that Holland suffered greatly as a result of the war; the Netherlands was so incapacitated in the wake of the Nazi occupation, Indonesians surmised, that it would take months or even years before the Dutch could assemble an army capable of reconquering the Indies. Indonesian spokesmen realized that any reassertion of Dutch control would be dependent on the attitude taken by the Allies, and particularly by the United States.[62]

The United States had unquestionably emerged as the greatest power in the Pacific at the end of World War II, and Indonesian nationalists appreciated the significance of this power shift for the independence movement. Buoyed by American anticolonial statements issued during the war, Indonesians hoped that the United States would take a sympathetic view of their fragile republic. They had listened intently to overseas broadcasts in which American spokesmen defended the principles of the Atlantic Charter and the Charter of the United Nations, and they believed that America's pledge of postwar independence for the Philippines would set an important precedent for all colonial peoples. Many Indonesians were convinced that

---

racy in Indonesia (Ithaca: Cornell University Press, 1962) pp. 2–3; Lawrence K. Rosinger, "Independence for Colonial Asia—The Cost to the Western World," *Foreign Policy Reports*, 19 (February 1, 1944):293–94; Andrew Roth, "Revolt in Asia," pt. 2, "Indonesia," *Nation*, November 10, 1945, pp. 493–95; Netherlands Indies Government Information Service, *What's It About in Indonesia?* (Batavia, 1947), p. 53; Charles Bidien, "Independence the Issue," *Far Eastern Survey*, 14 (December 5, 1945):345–48; Flora Bridges, "Indonesian Dilemma," *Current History*, 13 (September 1947):157; Vernon McKay, "Empires in Transition: British, French, and Dutch Colonial Plans," *Foreign Policy Reports*, 23 (May 1, 1947):37; B. H. M. Vlekke, "Present State of the Dutch Empire," *Asiatic Review*, 44 (January 1948):101.

[61]Gerbrandy, *Indonesia*, p. 26.

[62]Benedict R. O'G. Anderson, Introduction to Sutan Sjahrir, *Our Struggle* (Ithaca: Cornell University Modern Indonesia Project, 1968; 1945 reprint), pp 11–13.

Washington was genuinely opposed to European imperialism and that this attitude would naturally extend to the East Indies.[63] "Does not the 'Atlantic Charter,'" Hatta reasoned, "carry the solemn assurance of the Big Powers that they 'recognize the right of all peoples to live under a government of their own choice?'"[64]

Even Sjahrir, who was more skeptical about America's anti-colonial rhetoric, perceived the overwhelming significance that American, and to a lesser extent British, policy would have for the fledgling republic. "Indonesia is geographically situated within the sphere of influence of Anglo-Saxon capitalism and imperialism," he wrote in a highly influential pamphlet. "Accordingly Indonesia's fate ultimately depends on the fate of Anglo-Saxon capitalism and imperialism." Because Dutch rule in the Indies had formerly been dependent on British acceptance of that rule, Sjahrir reasoned it would now be dependent on American acceptance, since the United States had supplanted Britain as the leading Pacific power.[65] From whichever perspective they analyzed their chances for success or failure, then, Indonesian republicans recognized that the future of their republic and the course of American foreign policy would be inextricably linked.

[63]K'Tut Tantri, *Revolt in Paradise* (New York: Harper & Row, 1960), p. 175; Subandrio, "Social Reform in Indonesia," *Asian Horizon*, 1 (March 1948):33; Kahin, *Nationalism and Revolution*, pp. 129–30.

[64]Mohammed Hatta, "Indonesian Aims and Ideals," August 23, 1945, in *Portrait of a Patriot*, p. 501.

[65]Sjahrir, *Our Struggle*, pp. 24–25.

2

The United States, the East Indies, and the Colonial Question

The notion that the United States has been a sincere and determined foe of colonialism throughout its history has become virtually a staple of standard American ideology. Secretary of State John Foster Dulles succinctly summarized this belief when he proclaimed in 1954: "We ourselves are the first colony in modern times to have won independence. We have a natural sympathy with those who would follow our example."[1] Similarly, in a speech before the Senate in 1957 Senator John F. Kennedy invoked the traditions of anticolonialism in criticizing American policy toward the Algerian struggle. "If we are to secure the friendship of the Arab, the African, and the Asian," he said, "we cannot hope to accomplish it solely by means of billion-dollar foreign aid programs. . . . The strength of our appeal to these key populations—and it is rightfully our appeal, and not that of the Communists—lies in our traditional and deeply felt philosophy of freedom for all peoples everywhere."[2]

Many historians have firmly supported this view. "A product ourselves of revolt against colonial rule," wrote Julius Pratt, "we have tended to regard colonialism wherever practiced as unjust and to sympathize with those who would escape from it." According to this school of thought, American anticolonialism reached a peak during World War II, as President Franklin D.

[1] *U.S. Department of State Bulletin,* 30 (June 21, 1954):336.

[2] Remarks of Senator John F. Kennedy, July 2, 1957, 85th Cong., 1st Sess., *Congressional Record,* 103:10787.

Roosevelt led a vigorous assault on an oppressive European imperialist structure.[3]

This interpretation of American policy toward colonialism is certainly an oversimplification of a highly complex subject. Nevertheless, there has always been a significant strain of anticolonialist sentiment in American thought, and statesmen and historians are quite correct in pointing to the importance of this element of American ideology. Statements such as those above, however, overemphasize the moralistic and idealistic underpinning of this anticolonialism, almost to the exclusion of all other factors. In actuality, American anticolonialism often blended idealism with a strong element of economic self-interest.

The thought and policies of President Woodrow Wilson on the colonial issue offer an interesting case in point. To Wilson, American missionary idealism and economic self-interest were inseparable. The intensely moralistic president viewed traditional imperialism as the root cause of World War I. It was an atavistic system, he was convinced, which not only provoked highly dangerous international rivalry and competition, but also violently clashed with American open door trading principles, thus closing or restricting many of the world's markets to the peaceful penetration of American commerce. Accordingly, at the Versailles peace conference Wilson sought to reform the prevailing imperial structure through the mandate program of the League of Nations—a compromise between complete independence and continued imperial rule. Colonialism, Wilson believed, must be gradually liberalized; American commerce, as well as progressive American ideas and institutions, must be permitted to expand into the "backward" areas of the globe. This course, he reasoned, was in the interest not only of the

[3]Julius W. Pratt, "Anticolonialism in United States Policy," in Robert Strausz Hupé and Harry W. Hazard, eds., *The Idea of Colonialism* (New York: Praeger, 1958), p. 114. For the traditional interpretation of American anticolonialism, see Foster Rhea Dulles and Gerald A. Ridinger, "The Anti-Colonial Policies of Franklin D. Roosevelt," *Political Science Quarterly*, 70 (March 1955):1–18; Richard B. Morris, *Emerging Nations and the American Revolution* (New York: Oxford University Press, 1962), pp. 77–153; Thomas A. Bailey, *A Diplomatic History of the American People*, 9th ed. (Englewood Cliffs, N.J.: Prentice-Hall, 1970), pp. 787–88; Gary R. Hess, *America Encounters India, 1941–1947* (Baltimore: Johns Hopkins University Press, 1971), pp. 3–5.

United States, but of the dependent peoples themselves, and would promote world peace and stability as well.[4]

Despite such well-reasoned attacks on European imperialism, anticolonialism was never an overriding principle of American foreign policy, either before or during World War II. The need to balance other interests always tempered American anticolonial inclinations. Before the approach of the Pacific war, for example, the United States interest in the Netherlands East Indies lay primarily in maintaining equal access to the rich resources of the islands, especially their rubber, tin, and petroleum. Although American policy makers and businessmen often balked at the discriminatory trade practices of the Dutch, exclusionary commercial controls were a relatively minor irritant in U.S.–Dutch relations. Far more important was the order, stability, and development that the European colonial powers brought to Southeast Asia and other "backward" areas of the globe.

Throughout the nineteenth century, trade represented virtually the only focus of American interest in the Dutch East Indies, and this trade was relatively unimportant: the Indies supplied the United States with small amounts of such agricultural commodities as coffee, tea, sugar, and spices. Although the development of rich tin and rubber reserves in the Indies during the latter half of the century coincided with the growing need of American industry for those key raw materials, as late as 1896 coffee and sugar still accounted for over 90 percent of all the goods shipped from the Indies to the United States. American exports to the Dutch colony also remained insignificant throughout the nineteenth century.[5]

Commercial relations between the United States and the East Indies expanded considerably in the opening decades of the twentieth century, coincident with the emergence of the United States as a Pacific power. Trade reached a record high in 1920; American imports from the Indies amounted to $167 million in that year, while exports totaled $59 million. These figures con-

[4]N. Gordon Levin, Jr., *Woodrow Wilson and World Politics: America's Response to War and Revolution* (New York: Oxford University Press, 1968), pp. 236–51.

[5]John A. L. Sullivan, "The United States, the East Indies, and World War II: American Efforts to Modify the Colonial Status Quo," Ph.D. dissertation, University of Massachusetts, 1969, pp. 42–43.

tinued to grow throughout the decade, continually exceeding all previous records. Between 1925 and 1929, the average American share of the East Indian import market was 9.7 percent; its share of the East Indian export trade averaged 13.5 percent.[6]

The worldwide depression of the 1930s forced an abrupt but temporary contraction in trade between the two areas. By the middle of the decade, commercial relations again exceeded all previous records. In 1939 the United States absorbed 20 percent of all Indies exports, actually replacing the Netherlands as the colony's best customer. Partly as a result of the war in Europe, the United States became the leading supplier for the Indies in 1940, providing the archipelago with 23 percent of its imported goods. American exports to the Indies amounted to 1.3 percent of total American exports in 1940, and imports from the Indies to the United States in that year represented 6.7 percent of total imports—an indication of the growing economic importance of the East Indies to the United States on the eve of the Pacific war.[7]

Private American investment in the East Indies also increased considerably during this period. Just before the outbreak of hostilities in Southeast Asia, American firms had invested approximately $250 million in the Dutch colony. Such corporate giants as Standard Oil of New Jersey, General Motors, the U.S. Rubber Company, the Goodyear Rubber Company, Procter & Gamble, and the National Carbon Company had major investments in Indonesia.[8]

Despite these steadily improving prewar trade and investment patterns, American businessmen were often frustrated in

[6]U.S. Department of Commerce, Division of Regional Information, Bureau of Foreign and Domestic Commerce, Far Eastern Section, "Markets of the Netherlands East Indies," Trade Information Bulletin no. 509 (Washington, D.C.: U.S. Government Printing Office, 1928).

[7]U.S. Department of Commerce, Bureau of Foreign and Domestic Commerce, *Foreign Commerce Yearbook, 1939* (Washington, D.C.: U.S. Government Printing Office, 1942), pp. 281–82; U.S. Department of Commerce, Bureau of Foreign and Domestic Commerce, International Reference Service, *Trade of the United States with the Netherlands Indies in 1940* (Washington, D.C.: U.S. Government Printing Office, 1942), pp. 2, 45–46.

[8]U.S. Department of Commerce, Bureau of Foreign Commerce, *Investment in Indonesia: Basic Information for United States Businessmen* (Washington, D.C.: U.S. Government Printing Office, 1956), pp. 11–12; Netherlands Information Bureau, *Indonesia: Facts and Figures* (New York, 1948).

their attempts to expand commercial activities in the Indies by both Japanese competition and restrictive Dutch trading policies. During the 1930s, Japan emerged as a major rival to the United States for the rich East Indies market. Benefiting from their geographical proximity and the comparatively low price of their goods, Japanese merchants attempted to dominate trade with the East Indies and other Asian markets during that period. Statistics reveal their success in penetrating the East Indian import market: the Japanese share of East Indies imports grew from 10 percent in 1929 to 32 percent in 1933, providing a direct challenge to American commercial interests.[9]

Equally discouraging to American interests were the quota systems and other restrictive trade practices imposed by the Dutch government. The Dutch colony, like many of the world's markets during this time, was not organized on a free-market basis; instead, it was protected for the primary, if not exclusive, benefit of the European mother country, in obvious violation of the traditional American interest in open door trading principles. The Netherlands government promoted commerce between Dutch capitalists and the East Indies, at the expense of potential American competitors, through the widespread use of preferential trade arrangements. Even the production and price levels of such key commodities as rubber and tin—resources that American leaders considered vital to their nation's defense and security by the late 1930s—were set by international control committees dominated by the Dutch and other European colonial powers.[10]

Oil companies were among the first American industrial concerns to clash with the protective trading practices of the Dutch government. The Standard Oil Company of New Jersey made several attempts to explore the rich oil reserves of the archipelago during the nineteenth century, but it continually met with

[9]John C. LeClair, "Japan's Trade with the Netherlands Indies," *Foreign Affairs*, 15 (January 1937):381–83; Hubertus J. van Mook, *The Netherlands Indies and Japan: Their Relations, 1940–1941* (London: George Allen & Unwin, 1944); Rupert Emerson, *The Netherlands Indies and the United States*, (Boston: World Peace Foundation, 1942), pp. 48–53.

[10]Sullivan, "The United States, the East Indies, and World War II," pp. 47–48; Lloyd C. Gardner, *Economic Aspects of New Deal Diplomacy* (Madison: University of Wisconsin Press, 1964), pp. 64–67, 176.

obstruction from the colonial regime and the Royal Dutch Petroleum Company. When Standard managed to get a small foothold in the Indies, the Dutch passed laws that made it virtually impossible for it to compete with Dutch firms. In 1917 the States General of the Netherlands passed a law that not only required that all companies operating in the Indies be truly Dutch controlled and capitalized, but also gave the East Indies government the right to buy back and develop any promising oil fields uncovered by foreign firms.[11]

Not surprisingly, American oilmen balked at these discriminatory policies, and after Standard discovered the vast oil reserves of central Sumatra in 1918, the American government became actively involved. Both the State and Interior departments threatened retaliation against Royal Dutch operations in the United States if the Netherlands failed to alter its stand against Standard Oil and American capital in general. In 1920 Secretary of State Bainbridge Colby instructed the American minister in Holland to advise Dutch officials

> that this Government's interest is in the recognition of the principle of mutual or reciprocal access to vital natural resources by nationals of this and foreign countries. This Government is frank in saying that it believes that the granting of concessions to a single company covering all the best areas of the Dutch East Indies can hardly fail to be construed, whether rightly or wrongly, as a measure of exclusion and would at least seem to compromise in that region the principle of equal opportunity.[12]

After much diplomatic debate, the Dutch government and the Standard Oil Company reached a modus vivendi the following

[11]George Cyril Allen and Audrey Gladys Donnithorne, *Western Enterprise in Indonesia and Malaya: A Study in Economic Development* (London: George Allen & Unwin, 1957), pp. 176–79; Peter Mellish Reed, "Standard Oil in Indonesia, 1898–1928," *Business History Review*, 32 (Autumn 1958):329–37; Massachusetts Institute of Technology (MIT), Center for International Studies, Indonesia Project, *Stanvac in Indonesia* (New York: National Planning Association, 1957).

[12]Bainbridge Colby to William Phillips (minister, Netherlands), September 4, 1920, in *Foreign Relations of the United States* (Washington, D.C.: U.S. Government Printing Office, 1936), 3:276. Hereafter volumes in this series will be cited as *FR*, followed by the year.

year which recognized Standard's right to operate in the East Indies.[13]

In 1933 Standard merged its Far Eastern holdings with the Socony Mobil Oil Company to form the Standard-Vacuum Oil Company (Stanvac), which by 1941 was producing 25 percent of the petroleum in the Indies, with the Royal Dutch Company producing the remainder. By 1936 Standard-Vacuum's properties in the Indies were valued at approximately $70 million, representing the single largest investment of American capital in the Indies before the war. But the Dutch had closed the door tightly behind Stanvac, to the dismay of other American oil companies, such as American, Sinclair, Standard of California, Texaco, and Gulf, which tried and failed to expand their operations into the Indies in the 1920s and 1930s.[14]

Equally restrictive and detrimental to American interests were rubber and tin import regulations. Rubber was essential to American industry, and until the development of synthetic rubber during World War II, the United States depended on Southeast Asia as the world's largest supplier of this indispensable raw material. The sharply reduced demand for both rubber and tin during the world depression resulted in surplus production and steadily declining prices. Consequently, in 1933 Great Britain, the Netherlands, and France, the colonial nations that controlled the production of rubber in Southeast Asia, formed the International Rubber Committee to "regulate" production and pricing in the rubber commodity markets. Secretary of State

[13]Gerald D. Nash, *United States Oil Policy, 1890–1964* (Pittsburgh: University of Pittsburgh Press, 1968), pp. 61–68; Reed, "Standard Oil in Indonesia," pp. 329–37; Sullivan, "The United States, the East Indies, and World War II," pp. 49–52; Joan Hoff Wilson, *American Business and Foreign Policy, 1920–1933* (Lexington: University of Kentucky Press, 1971), p. 198. See also *FR*, 1920, 3:260–91 and 2:528–53.

[14]U.S. Department of Commerce, *Investment in Indonesia*, p. 11; U.S. Office of Strategic Services (OSS), "Pre-War Petroleum Statistics," Research and Analysis Report no. 1900, April 20, 1944, in U.S. Department of State Records, National Archives, Washington, D.C. (hereafter cited as DSR); Helmut G. Callis, *Foreign Capital in Southeast Asia* (New York: Institute of Pacific Relations, 1942), pp. 31–32; MIT, *Stanvac in Indonesia*, p. 20; Malcolm Caldwell, "Oil and Imperialism in East Asia," *Journal of Contemporary Asia*, 1 (1971):8; Irvine H. Anderson, Jr., *The Standard-Vacuum Oil Company and United States East Asian Policy, 1933–1941* (Princeton: Princeton University Press, 1975), pp. 31–37.

Cordell Hull protested vigorously against the formation of the organization, arguing that it would increase the price of rubber and reduce the supply. "The plan would provide for a pivotal price without prior consultation with consuming interests," he complained, "and the operation of the agreement would be entirely in the hands of an international committee representative solely of producer groups." Such "monopoly conditions," he warned, "naturally would be regarded with anxiety in this country."[15]

American opposition was ineffectual, however, and before long Hull's worst suspicions were confirmed: not only did the price of rubber rise rapidly, but production quotas imposed by the cartel thwarted American efforts to stockpile this precious commodity. "At the present time," Hull lamented in February 1937, "the American consumers of rubber find that . . . they are faced with a situation wherein world stocks and their own stocks are continuing to decline and control of available supplies of rubber for the next few months is very eagerly in the hands of speculative interests which rely upon continued narrow restrictions to insure a further marked increase in price."[16] In that year the stockpiling program of the U.S. government could develop only a four-and-one-half-month supply of rubber; the production quotas and price controls of the International Rubber Committee had clearly taken their toll. "Constantly rising prices under conditions of strict control," Hull reminded the Dutch and the British, "will strengthen the impression both in this country and elsewhere that private interests are generally using their control over a volume of raw material for their special advantage." The secretary emphasized that "this will cause increasing dissatisfaction throughout the United States."[17] Even with the impending threat of war in the Far East, the committee refused to increase world rubber production, despite the State Department's exhortations. The American economy again suffered as a result of the European colonial powers' control over a

[15]Cordell Hull to Laurits S. Swenson (minister, Netherlands), January 23, 1934, in *FR*, 1934, 1:621. See also ibid., pp. 615–63.

[16]Hull to Grenville T. Emmet (minister in Netherlands), February 23, 1937, in *FR*, 1937, 1:890. See also ibid., pp. 874–919.

[17]Hull to Emmet, January 23, 1937, in *FR*, 1937, 1:876.

vital resource—a condition that American officials would not soon forget.[18] As one American diplomat later recalled: "We objected to the pre-war rubber cartel and the pre-war tin cartel"; after the war, "I wanted that we should not be in a position where we could be shut out. . . ."[19]

The importance of American trade with the East Indies, especially in the key strategic commodities of tin and rubber, became critical as the likelihood of war with Japan increased. In a letter to President Franklin D. Roosevelt on May 1, 1940, Under Secretary of State Sumner Welles emphasized American dependence on East Indian and Malayan sources:

> The problem of our continued supply of strategic materials has once more come to the fore because of recent developments. The materials which are of greatest concern to us at the present moment are tin and rubber . . . which would be difficult to secure if hostilities broke out in that area or if there were any interruption to shipping over the very long supply routes from the Netherlands Indies and British Malaya.[20]

By 1940 American efforts to build up stockpiles of strategic materials had catapulted the East Indies into an area of primary interest to the United States; between 35 and 40 percent of American rubber was imported from the Indies in that year.[21]

Japan was equally covetous of the valuable resources of the Indonesian archipelago, especially its oil. While the East Indies

[18] See, for example, "Economic Program with Reference to the Netherlands East Indies," report prepared by the Foreign Economic Administration (FEA), August 1, 1944, in folder labeled "Economic Programming," Box 3041, FEA Records, RG 169, Washington National Record Center, Suitland, Md.; Walter A. Foote (consul general in East Indies) to Under Secretary of State Dean Acheson, August 20, 1946, 656E.1112/8-2046, DSR.

[19] Interview with Abbot Moffat (chief, Southeast Asian Division, Department of State), November 14, 1975.

[20] Quoted in Robert K. Wolthuis, "United States Foreign Policy towards the Netherlands Indies, 1937–1945," Ph.D. dissertation, Johns Hopkins University, 1968, pp. 16–17.

[21] U.S. Department of Commerce, Bureau of Foreign and Domestic Commerce, Industrial Reference Service, "U.S. Trade with the Netherlands Indies in 1940" (Washington, D.C.: U.S. Government Printing Office, 1941), p. 4, and *Summary of the Foreign Trade of the United States, Calendar Year 1940* (Washington, D.C.: U.S. Government Printing Office, 1950), pp. 7–25.

accounted for only 2.7 percent of world oil production in the years before the war, the rich oil fields of Sumatra were the only major source of petroleum in the Far East. Japan, an oil-poor nation, was particularly eager to guarantee its access to these reserves, and as relations with the United States, Japan's principal supplier of oil, grew increasingly bitter, the petroleum of the Indies took on added significance for Tokyo.[22]

Japanese designs on the Netherlands East Indies became a critical concern for the United States during 1940 and 1941. On April 17, 1940, Hull released a statement to the press which outlined the American position toward Japanese expansion into the archipelago:

> The Netherlands Indies are very important in the international relationships of the whole Pacific Ocean. . . . They are also an important factor in the commerce of the whole world. They produce considerable portions of the world's supplies of important essential commodities such as rubber, tin, quinine, copra, et cetera. Many countries, including the United States, depend substantially upon them for some of these commodities. Intervention in the domestic affairs of the Netherlands Indies or any alteration of their *status quo* by other than peaceful processes would be prejudicial to the case of stability, peace, and security not only in the region of the Netherlands Indies but in the entire Pacific area.[23]

In private negotiations, American diplomats tried to secure Japanese assurances that the status quo would be maintained and that all nations would have equal commercial opportunity in the East Indies. "As the Japanese Government is aware," Hull telegrammed Joseph Grew, the American ambassador in Tokyo, in July 1940,

> the products of the Netherlands East Indies enter prominently into the economy of many countries. The United States maintains important commercial relations with the Netherlands East Indies and there exists there a substantial American enterprise. According to the statistics of this Government for 1937, the latest year for which

[22]Anderson, *Standard-Vacuum*, pp. 4, 81–82; OSS, "Pre-War Petroleum Statistics."

[23]*U.S. Department of State Bulletin*, 2 (April 20, 1941):411.

> complete statistics are available, of the total foreign trade of the Netherlands East Indies 15.8 percent by value was with the United States as compared with 11.6 percent with Japan. Consequently, the Government of the United States has a substantial interest in the Netherlands East Indies, as well as elsewhere, of the principle and practice of equality of opportunity in trade and enterprise.[24]

On this and other major issues, the United States and Japan tragically failed to reach an agreement. On December 7, 1941, the Japanese struck at Pearl Harbor; shortly thereafter they moved into Southeast Asia. They secured control of the Indonesian archipelago in March 1942.[25]

The Pacific war completely transformed American–East Indian relations. For some weeks after Pearl Harbor the United States gave a great deal of attention to the Netherlands East Indies, observed Stanley Hornbeck, director of the State Department's Office of Far Eastern Affairs, "but from the moment when they were occupied by the Japanese we for three years gave them thought only as part of an ultimate military problem."[26] Hornbeck's statement, while reflective of official priorities, is only partially true. While military considerations obviously dwarfed all others during the war, political planning for the postwar world began seriously in 1942 and was carried on with great intensity throughout the war period; and the East Indies, as one of the European colonies overrun by the Japanese, figured prominently in the deliberations of the var-

[24]Hull to Grew, July 4, 1940, in *FR*, 1940, 4:383. On the growing importance of the Netherlands East Indies to the United States in 1940 and 1941, see especially the material in folder labeled "Netherlands East Indies," Box 311, Stanley K. Hornbeck Papers, Hoover Institution on War, Revolution, and Peace, Stanford University.

[25]Most historians recognize that while the Japanese threat to the East Indies was not the primary cause of war between the United States and Japan, it was certainly a major contributing factor. See, for example, Herbert Feis, *The Road to Pearl Harbor* (Princeton: Princeton University Press, 1950), pp. 51–59, 244–48; Paul W. Schroeder, *The Axis Alliance and Japanese-American Relations* (Ithaca: Cornell University Press, 1958), pp. 14–18, 173–74; Anderson, *Standard-Vacuum*, pp. 195–200; Sullivan, "The United States, the East Indies, and World War II," pp. 57–69; Wolthuis, "United States Foreign Policy," chaps. 2–13.

[26]Stanley K. Hornbeck, "The United States and the Netherlands East Indies," address delivered at the University of Michigan, July 2, 1947, in folder labeled "Netherlands (1947–1948)," Box 310, Hornbeck Papers.

ious postwar planning committees.[27] Indeed, the future of the colonial empires was one of the most fundamental and complex problems facing American planners: Would the United States favor a policy of liberation and self-determination for colonial peoples, in line with its traditional anticolonialist ideals? Or would the United States use its influence to help enforce a policy of colonial reconquest, supporting the position of its European allies? Much depended on the attitude Washington would take toward the future of the colonial territories, and colonial peoples and European imperial powers alike anxiously waited to see how American policy would develop toward this critical question.

The Roosevelt administration gave numerous strong indications during the war that it sought the eradication of what it believed to be an outdated colonial system. Speaking before the White House correspondents on March 15, 1941, Roosevelt said, "There never has been, there isn't now and there never will be any race of people of the earth fit to serve as masters over their fellow men. . . . We believe that any nationality, no matter how small, has the inherent right to its own nationhood."[28] The Atlantic Charter, signed by Roosevelt and British Prime Minister Winston Churchill in August 1941, further developed this commitment by calling for the "right of all people to choose the form of government under which they will live."[29] As if to clear up any possible ambiguity, on several occasions during the war American officials pointed to the universal applicability of the

[27]The best source for an analysis of the postwar planning committees is Wm. Roger Louis, *Imperialism at Bay: The United States and the Decolonization of the British Empire, 1941–1945* (New York: Oxford University Press, 1978).

[28]*New York Times*, March 16, 1941, p. 1. For the view that Roosevelt was a genuine and persistent foe of colonialism, see Dulles and Ridinger, "Anti-Colonial Policies," pp. 1–18; Willard Range, *Franklin D. Roosevelt's World Order* (Athens: University of Georgia Press, 1959), pp. 102–19; Robert C. Good, "The United States and the Colonial Debate," in Arnold Wolfers, ed., *Alliance Policy in the Cold War* (Baltimore: Johns Hopkins University Press, 1959), pp. 226–27; Pratt, "Anticolonialism," pp. 127–30; Elliot Roosevelt, *As He Saw It* (New York: Duel, Sloan & Pearse, 1945), pp. 74ff.; Gaddis Smith, *American Diplomacy during the Second World War* (New York: Wiley, 1965), pp. 81–83; Gary R. Hess, "Franklin Roosevelt and Indochina," *Journal of American History*, 59 (September 1972):353–68.

[29]U.S. Department of State, *Peace and War: United States Foreign Policy, 1931–1941* (Washington, D.C.: U.S. Government Printing Office, 1943), p. 719.

Atlantic Charter. Roosevelt himself, in a radio address to the nation on February 23, 1942, declared that "the Atlantic Charter not only applies to the parts of the world that border on the Atlantic, but to the whole world."[30] In a Memorial Day speech in 1942, Sumner Welles suggested that the war should ensure the sovereign equality of all peoples and should be followed by "the liberation of all people." He continued: "The age of imperialism is ended. The right of people to their freedom must be recognized, as the civilized world long since recognized the rights of an individual to his personal freedom. The principles of the Atlantic Charter must be guaranteed to the world—in all oceans and continents."[31]

Government spokesmen often pointed to the American experience with the Philippines as an appropriate model for European colonial nations to follow. In a radio address on July 23, 1942, Hull referred to the traditional American support of liberty for all peoples. "We have strived to meet squarely our own responsibility in this respect," he said, "in Cuba, in the Philippines and wherever else it has devolved upon us." He continued the address with the assurance that a goal of American policy had always been, and would remain, "to use the full measure of our influence to support attainment of freedom by all peoples. . . ."[32] The secretary of state returned to this theme on November 20, 1942, when he stated:

> "The President and I and the entire Government, earnestly favor freedom for all dependent peoples at the earliest date practicable. Our course in dealing with the Philippines situation in this respect, as in all other important respects, offers, I think, a perfect example of how a nation should treat a colony or a dependency in cooperating with it in all essential respects calculated to assist it in making all necessary preparation for freedom."[33]

[30]*New York Times*, February 24, 1942, p. 4.

[31]*New York Times*, May 31, 1942, p. 1.

[32]*U.S. Department of State Bulletin*, 7 (July 25, 1942):642.

[33]Hull to John Winant (ambassador, Great Britain), November 20, 1942, in *FR*, 1942, 1:746–47. A summary of U.S. wartime statements regarding colonial matters, entitled "Summary of Official Policy with Respect to the Post-War Administration of Dependent Areas," dated March 15, 1944, is in Records of the Policy and Planning Committees, Box 131, Harley A. Notter Files, RG59, DSR.

These American pronouncements during World War II, coupled with the promise of early independence for the Philippines and what colonial nationalist leaders perceived to be a traditional American antipathy toward imperialism and support for self-determination, had a profound impact on Asian independence movements. Ho Chi Minh, the leader of the Vietnamese nationalist movement and an avowed Communist, expressed a great deal of admiration for Jefferson, Lincoln, and the traditional American devotion to freedom, believing that the United States would oppose the reimposition of colonial rule in Asia. The opening words of the Vietnamese proclamation of independence of September 2, 1945, which borrowed liberally from the American Declaration of Independence, unmistakably illustrate the influence of American ideas.[34] Indonesian nationalists similarly expressed great admiration for the United States. As a report prepared in 1942 by the Office of Strategic Services (OSS) observed: "They are grateful for American policy in the Philippines which has helped guide movements for self-government in the East Indies."[35] When British troops landed in Java in September 1945, they found scrawled on the walls of public buildings statements such as "We are fighting for government for the people, by the people, of the people"; "We are fighting for our inalienable right to life, liberty, and the pursuit of happiness"; and "Give us liberty or give us death." As one British officer grumbled at the time, "Your damned American revolution is still giving us trouble."[36]

And it was. All across the continent of Asia nationalist leaders

[34]Bernard B. Fall, ed., *Ho Chi Minh: On Revolution* (New York: Praeger, 1967), p. 143; Allen W. Cameron, ed., *Viet-Nam Crisis: A Documentary History* (Ithaca: Cornell University Press, 1971), 1:52–54; Jean Lacouture, *Ho Chi Minh: A Political Biography* (New York: Random House, 1968), pp. 262–65, 267; William Warbey, *Ho Chi Minh and the Struggle for an Independent Vietnam* (London: Merlin Press, 1972), pp. 78–79; Robert Shaplen, *The Lost Revolution: America in Vietnam, 1946–1966,* rev. ed. (New York: Harper & Row, 1966), pp. 28–30; Richard B. Morris, *The Emerging Nations and the American Revolution* (New York: Harper & Row, 1970), pp. 3, 220.

[35]OSS, "Strategic Survey of the Netherlands Indies," Research and Analysis Report no. 707, January 31, 1941, DSR.

[36]Frederick E. Crockett, "How the Trouble Began in Java," *Harper's Magazine,* March 1946, pp. 279–80; Harold Isaacs, *No Peace for Asia* (New York: Macmillan, 1947), p. 122.

looked to the United States with great admiration and hope. Even the Chinese Communist leader Mao Tse-tung expressed great respect for American traditions and indicated a special admiration for George Washington.[37] The Atlantic Charter, the Charter of the United Nations, and the repeated anticolonial statements of the Roosevelt administration encouraged nationalists in dependent lands to believe that their respective causes would receive a sympathetic hearing in Washington. As Ho Chi Minh explained to a State Department representative: "My people look to the United States as the one nation most likely to be sympathetic to our cause."[38] If the United States believed in its stated principles, these nationalist leaders reasoned, then surely it would support self-government for colonial peoples.

American criticism of European colonialism was not restricted to pious public rhetoric. On the contrary, Roosevelt, Hull, and other high-ranking administration spokesmen reiterated the anticolonial theme in numerous conversations both among themselves and with various foreign leaders, especially during the first few years of the war. The views of Roosevelt himself, a man whose dominance over American foreign policy during this time was probably more complete than that of any other president in recent history, set the tone for the administration. His ideas on colonialism were perhaps most forcefully articulated during a brief trip to Africa in February 1942, en route to the Casablanca conference. After a short stopover in the British colony of Gambia, the president expressed his horror at the standard of living that he observed there. "Those people are treated worse than the livestock," he exclaimed to his son Elliott. "Their cattle live longer!"[39] In a letter to Churchill, the president labeled the area a "hell-hole."[40] Later, at a press conference, he vividly recalled his impressions of Gambia, emphasizing that it was "the most horrible thing I have ever seen in my life." Disease

[37]Edgar Snow, *Red Star over China* (New York: Grove Press, 1968), p. 138.

[38]Quoted in Gabriel Kolko, *The Politics of War: The World and United States Foreign Policy, 1943–1945* (New York: Random House, 1968), p. 609.

[39]Quoted in Elliot Roosevelt, *As He Saw It*, p. 75. On the importance of Roosevelt's trip to Africa, see especially Louis, *Imperialism at Bay*, pp. 226–27.

[40]Quoted in Louis, *Imperialism at Bay*, p. 227.

was rampant, he continued, and "the natives are five thousand years back of us."[41]

Those passionate remarks typified Roosevelt's general attitude toward European imperialism, a system that in his view brutally exploited the native population and at the same time created the seeds of future wars. "The colonial system means war," he insisted at one point. "Exploit the resources of an India, a Burma, a Java; take all the wealth out of those countries, but never put anything back into them, things like education, decent standards of living, minimum health requirements—all you're doing is storing up the kind of trouble that leads to war."[42] In meetings with Russian, Chinese, and British diplomats throughout 1942 and 1943, the president frequently gave vent to his anticolonialist sentiments, suggesting various plans for reform in the postwar world. Much to the dismay of the British, at one point he casually offered his prescription for the future of India, gleefully drawing a comparison with the American Revolution.[43] On another occasion he suggested to Foreign Minister Anthony Eden in his characteristically breezy manner that the British might consider returning Hong Kong to the Chinese as a gesture of "goodwill."[44] But his most strident denunciations of the colonial powers were reserved for the French in Indochina. "France has had the country—thirty million inhabitants—for nearly one hundred years, and the people are worse off then they were at the beginning," he said to the British ambassador. "France has milked it for one hundred years. The people of Indo-China are entitled to something better than that."[45] Precisely how such ideas could be translated into substantive, practical policies, however, was quite another story.

The anticolonialism of the Roosevelt administration can best be understood within the larger context of American postwar plans. During the war, American policy makers became convinced that the postwar prosperity of the United States and of

[41]Quoted in ibid., p. 356.
[42]Quoted in Elliot Roosevelt, *As He Saw It*, p. 74.
[43]Christopher Thorne, *Allies of a Kind: The United States, Britain, and the War against Japan, 1941–1945* (New York: Oxford University Press, 1978), pp. 242–43.
[44]Louis, *Imperialism at Bay*, pp. 227–29.
[45]Cordell Hull, *Memoirs*, 2 vols. (New York: Macmillan, 1948), 2:1597.

the world would depend to a large extent on open access to foreign markets and sources of raw materials. American leaders unequivocally agreed that disastrous depressions and world wars could be avoided in the future only by the universal adoption of the open door principle of nondiscrimination in foreign trade and investment. Cordell Hull accurately reflected the thinking of government spokesmen when he recalled in his autobiography that as early as World War I he had begun to realize that "unhampered trade dovetailed with peace; high tariffs, trade barriers, and unfair economic competition with war."[46] The lesson seemed simple: the 1930s had witnessed a multitude of discriminatory and monopolistic trade practices that contravened the essential principles of free trade, and consequently helped to create conditions of economic warfare and instability—conditions that proved to be a fertile breeding ground for radical ideologies and ultimately world conflict. American officials thus came to believe that the principle of nondiscrimination in foreign trade was a basic prerequisite for world peace, order, and stability.[47] As Dean Acheson observed in March 1945:

> The governments of the world have learned, as they have never learned before, all the tricks of economic warfare. . . . If the situation were spread throughout the world, it would have a devastating effect upon recovery from the war. Probably the only hope of maintaining stability—social, political, and economic—in the world, in the face of the great post-war troubles, is to adopt measures which will lead to an expansion of production, consumption, and trade.[48]

The existence of colonial trading blocs in which the colonial economies were almost completely geared to the needs of the mother country, serving primarily as sources of raw materials and labor and as protected markets for the manufactured goods

[46]Ibid., 1:81.

[47]Thomas G. Paterson, *Soviet-American Confrontation: Postwar Reconstruction and the Origins of the Cold War* (Baltimore: Johns Hopkins University Press, 1973), pp. 1–8; William A. Williams, *Tragedy of American Diplomacy*, 2d rev. ed. (New York: Delta Books, 1972), pp. 229–39; Lloyd Gardner, *Architects of Illusion: Men and Ideas in American Foreign Policy, 1941–1949* (Chicago: Quadrangle Books, 1970), pp. 203–5, 319.

[48]*U.S. Department of State Bulletin*, 12 (March 15, 1945):470.

of the metropolitan powers, represented one of the most glaring affronts to the American vision of an open world. In the Netherlands East Indies and other colonial areas, the United States had continually found itself faced with discriminatory commercial regulations that denied its exports equal access to colonial markets. With these lessons of history in mind, many American diplomats vigorously opposed the reestablishment of the colonial economic system, which—with its monopoly controls, quota restrictions, and preferential trade agreements—was so clearly incompatible with the American devotion to open door trading principles.[49]

Roosevelt administration officials did not believe that they were selfishly pursuing American economic advantage in this regard. On the contrary, many of these spokesmen sincerely believed that while a free world market would surely serve the economic interests of the United States—which by 1945 was producing an astonishing 50 percent of the world's goods—it was also necessary and desirable for the proper functioning of the international economy and the maintenance of global peace and prosperity. In this world view, American interests neatly coincided with those of the rest of the world, since, in the colorful words of Dean Acheson, "the United States was the locomotive at the head of mankind and the rest of the world was the caboose."[50]

Washington's anticolonialism was sharply limited, however, since American authorities were never willing to accept the logical extension of their own rhetoric—in short, full and immediate independence for all colonial territories. U.S. spokesmen always stopped well short of advocating rapid, unconditional independence, indicating instead that an appropriate period of preparation, or tutelage, would be necessary before

[49]Gardner, *Economic Aspects*, p. 176; Philip W. Bell, "Colonialism as a Problem in American Foreign Policy," *World Politics*, 5 (October 1952):87–88; *New Republic*, January 22, 1945, p. 105; Ernest B. Hoas, "The Attempt to Terminate Colonialism: Acceptance of the United Nations Trusteeship System," *International Organization*, 7 (February 1953):5; Lawrence K. Rosinger, "Independence for Colonial Asia—The Cost to the Western World," *Foreign Policy Reports*, 19 (February 1, 1944):303.

[50]Cited in Stephen E. Ambrose, *Rise to Globalism: American Foreign Policy, 1938–1970* (Baltimore: Penguin, 1971), p. 297.

self-government could be granted. In repeatedly pointing to the American record in the Philippines as a model, the Roosevelt administration made this point quite clear; after all, the United States had been preparing that colony for independence for almost fifty years. The very concept of total independence for colonial territories was still regarded as a radical idea; most American policy makers, while eager to effect a fundamental change in the traditional colonial system, simply did not believe that the underdeveloped world was prepared to accept the responsibilities and burdens that self-rule would inevitably bring. As Roosevelt himself once commented: "For a time at least there are many minor children among the peoples of the world who need trustees . . . just as there are many adult nations or peoples which must be led back into a spirit of good conduct."[51] In short, like Wilson, Roosevelt was a gradualist. It should not be surprising, then, that the Roosevelt administration at no time pressed Britain, France, or the Netherlands for an immediate grant of self-government to their colonies. "Our thought was that it would come after an adequate period of years," Hull later explained, "short or long depending on the state of development of respective colonial peoples, during which these people would be trained to govern themselves."[52]

Between the twin evils of early independence without adequate preparation and complete restoration of the European colonial structure, American policy makers sought alternatives. The compromise position that seemed to avoid both of these extremes, and which appeared most attractive to State Department experts, was international trusteeship. If formerly dependent areas were placed under a system of international trusteeship, an adequate period of preparation for self-rule would be provided, and yet the ultimate dismemberment of the European empires would be ensured. As Welles argued before one of the postwar planning committees, "The liberation of peoples

[51]Quoted in Ruth B. Russell, *A History of the United Nations Charter: The Role of the United States, 1940–45* (Washington, D.C.: Brookings Institution, 1958), p. 43.

[52]Hull, *Memoirs*, 2:1601. See also Pratt, "Anticolonialism," p. 132; OSS, "British and American Views on the Applicability of the Atlantic Charter to Dependent Areas," August 30, 1944, Research and Analysis Report no. 1972, DSR; Harold M. Vinacke, "United States Far Eastern Policy," *Pacific Affairs*, 19 (December 1946): 351–52.

should be the main principle. Many of the peoples cannot undertake self-government at this time. This is where trusteeship comes in. The United Nations should endeavor to develop the ability of these peoples to govern themselves as soon as possible."[53] On March 17, 1943, Hull presented Roosevelt with an outline of the State Department's recommendations on this question. For a trusteeship system to succeed, the secretary of state observed, colonial administrators would have to take at least four steps: provide protection and opportunity for the colony to advance its general welfare; allow colonial peoples a larger share in local government; establish dates when the colonies would become independent; and pursue development of the colonies and their resources over which natives may have decisive influence.[54]

Roosevelt himself took the lead in advocating the trusteeship concept, although he never allowed himself to be tied down to specifics, as Hull's various memoranda recommended. During Eden's visit to Washington in March 1943, the president first unveiled his thinking on the subject, proposing a grand reorganization of the colonial world; his plan included postwar trusteeship for Indochina and Korea, among other areas.[55] He continued to explore these ideas at the wartime conferences at Cairo and Tehran and in numerous conversations with foreign and administration officials. At various times he advocated that Indochina, part of the East Indies, and all of the Japanese-mandated islands in the Pacific, along with selected other territories, be placed under a system of international trusteeship. From its very inception, however, the trusteeship scheme was marred by the president's vague and often inconsistent proposals on the matter. At no time did he use his leadership to translate such concepts and notions into concrete, workable policies,

[53]Minutes of the Advisory Committee on Postwar Foreign Policy, August 8, 1942, in Box 66, Notter Files, DSR. For similar statements, see Committee on Colonial Problems, minutes, October 29, 1943, in Box 70, ibid.

[54]Hull to Roosevelt, March 17, 1943, cited in Harley Notter, *Postwar Foreign Policy Preparation, 1939–1945* (Washington, D.C.: U.S. Government Printing Office, 1950), p. 471; Hull, *Memoirs*, 2:1600.

[55]Memorandum by Hull of a conversation with Roosevelt, Eden, and others, March 27, 1943, in *FR*, 1943, 3:36–38; memorandum by Harry Hopkins of a conversation with Roosevelt, Eden, and others, March 27, 1943, in ibid., pp. 38–40; Louis, *Imperialism at Bay*, pp. 227–29.

nor was he able to heal the deep divisions within his own government over the future of the colonial empires.[56]

No area of the world better illustrates the ambiguities and inconsistencies of Roosevelt's trusteeship planning than the East Indies. It is extremely difficult, first of all, to gauge how thoroughly the president ever committed himself to the trusteeship concept for the East Indies. On April 6, 1942, for instance, he assured Queen Wilhelmina in a personal letter that the islands would be returned to the Dutch after the war, with no mention of trusteeship or eventual self-rule.[57] But three months later, while Roosevelt was entertaining the queen and her family at his estate in Hyde Park, New York, he urged her to make a definite commitment to postwar self-government for the Indies.[58] One of the few times he explicitly applied trusteeship to the Indonesian archipelago was during a White House meeting on October 5, 1943; then he informed Hull and Admiral William Leahy that he would like to see "appropriate points in the Dutch East Indies" placed under international trusteeship.[59] Yet the available evidence hardly suggests that Roosevelt vigorously pursued this objective; instead, it appears that he believed his aims for the future of colonialism—a gradual liberalization of imperial rule leading to eventual self-government—were not incompatible with the policy plans of the Dutch. He was apparently quite pleased when Queen Wilhelmina made a major policy pronouncement about the future of the Dutch colony in December 1942; in a speech clearly designed with an American audience in mind, she pledged—albeit vaguely—that her government would grant increasing powers of self-rule to native nationalists.[60]

Unquestionably, Roosevelt never promoted trusteeship for

[56]Walter LaFeber, "Roosevelt, Churchill, and Indochina: 1942–45," *American Historical Review*, 80 (December 1975):1277–95; Louis, *Imperialism at Bay*, pp. 274–86, 356–58; Robert Dallek, *Franklin D. Roosevelt and American Foreign Policy, 1932–1945* (New York: Oxford University Press, 1979), pp. 429–30.

[57]Roosevelt to Wilhelmina, April 6, 1942, in *FDR: His Personal Letters*, ed. Elliott Roosevelt, vol. 4 (New York, 1950).

[58]Hull, *Memoirs*, 2:1595–96; Louis, *Imperialism at Bay*, p. 437.

[59]Sumner Welles, *Seven Decisions That Shaped History* (New York: Harper, 1950), p. 150.

[60]Thorne, *Allies of a Kind*, p. 219; OSS, "Background Information on Dutch Promises Regarding the Netherlands Indies," Research and Analysis Report no. 478, January 25, 1943, DSR.

the Dutch East Indies as forcefully and consistently as he did for French Indochina. His violent antipathy to the French—which extended quite naturally to their valuable colony in Southeast Asia—led him to oppose the reestablishment of French rule in Indochina. This staunch opposition to the reimposition of French imperialism was in no way comparable to the president's views about the Dutch or Dutch colonialism. A combination of factors—his Dutch ancestry, his close personal relations with the Dutch royal family, and his view that the Dutch, as opposed to the French, were liberal colonialists sincerely committed to reforming past abuses—led the president to differentiate sharply between French and Dutch colonialism.[61] Indeed, Roosevelt tended to view Dutch plans for the future of the East Indies in a somewhat favorable light. In 1943 he again met with Wilhelmina in Washington and they discussed the colonial issue in great depth. Elliott Roosevelt later reported his father's account of the meeting:

> You know it was just about a year ago [1943] that Queen Wilhelmina was here. In the White House. For a visit. And we got to talking . . . I should say, I got *her* to talking, about the Dutch colonies, and what was going to happen to them after the war. Java, Borneo—all the Netherlands East Indies. Talked back and forth for more than six hours, over two or three evenings. I made the point that it was American arms that would be liberating those colonies from the Japanese. American soldiers and sailors and marines. I mentioned the Philippines. . . . She agreed that the policy we have in the Philippines would be the pattern she would follow in the Dutch East Indies, after the war. She promised me that her government would announce immediately after victory in Japan, that they were going to grant the people of the Dutch East Indies first dominion status, with the right of self-rule and equality.
>
> Then after their government has been established, if the people, by free vote, decide that they want complete independence, they shall be granted it. Just as we are granting it in the Philippines.

[61] Abbot L. Moffat to Joseph Ballantine (Office of Far Eastern Affairs), January 17, 1945, in folder labeled "Indochina, Political: French Postwar Policy," Box 9, Records of the Office of Philippine and Southeast Asian Affairs (PSA), Lot 54 D 190, RG59, DSR: LaFeber, "Roosevelt, Churchill, and Indochina," pp. 1285–86; Thorne, *Allies of a Kind*, pp. 217–18; Robert J. Leupold, "The United States and Indonesian Independence, 1944–1947: An American Response to Revolution," Ph.D. dissertation, University of Kentucky, 1976, pp. 44–46.

That's a commitment. And it means a sharp break away from the leadership of the British.[62]

Similarly, in a discussion with Australian Ambassador Sir Frederick Eggleston in November 1944, Roosevelt mentioned that he would support Dutch efforts to retain control of the East Indies because he believed that they were sincere in their pledges to bring democracy to Southeast Asia. In sharp contrast, he quickly added, were the British; while he wished that they would do the same for Burma and Malaya, he admitted that he had little hope.[63]

The vague and often contradictory nature of the president's thinking on the subject was only one of a series of problems that plagued the trusteeship program from its very inception. Even more serious was the staunch opposition of the European powers to trusteeship or any other formula that would challenge their colonial sovereignty. Great Britain sharply differed with the United States on this issue, preferring to talk about eventual colonial self-government rather than total independence, and favoring a single power exercising trusteeship authority in any given area rather than an international agency of control. In a celebrated speech, Churchill gruffly declared in 1942 that he had not become the king's first minister "in order to preside over the liquidation of the British Empire."[64] When Stanley Hornbeck brought up the status of Hong Kong during a discussion with British officials in London, he recorded that a "discordant note was struck" which had "an electrifying effect."[65] In the same vein, Churchill exclaimed angrily at Yalta, "Under no circumstances would [I] ever consent to forty or fifty nations thrusting interfering fingers into the life's existence of the British Empire."[66]

Churchill's remarks typified the general attitude of the European colonial powers toward the American trusteeship proposals. Many European leaders believed that anticolonial rhetoric

[62]Elliott Roosevelt, *As He Saw It*, p. 223.

[63]Louis, *Imperialism at Bay*, p. 424.

[64]*Times* (London), November 11, 1942, p. 1.

[65]Undated memorandum by Hornbeck of a conversation with Salisbury and Sir Stafford Cripps, in folder labeled "Autobiography 1942–44," Box 497, Hornbeck Papers.

[66]*FR*, 1945, *The Conferences at Malta and Yalta*, pp. 844, 858.

only masked underlying economic interests and feared that Washington would seek to expand its power and influence in the colonial areas of Southeast Asia at the conclusion of the war. Others wondered if misplaced American idealism and naiveté might not wreak havoc on the entire colonial system.[67] Dutch Ambassador Alexander Loudon spoke very bluntly and very strongly to Hull on at least one occasion about the constant "propaganda" in the United States regarding imperialism and racial equality. Such irresponsible statements had an extremely harmful effect on the East Indies, he complained; it was grossly unfair "that the Dutch East Indies are being held up as a horrible example of imperialism and other aggravated violations of all the liberal policies that should govern international relations and peoples in every part of the world."[68]

U.S. officials sought on numerous occasions to gain European acceptance of their trusteeship plans, but they encountered only icy hostility whenever they broached the subject. This opposition had to be taken quite seriously, since it threatened to create severe strains within the wartime alliance, and since the postwar plans of the United States depended to a great extent on harmonious relations with the Western European nations. Later, Hull emphasized this point when he wrote, "We had frequent conversations with these parent countries, but we could not press them too far with regard to the Southwest Pacific in view of the fact that we were seeking the closest possible cooperation with them in Europe. We could not alienate them in the Orient and expect to work with them in Europe."[69]

Further opposition to the trusteeship concept came from within the U.S. government itself. The War and Navy departments protested that Hull's trusteeship proposals conflicted with larger national security interests. American military planners were convinced that postwar security required exclusive American control over the Japanese-mandated islands; international or United Nations supervision was completely unacceptable from their perspective. In a conversation with Secretary of the Navy

[67]Louis, *Imperialism at Bay*, pp. 38–40; Thorne, *Allies of a Kind*, pp. 218–23.

[68]Memorandum by Hull of a conversation with Loudon, June 5, 1942, 856D.00/153, DSR.

[69]Hull, *Memoirs*, 2:1559.

James Forrestal on March 30, 1945, Secretary of War Henry Stimson expressed fears "that we might be tempted into making quixotic gestures the net result of which might be that we would surrender the hardly won islands which we had taken in the Pacific to the principle of trusteeship, whereas the British, Dutch and French would not."[70] The Joint Chiefs of Staff urged Roosevelt to formulate general principles on the trusteeship issue, but to avoid making any specific commitments or placing any specific territories under international trusteeship; all "territorial settlements," the Joint Chiefs urged, should "be delayed until after the defeat of Japan."[71]

Not even the State Department was unified on the increasingly tangled colonial question. Certain elements within the department, centered especially in the Office of European Affairs, looked with askance on any plans to remove from the European powers one of their principal sources of strength. Convinced that American plans for the postwar world would require European friendship and cooperation, the department's "Europeanists" insisted that the colonial powers must have their sovereignty restored unconditionally. Led by influential Assistant Secretary of State James Clement Dunn, these officials believed that any meddling in colonial affairs would only risk the alienation of Washington's traditional allies. To press such a potentially divisive issue during wartime, moreover, would represent the height of diplomatic impropriety. European-oriented by virtue of experience, education, and temperament, these men were horrified by many of Roosevelt's and Hull's plans. Unfamiliar with the Third World, they were hardly sympathetic to the cause of colonial nationalism. "Why are you fussing with Indonesia," Dunn contemptuously asked a State Department officer on one occasion. "It's only a Dutch colony."[72] Despite all

[70]James Forrestal, *The Forrestal Diaries*, ed. Walter Millis (New York: Viking, 1951), p. 37. See also Henry L. Stimson and McGeorge Bundy, *On Active Service in Peace and War* (New York: Harper, 1948), p. 601; Notter, *Postwar Foreign Policy Preparation*, pp. 276, 295–96.

[71]Memorandum from James Dunn (chairman, State-War-Navy Coordinating Committee) to Secretary of State Edward R. Stettinius, Jr., February 26, 1945, in Box 9, Records of the State-War-Navy Coordinating Committee, RG 334, DSR (hereafter cited as SWNCC Records).

[72]Quoted in Martin Weil, *A Pretty Good Club: The Founding Fathers of the U.S. Foreign Service* (New York: Norton, 1978), p. 217. See also Laurence Salisbury,

obstacles, they managed to maintain the most friendly and cordial relations with European diplomats. And while never actually disloyal to Roosevelt and Hull, the department's Europeanists fought in effect a rear-guard action throughout the war years, maneuvering to modify and compromise the administration's anticolonial stance whenever possible.

Aside from Hull, whose opposition to European colonialism was rooted in his devotion to free trade, the principal support for anticolonialism within the State Department came from its Asian experts. Generally junior Foreign Service officers or academic specialists brought into the department during the war, these "Asianists" were men far removed from the traditional centers of power in that most traditional of executive agencies. Yet in many ways their ideas were more in line with those of the president and were considerably more farsighted than those of their senior colleagues. Convinced that the United States had already made a firm and irrevocable commitment to colonial self-rule in its wartime pronouncements on the subject, they feared that a general retreat from those liberal principles would have a poisonous effect on the underdeveloped world. Since American men and matériel would be liberating most of the Southeast Asian colonies from the Japanese, they believed that Washington could not escape blame in the eyes of native nationalists if the colonial systems there were restored intact. "The return to European Governments of colonies in Asia taken from the Japanese by American forces," argued Laurence Salisbury, chief of the small Division of Southwest Pacific Affairs,

> or with American participation, without definite and strong intimation from us that we look forward to progressive improvement in the condition of the natives of those colonies will have a profound effect upon the attitude of all Asiatics, including the Chinese, toward the United States. Mistrust of the United States, already prevalent among some of the peoples of Asia, will increase; Asiatics will be encouraged to believe that their future lies in unity against the Occidentals; and a greater semblance to truth will be

"Personnel and Far Eastern Policy," *Far Eastern Survey*, 14 (December 19, 1945):361–64.

> given to the propaganda which the Japanese have been assiduously disseminating among the Asiatic peoples.[73]

For a combination of reasons—political, economic, and strategic—these officials believed that European imperialism could not long withstand the force of Asian nationalism in the postwar world and that the United States had best align itself with the wave of the future rather than that of the past. "The British, French and Dutch imperialist systems are probably on the way out in Asia," argued Far Eastern expert Raymond Kennedy. "We must not commit ourselves to underwriting these systems indefinitely."[74] China hand John Paton Davies echoed the theme. "We cannot afford to align ourselves in an Anglo-American bloc which would place us in opposition to the rise of nationalism in Asia," he wrote. "We must not put ourselves in a position where we cannot move with the historical stream rather than attempting to block a force which might prove too strong for us."[75] The consequences of alienating the peoples of Asia, in the view of these Far Eastern specialists, would be disastrous. One of the department's Asianists warned that unless a prompt reform of the colonial system were effected after the war, "there can be expected from the native peoples increasing bitterness and antagonism. The United States, as the close associate and ally of the colonial powers, will share with the latter that enmity." In addition, he pointed out, the Soviet Union, whose "policies and ideologies have gained a real hold over many progressive leaders in Asia and nearby areas," would stand to increase its power and influence in the area.[76]

[73]Memorandum by Salisbury, February 5, 1944, 856D.00/2-544, DSR.

[74]Memorandum by Raymond Kennedy, "American Interests in Southeast Asia," March 26, 1945, in folder labeled "Southeast Asia, 1946–1948, U.S. Policy," Box 5, PSA Records, DSR.

[75]Quoted in ibid. On this point, see also OSS, "Political Strategy for the Far East," Research and Analysis Report no. 2666, October 28, 1944, DSR.

[76]Memorandum by the Department of State's Liberated Areas Division, "Imperialism versus an Enlightened Colonial Policy in the Area of the South East Asia Command," January 2, 1945, enclosed in M. B. Hall to Moffat, January 13, 1945, in folder labeled "Southeast Asia, 1946–1948, U.S. Policy," Box 5, PSA Records, DSR.

Abbot Low Moffat, Salisbury's successor as chief of the Division of Southwest Pacific Affairs and a forthright advocate of trusteeship, summarized the concerns of the Asianists in a memorandum that was forwarded to Roosevelt by Hull on September 8, 1944. "It would seem of substantial military importance," the memorandum began, "to secure for the United Nations the good will of the native peoples of southeast Asia among whom, for some years, there has been increasing nationalistic sentiment, and who, for the past three years, have been subjected to intense Japanese propaganda exploiting the old slogan of 'Asia for the Asiatics'." The memorandum suggested "that early, dramatic and concerted announcements by the nations concerned making definite commitments as to the future of the regions of southeast Asia would save many American and Allied lives and facilitate military operations." It recommended that these announcements include specific dates when independence or self-government would be accorded, steps to be taken to develop the native capacity for self-rule, and a pledge of economic autonomy and equality of economic treatment toward other nations. These announcements would be further enhanced, Moffat suggested, if each of the colonial powers pledged a formal declaration of trusteeship under an international organization for the period of tutelage. Such a program would serve the postwar interests of the United States for the following reasons:

> These areas are sources of products essential to both our wartime and peacetime economy. They are potentially important markets for American exports. They lie athwart the southwestern approaches to the Pacific Ocean and have important bearing on our security and the security of the Philippines. Their economic and political stability will be an important factor in the maintenance of peace in Asia. Emergence of these regions as self-governing countries would appear desirable as soon as they are capable of self-rule, either as independent nations or in close voluntary association with western powers, for example as dominions. . . . Failure of the western powers to recognize the new conditions and forces in southeast Asia and an attempt to reestablish prewar conditions will

almost surely lead to serious social and political conflict and may lead to ultimate unifying of oriental opposition to the west.[77]

The arguments of Hull and Moffat for an aggressive anticolonial policy were compelling—and, in retrospect, remarkably prescient—but by late 1944 such ideas were clearly out of touch with the thinking of the administration as a whole. Larger political, strategic, and military concerns had already muted the administration's anticolonial rhetoric and forced a retreat in its trusteeship planning. The intransigence of the European powers and the overriding importance of maintaining harmony within the Western Alliance had induced the Roosevelt administration to take what it considered to be a more gradual and conciliatory attitude toward the problem of the colonial empires. The military's insistence that national security interests demanded a string of postwar bases in the Pacific, a need that could not be foolishly compromised by abstract trusteeship principles, also contributed to this new approach. Significantly, in deference to the military viewpoint Roosevelt instructed the American delegation to the Dumbarton Oaks Conference of 1944 to avoid all discussion of trusteeship and related matters.[78] This retreat from an anticolonial policy, which was increasingly evident by the end of 1944, was also dictated in part by military expediency. Army Chief of Staff George Marshall and the military favored bringing the war to a speedy close without becoming involved in the political and economic problems facing the imperial powers. General Marshall believed that the United States should neither assist nor interfere with the reestablishment of the colonial regimes in Asia; and since the dependent territories there fell under the jurisdiction of the Joint Chiefs of Staff

[77]Draft memorandum for the president, by Moffat, September 8, 1944, 856D.01/10-544, DSR; memorandum from Hull to Roosevelt, September 8, 1944, Map Room Files, Box 166, Roosevelt Papers, Franklin D. Roosevelt Library, Hyde Park, N.Y.

[78]Stettinius to Forrestal, December 30, 1944, Box 9, SWNCC Records, DSR; minutes of a meeting of the Committee of Three (Stimson, Stettinius, and Forrestal), January 2, 1945, in Stimson-Forrestal Meetings folder, Box 732, Edward R. Stettinius, Jr., Papers, University of Virginia Library, Charlottesville; memorandum from Stimson, Forrestal, and Stettinius to President Harry S. Truman, April 18, 1945, in International Trusteeship folder, Box 735, Stettinius Papers.

through the duration of the war, the military could override any conflicting State Department proposals.[79]

Hull and the Asianists within the State Department continued to resist this more accommodating policy toward European colonialism. In the case of the East Indies, their efforts focused on proposed civil affairs procedures. The Netherlands East Indies, except for Sumatra, fell under the military jurisdiction of General Douglas MacArthur's Southwest Pacific Area Command (SWPA) through the duration of the war; accordingly, the civil affairs procedures adopted as parts of the Indies were reconquered from the Japanese would set an extremely important precedent for future American policy toward Dutch colonial rule. In February 1944 MacArthur concluded a preliminary civil affairs agreement with Lieutenant Governor Hubertus van Mook, which provided that "the full sovereignty of the Netherlands Government will be restored to the Netherlands Indies as soon as the military situation, in the judgment of the Commander-in-Chief, permits." It also stipulated that Dutch civil affairs officers would be used to the fullest extent possible during the liberation and reoccupation of the islands.[80] Hull and the Asianists protested vigorously against the draft agreement; they believed, quite correctly, that such an agreement would subvert trusteeship planning. In a letter to General J. H. Hilldring, director of the Civil Affairs Division of the War Department, Hull conceded that the State Department recognized Dutch sovereignty over the East Indies—a legal question—but added some important qualifications:

> However, in any military agreement of the nature under consideration no commitments should be made which would prejudice the right of the Government of the United States to bring up either

[79]Maurice Matloff, *Strategic Planning for Coalition Warfare, 1943–1944,* vol. 3 of U.S. Department of War, *United States Army in World War II* (Washington, D.C.: Office of the Chief of Military History, 1959), pt. 2, pp. 527–28.

[80]"Principles Governing Arrangements for Civil Administration and Jurisdiction in Netherlands Territory in the Southwest Pacific Area," December 10, 1944, in *FR,* 1944, 5:1286–89; memorandum from Joint Chiefs of Staff to Hull, May 14, 1944, in ibid., pp. 379–85; Marshall to MacArthur, January 19, 1944, and MacArthur to Marshall, January 25, 1944, both in Box 3A, RG 4, Douglas MacArthur Memorial Archives, Norfolk, Va.; J. C. Dunn to J. H. Hilldring, December 2, 1944, 856D.01/12-444, DSR.

> prior to or after the resumption of sovereign rights by the Netherlands Government certain proposals for discussion and agreement of a general character which it may be believed to be of rightful concern to the United States Government and to all Governments which have subscribed to the principles of the Atlantic Charter, and to the Four-Nation Declaration at Moscow, and certain particular proposals which may be of special mutual concern to the people of the Netherlands Empire and the people of the United States.[81]

Hull's arguments were to no avail. On December 10, 1944, his successor as secretary of state, Edward R. Stettinius, Jr., quietly approved the civil affairs agreement with the Netherlands. Without Hull's strong advocacy, the position of the Asianists was of little consequence; the new secretary, moreover, leaned heavily on Dunn and the Europeanists in important policy matters.[82] As a result of this decision, the Roosevelt administration, disregarding its own public pronouncements, the Atlantic Charter, and the Charter of the United Nations, placed its prestige and military power behind a policy of restoring the status quo ante bellum to the liberated territories of Southeast Asia.

A final step in the retreat from anticolonialism came at the Potsdam Conference of July 1945. There the Combined Chiefs of Staff, with American approval, removed the East Indies from American military jurisdiction and transferred the islands to the British Southeast Asia Command. This decision virtually isolated U.S. forces from future involvement in the internal affairs of the Indies, presumably leaving the Dutch to restore prewar conditions without American interference or international accountability. At the same time, since British forces were grossly unprepared for such an assignment, the transfer in command provided unparalleled opportunities for the Indonesian independence movement.

[81]Quoted in Wolthuis, "United States Policy," pp. 377–78. See also memorandum from Hornbeck to Hull, February 3, 1944, in James Clement Dunn folder, Box 151, Hornbeck Papers.

[82]Leupold, "United States and Indonesian Independence," pp. 110–11.

3

Reoccupation: August–December 1945

Most senior American officials were quite unprepared for the nationalist rebellions that erupted in Indochina and the East Indies in the wake of the Japanese surrender. Despite the warnings of a handful of State Department specialists who insisted that the war had irrevocably shattered the European colonial order, top policy makers anticipated that the reassertion of European rule would be relatively smooth and orderly. One intelligence estimate even predicted that the Indonesians would warmly embrace the returning Dutch rulers as liberators.

The views of Walter Foote in this regard, though perhaps a bit extreme, were not untypical. As consul general in the Indies, Foote had spent fifteen years in the islands, longer than any other State Department official. Comfortable with the colonial lifestyle and close to many Dutch leaders, he considered the statements floating around Washington about the future of the European colonies to have no relevance to the Indies. "The natives of the Netherlands Indies," he reported confidently in June 1942, "are most definitely not ready for independence. That condition is fifty or seventy-five years in the future. . . . The only feasible solution is for the Indies to remain under Netherlands sovereignty."[1] From his vantage point in Australia, where he spent the war years, Foote elaborated on this theme in a report he prepared for General Douglas MacArthur in early 1944. In-

[1]Walter A. Foote, "Future of the Netherlands Indies," June 27, 1942, 856D.001/154, in U.S. Department of State Records, National Archives, Washington, D.C. (hereafter cited as DSR).

donesian political parties, he said, were too small to have any influence or importance.

> The reason for this was that the natives were docile, peaceful, contented, and apathetic towards politics. They were sociable, fun loving, and witty, but exhibited little or no interest in political affairs. This is easily understood when it is realized that the natives of the East Indies, practically without exception, are polite, mild, docile, friendly, and possess a sense of humor somewhat akin to our own. Their main interests in life are their wives; children; rice fields; carabaos; chickens; a bamboo hut in a garden of banana and cocoanut trees; an occasional visit to the moving pictures (especially when "Westerns" are shown); [and] a new sarong now and then, especially around their New Year.

By the way of illustration, Foote pointed out that he had had the same servants for nearly fifteen years and "found them to be rather proud, brave, loyal, ready to accept just reproof calmly, but highly resentful of a personal injustice." He was "convinced that the news of the first landing of troops in the Indies will spread like wild fire and will be the signal for jubilation."[2]

Although few officials in Washington were quite so complacent as Foote, most were convinced that the Dutch would encounter little resistance to the restoration of their control over the islands. Indeed, American postwar plans for the Indies were based on the twin assumptions that the Indonesians were politically apathetic and that they would be incapable of self-government for decades to come. American policy makers believed that independence for the Indies was a distant goal, not a serious consideration for the present; it was inconceivable to them that native nationalists would mount a broad-based challenge to the reassertion of Dutch sovereignty. Still, the desire to avoid any potentially awkward American entanglement in the colonial problems of Southeast Asia was strong. This concern probably reinforced the important military and strategic considerations that led at Potsdam to the transfer of the East Indies and

[2]Foote to MacArthur, January 29, 1944, 856D.00/166, DSR. See also excerpts from Walter Foote's diary, July–September 1942, in Walter A. Foote folder, Box 167, Stanley K. Hornbeck Papers, Hoover Institution on War, Revolution, and Peace, Stanford University.

other areas from an American to a British theater of operations.

Throughout most of World War II, MacArthur's Southwest Pacific Area Command (SWPA) retained military jurisdiction over the entire Indonesian archipelago, with the exception of Sumatra. SWPA was responsible for liberating all of the Japanese-occupied areas within its boundaries. Both American and Dutch officials assumed that this responsibility would include the restoration of Dutch sovereignty in the East Indies; their plans were set forth in the van Mook–MacArthur civil affairs agreement of December 1944. The Indies, except for Sumatra, remained within MacArthur's theater of operations until the Potsdam Conference of July 1945. At Potsdam the Anglo-American Chiefs of Staff suddenly agreed to transfer the Dutch East Indies, along with Thailand (Siam) and the southern half of Indochina, to the Southeast Asia Command (SEAC) of British Admiral Lord Louis Mountbatten—a decision that was to have far-reaching political consequences.[3]

The precise origins of the Potsdam transfer remain somewhat cloudy, despite the profound implications of the decision. It is clear that in the closing years of the conflict British leaders actively began to press Washington for increased responsibility in the direction of Allied operations against Japan. Speaking before the House of Commons on December 14, 1943, Foreign Secretary Anthony Eden insisted that "even if we are compelled, for the time being, to devote the greater part of our human and material resources to the task of defeating Germany, we are still principals in the Far Eastern War."[4] Great Britain's interest in an expanded role in Southeast Asia was clear-cut: not only was London eager to recover its damaged prestige in that part of

[3]F. S. V. Donnison, *British Military Administration in the Far East,* in J. R. M. Butler, ed., *History of the Second World War,* United Kingdom Military Series (London: Her Majesty's Stationery Office, 1956), p. 415; Idrus N. Djajadiningrat, *The Beginnings of the Indonesian-Dutch Negotiations and the Hoge Veluwe Talks* (Ithaca: Cornell University Modern Indonesia Project, 1958), pp. 7–8; Alastair M. Taylor, *Indonesian Independence and the United Nations* (Ithaca: Cornell University Press, 1960), pp. 5–6.

[4]*Parliamentary Debates, 1943* (Official Record of the House of Commons), vol. 395, col. 1427; John Ehrman, *Grand Strategy, August 1943–September 1944,* vol. 5 of Butler, ed., *History of the Second World War,* pp. 438–50; Robert K. Wolthuis, "United States Foreign Policy towards the Netherlands Indies, 1937–1945," Ph.D. dissertation, Johns Hopkins University, 1968, pp. 408–9.

the world and to restore British sovereignty over its own colonies, but it was equally concerned that American anticolonial inclinations, if left unchecked, might threaten the very survival of the British Empire. As the British Joint Planning Staff noted in a position paper prepared in April 1945: "It is desirable that the French and the Dutch should deal with us rather than the Americans on questions concerning the recovery of their possessions."[5]

At first, American officials opposed any boundary changes in the Pacific. When the question was introduced at the Hawaii military planning conference of July 1944, MacArthur argued that the British should not be allowed to assume control of any territory that the United States recaptured from the Japanese. He objected to a proposal that military control over the East Indies be transferred to the British, contending that past experience taught that if the British regained control of Dutch territory, it might be difficult ever to pry them loose. Despite this initial cold reception, however, London continued to explore with Washington the possibilities of an alteration in the command structure.[6]

The British also approached the Dutch at this time in order to solicit their views on a possible jurisdictional change. In May 1944 Mountbatten raised this question with Hubertus J. van Mook, who was still serving as lieutenant governor general of the East Indies. Van Mook's primary concern was the successful liberation of the Indonesian islands, and he realized that American military forces were far better equipped for that hazardous assignment than were the relatively ill-prepared British troops. Consequently, he and Eelco van Kleffens, the minister for colonies and foreign affairs in the wartime Dutch government, favored keeping the archipelago under U.S. military jurisdiction.[7] Peter S. Gerbrandy, the wartime prime minister, and

[5]Ehrman, *Grand Strategy, October 1944–August 1945,* vol. 6 of Butler, *History of the Second World War,* p. 229. See also Akira Iriye, *The Cold War in Asia: A Historical Introduction* (Englewood Cliffs, N.J.: Prentice-Hall, 1974), pp. 86–88.

[6]MacArthur to Marshall, August 1, 1944, WAFPAC Correspondence, Box 3B, RG 4, Douglas MacArthur Memorial Archives, Norfolk, Va.; William D. Leahy, *I Was There* (New York: Whittlesey House, 1950), pp. 251–55.

[7]Eden to Churchill, September 13, 1944, in Prime Minister's Records (PREM) 3/326, Public Record Office, London (hereafter cited as PRO); Djajadiningrat,

other members of his cabinet took a different view of the proposal; they believed that a transfer to British control might actually be politically advantageous to Holland, partly because Churchill had assured Gerbrandy that "he was going to stand up for the Dutch Empire after the war."[8] Even though the final decision on a boundary change would of course be made by the American and British governments, the Dutch forfeited an opportunity to influence that decision by allowing these sharp divisions within their government to prevent it from pursuing a unified policy.

Meanwhile, key American military spokesmen were beginning to reconsider their earlier position. Secretary of War Stimson noted in his diary entry for November 1, 1944, that General Marshall now favored an expanded British role in the Pacific operations. Concerned with the projected invasion of Japan and eager to curtail American loss of life in the Far East, Marshall "suggested the laying of a new line of demarcation which will cut those territories outside of the southwestern Pacific jurisdiction which MacArthur has charge of and leave him the Philippines." Aware of a long-standing rivalry between the two prominent generals, Stimson anticipated that MacArthur might oppose this adjustment, but added that "we all agree that that ought to be done."[9]

As Stimson feared, MacArthur continued to oppose any proposed transfer of part of his command to SEAC. When Marshall informed him on February 7 that the Joint Chiefs of Staff wished "to avoid the use of U.S. troops in mopping up the Netherlands East Indies area,"[10] MacArthur replied that his forces should at

---

Beginnings, p. 9. Van Mook has written that the Dutch government was not consulted about the change in command: "The political and military reasons for this important realignment had little to do with the interests of the nations and the people concerned. The Dutch government was neither consulted nor advised about the impending change; neither, probably, was the French" (*The Stakes of Democracy in Southeast Asia* [New York: Norton, 1950], p. 174).

[8]Meeting between Churchill and Gerbrandy, February 11, 1944, PREM 3/326, PRO; Taylor, *Indonesian Independence*, p. 6.

[9]Stimson diary, November 1, 1944, in Henry Stimson Papers, Yale University Library.

[10]Marshall to MacArthur, February 7, 1945, in War Department Messages, Box 3B, MacArthur Archives.

least help to reestablish the Netherlands East Indies government in Batavia before any responsibility was transferred to the British, since restoration of the Dutch "would bring about the most favorable repercussions throughout the Far East and would raise the prestige of the United States to the highest level with results that would be felt for a great many years."[11]

Despite his protests, the Joint Chiefs of Staff argued that in order to prepare for the projected invasion of Japan, the Southwest Pacific Area should be dissolved and all responsibility for territory south of the Philippines should be transferred to British and Dutch authorities. On April 13, 1945, they officially submitted this proposal to the British Chiefs of Staff. The memorandum read in part: "U.S. Chiefs of Staff clearly felt that the sooner changes on these lines could be introduced the better. They are not wedded to any particular line of demarcation and would no doubt be ready to consider any alternative you might like to suggest. They appreciate of course that they are setting you a difficult problem."[12]

Gradually even MacArthur began to accept the logic of an alteration in the command structure. As military plans for the operation against the Japanese home islands crystallized, he realized that his command might be dangerously overextended if he continued to insist on maintaining the East Indies within his theater. On May 30 he informed Marshall that the preparation for the execution of "Olympic"—the code name for the invasion of Japan—"will absorb completely all of the theater's United States resources even under existing conditions," and that "the utmost effort must be exerted to complete adequate preparations for and execute Olympic on time." Any attempt to divert those resources to Java or Borneo, he added, "will prevent the execution of Olympic at the time scheduled."[13]

Ironically, while the United States was gravitating toward the British point of view, British authorities were beginning to ques-

[11]MacArthur to Marshall, February 26, 1945, in War Department Messages, Box 3B, MacArthur Archives. See also interview with MacArthur by Lieutenant General Sir Hastings Ismay, August 1, 1944, Cabinet Records (CAB) 127/33, PRO.

[12]Quoted in Ehrman, *Grand Strategy*, 6:228.

[13]MacArthur to Marshall, May 30, 1945, in WAFPAC Correspondence, Box 3B, MacArthur Archives.

tion the wisdom of their own recommendation. While still favoring a shift in the command structure in Southeast Asia, they had become more cognizant of some of the logistical difficulties involved in such a plan. In a memorandum to the Chiefs of Staff, the British Joint Planning Staff recommended that the British "assume control of the proposed area as soon as practicable," but added a note of caution: "We should not take over the area before we are assured that the necessary resources, which we cannot provide and are now in the theatre, will be made available and that the United States will continue to allot maintenance requirements and shipping."[14] Mountbatten also advised extreme caution in accepting the transfer of jurisdiction, notifying MacArthur that he was unprepared for such a large expansion in his command and could not be ready to accept a transfer until October at the earliest.[15]

Nonetheless, the British Chiefs continued to urge as early a transfer as possible. At the Potsdam Conference they submitted a memorandum to the Combined Allied Chiefs of Staff, proposing that the British should assume "a greater share of the burden of strategic decisions" related to the war against Japan. "Although our contribution in the Pacific must always remain small in comparison with that of the United States," they asserted, "it is natural that our interests and concern should grow as more of our forces begin to be deployed in the Pacific area."[16] Now that the European war was concluded, Britain was evidently prepared to resume its presence in Southeast Asia in an effort to protect the interests of the British Empire. According to some American officials in the Pacific, SEAC really stood for "Save England's Asian Colonies."[17]

[14]Quoted in Ehrman, *Grand Strategy*, 6:230.

[15]Vice-Admiral the Earl Mountbatten of Burma, *Report to the Combined Chiefs of Staff by the Supreme Allied Commander Southeast Asia, 1943–1945* (New York: Philosophical Library, 1951), p. 183; Supreme Allied Commander's (SAC) 270th Meeting, August 20, 1945, Box 83, SEAC War Diaries, RG 331, Washington National Record Center, Suitville, Md. (hereafter cited as WNRC).

[16]Memorandum from British Chiefs of Staff to Combined Chiefs of Staff, in *Foreign Relations of the United States: Conference of Berlin (Potsdam) 1945*, 2 vols. (Washington, D.C., 1960), 2:1313–14. Hereafter volumes in this series will be cited as *FR*, followed by the year.

[17]British Chiefs of Staff Committee, "British Participation in the War against Japan," June 30, 1945, in PREM 8/29, PRO; Meeting of Cabinet Defense Commit-

On July 17, the American Chiefs of Staff approved the British proposal and agreed to a rapid command shift in order to free American troops for the offensive against Japan. They stated: "The objective of the United States Chiefs of Staff in proposing the transfer has been to release United States resources and commanders from the responsibility for containing and mopping up the Japanese forces in the area in order that they might concentrate on the main effort. Hence they have proposed 15 August as the date of turnover."[18] Although some minor technical details had to be worked out before the transfer became official, Prime Minister Churchill and President Harry S. Truman formally consented to the boundary change on July 24. The United States was now freed from all of its responsibilities in the Netherlands East Indies.

While Great Britain's motives in pressing for the jurisdictional change are easily explicable, American motives appear to be more complex. Part of the rationale for the American position, surely, was the expressed one: by late 1944 and early 1945, the overriding concern of the United States was the preparation for an offensive against Japan; any theater of operations that siphoned troops and supplies away from that primary goal was of peripheral interest. These military considerations, however, were almost certainly reinforced by political considerations. It is unlikely that American leaders would have made such a critical decision in ignorance of the unsettled conditions in both the Dutch East Indies and French Indochina. In both areas, active nationalist movements had aspired to independence for decades, and it would have been foolish indeed to expect their peaceful acquiescence to a reimposition of Dutch and French imperial rule. As early as 1943, John Paton Davies, one of the State Department's Asianists, had warned of such dangers:

> In so far as we participate in SEAC operations, we become involved in the poltically explosive colonial problems of the British, Dutch

tee, August 8, 1945, in ibid.; Walter LaFeber, "Roosevelt, Churchill, and Indochina: 1942–45," *American Historical Review*, 80 (December 1975), 1280; Christopher Thorne, "Indochina and Anglo-American Relations, 1942–1945," *Pacific Historical Review*, 45 (February 1976):75.

[18]Memorandum from U.S. Chiefs of Staff, July 17, 1945, in *FR*, 1945, 1, pt. 2:1313–14.

> and possibly French. In doing so, we compromise ourselves not only with the colonial peoples of Asia but also the free peoples of Asia, including the Chinese. Domestically, our Government lays itself open to public criticisms—"Why should American boys die to recreate the colonial empires of the British and their Dutch and French satellites?" Finally, more Anglo-American misunderstanding and friction is likely to arise out of our participation in SEAC than out of any other theater. Therefore we should concentrate our Asiatic efforts on operations in and from China.[19]

During the war, the United States had tried to play both sides of the colonial issue. While ostensibly promoting the aspirations of colonial nationalist movements, Washington had quietly reassured the Dutch and French that it would not contest their right to reestablish sovereignty over their colonies. If the change in command structure had not occurred, then, the United States would have faced a profound dilemma: either to honor its commitment to its European allies—even if that course entailed suppression of a popular national liberation movement—or to back the cause of colonial self-determination. The first position would have risked forfeiting the respect and goodwill that the United States had been building up in the underdeveloped world as a result of its anticolonial posture; the latter policy would have risked alienating the European imperial powers, whose support in Europe was considered essential to the success of America's postwar plans. A far easier solution, it seemed, was to avoid any involvement in internal colonial politics. By transferring its military commitment to the British, who had themselves requested the change, the United States could sidestep any awkward entanglement in Southeast Asia and continue to play both

[19]Memorandum by John Paton Davies, in *FR*, 1943, 6:188. For similar indications of American concern about involvement in Southeast Asia and possible political ramifications, see memorandum from C. D. Glover to Commander in Chief, Naval Plans Division, June 15, 1945, in Box 173, Strategic Plans Division File, Naval Operational Archives, Washington Navy Yard; memorandum from M. M. Dupre, Jr., to Assistant Chief of Staff, Naval Plans Division, in Box 172, ibid.; "Imperialism versus an Enlightened Colonial Policy in the Area of the South East Asia Command," Department of State memorandum, January 2, 1945, enclosed in M. B. Hall to Abbot Moffat, in file labeled "Southeast Asia, 1946–1948, U.S. Policy," Box 5, Records of the Office of Philippine and Southeast Asian Affairs, DSR (hereafter cited as PSA Records).

sides of the colonial question. An intelligence report on conditions in the Netherlands East Indies, prepared by the State Department in August 1945, accurately reflected this thinking:

> In the event of considerable resistance, which may involve suppression by force of arms and harsh reprisals against leading Indonesians, the liberation of the Indies may assume the aspect of a reconquest of a colony, possibly with the participation of non-Netherlands military forces. The presence or absence of U.S. personnel will then be given a certain interpretation by the local population and influence its future attitude towards the U.S.[20]

But in avoiding one problem the United States created an even more serious one, for the British were woefully unprepared for the magnitude of the task they had assumed. They were now responsible for liberating from the Japanese an area whose size alone was staggering: it included 1.5 million square miles of land area with a population of more than 128 million people. Moreover, "throughout this vast area there existed no reliable civil police," according to Mountbatten, "and (except in Siam) no civil government with even a shadow of independent administration."[21] The sudden capitulation of the Japanese on August 14 further complicated the problem. Mountbatten found his command short of the men and shipping necessary to fulfill its expanded responsibilities and lacking any reliable intelligence estimates in regard to actual conditions in the East Indies. Since the liberation of the British colonies of Malaya and Singapore was SEAC's top priority, the reoccupation of the Indies was

[20]Office of Strategic Services (OSS), "Problems Arising from a Sudden Liberation of the N.E.I.," Research and Analysis Report no. 3229, August 13, 1945, DSR. Charles Wolf, who served as American vice-consul in the East Indies, has suggested that political factors may well have reinforced the decision to change the command structure. See Charles Wolf, *The Indonesian Story: The Birth, Growth and Structure of the Indonesian Republic* (New York: John Day, 1948), p. 16. See also Amry Vandenbosch and Richard A. Butwell, *Southeast Asia among the World Powers* (Lexington: University of Kentucky Press, 1957), p. 292; Harold M. Vinacke, "United States Far Eastern Policy," *Pacific Affairs*, 19 (December 1946):351–52.

[21]Mountbatten, *Post Surrender Tasks: Section E of the Report to the Combined Chiefs of Staff by the Supreme Allied Commander Southeast Asia, 1943–1945* (London: Her Majesty's Stationery Office, 1969), p. 282.

delayed even further. It was not until September 29 that the first full contingent of British troops landed in the East Indies—six weeks after Japan's surrender and the Republic of Indonesia's proclamation of independence. Regardless of the motives of those responsible for the abrupt change in the command structure, then, the net effect of that decision was to create a political and military vacuum in Indonesia—a vacuum that was quickly filled by the Indonesian nationalists.[22]

The six-week interval between the proclamation of the republic and the arrival of the initial British occupation forces provided the nationalists with a unique opportunity to stabilize their newly formed government. The Indonesians feverishly attempted to create the first alternative to alien rule in their homeland in over three hundred years. After the birth of the Republic of Indonesia on August 17, the Independence Preparatory Committee convened and quickly named Sukarno and Hatta president and vice-president respectively; the two veteran nationalists were obvious and unanimous choices for the top leadership positions. The committee then appointed a commission to make final changes in the national constitution, a project begun during the last month of the war. Within a week, a final draft of the constitution was completed and promulgated throughout the archipelago. Under the prevailing emergency conditions, President Sukarno dissolved the Independence Preparatory Committee on August 29 and replaced it with the Central Indonesian Committee, a body composed of 135 prominent nationalists chosen by Sukarno and Hatta from among the leading ethnic, religious, social, and economic groups in the East Indies and responsible for advising the president and his cabinet.[23]

Before its dissolution, the Preparatory Committee took several other major steps. By decree it divided the republic into eight

[22]Calvin H. Oakes to State-War-Navy Coordinating Committee, August 11, 1945, in Box 30, Records of the State–Army–Navy–Air Force Coordinating Committee, DSR (hereafter cited as SWNCC Records); SEAC Operational Directive no. 38, August 17, 1945, in Box 82, SEAC War Diaries, WNRC; Donnison, *British Military Administration*, pp. 421–22.

[23]Wolf, *Indonesian Story*, pp. 16–17; George McTurnan Kahin, *Nationalism and Revolution in Indonesia* (Ithaca: Cornell University Press, 1952), pp. 138–40; Benedict R. O'G. Anderson, *Java in a Time of Revolution, Occupation, and Resistance, 1944–1946* (Ithaca: Cornell University Press, 1972), pp. 87–91.

provinces, each to have a governor appointed by Sukarno. The committee also made provision for a cabinet of twelve ministers, all responsible to the president. Finally, using the Japanese-created military and youth groups as a base, the Preparatory Committee began to establish an embryonic Indonesian army—or, more properly, an auxiliary police force. The Badan Keamanan Rakjat or People's Peace-Preservation Corps (BKR) was composed of highly autonomous—indeed, virtually independent—constituent units, having a territorial base and subject to no real central control. This newly formed "army" quickly joined the revolutionary struggle, helping to seize government buildings from the Japanese and to arrest people who refused to leave them.[24]

Most of the Indonesian administrators who had worked for the Japanese immediately declared their allegiance to the republic; some were even appointed by Sukarno to serve in his first cabinet. As of September 1, 1945, the Indonesian department heads who had been serving in the Japanese military government, along with the new department heads named by Sukarno, became ministers of the Republic of Indonesia. Likewise, Sukarno decreed that all Indonesian civil servants should now ignore Japanese orders and obey only the directives of the new republican government. In response to this decree, the republic gained the immediate and enthusiastic backing of almost all Indonesian government personnel. The Japanese were powerless to check the desertion of their administrative functionaries, and without these personnel the Japanese administration quickly collapsed.[25]

The rapid establishment of the republican government placed the Japanese military command in a quandary. The Allied Southeast Asia Command had explicitly ordered the Japanese to maintain the status quo in Indonesia before the arrival of Allied troops. The Japanese believed, however, as Sukarno had repeatedly

[24]Anderson, *Java*, pp. 103–5; Kahin, *Nationalism and Revolution*, pp. 140–41. On October 5, 1945, the name of the national army was changed to Tentara Keamanan Rakjat (People's Peace-Preservation Army), or TKR. Later, as the army became more centralized, its name was changed first to Tentara Republik Indonesia (Army of the Republic of Indonesia), or TRI, and then to Tentara National Indonesia (TNI).

[25]Kahin, *Nationalism and Revolution*, p. 139.

stressed, that any effort to suppress the infant republic would lead to a costly and bloody struggle. Anxious to avert such a clash, the Japanese vacillated: while trying to halt the growth of Indonesian military power, they chose not to contest the establishment of the republican government. But this strategy backfired, as Japanese attempts to thwart the growing military strength of the republic led to fighting throughout late August and September 1945. These armed clashes, which were usually spurred by Indonesian attempts to secure Japanese arms, continued to rage at the time the first major contingent of British troops landed in Java, on September 29, 1945.[26]

The British were bewildered by the state of affairs they found in the East Indies. Contrary to their intelligence reports, which Mountbatten angrily criticized as "patently inadequate and erroneous," they found a functioning native government, actively supported by the great majority of politically conscious Indonesians and operating at a high degree of efficiency.[27] As defined by the Combined Chiefs of Staff, the Southeast Asia Command had three major responsibilities in the East Indies: to enforce the surrender and disarmament of the Japanese armed forces; to release the Allied prisoners of war and internees; and to establish and maintain law and order in the country until the Dutch administration could function effectively. The completely unexpected strength and popular support of the republic would necessitate a significant modification in those original instructions.[28]

Lieutenant General Sir Philip Christison, commander of the Allied Forces in the Netherlands East Indies, gave the first indication of a modification of British goals in Indonesia. On September 29, before he arrived in Java, he explained at a press conference that his only task was to rescue prisoners of war and

[26]Ibid., pp. 137–38, 141.

[27]Mountbatten to British Chiefs of Staff, September 29, 1945, in Box 90, SEAC War Diaries, WNRC; SAC's 29th Miscellaneous Meeting, September 29, 1945, in ibid.; SAC's 286th meeting, September 28, 1945, in ibid.; David Wehl, *The Birth of Indonesia* (London: George Allen & Unwin, 1948), pp. 37–38.

[28]Mountbatten, *Post Surrender Tasks*, p. 282; van Kleffens to van Mook, August 14, 1945, in S. L. van der Wal, ed., *Officiele Bescheiden Betreffende de Nederlands-Indonesische Betrekkingen, 1945–1950* (The Hague: Martinius Nijhoff, 1971), 1:25–26 (hereafter cited as *Officiele Bescheiden*).

internees and to disarm the Japanese. "We have no interest in their politics," Christison declared. "British and Indian troops will not become involved in internal politics." He further noted that the nationalist forces would be given a share in the responsibility for maintaining law and order. Moreover, Christison said that he had insisted on a conference between Indonesian nationalist leaders and Dutch colonial administrators and was now urging The Hague to make a statement clarifying its plans for the East Indies. "What form of government the Dutch are going to give them," added the outspoken general, "I don't know. They'll certainly have to give them something."[29] British Secretary of War J. J. Lawson was quoted the same day as having stated that "Britain's obligation does not involve fighting for the French against the people of Indo-China or for the Dutch against Javanese nationalists."[30] Both of these widely quoted statements were unmistakable indications that the initial role of the British forces in Indonesia would be limited.

Indonesians quickly seized on Christison's remarks as according de facto recognition to their fledgling government. It is highly unlikely that this was the general's intention, but his statement certainly conferred an aura of legitimacy on the young republic.[31] Dutch authorities were infuriated by Christison's

[29]Extract from SEAC War Diary, September 30, 1945, in Box 90, SEAC War Diaries, WNRC; *Times* (London), October 1, 1945, p. 3; *New York Times*, September 30, 1945, p. 30. See Anderson, *Java*, pp. 135–36, for an examination of the controversy surrounding the remarks. Christison claims that he was misquoted. See, for example, Mountbatten, *Post Surrender Tasks*, p. 290; Taylor, *Indonesian Independence*, p. 7.

[30]*New York Times*, September 30, 1945, p. 30. Lawson is also quoted in U.S. Department of State, Interim Research and Intelligence Service, "British Policy toward Nationalists in Indonesia Strengthens Sukarno's Position," Research and Analysis Report no. 3270, October 5, 1945, DSR.

[31]Ide Anak Agung Gde Agung, *Twenty Years Indonesian Foreign Policy, 1945–1965* (The Hague: Mouton, 1973), p. 18. An American intelligence report noted the profound political implications of Christison's statement: "The nationalist group is therefore now receiving recognition, if not as a government, as the nationalists originally desired, then at least as representatives of the Indonesian people, specifically of the national groups. This in itself is an enormous victory for Sukarno." See U.S. Department of State, Interim Research and Intelligence Service, "British Policy toward the Nationalists." The British Foreign Office was quite upset by Christison's blunt remarks. See J. C. Sterndale Bennett to British Chiefs of Staff, September 30, 1945, FO 371, F/7655/6398/61, PRO; I. A. Wilson Young to Maberly E. Dening, September 30, 1945, FO 371 F/7608/6398/61, PRO.

apparent lack of sympathy for their weak position. "If newspapers and broadcasts are true," van Mook complained to Mountbatten, "your commander in Batavia created an impression of virtually recognizing the Indonesian republic. I can hardly believe this public action was taken with your consent and without even previous notice to my government or myself."[32]

Despite the Dutch charges, the British never actually questioned Dutch sovereignty over the East Indies. In fact, Christison was bluntly reminded by the Foreign Office and Mountbatten on October 1 that he was to recognize only the Netherlands government in Indonesia.[33] Christison's pragmatic, if undiplomatic, approach was simply an early attempt to cope with the new realities in the Indonesian archipelago. Reports from Java during the next few weeks frequently pointed to the surprising strength and popular support of the republic. British commanders believed that only a policy of strict nonintervention in Indonesian internal affairs could allow them to carry out their main tasks of freeing the prisoners of war and internees and disarming the Japanese; any involvement in political matters would only complicate their duties and overextend the British commitment. As Mountbatten frankly explained to Dutch representatives on September 30, the British "were willing to help the Netherlands Government back to its lawful position, but could not get involved in civil war as a consequence of an internal policy which seems unsuitable to them."[34] An added

[32]Van Mook to Mountbatten, September 30, 1945, in *Officiele Bescheiden*, 1:193. Van Mook later wrote: "By taking this precipitate step the Republic of Indonesia—which at that time was neither an administration nor even a unified movement—acquired a kind of international recognition which irrevocably prejudiced the future, and about which no previous consultation with the Dutch Government or its representative had taken place" (*Stakes of Democracy*, pp. 187–88). Peter Gerbrandy later wrote: "British policy was the primary, if not the sole, cause of the collapse of the once stable kingdom of the Netherlands. That much is incontrovertible" (*Indonesia* [London: Hutchinson, 1950], p. 105). See also memorandum from J. Webb Benton (chargé, Netherlands) to James Byrnes, October 10, 1945, 856E.00/10-1045, DSR; memorandum from Stanley Hornbeck (ambassador, Netherlands) to Byrnes, October 14, 1945, 856D.00/10-1445, DSR.

[33]Mountbatten to Christison, September 30, 1945, in Box 90, SEAC War Diaries, WNRC; Mountbatten to Christison, October 1, 1945, *Officiele Bescheiden*, 1:218–19; Foreign Office to Dening, October 1, 1945, FO 371 F7649/6398/61, PRO.

[34]Minutes of meeting between British and Dutch officials, September 30, 1945, in *Officiele Bescheiden*, 1:200; SAC's 30th Miscellaneous Meeting, September 28, 1945, in Box 90, SEAC War Diaries, WNRC.

complication was that a large percentage of the occupying forces was composed of Indian troops. British authorities questioned the wisdom of using Indians to suppress fellow Asians, and were especially worried about the political effect that such circumstances would undoubtedly have in India, where the clamor for independence was growing louder.[35]

Aware of these problems, Mountbatten instructed Christison to avoid any interference in the political affairs of the archipelago. At the same time, he began to press Dutch officials to meet with representatives of the republic. Mountbatten defended this policy in purely military terms: if the Dutch and Indonesians did not negotiate, disorders might easily occur which the Dutch themselves had inadequate forces to control. This attempt to bring the two parties to the bargaining table, the admiral informed the British Chiefs of Staff on October 5, "was purely for the maintenance of law and order as an impartial and humanitarian process directed at enabling the people to live their lives without fear of bloodshed."[36] He asserted that the British should establish quite clearly the distinction between maintaining law and order and any policy of suppressing the Indonesian independence movement on behalf of the Netherlands government. In effect, Mountbatten urged the Foreign Office to pressure the Dutch into making some guarantee of limited independence to Indonesia. "I consider it militarily essential," he declared, "that Netherlands pronouncements of the political future of N.E.I. are imaginative and generous to avoid bloodshed which would inevitably involve British and Indian troops."[37]

Initially the Foreign Office believed that the Southeast Asia Command "was going much too far" in advocating that the British pressure the Dutch to grant some form of Indonesian self-rule. In a letter to Maberly E. Dening, chief political adviser to Mountbatten, the Foreign Office warned that the arguments

[35]Mountbatten to British Chiefs of Staff, September 29, 1945, FO 371 F7652/6398/61, PRO; Anderson, *Java*, pp. 132–35.

[36]Mountbatten to British Chiefs of Staff, October 5, 1945, FO 371 F8071/6398/61, PRO.

[37]Mountbatten to Foreign Office, October 11, 1945, FO 371 F83051/6398/61, PRO; memorandum from representatives of British Chiefs of Staff to Combined Chiefs of Staff, "The Situation in the Netherlands East Indies," October 30, 1945, CCS 932, Operation and Planning Division Files, RG 165, Modern Military Branch, National Archives.

favoring nonintervention in the East Indies must be balanced against the very harmful effect that such a policy might have on Anglo-Dutch relations, particularly if the British appeared to take no interest in the restoration of Dutch territory and thereby to encourage consolidation of the nationalist movement.[38]

Only gradually did the Foreign Office come to accept the logic of Mountbatten's position. It sent Dening to Java to assess conditions, and his reports consistently corroborated the viewpoint of the British military commanders. Nobody in Indonesia wanted "the old gang" back, Dening observed. The danger from the British point of view was "that we shall be accused—and not entirely without reason—of holding the lists until the Dutch could do the shooting." He insisted that the Dutch must be convinced that they are no longer welcome in Indonesia and that they must clarify their future plans. "The Dutch have an opportunity," Dening pointed out, "but their present attitude is not encouraging. The remedy lies with them, but if they do not apply it, and soon, we will also become involved."[39]

The Defense Committee of the British cabinet discussed Indonesian policy at a meeting on October 10, 1945. London's ultimate policy objective was to restore law and order as soon as possible; to effect the release of all prisoners of war and internees and the disarmament of the Japanese; and then to transfer the territory to the Dutch and withdraw. The British task was complicated because any appearance of restoring the Dutch administration by force might have dangerous repercussions for Britain's general position in the Far East, yet "any appearance of surrender to the extremists and failure to restore Dutch administration would have equally wide and undesirable repercussions." The Chiefs of Staff cautioned that the archipelago was perfectly suited for guerrilla tactics that would require forces far in excess of those that Mountbatten had for combat. Foreign Secretary Ernest Bevin, bemoaning the hazardous British position, suggested that the cabinet accept Mountbatten's recom-

[38]Foreign Office to Dening, October 1, 1945, FO 371 F7649/6398/61, PRO. See also memorandum from Sterndale Bennett to Foreign Office, October 9, 1945, FO 371 F7659/6398/61, PRO.

[39]Dening to Foreign Office, October 11, 1945, FO 371 F8216/6398/61, PRO.

mendation and urge the Dutch to explore "talking points" with the republicans.[40]

In a memorandum prepared for Prime Minister Clement Attlee on October 15, the Foreign Office clarified this position: "We naturally want the N.E.I. restored to the sovereign power. But we cannot accept the theory that we have a definite responsibility to restore it at all costs in the face of local opposition." Though any dispute between the Dutch and the people of the East Indies was not a British affair, the maintenance of law and order "may involve British troops in extensive fighting and the British Government in many political complications." The particularly sensitive subject of Indian soldiers was also a major concern; the use of Indian troops against fellow Asians would place Britain in an extremely awkward position. British policy, the Foreign Office brief summarized, had two complementary aims: to minimize the risk of having to use armed force and to urge the Dutch to negotiate with the republicans.[41] In a meeting that day with the Dutch ambassador, Attlee stressed these points. He explained that while the British would carry out their obligations to the Dutch, "they could not assume an unlimited liability."[42]

The Netherlands government at first vehemently opposed any negotiations with the republicans. The Dutch position was simple: the republican government was a Japanese-created puppet state; Sukarno and Hatta were quislings at best and war criminals at worst; Dutch sovereignty over the archipelago was unquestionable. "The Netherlands Government desires to stress the fact," a Dutch Foreign Office memorandum to the British asserted, "that the so-called Sukarno-government in Java is by no means the outcome of a spontaneous and widespread popular movement but, as clearly proved by the facts, a Japanese puppet-Government of the Quisling type (which has accepted the maxim 'to do or die with Japan'), and outspokenly totali-

[40]Minutes of cabinet defense meeting, October 10, 1945, FO 371 F8658/6398/61, PRO. See also British Chiefs of Staff to Mountbatten, October 10, 1945, in *Officiele Bescheiden*, 1:299–300.

[41]Brief for Prime Minister from Foreign Office, October 15, 1945, FO 371 F8426/6398/61, PRO.

[42]Record of a conversation between Attlee and the Netherlands ambassador, October 15, 1945, PREM 8/70, PRO.

tarian in character."[43] Added van Mook: "Sukarno's regime is wholly unable to install order and prosperity to the Indies, and would, if left alone, succumb after a short time through internal dissensions."[44] The Dutch were quite out of patience with the British, who, they felt, had unwittingly aided the cause of the nationalists. "It is well known," complained the Netherlands Foreign Office,

> that the present disability of the Netherlands to re-occupy Java with their own forces is caused by the fact that they were the last to be liberated from German occupation and have ever since been dependent on the aid of their Allies for the rebuilding of their army and navy. They have, moreover, continually been hampered by the fact that during the war and later under the demobilisation afterwards, only very low priorities were granted to their interests. . . . The Netherlands Government feels that their alliance with Great Britain entitles them to the fullest help of the British Government and that they should not be abandoned for the time being to their own slender resources in finishing off the war with Japan and the Japanese policy of a greater East Asia of which the Sukarno incident forms an integral part.[45]

While Dutch plans for the future of the East Indies had not yet crystallized, the Dutch did envision granting their rich colony some degree of autonomy in the not too distant future. Queen Wilhelmina's speech of December 6, 1942, still served as the basis for this expectation. The queen's rather vague pronouncement had called for a postwar conference to explore the possibilities of a change in colonial policy; she had indicated that Holland would accept a commonwealth or federated structure based on the British model.[46] Referring to the queen's declara-

[43] Memorandum from Dutch Foreign Office to British Foreign Office, in *Officiele Bescheiden*, 1:188–89.

[44] Memorandum from van Mook to Dutch Foreign Office, enclosed in memorandum by Dean Acheson, October 10, 1945, in folder labeled "S.E.A. Civil Affairs Administration, 1944–46," Box 11, PSA Records, DSR.

[45] Memorandum from Dutch Foreign Office to British Foreign Office, in *Officiele Bescheiden*, 1:189.

[46] *The Netherlands Commonwealth and the Future: Important Statements of Her Majesty Queen Wilhelmina on Post-War Aims* (New York: Netherlands Information Bureau, 1945), pp. 20–22.

tion, one prominent Dutch authority had assured American diplomats in March 1945 that "the basis of a sound colonial policy . . . is to give the more primitive societies a secure foundation for future progress and development, to which we add that this should lead to self-expression and self-government."[47] But any liberalization of Dutch policy would occur gradually; few, if any, leading Dutch officials were thinking in terms of an independent Indonesia. Most believed that Indonesia was indispensable to the Dutch economy and would continue to be indispensable in the postwar period, especially in view of the desperate needs of their war-ravaged homeland. The very nature of the Dutch government, moreover, militated against a more progressive approach to the colonial question: it was a provisional, emergency administration without an electoral mandate, and the Dutch constitution specifically stated that no fundamental change in colonial policy could be instituted before the Dutch people had a chance to express their opinion on the issue.[48]

Events in Indonesia, however, rapidly undermined the Dutch position. A gradual, evolutionary approach was quite obviously insufficient to stem the tide of revolutionary upheaval. The British immediately grasped this reality and attempted to adjust their policy accordingly. From their perspective, the logic of negotiations was inescapable. Mountbatten held a conference in

[47]Press interview of A. J. Lovink (Dutch Foreign Office), enclosed in George Atcheson (chargé, China) to Secretary of State, March 8, 1945, 856D.00/2-2345, DSR.

[48]Hornbeck to Secretary of State, October 1, 1945, 856E.00/10-145, DSR; memorandum by Wilson Young of a conversation with J. H. A. Logemann (Dutch minister for overseas territories), September 29, 1945, FO 371 F7656/6398/61, PRO; memorandum by Acheson of a conversation with Alexander Loudon, October 10, 1945, *FR*, 1945, 6:1163–64; Leslie H. Palmier, *Indonesia and the Dutch* (New York: Oxford University Press, 1962), p. 47; U.S. Forces, European Theater, Mission to the Netherlands, Monthly Report, November 27, 1945, in Chief of Naval Operations Records, Naval Operational Archives, Washington Navy Yard. The *New York Times* reporter in Amsterdam asserted that many Dutch considered the loss of the Indies to be more devastating to the Netherlands than World War II. "It is feared that unrest may retard the recovery of the East Indies to a point where it affects recovery of the Netherlands. This margin is slender since the economy of the mother country is blended with and probably dependent on that of the colonies." He went on to say: "There are disquieting possibilities of native control of exports, which in the opinion of businessmen here would be 'disastrous' to the Netherlands" (*New York Times*, October 21, 1945, p. 31).

Singapore on October 10–11, 1945, at which time he tried to persuade Dutch representatives to meet with leading republicans. It was the only solution, he insisted, because armed clashes between Indonesian and Allied soldiers were already occurring, and until the Dutch clarified their policy toward the new government, such incidents threatened to become more serious.[49]

Annoyed by the "high-handed" approach of the British, Lieutenant Governor van Mook nevertheless realized that the Dutch were dependent on British policy—at least until the Dutch themselves were capable of fielding an adequate military force. He explained to his government that talks with the republicans had become a *conditio sine qua non* for continued British military support. The Netherlands government accordingly allowed van Mook to meet with Indonesian nationalists, but stressed that he should not meet with Sukarno, Hatta, or any other Japanese "collaborators." This stance was completely unrealistic: Sukarno was the head of the government, and to refuse to talk with him was tantamount to rejecting all contact with the republic. As Mountbatten had informed London, it was absolutely essential that the Dutch government give van Mook "a completely free hand as to whom he sees."[50] General Christison subsequently arranged two informal sessions on October 23 and October 31 between van Mook and top republican spokesmen, including Sukarno. When word reached The Hague that Sukarno had been present at the talks, the Dutch government sharply rebuffed van Mook and issued an official statement explaining that he had been acting outside his authority. The stalemate continued.[51]

The British were piqued by the Dutch failure to face realities.

[49]Records of 34th and 35th meetings of Supreme Allied Commander, October 10 and 11, 1945, in *Officiele Bescheiden*, 1:300–318.

[50]Mountbatten to British Chiefs of Staff, October 11, 1945, in *Officiele Bescheiden*, 1:338; SAC's 291st meeting, October 17, 1945, in Box 93, SEAC War Diaries.

[51]Djajadiningrat, *Beginnings*, pp. 30–31; Sir Neville Bland (British ambassador, Netherlands) to the Foreign Office, November 3, 1945, FO 371 F9454/6398/61, PRO; *New York Times*, November 1, 1945, p. 1. Van Mook defended his action in meeting with Sukarno. "Somehow," he wrote, "a bridge had to be built between the two parties if we wanted to explore the possibilities of reconstruction" (*Stakes of Democracy*, pp. 211–12).

A British intelligence report dryly described Dutch policy as "characterized by an unwillingness to realize the actualities of the situation."[52] Dening hoped that negotiations with the Indonesians might break the impasse, but he had serious doubts. "I am unable to rid myself of the impression," he cabled the Foreign Office, "that the Dutch will wish to rule Indonesia for the benefit of Holland and that they intend to rule it from Holland and not from here." He added that "if the Dutch cannot be persuaded of the truth that the East has changed and changed radically as a result of the war then a satisfactory solution is unlikely."[53] Dening perceived that the Dutch were unwilling to recognize the legitimate aspirations of the Indonesians to self-rule. There has been no indication, he commented, that the nationalists were being invited to participate in any arrangement that might lead to self-government. Assessing the gloomy prospects for a settlement, Dening concluded: "Unfortunately there are far too many Dutchmen here who . . . still live in the past to offer much hope that they will achieve success in the future. I hope we will not associate ourselves with any attempt the Dutch may make (and I am afraid they will make one) to force the Indonesians into submission."[54]

Indonesian leaders were also becoming increasingly disheartened by Dutch policy. In a letter to General Christison on October 9, Sukarno eloquently pleaded for his nation's independence. "Is liberty and freedom only for certain favored peoples of this world?" he asked. "Indonesians will never understand why it is, for instance, wrong for the Germans to rule Holland if it is right for the Dutch to rule Indonesia. In either case the right to rule rests on pure force and not on the sanction of the populations." He warned the British military commander that the

[52]Memorandum from Director of Intelligence of British Army, "Situation in the Netherlands East Indies," October 27, 1945, FO 371 F9770/6398/61, PRO.

[53]Dening to Foreign Office, October 24, 1945, FO 371 F8889/6398/61, PRO.

[54]Dening to Foreign Office, October 28, 1945, FO 371 F9031/6398/61, PRO. An American intelligence report indicated a similar concern that the Dutch might resort to armed force: "Since the Nationalists have no intention of submitting to dictation, it is expected that the Dutch will resort to a bloody campaign of military suppression" (U.S. Department of War, Strategic Services Unit, Research and Analysis Branch, "Indonesian Nationalist Opinions," December 9, 1945, XL 32100, RG 226, Modern Military Branch).

Dutch underestimated the spirit of the Indonesians and their capacity to wage a long and bloody struggle.[55] Mohammed Hatta similarly berated Dutch policy on several occasions. In a statement issued on October 18, the republican vice-president noted sarcastically that while van Mook "came here with the avowed aim of reimposing Dutch rule on us he is pained to find the Dutch about as popular as the pox."

> On examination we find that the autonomy offered us by Dr. van Mook is as different from true autonomy as chalk is from cheese. Under fancy titles and a gilded facade Dr. van Mook is out to impose on us a streamlined version of the old Dutch colonial policy—something far, far less than what we already hold. The Dutch are graciously permitting us entry into the basement while we have climbed all the way to the top floor and up to the attic.[56]

Officials in the United States, following developments in the East Indies closely, were equally disappointed with the limited vision of Dutch leaders. One State Department officer stressed that few Dutch representatives "either at home or in the area appear to grasp the seriousness of the situation or to admit the sincerity of the Nationalists"; it was unlikely, he speculated, that The Hague would make sufficient concessions to satisfy the republicans without either further hostilities or firm pressure by world opinion.[57] A report prepared by the State Department's Research and Intelligence Branch concluded that "unless some decisive and constructive steps to break the deadlock are taken in the near future, the situation may degenerate into more widespread violence, which in turn may result in a pacification campaign necessitating armed action by British and Dutch troops

[55]Sukarno to Christison, October 9, 1945, FO 371 F9462/6398/61, PRO.

[56]OSS, Research and Analysis Branch, "Statement by Mohammed Hatta," October 18, 1945, XL 24686, Modern Military Branch. See also Hatta to Christison, November 9, 1945, in U.S. Department of War, Strategic Services Unit, XL 32951, Modern Military Branch; Sukarno to Christison, October 6 and October 9, 1945, in *Officiele Bescheiden*, 2:259, 285–90; Hatta to Brigadier General R. M. C. King, October 11, 1945, in *Officiele Bescheiden*, 1:340–41.

[57]Charles W. Yost (American representative to SEAC) to Byrnes, "Situation in French Indochina and Netherlands East Indies," October 23, 1945, 851G.00/10-2345, DSR. For a similar view, see Commanding General, U.S. Forces, India-Burma Theater, to War Department, October 9, 1945, in folder labeled "Messages via War Department," Box 8, PSA Records, DSR.

against resisting Indonesians."[58] Nevertheless, Washington had no interest in getting involved in the Indonesian upheaval. "It would seem important to avoid any entanglement in the colonial problems of western powers in Southeast Asia," advised Abbot Moffat, chief of the State Department's Division of Southeast Asian Affairs, "unless essential to protect American security interests from some threat not presently visible."[59]

The long-feared clash between British troops and Indonesian nationalists erupted in late October 1945. In order to comply with its appointed tasks, the British military command had been occupying key cities in Java for several weeks. Indonesians were irritated by these British actions, believing them to be thinly veiled attempts to bring in Dutch troops under British cover. At Surabaya, in eastern Java, the powder keg exploded. Ragged Indonesian soldiers mounted a ferocious assault on the occupying British forces in a desperate attempt to halt their advance. Heavy casualties occurred on both sides and a British brigadier general, William Mallaby, was killed. By early November, with the aid of air and sea support, the British had finally gained control of the city, but only at tremendous cost.[60] The impact of the battle—regardless of who won or lost in conventional terms—cannot be overestimated: it demonstrated to the British that the republic was enthusiastically backed by the Indonesian people, and that many would sacrifice their lives if necessary for their new nation. The events at Surabaya shocked the British into realizing that without a substantial commitment of more troops and equipment they would have to reach some form of modus vivendi with the republic. The alternatives for British policy makers were now evident: if they could not persuade the

[58]U.S. Department of State, Interim Research and Intelligence Service, Research and Analysis Branch, "Problems Facing the Allies in the N.E.I.," October 16, 1945, XL 23086, Modern Military Branch, and "The Political Issues and Occupation Problems in the N.E.I.," Report no. 3279, October 19, 1945, DSR.

[59]Moffat to John Carter Vincent (director, Office of Far Eastern Affairs), October 12, 1945, in folder labeled "N.E.I. Arms–Surplus Property Disposal," Box 11, PSA Records, DSR.

[60]Djajadiningrat, *Beginnings*, pp. 35–39; Wehl, *Birth of Indonesia*, pp. 52–56; Anthony J. S. Reid, *Indonesian National Revolution, 1945–50* (Hawthorn, Australia: Longman, 1974), pp. 49–53. For the controversy surrounding Mallaby's death, see J. G. A. Parrott, "Who Killed Brigadier Mallaby?," *Indonesia*, no. 20 (1975), pp. 87–110.

Dutch to make an accommodation with the nationalists, they would have to decide whether to withdraw or to reimpose Dutch sovereignty by force.[61]

Editorial opinion in the United States reacted sharply to the outbreak of hostilities in Indonesia. "It is difficult to see," wrote the *New Republic,* "what 'moral obligation' the British Labor government—theoretically opposed to colonial oppression—is under to maintain the Dutch empire by force." "The reports from Surabaya," bluntly observed the *St. Louis Post-Dispatch,* "bear a sickening resemblance to the news from Warsaw, Rotterdam, Belgrade, Athens, Coventry and London when they were subjected to the bombs of the Nazis." Great Britain, the newspaper charged, was simply "doing the dirty work for the rich islands' overlords." *The Nation* similarly bemoaned "the slaughter of hapless Indonesians at Surabaya." By backing "the principle of imperialist solidarity with unlimited force, instead of insisting that the Dutch authorities negotiate with the Java nationalists, Britain's Labour government embarked on seas which may wreck it." Added the *Chicago Tribune*: "Obviously the Dutch and the French are unable to restore their hated rule over the Netherlands East Indies and French Indo-China without outside aid. No such aid should be given them."[62]

American officials also viewed the crisis in Indonesia with growing alarm. Although the United States never questioned Dutch sovereignty over the East Indies, American policy makers were concerned with the apparent inability and unwillingness of the Dutch to deal constructively with the republicans. State Department analysts appreciated the deep roots of the nationalist movement; they understood that it was not simply a Japanese creation, as the Dutch claimed. They also realized that Sukarno was not a quisling, but an authentic nationalist spokes-

[61] U.S. Department of State, Interim Research and Intelligence Service, "Fighting at Soerbaja [sic] Postpones NEI-Indonesian Negotiations," November 2, 1945, Research and Analysis Report no. 3287, DSR; Mountbatten to British Chiefs of Staff, November 5, 1945, in *Officiele Bescheiden,* 1:527–30; Mountbatten to Cabinet, November 9, 1945, FO 371 F9918/6398/61, PRO; Kahin, *Nationalism and Revolution,* pp. 144–45.

[62] "Revolution in Indonesia," *New Republic,* October 29, 1945, pp. 558–59; *St. Louis Post-Dispatch,* October 27, 1945, p. 10; *Nation,* November 17, 1945, pp. 509–10; *Chicago Tribune,* November 1, 1945, p. 12.

man who had a long prewar record as a champion of Indonesian independence. The only alternative for the Dutch, in their view, was to negotiate with the republicans in good faith; only if The Hague expressed a willingness to offer some degree of home rule to the Indies could a potentially explosive deadlock be averted. This assessment was based on American intelligence reports of the republican government's strength.[63] "It is well organized, disciplined, armed at least for guerrilla warfare, and above all unified," one State Department report estimated. "The economic weapons at their command are enormous and they are well aware of them." Furthermore, the Dutch were seen as incapable of quashing the republic: "If the movement is put down by force now it will rise again. . . . The Dutch will never be strong enough now to keep 70 million people under martial law indefinitely."[64]

The State Department followed developments in Indonesia closely, but studied noninvolvement remained the keynote of American policy toward the conflict. Given the larger interests of American foreign policy at the time, this position was quite realistic. Colonial disputes, such as those simmering in the Dutch East Indies and in French Indochina, posed an insuperable dilemma to American authorities. On the one hand, Washington was eager to maintain friendly relations with the underdeveloped world, and active support for a reimposition of the imperialist order in Southeast Asia would surely incur the wrath of Asian nationalists. As one member of the State Department's Far Eastern Division explained, "The traditional position of the United States as the champion of freedom and national self-determination has given the United States a place of disinterested prestige in many parts of the world, which can be very

[63]Memorandum by John Cady (Southeast Asia Division) of a conversation with Jay Reid of *New York Herald Tribune*, October 15, 1945, 856D.00/10-1545, DSR; OSS, "Transitional Period in Indonesia's Internal Political Situation," August 24, 1945, Research and Analysis Report no. 3232; "Indonesian Unrest Portends Most Critical Situation in Southeast Asia Command," September 28, 1945, Research and Analysis Report no. 3265; and "A 'Government of the Republic of Indonesia' Confronts Allied Reoccupation Forces in the Netherlands East Indies," September 14, 1945, Research and Analysis Report no. 3255, all in DSR.

[64]OSS, "Situation Report" (by Jane Foster), October 15, 1945, XL 24208, Modern Military Branch.

gravely prejudiced by ill-considered action on our part and almost equally seriously prejudiced by inaction."[65]

On the other hand, any expressions of outright support for the colonial independence movements would seriously undermine cooperative relations with Holland, Great Britain, and the other European imperial powers. In a preliminary position paper entitled "Basic Policies and Objectives of the U.S. in the Pacific and the Far East," the State-War-Navy Coordinating Committee (SWNCC) elucidated this central dilemma: "A problem for the United States is to harmonize, so far as possible and without prejudice to its traditional position, its policies in regard to the two objectives: increased political freedom for the Far East and the maintenance of the unity of the leading United Nations." In order to balance those seemingly contradictory goals, the SWNCC memorandum recommended that the United States avoid intervention in the British, French, and Netherlands dependencies in the Far East and the Pacific: American interests would be best served, it suggested, by "a Far East progressively developing into a group of self-governing states—independent or with Dominion status—which would cooperate with each other and with the Western powers on a basis of mutual self-respect and friendship."[66]

This rather vague policy objective left one major question unanswered. Put simply: was this neutral stance consistent with the anticolonial pronouncements of the war years? In a memorandum of October 5, 1945, Under Secretary of State Acheson urged SWNCC to clarify American aims in regard to the colonial issue. "The Atlantic Charter commits us, among other things,"

[65]"United States Policy toward the Netherlands Indies and Indochina," December 18, 1945 (prepared by Rupert Emerson), enclosed in Gordon Strong (Economic Division) to Oliver C. Lockhart (Economic Division), December 20, 1945, 856E.01/12-2945, DSR.

[66]Preliminary Report by SWNCC, "Basic Policies and Objectives of the U.S. in the Pacific and the Far East," August 31, 1945, in Box 99, SWNCC Records, DSR. For an earlier version of this policy statement, see policy paper prepared in Department of State: "An Estimate of Conditions in Asia and the Pacific at the Close of the War and the Objectives and Policies of the United States," June 22, 1945, in *FR*, 1945, 6:556–58, 574–78. For a similar analysis of American interests in regard to the colonial conflicts in Southeast Asia, see Office of Naval Intelligence, "Basic Factors in World Relations," December 1945, in Box 106, Strategic Plans Division Records, Naval Operational Archives.

he reminded SWNCC representatives, "to a respect for the right of all peoples to choose the form of government under which they will live, and to the desirability of securing for all peoples improved labor standards, economic advancement and social security." He asked pointedly: "To what lengths will we go to further these general objectives in the dependent areas of the Far East?"[67] As this fundamental question remained unanswered, America's drift away from anticolonialism was steadily becoming more evident.

Still, State Department spokesmen insisted that the United States had not abandoned its commitment to the principles of independence for colonial peoples. They cautioned, however, that this continued dedication to anti-imperialism did not mean that the United States could interfere in the internal affairs of friendly powers any more than Great Britain, for example, could interfere in Puerto Rico.[68] Speaking in New York City on October 20, 1945, John Carter Vincent, director of the State Department's Office of Far Eastern Affairs, reaffirmed the American devotion to self-determination, indicating that the United States continued to pursue colonial questions in terms of its experience in the Philippines. "Do we feel that recognition given to the self-governing aspirations of dependent peoples will be conducive to peace and well-being in the Far East?" he inquired rhetorically. "I believe we do. It is not our intention to assist or participate in forceful measures for the imposition of control by the territorial sovereigns, but we should be prepared to lend our assistance, if requested to do so, in efforts to reach peaceful agreements in these disturbed areas."[69]

In a speech on October 24, Sukarno expressed his hope that Vincent's statement signaled a new U.S. policy toward the Indonesian conflict. "I appeal to the U.S.A. to enact and act as mediator in the present political dispute in this part of the Pacific," he declared. "I am convinced that the American peo-

[67]Memorandum from Acheson to SWNCC, October 5, 1945, in Box 99, SWNCC Records, DSR.

[68]U.S. Department of State, Interim Research and Intelligence Service, "Problems Facing the Allies"; memorandum by Kenneth Landon (Southeast Asia Division) of a conversation with Sharp and Mr. Fitzmaurice of *Newsweek*, October 18, 1945, 856D.00/10-845, DSR.

[69]*U.S. Department of State Bulletin*, 13 (October 21, 1945), 644–48.

ple who have fought and won this war for the realization of the great human ideals of justice and freedom will impartially deal with all matters connected with the Indonesian problem in the interest of world peace."[70] The Dutch, who were initially perturbed by Vincent's speech, were quickly reassured by Secretary of States James Byrnes's statement of the American position: a request for mediation would have to come from the "territorial sovereign." Since The Hague considered the Indonesian crisis a strictly internal affair, American intervention was completely out of the question. Washington thus rejected Sukarno's request.[71]

This snub came as a bitter disappointment to Indonesian nationalists, many of whom still clung to the hope that the United States would honor its wartime pledges and champion the republican cause. Instead, Washington insisted on a policy of strict neutrality. But Indonesians were convinced that even this "neutrality" was being violated by American actions: not only was the United States fully recognizing the right of the Netherlands to restore its prewar rule, it was also actually supplying the Dutch with surplus lend-lease equipment while continuing to train a small contingent of Dutch troops in the United States. In a radiogram to President Truman, Sukarno complained that some Dutch troops in the Indies were using American arms, munitions, and trucks. "Asiatic goodwill toward Americans," the Indonesian president warned, "is endangered by the fact that the Dutch continue to wear U.S. army uniforms and canteens marked 'USA.'"[72]

American officials justified the granting of lend-lease material and surplus property credits to the Netherlands on the grounds that it was consistent with American policy to assist a friendly ally whose sovereignty over its colonial dependency the United

[70]Quoted in van Kleffens to John Morgan (Northern European Division), October 25, 1945, 856D.00/10-2445, DSR. Sukarno telegramed a similar message directly to Truman on October 26, 1945 (856E.00/10-2645, DSR).

[71]Byrnes to Walter Foote (American consul general, East Indies), October 31, 1945, 856E.00/10-2845, DSR; memorandum by Vincent, October 22, 1945, in *FR*, 1945, 6:1167–68; memorandum to Douglas MacArthur (from THS?), October 25, 1945, in folder labeled "Indochina (general) 1940–45," Records of the Office of French and Iberian Affairs, DSR (from the notes of Lisle A. Rose).

[72]*New York Times*, October 21, 1945, p. 1, and November 9, 1945, p. 2.

States had never questioned. Nonetheless, this aid to the Dutch, which over the next two years totaled over $100 million, raised a storm of controversy in the United States.[73] "In the Far East," remarked Major General Patrick Hurley, "we are furnishing lend-lease supplies and using all our reputation to undermine democracy and bolster imperialism and communism." Hugh de Lacy, congressman from Washington, called attention on the floor of the House of Representatives to "the use of American lend-lease in the suppression of the liberties and freedoms of the peoples of that land." Since the official policy of the U.S. government, commented California Representative Ellis E. Patterson, is "not to interfere in other nations' internal affairs, and the upholding of all peoples' right of self-determination, I am amazed that our Navy Department helped arm, train, and equip Dutch troops who are now fighting the Indonesian people in the Netherlands East Indies." Added Congresswoman Clare Boothe Luce of Connecticut: "Nowhere does the weakness of our foreign policy show up more clearly than in our present bewildered inactivity about the tragic situation in Indonesia."[74]

In the face of this sharp criticism, the State Department asked the Dutch and British to remove American labels from all military equipment being used in the East Indies. This maneuver failed to stem the wave of criticism, however. In fact, one observer ridiculed it as a "Pontius Pilate gesture." Added *The Nation*: "Our own government has . . . a responsibility which cannot be dodged by removing American tags from tanks used to crush Indonesian insurgency."[75] In November the State Department finally ordered the termination of further sales of arms and military equipment to the Dutch, but the sale of nonmilitary material—material that at least indirectly continued to benefit the

[73]For exact figures on American aid to the Netherlands, see SWNCC, Subcommittee on Far Eastern Affairs, Special Ad Hoc Committee Country Report on Indonesia, July 22, 1947, in Box 109, SWNCC Records, DSR. See also Acheson to Forrestal, December 10, 1946, in folder labeled "NEI: American Surplus Property Disposal," Box 11, DSR.

[74]U.S. Congress, Senate, 79th Cong., 2d sess., *Congressional Record*, vol. 41, pt. 13, pp. A5318, A5765, A5426, A5318.

[75]Excerpt from memorandum of State Department Press and Radio News Conference, October 24, 1945, in folder labeled "Indonesia General (1945–46)," Box 11, PSA Records, DSR; Junius B. Wood, "Twilight of Empire," *Nation's Business*, March 1946, p. 89; *Nation*, November 17, 1945, 510.

position of the Dutch vis-à-vis the Indonesians—remained unaffected by this decision.[76] According to American officials, this course was entirely consistent with the larger aims of American policy, which, as a State Department memorandum spelled out, required "establishing a realistic settlement of the problems of Southeast Asia with a view to protecting the security, the interests, and the influence of the Western Powers in that section of Asia."[77]

On several occasions the Indonesian Republic accused the United States of pursuing a pro-Dutch policy; these protests were relatively mild, however, because the republic was unwilling to risk alienating Washington. The republicans sought to achieve independence through diplomacy. From the outset of their independence struggle, republican leaders were forced to choose between two alternative policies: *diplomasi* or *perdjuangan* (struggle). Such spokesmen as Sukarno, Hatta, and Sjahrir believed that the military, organizational, and ideological weakness of the republic necessitated a diplomatic policy. Broadly conceived, their view was that the republic must rely primarily on achieving a negotiated settlement with the Dutch which would be guaranteed by the great powers; everything else would have to be subordinated to that central goal. Once a settlement had been attained, the nation could return to the tasks of transforming and democratizing Indonesian society. The logic of diplomacy thus demanded that any radical or revolutionary tendencies within the nationalist movement be suspended or suppressed to appease international opinion. The republic, according to this viewpoint, had to demonstrate that it was a responsible, capable, and stable government. By promising to protect foreign properties and displaying a willingness to welcome foreign investments—as it did in its political manifesto

[76]Memorandum for the President: "Policy with Respect to Shipment of Military Equipment to Dutch Territories," December 22, 1945, in folder labeled "NEI: American Surplus Property Disposal," Box 11, DSR; Southeast Asian Division draft memorandum, December 18, 1945, in ibid.; Lisle A. Rose, *Roots of Tragedy: The United States and the Struggle for Asia, 1945–1953* (Westport, Conn.: Greenwood Press, 1976), p. 87.

[77]Southeast Asian Division draft memorandum, December 18, 1945, in PSA Records, DSR.

of November 1—the Republic of Indonesia vied to project this image to the world.[78]

The danger inherent in a policy of diplomasi was that the achievement of international recognition, if the policy succeeded, might occur at the expense of internal social reform. Perdjuangan, the alternative strategy, based its hopes instead on the strength of the national revolutionary movement. Its chief advocate, Communist leader Tan Malaka, stressed the inevitability of armed struggle; he refused to believe that true independence could be bestowed as a gift from the Western powers. Only through struggle to attain a common goal, he insisted, could Indonesian society be transformed and a cohesive, organized sense of purpose be created out of the formless national movement.[79]

While these conflicting strategies continued to compete for popular support, the early triumph of the diplomasi forces soon became apparent. Sukarno expressed his government's willingness to pursue diplomatic channels in a statement issued on October 25:

> Indonesia's interests do not only concern the development of a new world structure but also the achievement of a basis for lasting peace in the Pacific. Based on this precept the Government of the Republic of Indonesia is of the opinion that discussions to solve the

[78]Anderson, *Java*, pp. 307–8. The Political Manifesto of the Republic of Indonesia is reprinted in Wolf, *Indonesian Story*, pp. 172–75. For American intelligence analyses of the republic's desire to attract American and Western investment, see OSS, "Program of Nationalists," September 28, 1945, XL 18340, Modern Military Branch; U.S. Department of State, Interim Research and Intelligence Service, "The Economic Situation in Java and Prospective Business Policies," Research and Analysis Report no. 3288, November 2, 1945, DSR.

[79]Anderson, *Java*, p. 308. John R. W. Smail has produced the most convincing analysis of the genuine revolutionary forces present within Indonesian society. He argues, much as Carl Becker did about the American Revolution, that two separate revolutions were taking place simultaneously: one over home rule and one over who would rule at home. "The difficulty with this 'diplomatic' policy," he contends, "was that the Republic could not be maintained successfully against the Allies or the Japanese without the dynamism of the *perdjuangan*, itself necessarily subversive of the domestic status quo" (*Bandung in the Early Revolution, 1945–1946: A Study in the Social History of the Indonesian Revolution* [Ithaca: Cornell University Modern Indonesia Project, 1964], p. 62).

> Indonesian problem can only succeed and guarantee lasting peace if they are conducted before the world at large.[80]

He stressed that the starting point of such negotiations would have to be the right of the Indonesian people to self-determination; that concept was not negotiable. On November 1 the republic issued its carefully worded political manifesto, giving further evidence of the government's eagerness to seek international acceptance.

Then on November 9, in another maneuver designed to court world opinion, Sukarno designated Sjahrir to head the first parliamentary cabinet of the republic. The appointment was prompted partly by internal political considerations, but, more important, the Western-educated Sjahrir, an adept negotiator with a polished and engaging style, was far more acceptable to the Dutch than the mercurial Sukarno, who would be forever tainted in Dutch eyes by his wartime collaboration with the Japanese. Sukarno remained titular president, but he surrendered the day-to-day governing responsibilities to Sjahrir.[81] This governmental change greatly pleased American observers. "The moderate and non-collaborationist character of the new group," predicted Abbot Moffat, "will probably satisfy Dutch objections to negotiating with Sukarno, although the fact that the President has not relinquished his office may provide grounds for further objections from The Hague."[82]

In actuality, the Dutch continued to move with extreme caution. J. H. A. Logemann, minister for overseas territories in the Netherlands government, told a reporter for the *New York Times* that he expected the Indies to gain something akin to dominion status in his lifetime, but not independence. Presumably he

[80]Quoted in Djajadiningrat, *Beginnings*, p. 40.

[81]Kahin, *Nationalism and Revolution*, pp. 153–54, 168–69; Anderson, *Java*, pp. 180–89; Anak Agung, *Twenty Years Indonesian Foreign Policy*, pp. 19–20. There are many indications that the Dutch were pleased with Sjahrir's ascendancy. See, for example, van Mook, *Stakes of Democracy*, p. 211; Hornbeck to Byrnes, November 16, 1945, 856E.00/11-1645, DSR; Chester Wilmot's BBC interview with J. H. A. Logemann, November 28, 1945, cited in Bland to William Schermerhorn, December 2, 1945, in *Officiele Bescheiden*, 2:265.

[82]Memorandum from Moffat to Vincent, November 21, 1945, in folder labeled "NEI: September 1944–1947, Indonesian Parties and Leaders," Box 11, PSA Records, DSR.

meant twenty to thirty years, and Logemann, remarkably, was reputed to represent the liberal wing of Dutch opinion.[83] This stubborn failure to deal with the realities of Indonesian nationalism characterized the long-awaited policy statement on Holland's future plans for the East Indies. Issued by van Mook on November 6, the statement declared that Dutch objectives for the Indies continued to be based on the principles proclaimed by Queen Wilhelmina in December 1942. The Netherlands expressed its willingness to expand Indonesian representation in the Volksraad, but that body would remain a pseudo-parliament with no real legislative function. Indonesians would be appointed to head certain governmental ministries, although they would still be subordinate to the Dutch governor general. In effect, the Dutch offered cosmetic changes in the governmental structure while maintaining for themselves the real power in the archipelago.[84] British spokesmen regarded the Dutch proposals as a "reasonable offer," but to Indonesians the Dutch statement of November 6 was an insulting "compromise" that suggested nothing less than a return to the old colonial relationship. "It is only a going-over of the old familiar statement of the Queen," remarked Sukarno. "We do not want anything to do with the Netherlands Kingdom."[85]

The Dutch position was weakened, though, by its continued dependence on British military support. Van Mook reported to The Hague in early November that he and the Dutch military commanders agreed that a force of approximately 75,000 men would be required to reestablish Dutch control over the East Indies. After careful consideration the Netherlands government ascertained that no more than 30,000 soldiers could be available for duty in Indonesia by October 1946. With such an inadequate force at their disposal, Dutch officials remained highly vulnerable to British advice.[86]

[83]*New York Times*, October 28, 1945, p. 4.

[84]Djajadiningrat, *Beginnings*, p. 41; Hornbeck to Byrnes, November 10, 1945, 856D.00/11-1045, DSR.

[85]Meeting between British, Dutch, and Indonesian representatives, November 17, 1945, in *Officiele Bescheiden*, 2:100; *New York Times*, November 7, 1945, p. 13.

[86]Djajadiningrat, *Beginnings*, pp. 42–43; memorandum from General Hull to Chiefs of Staff, September 21, 1945, OPD 336.2TS 2/56, Operation and Planning Division Files, Modern Military Branch.

The British government, meanwhile, was undertaking a complete reevaluation of its policy. On December 2 the Joint Planning Staff issued a detailed analysis of London's long-term policy objectives in the East Indies. The report contended that the British had successfully fulfilled two of their assigned tasks in Indonesia—enforcing the surrender and disarmament of the Japanese and releasing Allied prisoners of war and internees—but had encountered considerable difficulty with the third assignment of transferring the country to Dutch civil authorities. The latter task had become a far more complex commitment than had been anticipated when the original directive was drafted. The military prognosis in Java appeared bleak; the fighting at Surabaya had unmistakably demonstrated the strength and determination of the nationalist forces. "At no time," the Planning Staff pointed out, "have we stated that we intend to enforce Dutch rule on the Indonesians by force of arms." Britain was legally obliged, noted the report, only to *allow* the Dutch to resume effective control; it was not obliged to *place* the Dutch in control against the opposition of the local population. Moreover, the use of Indian troops in Indonesia compounded the problem: British authorities were concerned that the prolonged use of Indians to suppress the nationalists might sour British–Indian relations.

The arguments against withdrawal, however, were equally compelling. British policy makers acknowledged that they had a deep moral obligation to the Dutch as allies and would surely be accused by them of breaking faith in the event of an abrupt British withdrawal. Britain's long-term interests also dictated the cultivation of a friendly relationship with Holland in Europe. Another argument advanced by the Joint Planning Staff against a precipitous withdrawal from the East Indies was the dangerous precedent that such a move might set. "The peoples of India, Ceylon, Burma, and Malaya would undoubtedly draw the inference," the report warned, "that by using a sufficient degree of violence it was possible to attain complete independence. This would probably result in an increase in our military commitment in these areas." Finally, the Planning Staff pointed out that British strategic interests in the Far East required a strong and friendly government in the East Indian islands, which would not be the case if the republicans were in power.

Caught between the equally unattractive prospects of an early withdrawal or an increased military commitment, the report urged a middle course. The Planning Staff recommended a policy first suggested by Mountbatten: holding a position in West Java until the Dutch were strong enough to replace the British. The advantages of maintaining a foothold in West Java were fivefold: (1) the British could then limit their present commitment; (2) their forces in West Java would then be strong enough to control events there; (3) West Java was easily defensible and contained the main resources of that key island; (4) by strengthening their position there the British could then help Indonesian moderates to establish influence over the republican government; and (5) the Dutch administration would then have an opportunity to establish its administration behind the British forces in Java.[87]

London quickly adopted the report of the Planning Staff as official policy, but not without some serious objections. J. C. Sterndale Bennett of the Foreign Office argued that such a limited policy would be unwelcome to the Dutch government because it would leave the nationalists free to consolidate their strength in the greater part of Java, from which it would be difficult to dislodge them. Conversely, he reasoned that the modification of British goals in the East Indies could be interpreted as a defeat for Great Britain. "It will be regarded as a victory by the extremists," he observed, "and, while we have to put the best face possible on this in our propaganda, it will in fact be a victory."[88] The British government countered these reservations with the hope that a negotiated settlement between the Dutch and the Indonesians could still be worked out.

Plagued by a wave of international criticism—from the supporters of both the Dutch and the Indonesians—for their policy in the East Indies, British diplomats increasingly looked to the United States for comfort. On November 9 Lord Halifax, the British ambassador in Washington, met with Secretary of State

[87]Report by Joint Planning Staff, "Long Term Policy in the Netherlands East Indies," December 2, 1945, FO 371 F11234/6398/61, PRO.

[88]Sterndale Bennett to Foreign Office, December 3, 1945, FO 371 F11920/6398/61, PRO.

Byrnes to explain his government's actions and difficulties. He reminded Byrnes that Great Britain was performing a task defined by the Allied Combined Chiefs of Staff—an assignment that had originally been an American responsibility. The secretary agreed that Britain was acting for the Allies, but in response to Halifax's request for some indication that the United States appreciated Britain's predicament—a statement of support, presumably—the American government remained strangely silent. British Foreign Office officials considered offering to share arbitration duties with the United States in the East Indies, but they ultimately scrapped this plan. The British were too wary of America's identification with the anticolonial cause to invite its entry into a colonial dispute. As Sterndale Bennett saw it: "The Americans did not approach these things in the same objective manner as we were trying to do and their support would probably be all on the side of the Indonesians."[89]

In fact, nothing was further from the truth. Despite paying occasional obeisance to the principles of self-determination, as in Vincent's speech of October 20, American officials consistently refused to give any positive support to colonial nationalist movements. At the same time, Washington reassured the European imperial powers that it recognized their sovereignty over their former colonies. Under Secretary of State Acheson spelled out the American position in response to a query from an interested congressman: "While the U.S. recognizes the sovereignty of Great Britain, France and the Netherlands in their colonial territories in Southeast Asia, it is not the policy of this Government to assist the colonial powers to reestablish by force their position in those territories."[90] Although quickly dissociating itself from any possible military confrontations, the United States clearly aligned itself with the colonial nations in opposition to the nationalists; its unwillingness to question the

[89]Lord Halifax to Foreign Office, November 10, 1945, FO 371 F9862/6398/61, PRO; memorandum by Sterndale Bennett to Foreign Office, December 4, 1945, FO 371 F11236/6398/61, PRO; Sterndale Bennett to Foreign Office, December 3, 1945, FO 371 F11920/6398/61, PRO; memorandum by I. A. Wilson Young of a conversation with John M. Allison (of American Embassy, London), November 24, 1945, FO 371 F10466/6398/61, PRO.

[90]Acheson to Representative Frank R. Havenner, December 20, 1945, 856D.00/11-2645, DSR.

rights of the territorial sovereigns along with its lend-lease aid to the Dutch belied any official professions of American "neutrality."

On December 19, 1945, the State Department finally responded to the British request for an official public statement on the Indonesian conflict, breaking two months of silence: "The United States Government has viewed with increasing concern recent developments in the Netherlands East Indies. It had hoped the conversations between the Indonesians and the Netherlands authorities would have resulted in a peaceful settlement recognizing alike the natural aspirations of the Indonesian peoples and the legitimate rights and interests of the Netherlands." Expressing disappointment with the breakdown of negotiations, the State Department indicated its interest in an early agreement between "the Netherlands authorities, as representatives of the territorial sovereign, and the Indonesian leaders. Such a settlement can be attained only through a realistic, broadminded and cooperative approach on the part of all concerned and a will to reconcile differences by peaceful means."[91]

Despite the rather innocuous language, the press release was extremely significant—as much for what it did not say as for what it did say. There was no longer any mention of the principles of self-determination or self-government, or any expression of willingness to arbitrate the dispute. Still trying to straddle the fence on the sensitive subject of colonial relations, the United States attempted to balance its position between "the natural aspirations of the Indonesian peoples and the legitimate rights and interests of the Netherlands." The balance was distorted, though, for American recognition of the rights of the Netherlands as the "territorial sovereign" amounted to a denial of the republic's quest for status as an equal party to the dispute. Significantly, there was no mention of the Indonesian Republic itself in the American statement.

Nevertheless, the State Department press release of December 19 was a diplomatic triumph for the United States: it encouraged the resumption of negotiations without alienating any of the interested parties, a considerable accomplishment indeed.

[91] *U.S. Department of State Bulletin*, 13 (December 23, 1945), 1021–22.

General Christison and his staff regarded it as a "perfect and will-timed document" that not only strengthened Britain's position but also upheld van Mook's efforts to convince his government of the need to reach an accommodation with the nationalists.[92] For its part, the Dutch Foreign Office commented that the American policy statement was helpful since it showed an appreciation of the difficulties that the Dutch were encountering in the East Indies. The Dutch also realized, however, that the United States was making a friendly but firm suggestion that they return to the conference table with a willingness to make definite concessions to Indonesian nationalism.[93] Even the Indonesians—whatever private doubts they might have held about the American position—officially expressed their gratitude for the policy statement. Sutan Sjahrir sent an appreciative Christmas telegram to President Truman. "The last message of good will and encouragement issued by your State Department," Sjahrir remarked, "has given us great comfort in the struggle we are waging to establish freedom, justice and democracy in Indonesia." He added: "We look to you, as the head of a country that has always been in the forefront of the fight for liberty, justice, and self-determination, to use the benefit of your influence to stop the present bloodshed in Indonesia."[94]

Finally, the Dutch began to realize that the initiative to break the deadlock with the republicans would have to come from them. London had made clear that its continued support for the Dutch was contingent on the reopening of talks with the republicans, and now Washington had pointedly expressed a similar wish. This pressure forced the Dutch to act. On December 25 a conference of Dutch and British officials was held at Chequers, the official country residence of the British prime minister. At the conclusion of the meeting a joint comminiqué was issued:

> The respective governments were agreed that a solution of the political problem should be considered as an essential contribution to the successful implementation of the task entrusted by the Su-

[92]Foote to Byrnes, December 23, 1945, 856.00/12-2345, DSR.
[93]Hornbeck to Byrnes, December 21, 1945, 856E.00/12–2145, DSR; Djajadiningrat, *Beginnings*, p. 50.
[94]Sjahrir to Truman, December 25, 1945, in *FR*, 1945, 6:1186.

> preme Allied command to Great Britain in order to liquidate the Japanese occupation of these territories, and, so far as this is concerned, it is the joint task of the British and the Netherlands Governments and of the Indonesian people. The British and Netherlands Governments are therefore agreed on the course of conduct to promote that the leaders of the nationalist movement will come to an agreement with the Netherlands authorities.[95]

The new year thus began on a hopeful note as the Dutch pledged to enter into constructive negotiations with the republicans.

[95] Communiqué on a meeting between Prime Minister and Dutch ministers at Chequers, December 27, 1945, in *Officiele Bescheiden*, 2:468–69; Djajadiningrat, *Beginnings*, p. 50.

4

Toward the Linggadjati Agreement: January–November 1946

The year 1946 was a trying one for President Truman and his foreign policy advisers. The wartime alliance with the Soviet Union had shattered, leaving broad areas of disagreement between the two superpowers on virtually every major issue. In Eastern Europe, in Iran, in Germany, in Greece, even in China, American and Soviet interests clashed. The devastating effects of World War II, moreover, left much of Western Europe in economic ruin. The demands on American policy makers were staggering.

Given these pressing problems, it is hardly surprising that senior American officials paid little attention to a colonial conflict in far-off Southeast Asia. Developments in Indonesia, of course, could not be isolated from other, more central concerns of American diplomacy. Even so, American policy makers assigned very low priority to Southeast Asia, a region that had never been a traditional area of interest for the United States. Washington took comfort in the fact that its closest ally, Great Britain, was endeavoring to achieve a liberal, negotiated settlement between the Dutch and the Indonesians. There was no reason to believe that London would fail in its appointed task, nor was there any reason to believe that Washington could improve on London's performance. The chief American interest in the Dutch–Indonesian conflict at this time was to ensure that it did not become a major international crisis, or become yet another bone of contention between the West and the Soviet Union.

Ironically, the promising results of the Chequers conference had hardly been announced when the conflict in the East Indies suddenly did threaten to explode into a major international crisis. On January 17, 1946, the delegates to the inaugural session of the United Nations Security Council began debate on their very first agenda item: a complaint by Iran that the continued presence of Soviet troops within its borders constituted interference in Tehran's internal affairs. The Soviet Union countered this charge with an accusation of its own: that the British had been employed by "reactionary" elements against the "democratic forces" of Greece. Ukranian delegate D. Z. Manuilsky proposed that the Security Council examine the threat to world peace posed by British military operations in Indonesia. He argued that the problem could not be considered an internal affair of the Netherlands, since British and Japanese soldiers were fighting the Indonesian people. Manuilsky appealed to the council to "carry out the necessary investigation" in an effort to end the fighting.[1]

Before this verbal assault on Great Britain in the United Nations, the Soviet Union had pursued a cautious policy toward colonial issues. During the autumn of 1945, Russian comment on the Indonesian conflict had been minimal, limited to mild criticism of the Dutch and British roles and the American "hands-off" posture. At the Moscow Foreign Ministers' Conference in December, Soviet Foreign Minister V. M. Molotov had shown considerable interest in the Netherlands East Indies, suggesting at one point that the withdrawal of British troops from Java parallel the withdrawal of Soviet troops from Manchuria and American troops from North China. The Soviets quickly dropped this proposal, however, when the British registered their firm opposition to it.[2] This relatively conciliatory policy probably reflected the Kremlin's reluctance to put any further strain on the wartime alliance. A strong Soviet condemnation of the European imperial powers would have represented a significant step toward a complete dissolution of that alliance, and

[1]United Nations Security Council, *Official Records*, 1st yr., Supplement no. 1, Annex 4, p. 76 (hereafter cited as SCOR).

[2]Minute by Sterndale Bennett, December 29, 1945, FO 371 F81/1/61, Records of the British Foreign Office, Public Record Office, London (hereafter cited as PRO).

Moscow, which sought Western recognition of its emerging sphere of influence in Eastern Europe, wanted to minimize any possible areas of friction with the West. By early 1946, however, East–West tensions were increasing, leading to this initial confrontation in the United Nations. As political commentator James Reston noted in the *New York Times*, the Soviet indictment of British policy in Greece and Indonesia appeared to be one of the first cracks in postwar solidarity.[3]

Debate over the Ukranian complaint began on February 7. Manuilsky and his Russian counterpart, Andrei Y. Vyshinsky, alleged that British and Japanese troops were waging war for the purpose of suppressing the "Indonesian national liberation movement."[4] British Foreign Secretary Ernest Bevin scoffed at this charge, insisting that there were hardly enough British troops in the area "to interfere with anybody," and assuring his adversaries that as soon as negotiations were concluded in Indonesia, Britain would be very glad to withdraw its troops. Since Dutch sovereignty over the East Indies had not been questioned, Bevin wondered how the Security Council could legally send a commission to investigate a problem that fell under the jurisdiction of a sovereign power, a position the Dutch delegate warmly embraced.[5] Privately, Bevin suggested that the real objective of the Soviet government was to secure a foothold in Southeast Asia. If the Soviets succeeded in their demand for an independent inquiry into the conduct of British troops in the Dutch East Indies, he warned the cabinet, an unfortunate precedent would be set: a similar commission of inquiry could be demanded should disorders break out in India.[6]

For its part, the United States decided, in the words of Secretary of State Byrnes, that "we have got to go along with Britain as

[3]*New York Times*, February 10, 1946, IV, p. 5; Ruth T. McVey, *The Soviet View of the Indonesian Revolution* (Ithaca: Cornell University Modern Indonesia Project, 1957), pp. 3–12. For the view that the Soviet action in the Security Council was a retaliatory measure for Western criticism of Russian moves in Iran, see Alastair M. Taylor, *Indonesian Independence and the United Nations* (Ithaca: Cornell University Press, 1960), pp. 14–15; William Henderson, *Pacific Settlement of Disputes: The Indonesian Question, 1946–1949* (New York: Woodrow Wilson Foundation, 1954), p. 13; Philip C. Jessup, *The Birth of Nations* (New York: Columbia University Press, 1974), p. 43.

[4]SCOR, 1st yr., 14th meeting, February 10, 1946, pp. 205–6.

[5]Ibid., 11th meeting, February 7, 1946, p. 180.

[6]Cabinet Records (CAB) 128, Confidential Annex, January 1, 1946, PRO.

far as we can."[7] American delegate Edward R. Stettinius accordingly expressed the view that the best hope for an amicable settlement lay in a successful conclusion of negotiations then in progress. Those talks, he argued, would achieve results in harmony with the purposes of the United Nations Charter and "meet the legitimate aspirations of the Indonesian people for self-government." When put to a vote, the Ukranian draft resolution to establish a commission of inquiry was resoundingly defeated, much to the delight of the Western powers, receiving support only from the Soviet Union and Poland.[8] Nevertheless, the significance of this episode cannot be discounted. "The practical effect of the USSR-Ukranian move," suggested a State Department intelligence report, "is to exert some additional pressure on the Netherlands and Great Britain to achieve a speedy solution of the conflict in Java."[9]

Both Washington and London were hopeful, as they pointed out in the Security Council debates, that Dutch–Indonesian differences would be bridged satisfactorily in the very near future. At Chequers, Dutch spokesmen had agreed to resume serious discussions with republican representatives, giving rise to much optimistic speculation. The Dutch, moveover, had yielded to London's suggestion that it appoint a respected British diplomat to lend advice and assistance at the upcoming talks. In the view of some American and British analysts, the initially rigid Netherlands position was softening considerably.[10] Statements by

[7]Memorandum by Benjamin V. Cohen (counselor, State Department) of a telephone conversation with Byrnes, February 12, 1946, 856D.00/2-1246, in U.S. Department of State Records, National Archives, Washington, D.C. (hereafter cited as DSR).

[8]SCOR, 1st yr., 16th meeting, February 11, 1946, pp. 235–37; Taylor, *Indonesian Independence*, p. 389; memorandum prepared in Department of State, December 26, 1945, in *Foreign Relations of the United States* (Washington, D.C., 1971), 8:787–89 (hereafter volumes in this series will be cited as *FR*, followed by the year); memorandum by Moffat of a conversation with Bohlen, Vincent, and Cumming, February 7, 1946, in folder labeled "N.E.I. 1945–1946, British Relations," in Box 12, Records of the Office of the Philippines and Southeast Asian Affairs, DSR (hereafter cited as PSA Records); J. Foster Collins, "The United Nations and Indonesia," *International Conciliation*, March 1950, pp. 118–19.

[9]U.S. Department of State, Office of Research and Intelligence (ORI), Division of Far East Intelligence, Situation Report—Southern Areas, no. 3480, January 23, 1946, RG 59, DSR.

[10]Hornbeck to Byrnes, January 17, 1946, in *FR*, 1946, 8:797, Dening to Foreign Office, FO 371 F1193/1/61, PRO.

Dutch political leaders fueled this optimism. On January 17, for example, J. H. A. Logemann, the Dutch minister for overseas territories, declared that his government was prepared to accord "the nationalist conception a fully recognized status within the Kingdom." Logemann contended that in an international sense his nation was rowing against the tide; it was no use, he said, to talk about what his country had achieved in the Indies, as the colonial relationship was now outdated and the world expected the Netherlands to steer a new course.[11]

Other indications, however, continued to point in the opposite direction. The undisciplined actions of Dutch troops in Java, some of whom actually made several attempts on the life of Prime Minister Sjahrir, particularly concerned British officials. On January 6 Sir Neville Bland, the British ambassador to the Netherlands, caustically informed The Hague that the behavior of Dutch troops was adversely affecting the prospects for serious negotiations.[12] His remarks only heightened the ire of Dutch diplomats, who already believed the British guilty of undue meddling in their affairs. Tension between the two former allies was now reaching unprecedented proportions; British contempt for the Netherlands' position was growing increasingly evident while the Dutch continued to believe that British actions in Indonesia were seriously compromising their hopes for a liberal settlement in the Indies. Reflecting the prevailing British viewpoint, Dening commented that "internal dissension, both in Holland and in Batavia, seems to render it impossible to determine a settled policy towards the Indonesian question."[13]

At a meeting of the cabinet on January 15, Bevin said that The Hague's delay in fulfilling its Chequers pledges was unfortunate "since it was most important, both for financial reasons and because of political reactions in India, that we should reduce as quickly as possible our military commitments in the Dutch East Indies."[14] The most pressing of London's concerns remained the

[11]Quoted in ibid. For Logemann's view of Dutch–Indonesian relations, see J. H. A. Logemann, "The Indonesian Problem," *Pacific Affairs*, 20 (March 1947), 30–41.

[12]Bland to Foreign Office, January 6, 1946, FO 371 F310/1/61, PRO; Bland to Foreign Office, January 6, 1946, FO 371 F311/1/61, PRO.

[13]Dening to Foreign Office, January 22, 1946, FO 371 F1250/1/61, PRO.

[14]CAB 128/5, January 15, 1946, PRO.

need for a prompt withdrawal of Indian troops from the East Indies; their continued service in a colonial context was stirring vigorous protests in India, and the British viceroy repeatedly urged his government to withdraw them.[15]

Largely owing to British pressure, on February 10, 1946, the Netherlands finally reopened formal talks with Indonesian representatives. Van Mook and Sjahrir headed the Dutch and Indonesian delegations, respectively, while the seasoned British diplomat Lord Inverchapel served as mediator. Inverchapel (formerly Sir Archibald Clark Kerr) had accepted the unenviable task of attempting to reconcile two widely divergent points of view. As he was leaving his former post as ambassador to the Soviet Union, no less experienced a negotiator than Joseph Stalin warned him that his new position would be an extremely trying one.[16] From the outset, Inverchapel insisted that his role would be quite limited; he would help the Dutch and Indonesians to settle their principal differences, but the basic constitutional issues could be resolved only by the parties themselves. London's chief concern, Bevin had instructed him, lay not in resolving intricate constitutional issues but in avoiding the disastrous consequences of a continued failure to reach any settlement.[17]

Van Mook chose this inaugural meeting to submit to the republic an integrated Dutch plan for the future of the East Indies. He proudly announced that the proposal represented a new departure in the relationship between the Netherlands and Indonesia. "For the first time in the history of that relationship," he declared, "a definite goal is set for the political development of Indonesia. Recognizing the right of self-determination for the citizens of this country, the proposals embody a clear and workable way towards democratic liberty." The gist of the Dutch plan was that the people of Indonesia would freely decide their political destiny after a given preparatory period. During the transi-

[15]Record of a meeting at 10 Downing Street, January 9, 1946, FO 371 F684/1/61, PRO; report by Joint Planning Staff, "Indian Troops in Java," January 1946, FO 371 F748/1/61, PRO; Bevin to Bland, January 18, 1946, FO 371 F1202/1/61, PRO.

[16]Draft letter from Inverchapel to Stalin, February 2, 1946, in Inverchapel Papers, FO 800, PRO.

[17]Bevin to Clark Kerr, January 25, 1946, FO 371 F1089/1/61, PRO.

tion period, the Netherlands government intended to create a Commonwealth of Indonesia that would be a partner in the Kingdom of the Netherlands and would be "composed of territories possessing different degrees of autonomy." The domestic affairs of the commonwealth were to be "managed independently by the Commonwealth's own institutions," but a representative of the Dutch crown was still to have "special powers to guarantee fundamental rights, an efficient administration and sound financial management."[18] Significantly, the proposals did not specifically state when the Indonesians would be "enabled freely to decide their political destiny," although a subsequent clarification by Dutch officials nebulously defined the transition period as terminating before the present generation had reached retirement age.[19]

The *New York Times* announced that the Netherlands plan "definitely ends the colonial era in Indonesia,"[20] but British and Indonesian spokesmen remained skeptical. Richard Allen of the British Foreign Office pointed out that "the statement appears to be for the most part only an amplification of earlier statements without any basic change of policy." What was offered to Indonesia, he noted, was status between a colony and a dominion.[21] Sjahrir complained that the new proposition provided only for Dutch domination of the archipelago and the virtual liquidation of the republic. He stressed that Indonesia had no interest in the proposed kingdom and would accept nothing less than commonwealth status similar to Australia's in the British Empire. The Indonesian prime minister intimated to

[18]U.S. Department of State, ORI, "Netherlands Proposals for the Future Status of Indonesia," Report no. 3507A, March 15, 1946, DSR; *New York Times*, February 11, 1946, p. 2. See also Taylor, *Indonesian Independence*, pp. 20–21; David Wehl, *The Birth of Indonesia* (London: George Allen & Unwin, 1948), pp. 109–11; Raymond Kennedy, "Dutch Plan for the Indies: A Bargaining Offer," *Far Eastern Survey*, 15 (April 10, 1946), 97–102.

[19]Idrus N. Djajadiningrat, *The Beginnings of the Indonesian-Dutch Negotiations and the Hoge Veluwe Talks* (Ithaca: Cornell University Modern Indonesia Project, 1958), p. 52.

[20]*New York Times*, February 12, 1946, p. 24.

[21]Quoted in Byrnes to Hornbeck, February 7, 1946, 856E.00/2–846, DSR. See also U.S. Department of State, ORI, Division of Far East Intelligence, "Progress of Netherlands-Indonesian Negotiations," Situation Report—Southern Areas, no. 3480.4, February 20, 1946, DSR.

American Consul General Walter Foote that acceptance of the Dutch offer would surely lead to the fall of his parliamentary government.[22] Inverchapel agreed that the Dutch terms were unacceptable in their present form, but he urged Sjahrir to consider them as a basis for discussion. In a subsequent conversation with Foote, Inverchapel expressed his belief that the Indonesians would gain by stalling because the British would not fight and the Dutch were unable to. "My opinion," Foote cabled the State Department, is that "Indos hold all four aces."[23]

As Sjahrir explained to Inverchapel, his freedom to accept the Dutch concessions was severely circumscribed by virulent domestic opposition to his diplomatic policy.[24] His accession to the prime ministership in November had signified a temporary setback for the proponents of perdjuangan, but in the succeeding months their strength had steadily grown. The opposition to diplomasi and Sjahrir coalesced around the program of Tan Malaka's Persatuan Perdjuangan (Fighting Front, or PP), which demanded complete independence as its minimal goal. Tan Malaka outlined the PP's policy in a January speech:

> We are not willing to negotiate with any one else before we obtain our 100 per cent freedom and before our enemy has left our shores and our seas in good order. We are not willing to negotiate with a thief in our house. Let us not have the idea that the public does not understand diplomacy. We are not willing to negotiate as long as the enemy is still in our country. If we are willing to hold negotiations, we are doing it against the will of the general public.[25]

[22]Foote to Byrnes, February 14, 1946, in *FR*, 1946, 8:810. Van Mook, on the other hand, considered the Dutch offer to be eminently reasonable. "The only difference between the Indonesian demand of immediate independence and the Netherlands proposals," he insisted, "is a difference between the impossible and possible way of realizing the same ideal." See van Mook to Clark Kerr, February 25, 1946, in *Officiele Bescheiden Bettrefende de Nederlands-Indonesische Betrekkingen 1945–1950*, ed. S. L. van der Wal (The Hague: Martinius Nijhoff, 1971–76), 3:448–49.

[23]Foote to Byrnes, February 26, 1946, 856E.00/2-2646, DSR. See also Benedict R. O'G. Anderson, *Java in a Time of Revolution; Occupation, and Resistance, 1944–46* (Ithaca: Cornell University Press, 1972), p. 304.

[24]Clark Kerr to Foreign Office, February 23, 1946, FO 371 F2887/1/61, PRO.

[25]Quoted in George McTurnan Kahin, *Nationalism and Revolution in Indonesia* (Ithaca: Cornell University Press, 1952), p. 173.

A groundswell of popular support greeted the promulgation of the PP's program; nearly all Indonesian political parties, along with most senior officers of the army, pledged their support to Tan Malaka's burgeoning coalition. Sjahrir nonetheless clung to the belief that in view of Allied strength and British attitudes, there was no realistic alternative to immediate negotiations with the Dutch; but his power was steadily eroding. On February 23 Sjahrir bowed to PP pressure and reluctantly tendered a letter of resignation to President Sukarno. Sukarno then gave Tan Malaka the mandate to form a new cabinet. The PP, however, found itself unable to overcome severe internal divisions and incapable of translating its oppositionist front into a workable governing coalition. With the subsequent collapse of the PP's bid for power, Sukarno again turned to the former prime minister, and on March 12 Sjahrir skillfully formed a new cabinet.[26]

The failure of Tan Malaka's coalition to create a viable government vindicated the prime minister's diplomatic policy; Sjahrir's power base within Indonesia was correspondingly strengthened. The mandate of his second government called for "the conduct of discussions based on full recognition of the Republic of Indonesia." As van Mook later noted, "The fact that Sutan Sjahrir's cabinet had survived the first attacks on its moderation by the wilder elements in the interior made it possible to begin real negotiations in March."[27] When the talks with van Mook resumed on March 13, the republicans officially responded to the initial Dutch offer by demanding recognition of the republic's sovereign power over the entire archipelago. Rejecting The Hague's plan for a transitional period, Sjahrir suggested that the republic would entrust the conduct of foreign affairs and the defense of both countries, for a specified period, to a body composed of both Dutch and Indonesians. Last, the republican delegation proposed that all Netherlands troops withdraw from Indonesia immediately upon the conclusion of an agreement between the two parties.[28]

[26]Ibid., pp. 172–76; Anderson, *Java*, pp. 310–16.

[27]Hubertus J. van Mook, *The Stakes of Democracy in Southeast Asia* (New York: Norton, 1950), p. 213. See also U.S. Department of State, ORI, Division of Far East Intelligence, Situation Report—Southern Areas, no. 3480.7, April 10, 1946, DSR.

[28]Anderson, *Java*, pp. 316, 322; Taylor, *Indonesian Independence*, p. 20.

The Indonesian offer was completely unacceptable to the Dutch. But just as another deadlock appared unavoidable, an adventitious circumstance probably averted a breakdown of negotiations. On March 6, 1946, France had concluded an agreement with Vietnam which apparently solved a similar colonial problem; it had determined that Vietnam would be a free state in the Indochinese Federation, which in turn would constitute part of the French Union. Encouraged by this unexpected precedent, van Mook handed a translation of the settlement to the Indonesian representatives and suggested that they peruse it as a possible basis for healing the Dutch–Indonesian rift. Taking the initiative, van Mook then offered a fresh set of proposals based on the French–Vietnamese agreement. At the heart of van Mook's plan lay his willingness to recognize the de facto authority of the republic and his offer to the republic to become a partner in a federative Indonesian Free State. In turn, the republic would have to cease all hostilities and to join in general deliberations with representatives from all parts of the East Indies, and with minority groups, to determine the political structure of the future Indonesian state and its relations with the Netherlands. Van Mook pursued this new approach because he was deeply and sincerely concerned with the potentially grave consequences of a collapse of the talks. In addition, he was firmly convinced that the best hope of coming to terms with the republic lay in negotiations with the moderate Sjahrir government.[29]

For its part, the Sjahrir government was keenly aware that world opinion was gradually shifting and that the Dutch offer was increasingly regarded in the West as an honest and sincere effort to accommodate the nationalists' aspirations.[30] Wedded to its strategy of diplomasi, the republic could not risk forfeit-

[29]Clark Kerr to Foreign Office, March 21, 1946, FO 371 F4362/1/61, PRO; Djajadiningrat, *Beginnings*, pp. 54–56; van Mook, *Stakes of Democracy*, p. 213; Charles Wolf, Jr., *The Indonesian Story: The Birth, Growth, and Structure of the Indonesian Republic* (New York: John Day, 1948), p. 37; Anderson, *Java*, pp. 322–23. American officials were keenly aware that the Dutch were using the Franco–Vietnamese agreement as a model. See, for example, Foote to Byrnes, March 27, 1946, 856E.00/3-2746, DSR; Hornbeck to Byrnes, April 3, 1946, 856E.00/4-346, DSR; Foote to Byrnes, March 31, 1946, *FR*, 8:818.

[30]An editorial in the *New York Times*, February 17, 1946, p. 28, noted that "an almost worldwide recognition of the Dutch offer as a generous one" had resulted in "the greatest pressure for peace in Java."

ing international sympathy by appearing obstinate in the face of "generous" Dutch offers.[31] Moreover, Inverchapel alerted Sjahrir that the Indonesians could expect no further assistance from Great Britain in the negotiations unless they made significant concessions to the Dutch.[32] On March 27, aware of his government's precarious position, the prime minister submitted to the Dutch a fresh set of proposals that represented a marked retreat from the republic's earlier position. Instead of outright recognition of its sovereignty, the republic now demanded only that the Dutch recognize its de facto authority in Java and Sumatra, with the exception of areas under control of the Allied Military Administration.[33]

This conciliatory overture by the republic brought the two delegations close enough to justify a renewed effort to reach a formal agreement. Van Mook considered it necessary at this juncture to consult The Hague, since, as he reminded the republicans, the final decision regarding the preliminary agreement rested with the Netherlands government. He suggested that Sjahrir send an Indonesian delegation to Holland to elucidate the republican point of view. Sjahrir quickly appointed his minister of justice, Suwandi, to head a three-man republican negotiating team.[34] As both parties made arrangements for the trip to Holland, a general mood of optimism swept the proceedings. The Indonesian delegation was convinced that its trip would be crowned with success; van Mook similarly predicted an early agreement; even the normally skeptical Inverchapel believed that a settlement would probably be reached within a week to ten days.[35]

Despite this apparent breakthrough, the British were growing increasingly restive with the "leisurely fashion" in which the Dutch were conducting negotiations. The continued use of Indi-

[31]Dr. Sudarsono of the republican delegation explained to Djajadiningrat that his government adjusted its policy as a result of the international climate of opinion, which appeared to back the Dutch position. See Djajadiningrat, *Beginnings*, pp. 56–57.

[32]Foote to Byrnes, March 10, 1946, in *FR*, 1946, 8:814.

[33]Djajadiningrat, *Beginnings*, pp. 57–59; Taylor, *Indonesian Independence*, p. 21.

[34]Djajadiningrat, *Beginnings*, pp. 59–60.

[35]Ibid., p. 60; *New York Times*, April 14, 1946, p. 28; Foote to Byrnes, March 31, 1946, in *FR*, 1946, 8:817–18.

an troops in the East Indies remained a pressing problem for London; their prolonged deployment in Indonesia at the same time that Britain was engaged in delicate negotiations regarding the decolonization of India itself placed Britain in a compromising position. In addition, as Bevin pointed out, Indonesian operations "were already imposing an undue burden" on Britain's resources; it "should be made quite clear to the Dutch that if negotiations were to break down, we should not engage in operations to reinstate them."[36]

On March 25 Sterndale Bennett informed the Dutch ambassador that Britain would shortly begin a phased withdrawal of British and Indian troops from the East Indies. The Dutch government angrily protested that this decision would have an adverse effect on the negotiations and argued that British military tasks in Indonesia had not yet been completed. Attlee insisted that the Dutch had no grounds for complaint. He and Bevin patiently explained the British position to a high-level Dutch delegation at a tense meeting in London on April 12. The Dutch again protested Whitehall's decision, but the British were firm; any further delay in evacuating Indian toops, they stressed, would cause undue agitation in India. The first troop withdrawals were scheduled for early May and the British declared flatly that they planned to withdraw all of their forces before the end of 1946. A successful conclusion of the upcoming negotiations in Holland, they emphasized, was now imperative.[37]

When the Dutch–Indonesian conference convened on April 14, 1946, at the Hoge Veluwe, a hunting lodge outside Arnhem, the initial optimism quickly dissipated. After five minutes, recalled one republican delegate, it became clear to the Indonesians that their mission was doomed to fail. There were at least two major stumbling blocks. One was the question of Sumatra: the Dutch government was willing to recognize the republic's de facto authority only in Java, not in Sumatra. This unyielding

[36]Record by Sterndale Bennett of a conversation with the Dutch ambassador, March 25, 1946, FO 371 F4879/1/61, PRO; memorandum from Netherlands Foreign Office to British Foreign Office, March 27, 1946, FO 371 F5175/1/61, PRO; 49th meeting of Chiefs of Staff, March 28, 1946, FO 371 F5073/1/61, PRO; CAB 128/29, PRO.

[37]Record of a meeting at 10 Downing Street, April 12, 1946, Prime Ministers' Records (PREM) 8/263, PRO.

stand overturned van Mook's preliminary draft agreement and placed an insurmountable obstacle before the republic's negotiating team. It also overturned pledges that the Dutch had made to the British only two days earlier, much to London's dismay.[38] The Indonesians fully realized that by accepting that point they would not only overstep their own mandate, but also endanger the very survival of the Sjahrir government. They argued eloquently that the republic's authority in Sumatra was the only effective one on the whole island; indeed, an American intelligence report later pointed out that Dutch control in Sumatra was "almost non-existent."[39] Still, the Dutch refused to budge on that pivotal question. The second major controversy arose over the form of the agreement: the republican delegation sought a formal treaty, while the Dutch drafted their proposals in the form of a protocol. The distinction was more significant than mere diplomatic jargon. While the republicans desired a treaty agreement modeled after the Franco-Vietnamese settlement, which would have accorded them a status equal to that of the Netherlands government, The Hague balked at such a stipulation, insisting that under Dutch law the Netherlands could conclude a treaty only with a foreign power. With these fundamental issues separating the two sides, the talks ended in failure.[40]

The collapse of the Hoge Veluwe conference resulted largely from internal pressures on the Dutch government. Prime Minister William Schermerhorn's interim government anxiously awaited the results of the first postwar parliamentary elections, scheduled for May 1946. His extraparliamentary regime, which had been formed at the request of the queen after the liberation of Holland in June 1945, could not count on a majority in the

[38]Minute by Edward T. Lambert, May 4, 1946, FO 371 F6598/1/61, PRO.

[39]U.S. Department of State, ORI, Division of Far East Intelligence, "Current Developments in Dutch-Indonesian Relations," Situation Report—Southern Areas, no. 3480.11, June 5, 1946, DSR.

[40]The most informative account of Hoge Veluwe, based on Dutch summary records of the conference, can be found in Djajadiningrat, *Beginnings*, pp. 61–76. See also Foote to Byrnes, June 5, 1946, in *FR*, 1946, 8:826. For the official Dutch explanation for the collapse of the talks, see statement of Logemann in *Netherlands News Letter*, May 10, 1946 (New York: Netherlands Information Bureau), pp. 1–4.

States General, nor did it have a popular mandate to deal with the sensitive issue of colonial relations. The vehement public reaction within the Netherlands to a republic that many Dutch believed to be Japanese-created compounded the problem. These domestic constraints tugged at the Schermerhorn government, severely hampering its freedom of action.[41] Van Mook later suggested that the Dutch "national character, with its excess of caution and its deficiency of imagination, stood in the way of a large gesture that might have given the history of the conflict a turn for the better."[42] In the more prosaic words of Neville Bland, the Dutch simply got "cold feet" and were now content to await the outcome of the upcoming general elections.[43]

As a result of those elections, held on May 17, the Schermerhorn government was defeated and Louis J. M. Beel became prime minister. Beel quickly named Johannes A. Jonkmann to replace Logemann as minister of overseas territories and pledged a continuation of the previous government's efforts to reach an accommodation with the nationalists. Since the new Dutch government would not take office until July 2, the Schermerhorn government now assumed the character of a caretaker regime. Determined nonetheless to make a final effort to resolve the impasse with the Indonesian republicans, Schermerhorn authorized van Mook to present one more offer to the nationalists. This new proposal, which van Mook delivered to Sjahrir on May 19, officially expressed the Netherlands' willingness to accept de facto recognition of the republic's authority in Java, but it insisted that the republic must become part of a federated Indone-

[41]U.S. Department of State, ORI, Division of Europe, Near East, and Africa Intelligence, "Netherlands: Campaign for the National Elections," Situation Report—Western Europe, no. 1121.141, April 19, 1946, and "Netherlands: Parliamentary Debate on Indonesia," Report no. 1121.143, May 17, 1946, both in DSR; van Mook, *Stakes of Democracy*, pp. 214–15; Djajadiningrat, *Beginnings*, pp. 80–93, 90–94; Samuel J. Eldersveld, "Government and Politics in the Netherlands during Reconstruction," in James Kerr Pollock, ed., *Change and Crisis in European Government* (New York: Rinehart, 1947), p. 25; H. Arthur Steiner, "Postwar Government of the Netherlands East Indies," *Journal of Politics*, 9 (November 1947):624–51; Ronald S. Kain, "Netherlands and Indonesia," *Yale Review*, 36 (December 1946):295–96.

[42]Van Mook, *Stakes of Democracy*, p. 215.

[43]Bland to Foreign Office, April 30, 1946, FO 371 F6484/1/61, PRO.

sian state within the Dutch kingdom, moving eventually toward independence after a suitable interim period. This "new" approach in effect represented a substantial retreat from van Mook's earlier, unofficial offer. The Dutch remained intransigent on the key issue of Sumatra.[44] The "present Dutch offer," Foote tersely informed the State Department, "differs in no important respects from previous offers."[45]

Predictably, Sjahrir viewed this proposed settlement as "a definite step backwards." Stung by The Hague's rigidity, his government stiffened its own minimum demands. On June 17, 1946, Sjahrir issued a bold set of counterproposals that caught the Dutch by surprise. He now called for the enlargement of the republic's de facto authority to encompass all of Java and Sumatra, including Allied-occupied territory; this response reflected his government's apparent intention to prevent any further landing of Dutch troops. The prime minister also suggested that the republic form an alliance with, rather than a partnership under, the crown.[46] One Dutch spokesman immediately denounced the Indonesian proposals for their failure to acknowledge The Hague's sovereignty. "It is a serious assault on the basis on which the negotiations have so far been conducted," he stormed.[47] With the two parties further apart than ever, renewed efforts to break the deadlock awaited the organization of the newly elected Netherlands government. "The efforts of the past seven months," concluded one State Department assessment, "have proved futile."[48]

Meanwhile, events within Indonesia were rapidly moving the Dutch–republican negotiations off center stage. Opposition to Sjahrir's policy of diplomasi, seemingly defeated in March, was strengthened by the crushing diplomatic setback at Hoge

[44]Wehl, *Birth of Indonesia*, pp. 122–23; Taylor, *Indonesian Independence*, p. 25; Hornbeck to Byrnes, June 20, 1946, in *FR*, 1946, 8:830–31.

[45]Foote to Byrnes, May 27, 1946, 856E.00/5-2746, DSR.

[46]Minute by Lambert, June 22, 1946, FO 371 F9574/1/61, PRO; *New York Times*, May 26, 1946, p. 15; Anderson, *Java*, p. 381; Taylor, *Indonesian Independence*, pp. 24–25.

[47]*Netherlands News Letter*, July 15, 1946, p. 2; memorandum by Wilson Young, June 27, 1946, FO 371 F9598/1/61, PRO.

[48]U.S. Department of State, ORI, Division of Research for Europe, "The Beel Government," Situation Report—Northern and Western Europe, no. 1121.146, July 22, 1946, DSR.

Veluwe. Convinced that the Dutch were now preparing to launch a preemptive military strike against the republic, a coalition of key army leaders, major political parties, and youth groups demanded Sjahrir's ouster and insisted that the republic abandon diplomacy for armed struggle. Sjahrir found himself in a paradoxical position. While the continued existence of dissident forces within the republic, according to the Dutch, was the fundamental obstacle to a settlement, a major element in Sjahrir's political strength—his acceptability to Dutch political opinion—prevented him from building the solid base of support within Indonesia that would have calmed Dutch suspicions.[49]

This latest crisis erupted on June 27, when a small group of radical youths, supported by disaffected army officers, boldly kidnapped the Indonesian prime minister. Their action backfired, however, for Sukarno promptly declared an emergency and assumed all governmental powers for himself, as provided by the Indonesian constitution. On the evening of June 30 the president made a stirring speech on Indonesian radio. Pleading for stability, he insisted that political opposition must be orderly and based on democratic principles. The kidnapping of Sjahrir, Sukarno warned, would permit the Dutch to exclaim to the world that Indonesia could not rule itself, and that chaos and disorder prevailed everywhere. His appeal worked masterfully: the prime minister was returned the following day and opposition groups rallied around the government, tacitly agreeing that the policy of diplomasi would be allowed to continue without further obstruction. With order now restored, Sjahrir quickly consolidated his position, and by October 2 he had formed his third parliamentary government.[50]

At this juncture, with the two sides at a virtual impasse, Great Britain decided that only a renewed effort to bring the Dutch and the republicans back to the bargaining table could avert a complete breakdown of relations between the two parties. "The

[49]Anderson, *Java*, pp. 370–77.

[50]For a detailed examination of the "July crisis," see ibid., pp. 370–403. See also Kahin, *Nationalism and Revolution*, pp. 189–92; Bernhard Dahm, *History of Indonesia in the Twentieth Century* (New York: Praeger, 1971), pp. 123–24; Gilbert MacKereth (British consul general, East Indies) to Foreign Office, July 2, 1946, FO 371 F9778/1/61, PRO.

prolongation of the present state of tension and the probable outbreak of hostilities could only be disastrous for the Dutch, the Indonesians and ourselves," one senior Foreign Office official noted. "The fact remains that failure to reach a political settlement before we leave is almost bound to lead to bloodshed on a large scale."[51] Several British analysts feared that the Dutch were simply playing for time; their troops were gradually replacing British forces in the Indies and would soon be able to act without London's restraining hand. The Foreign Office realized, moreover, that if fighting did take place after the British withdrew, London would be greatly criticized by world opinion for its role in the Indies.[52] Whitehall's recent decision to evacuate all British and Indian troops from the islands by November 30, 1946, regardless of developments, underscored the urgency of the situation. Attlee summarized the problem in a July 1 letter to Australian Prime Minister Joseph B. Chifley. Both the Dutch proposals of May 9 and the Indonesian proposals of June 17 represented a marked retreat from the positions reached with such difficulty in April, he explained. Unless the two parties could be persuaded to return to those earlier positions, conditions in Indonesia would steadily deteriorate, and the British withdrawal in November would probably be the signal for bitter fighting.[53]

In order to get those discussions off the ground once more, London informed The Hague that it was appointing another experienced British diplomat to fulfill the role of mediator previously played by Inverchapel. In mid-August, Lord Killearn, Britain's special commissioner for Southeast Asia, arrived in Batavia. In a series of talks with the Dutch and the republicans, he impressed on them the significance of the imminent departure of British troops and the consequent urgency of resuming serious negotiations.[54]

The United States, which had carefully limited itself to the

[51]Memorandum by Wilson Young, June 27, 1946, FO 371 F9598/1/61, PRO.

[52]Ismay to Attlee, June 19, 1946, PREM 8/263, PRO.

[53]Attlee to Chifley, July 1, 1946, FO 371 F9684/1/61, PRO.

[54]Aides-mémoires from British government to Netherlands government, June 29 and July 3, 1946, *Officiele Bescheiden*, 6:588, 601; Acheson to Hornbeck, August 5, 1946, in *FR*, 1946, 8:840; Acheson to Foote, August 8, 1946, in *FR*, 1946, 8:841–42.

role of interested but uninvolved bystander ever since the inception of the tripartite discussions in February, was also disturbed by the continuing stalemate. Washington was particularly concerned that the lack of appreciable progress in Indonesia would lead the Soviet Union to reintroduce the question during the upcoming session of the United Nations. On August 5 the State Department instructed Ambassador Hornbeck to suggest informally to The Hague that it take a more conciliatory negotiating position in order to forestall such actions by the Soviets.[55] This point was reiterated in a conference with Ambassador Loudon in Washington the following week. During that meeting, John Hickerson and Hugh Cumming of the State Department's Office of European Affairs informed the Dutch ambassador that while as individuals they were good friends of the Netherlands, they had to tell him in all frankness that they believed The Hague was "on a bad wicket" in regard to worldwide opinion toward the Indonesian dispute. Since Moscow would almost certainly reintroduce the question at the upcoming session of the Security Council, the two diplomats pointed out, the Dutch should take "some constructive action looking to a satisfactory solution" before that time.[56]

These British and American representations helped to break the logjam in Holland. Eager to achieve a settlement before the British withdrawal, the newly organized Netherlands government appointed a commission general on September 2 to reach an agreement with the Indonesians. This official body, headed by former prime minister Schermerhorn, was fully authorized to negotiate a settlement with the republicans, although any agreement would not become valid until it was approved by the Dutch parliament. The appointment of the commission general was definitely a conciliatory gesture; British and American pressure had combined with the more realistic attitude of the Beel government to effect this modification of the Dutch position.[57] As Jonkmann later explained to Abbot Moffat, chief

[55]Acheson to Hornbeck, August 5, 1946, in *FR*, 1946, 8:840.

[56]Memorandum by Hickerson of a conversation with Loudon, August 15, 1946, in Box 3, Hickerson Files, Records of the Office of European Affairs, DSR.

[57]David J. McCallum (U.S. naval attaché, Batavia) to Chief of Naval Operations (CNO), September 8, 1946, Naval Attaché Reports File, Naval History Division,

of the State Department's Division of Southeast Asian Affairs, the Dutch government was unwilling to undertake a colonial war at this point for both national and international reasons and therefore considered it essential to reach a peaceful agreement with the Indonesians.[58] In addition, it must be pointed out, most informed observers agreed that the Dutch did not yet have the military capability to embark on an extensive pacification campaign.[59]

Another hopeful development came with the report of the Koets mission. At the invitation of the republic, Dr. P. J. Koets, the chief of van Mook's cabinet, headed a semiofficial party that undertook an exploratory trip into the center of Java to examine the republic's claim that its rule was secure and that peace and order prevailed throughout the island. To the astonishment of the Netherlands government, Koets, the first leadng Dutch official to visit the interior since the reoccupation, substantiated the republic's claims.[60] "The general picture we saw," explained Koets, "was that of a society which was not in the course of dissolution but which is being consolidated."[61] Koets's report had a profound effect on Dutch attitudes toward the Indonesian crisis; it contradicted the prevalent notion that the republic was about to fall apart, that Sjahrir had little support, and that economic life had come to a standstill. Walter Foote, the senior American diplomat in the East Indies, related this new develop-

---

Washington National Records Center, Suitville, Md. (hereafter cited as WNRC); Weekly Review, prepared by Southeast Asia Division, "Constructive Moves by Dutch in Indonesian Situation," July 31, 1946, in folder labeled "Political Miscellaneous," Box 12, PSA Records, DSR; *Netherlands News Letter*, August 15, 1946, p. 1; van Mook to Jonkmann, September 2, 1946, in *Officiele Bescheiden*, 5:288–90; Wehl, *Birth of Indonesia*, pp. 134–35.

[58]Memorandum by Moffat of a conversation with Jonkmann, November 16, 1946, 856E.00/10-2346, DSR.

[59]Report by Lieutenant General E. C. Mansergh (commander in chief, Allied forces in Netherlands East Indies), "Review of Situation of the Netherlands East Indies on the Conclusion of 'Exodus,'" October 8, 1946, enclosed in Killearn to Foreign Office, October 29, 1946, FO 371 F15667/1/61, PRO.

[60]Wehl, *Birth of Indonesia*, p. 141; Wolf, *Indonesian Story*, pp. 42–43.

[61]Quoted in Wolf, *Indonesian Story*, p. 42. See also "Report of the Inspection Tour Made by Dr. Koets' Party in the Republican Territory of Java from 15th to 20th of September 1946," enclosed in McCallum to CNO, October 15, 1946, in Naval Attaché Reports File, Naval History Division, WNRC; Killearn to Foreign Office, September 21, 1946, FO 371 F13867/1/61, PRO.

ment to the State Department: "Speaking with great sincerity and considerable enthusiasm, he [Koets] gave his listeners a picture of a young and dynamic government fully supported by the great mass of the population, and of a hard working people fired by a newly acquired sense of national dignity and self-respect, who had managed to achieve a remarkable degree of economic prosperity despite appalling handicaps." Foote commented optimistically that "in the short space of less than two months . . . the situation changed sharply from one of political deadlock and open warfare to one in which confident diplomatic negotiation is at last undisturbed by the clash of arms."[62]

Under the chairmanship of Lord Killearn, Dutch–Indonesian negotiations formally reopened on October 7. Progress now was rapid. For the first time the Dutch offered to accept the republic's de facto authority in Sumatra, and with that central issue resolved the talks proceeded smoothly. On October 14 the two parties took a major step by concluding a truce agreement; it provided for the stabilization of existing military positions and appointed a truce commission composed of Dutch, Indonesian, and British representatives to supervise the cease-fire. With both sides making significant concessions, the final meetings moved to the mountain resort of Linggadjati, about fifteen miles from the city of Cheribon. There, on November 15, 1946, the Netherlands and the republic initialed a draft agreement. Negotiations had triumphed—at least temporarily—over the threat of force.[63]

The Linggadjati agreement represented a series of compromises on the part of both the Indonesian delegation and the Dutch commission general. According to the first article of the agreement, The Hague agreed to recognize the republic as exercising de facto authority over both Java and Sumatra—the major stumbling block at Hoge Veluwe. The republicans made an equally significant concession by assenting to a federal form of government for the proposed United States of Indonesia

[62]Foote to Byrnes, October 23, 1946, 856E.00/10-2346, DSR.

[63]"Summary of Dutch-Indonesian Talks under Chairmanship of Lord Killearn," October 7, 1946, in *Officiele Bescheiden*, 5:502–10; Killearn to Foreign Office, October 15, 1946, in ibid., pp. 547–48; Taylor, *Indonesian Independence*, pp. 28–29.

(U.S.I.); Borneo and East Indonesia were to have the same juridical status as the republic in the new Indonesian state. Another key element in the draft agreement was the provision that any component state of the U.S.I. would have the option to decide by democratic means when and on what terms it would join the U.S.I. Linggadjati also provided that the U.S.I. was to be a sovereign and equal partner in a Netherlands Union—a point the republican delegation had demanded; but the union would be headed by the Dutch crown, which would administer areas of joint interest, such as defense and foreign affairs. Both parties were to "cooperate" in the rapid formation of the U.S.I., which was to be formed no later than January 1, 1949.[64]

The Dutch conceded a good deal more than they originally intended to, as one Foreign Office official noted, but they "succeeded in keeping the door open for the maintenance of Dutch influence, interests, and commercial predominance in the NEI."[65] The long delay in the granting of self-government was particularly puzzling to the British; Bland commented acidly that "the Dutch are slow but I never imagined they would be as slow as that."[66] Nevertheless, he believed that on the whole the Dutch had made real concessions and the Indonesians should trust them. The chief problem with the settlement lay in its considerable ambiguity; many of the accord's key sections were subject to interpretation, presaging later difficulties.

Despite its imperfections—and there were many—Linggadjati was universally hailed as a diplomatic breakthrough. It was, in the words of Sumner Welles, "the most encouraging development of recent months."[67] Nearly everyone on the scene fully realized that if a settlement had not been reached before the British troop withdrawal, armed conflict would almost surely

[64]For the text of the Linggadjati agreement, see "Dutch-Indonesian Draft Agreement," November 18, 1946, 856D.00/11-1846, DSR; it is reprinted in Wehl, *Birth of Indonesia*, pp. 146–49. See also van Mook, *Stakes of Democracy*, pp. 222–24; Wolf, *Indonesian Story*, pp. 43–44; W. H. van Helsdinger, "The Netherlands Indonesian Draft Agreement," *Pacific Affairs*, 20 (June 1947):184–87; *Economist*, November 23, 1946, p. 835.

[65]Minute by Allen, November 18, 1946, FO 371 F17212/1/61, PRO.

[66]Bland to Foreign Office, November 13, 1946, FO 371 F16409/1/61, PRO.

[67]*New York Herald Tribune*, Paris ed., November 27, 1946, quoted in Everett F. Drumright (first secretary, U.S. embassy, London) to Allen, November 27, 1946, FO 371 F17357/1/61, PRO.

have broken out. "Civil war between Dutch and Indonesians would have been certain," commented one British Foreign Office official, "and this would inevitably have spread over a large area of South East Asia."[68] Similarly, van Mook stated emphatically that the only alternative for the Dutch would have been war.[69] In contrast with the rapidly deteriorating situation in nearby Indochina between the French and the Vietnamese nationalists, Linggadjati indeed seemed to represent a hopeful and rational precedent for other imperial powers to follow.

Within days of the initialing of the Linggadjati agreement, the final contingent of British troops withdrew from the East Indies, terminating in dramatic fashion Britain's military commitment there. In little over a year, Great Britain had been forced to make decisions that would have a monumental impact on the future of Dutch–Indonesian relations. As a result of the abrupt alteration of the wartime command structure at Potsdam, the British had inherited an operation for which they had been woefully unprepared. Anticipating a relatively routine assignment, British occupying forces instead found themselves embroiled in a bitter and politically explosive colonial conflict. Confronted on the one hand with a surprisingly effective and popular government of native nationalists demanding independence and, on the other hand, with a friendly wartime ally that was unalterably opposed to any negotiations with what it considered to be a group of traitorous extremists, London had been compelled to tiptoe through a minefield of conflicting interests. Given Britain's limited resources, its urgent need to extricate Indian troops from an entangling colonial conflict, and the pressing nature of its own imperial problems, London succeeded admirably in maintaining an even-handed approach toward the Indonesian crisis. By insisting that the Dutch realize that the war had irrevocably upset the old colonial relationship and that only a sincere accommodation to Indonesian nationalism could prevent armed conflict, and by firmly and patiently explaining to

[68]Nash and P. J. Dixon (British delegates to Council of Foreign Ministers, New York) to Dening, November 16, 1946, FO 371 F16579/1/61, PRO. See also Killearn to Foreign Office, November 14, 1946, FO 371 F16544/1/61, PRO.

[69]Quoted in Michael R. Wright (Killearn's deputy) to Foreign Office, November 17, 1946, FO 371 F16578/1/61, PRO.

the Indonesians that a bid for 100 percent independence would be both unrealistic and self-defeating, the British managed to bring the two sides face to face, in the process helping to close the immense political and cultural gap between them. Inevitably Britain wound up alienating both parties at various times, engendering a particularly spiteful reaction on the part of the Dutch. Nevertheless, given the complexities of its position, Great Britain's accomplishments in the East Indies were considerable. It is interesting—albeit fruitless—to speculate on the role that American policy might have played in the unfolding drama in Indonesia had the Potsdam transfer not taken place.

Linggadjati, as the British keenly realized, represented only a small first step toward a meaningful colonial settlement. The possibility that the agreement would break down and actual warfare erupt was ever present; many British diplomats even believed war likely. Within the inner councils of the British government, contingencies for an appropriate response to future widespread fighting were considered and debated. While some policy makers argued that in such an eventuality Britain must be prepared to step in again as mediator, this was an unpopular minority view. With the conclusion of Linggadjati, most British officials were eager for a complete extrication from the Indies. Preoccupied with more pressing problems, they desired no further commitment in the area, suggesting instead either joint arbitration with the United States or United Nations intervention in case of further trouble. London, then, which had played such a dominant role in Indonesian developments ever since the close of the war, was leaving a significant power vacuum in the Indies. Only one nation had the interest, power, and capability to fill that vacuum—the United States.

5

From Negotiations to War: November 1946–July 1947

By 1947, Washington's interpretation of the Soviet threat had led to a radical redefinition of American national security interests. This redefinition would have a profound effect on the American view of developments in far-off Indonesia. No longer would such areas as Southeast Asia and the Middle East be seen as peripheral to vital American interests; and no longer would the United States be content to have the British maintain order and stability in those areas. On the contrary, all international crises were now viewed as potentially vital to American security interests. The new doctrine of national security taught that all areas of the globe were possible prizes or victims in the struggle against an expanding Communist movement; given the growing interrelationship of world events, American leaders ignored distant crises only at their peril. The concept of national security, according to historian Daniel Yergin, "postulates the interrelatedness of so many different political, economic, and military factors that developments halfway around the globe are seen to have automatic and direct impact on America's core interests."[1]

The United States was extremely pleased with the Linggadjati agreement. By providing for the peaceful evolution toward native self-rule while maintaining intact Dutch political, military, and economic influence in the Indies, it seemed to conform perfectly with American policy objectives for postwar Southeast Asia. The Department of State congratulated the Dutch and the

[1]Daniel Yergin, *Shattered Peace: The Origins of the Cold War and the National Security State* (Boston: Houghton Mifflin, 1978), pp. 195–96.

Indonesians on their "high statesmanship" in reaching such an amicable settlement. From the outset of the dispute, Washington had feared that the cirsis in the Indies might degenerate into full-scale war; now that a rational arbitration of the difficulties had evidently been achieved, it was greatly relieved.[2] Responding to a request by the British government, on December 17 the State Department issued a polite press release—its first official comment on developments in Indonesia in nearly a year—which expressed this point of view. The United States government hoped, it pointed out, that

> the basic principles of this agreement will enable the Dutch and Indonesian people to work together and in mutual respect for their welfare and for the prosperity and stability of Southeast Asia.
>
> The evidence of high statesmanship displayed by both Dutch and Indonesian delegations in negotiating the settlement gives promise that the agreement will be implemented with continuing regard for the welfare of the peoples concerned.
>
> The United States Government will watch with close interest the measures undertaken to make this agreement effective and progress toward the political stabilization and economic rehabilitation of the Indies which we hope will result therefrom.[3]

Throughout 1946, official American policy toward the Indonesian upheaval followed the policy developed during the closing months of 1945. While not questioning the right of Holland to restore its prewar rule, the United States indicated on several occasions that it would strongly disapprove of any attempt to reassert such control by force of arms, while suggesting, conversely, that it would warmly applaud any movement toward self-government in the Indies. Washington thus sought to maintain the appearance of neutrality, hoping that a nominally impartial stance would not alienate either of the concerned parties. Actually, American "neutrality" was still working to the distinct

[2]Memorandum from Vincent and Hickerson to Dean Acheson, November 27, 1946, in *Foreign Relations of the United States* (Washington, D.C., 1971), 8:855–56. Hereafter volumes in this series will be cited as *FR*, followed by the year.

[3]Substance of a telegram from State Department, November 19, 1946, FO 371 F16881/1/61, Records of the British Foreign Office, Public Record Office, London (hereafter cited as PRO); Foreign Office minute, November 21, 1946, ibid.; *U.S. Department of State Bulletin*, 15 (December 29, 1946), 1188.

advantage of the Dutch. Not only did the United States refuse to recognize the Republic of Indonesia as an equal party to the dispute—in direct contravention of its vigorous wartime support for the principle of self-determination—but it also generously extended lend-lease and surplus-property credits in excess of $100 million to the Netherlands, facilitating, at least indirectly, the Dutch effort to reimpose imperial control.[4] According to Stanley Hornbeck, who served as American ambassador to Holland during this period, the United States "in effect attempted to support neither side and yet favored one and hoped not unduly to offend the other."[5]

This policy was entirely consistent with the larger interests of the United States in Southeast Asia. Those interests required, first and foremost, stability. Failure on the part of the European powers to adapt to the demands of Asian nationalism, a failure that might in turn lead to anachronistic colonial wars, was from Washington's perspective the chief threat to stability in the region. The most hopeful long-range development would be the creation of moderate nationalist regimes, moving gradually toward self-government within a commonwealth or federation structure, with the respective European imperial powers maintaining considerable economic, political, and military influence in their former colonies. While British actions in Burma and in India generally pleased American policy makers as they appeared to move, however haltingly, toward these goals, the intransigence of the French in Indochina was viewed with keen disappointment. American policy toward the Philippines, which was formally granted independence on July 4, 1946, was again continually upheld as the beacon for other colonial powers to follow. Indeed, the postindependence relationship between the United States and the Philippines, in which the United States maintained its enormous influence over virtually all

[4]State–Army–Navy–Air Force Coordinating Committee (SWNCC), Subcommittee on Far Eastern Affairs, Special Ad Hoc Committee Report on Indonesia, July 22, 1947, in SWNCC Records, U.S. Department of State Records, National Archives, Washington, D.C. (hereafter cited as DSR).

[5]Stanley K. Hornbeck, "The United States and the Netherlands East Indies," *Annals of the American Academy of Political and Social Science*, 255 (January 1948): 132–33.

aspects of Philippine society, appears quite consistent with American objectives for the region as a whole.[6]

Of course the colonial problem in postwar Southeast Asia was an extremely complex and emotional one, and it is not surprising that there were sharp differences within the State Department over policy matters. The major bureaucratic conflict, as during the war, was between the Office of Far Eastern Affairs and the Office of European Affairs. Members of the former office generally had a broader understanding of the historical revolt of Asian peoples against Western colonialism; accordingly, they tended to be sympathetic toward the nationalist movements and regimes in Southeast Asia, believing that native aspirations toward self-government were both understandable and legitimate. At the same time, they tended to be harshly critical of past colonial rule and distrustful of European pledges of greater native self-rule. In short, the Office of Far Eastern Affairs, especially its small Division of Southeast Asian Affairs, clung to a liberal, anticolonial perspective. The Office of European Affairs was considerably less sympathetic to the nationalists. With little understanding of Asian affairs, policy makers within this office tended to view Asian events through a European lens. Convinced that the central focus of American foreign policy in the postwar years was, as always, Western Europe, these diplomats viewed the colonies in Southeast Asia as mere appendages of the European mother countries; they were convinced that the rehabilitation and reintegration of Western Europe was an overarching goal of American foreign policy in the postwar years, and considered the European colonies in Southeast Asia as significant only insofar as they could contribute to the economic recovery of the respective mother countries. The Europeanists believed that American cooperation with the European imperial powers, which was necessary for the

[6]Memorandum from Landon to Vincent, "General Political Situation in Southeast Asia," March 14, 1946, 890.00/3-1446, DSR; memorandum by Cady, "The Importance of the Philippines with Respect to United States Policy in Southeastern Asia," January 2, 1946, and memorandum by Moffat, "The Turning Point in Southern Asia," April 14, 1947, both in folder labeled "Southeast Asia, 1946–1948, U.S. Policy," Box 5, Records of the Office of the Philippines and Southeast Asian Affairs, DSR (hereafter cited as PSA Records).

success of Washington's postwar plans, would only be upset by any frivolous meddling in colonial affairs.

While these cleavages often led to intense squabbles over policy, their significance should not be exaggerated. Actually there was more agreement than disagreement over basic policy goals, and bureaucratic conflict appears to have had little effect on the larger framework of American policy toward Southeast Asia during these years. Despite the liberal, anticolonial ideals espoused by so many members of the Office of Far Eastern Affairs, none believed that native nationalists were prepared for immediate independence, nor did any believe that American interests would be served by a precipitous removal of European influence from that part of the world. Indeed, Abbot Moffat, head of the Southeast Asian Division and easily one of the most liberal advocates of the nationalist cause within the department, admitted that the larger aims of American policy required "establishing a realistic settlement of the problems of Southeast Asia with a view to protecting the security, the interests, and the influence of the Western Powers in that section of Asia." Both Europeanists and Asians, then, agreed that European influence and interests in their colonial territories should be maintained, and that colonial rule should be liberalized so as to prepare responsible native elites for eventual self-rule and to allow American commerce equal access to the rich colonial markets.[7]

As long as Great Britain was making the major decisions in the Indies, the United States could afford the luxury of remaining somewhat aloof from that conflict. As far as Washington was concerned, London was serving the policy interests of the United States quite well with its efforts to help negotiate an equitable settlement between the Dutch and the Indonesians. When the United States could support those efforts by representations toward either one or both of the contending parties, it generally did, but in a decidedly low-key manner. The great advantage of

[7]Testimony of Moffat, May 11, 1972, in U.S. Congress, Senate, *Causes, Origins, and Lessons of the Vietnam War: Hearings before the Committee on Foreign Relations*, 92nd Cong., 2d sess. (Washington, D.C.: U.S. Government Printing Office, 1973); Martin Weil, *A Pretty Good Club: The Founding Fathers of the U.S. Foreign Service* (New York: Norton, 1978), pp. 148–50, 217–19.

remaining on the sidelines was that it kept the United States out of yet another vexing international dispute; noninvolvement, moreover, enabled the United States to maintain its leverage and prestige with both parties. This position coincided closely with a report prepared by the Office of Naval Intelligence in December 1945. "In world politics," it had declared, "Britain is sufficiently dependent upon the United States to follow this country's basic objectives."[8] The British withdrawal from the Indies, as their later withdrawal from areas of the Near and Middle East would do, presented Washington with a new set of problems. The creation of power vacuums in Indonesia and elsewhere would increasingly be viewed by American policy makers against the backdrop of the deepening Cold War and would inevitably lead to intensified U.S. interest and involvement in those areas.

The Dutch–Indonesian struggle for control over the East Indian archipelago certainly did not emerge as an overarching concern of American diplomacy at this time. With tension growing between the United States and the Soviet Union over such troublesome areas as Eastern Europe, Germany, Iran, and Greece, American policy makers could hardly be expected to devote an inordinate amount of attention to the Indonesian imbroglio. On the other hand, Indonesia could not be isolated from other, more central issues. The political and economic stabilization of Western Europe—one of the most serious of all postwar problems for the United States—was inseparably linked to the tumultuous developments in Indonesia and elsewhere in Southeast Asia. Until the Netherlands, France, and Great Britain solved their colonial problems, the economy of the United States, as well as that of Europe, would be deprived of the key natural resources produced in that region. A report prepared for President Truman in 1947 by the newly created Central Intelligence Agency emphasized this interrelationship. "Of important concern in relation to Western European recovery," it noted, "is the existing instability in colonial (or former colonial) areas upon the resources of which several European powers (the United

[8]Office of Naval Intelligence, "Basic Factors in World Relations," December 1945, Post World War II Command File, Naval Operational Archives, Washington Navy Yard.

Kingdom, France, and the Netherlands) have hitherto been accustomed to depend. . . . The continuance of unsettled conditions hinders economic recovery and causes a diversion of European strength into efforts to maintain or reimpose control by force."[9] The rehabilitation and reintegration of Western Europe, the expansion of world production and trade, the competition with the Soviet Union for the loyalty and resources of the underdeveloped world—all of those vital concerns of American foreign policy were directly affected by the upheaval in Indonesia. "World politics and international relations," Hornbeck observed in 1948, "are a chain-woven fabric. Effective conducting of foreign relations calls for constant and skillful correlating of many strands and links."[10]

In an increasingly interdependent world economy, one of those crucial links was the relationship between the needs of the industrialized Western economies for raw materials and the underdeveloped world that produced so many of those essential commodities. Assistant Secretary of State William Clayton, in a major speech delivered before the Foreign Trade Convention on November 13, 1946, warned that an expanding domestic economy along with "the depletion of our natural resources" would make the United States considerably more dependent on the importation of raw materials and minerals. He added that many of those resources would have to come from the newly emerging areas of the world. "Because of our dependence upon imports of strategic metals and minerals," Clayton emphasized, "what happens to American-owned reserves of such materials abroad is a matter of national concern."[11]

[9]Central Intelligence Agency, "Review of the World Situation as it Relates to the Security of the United States," CIA 1, September 26, 1947, in President's Secretary's Files (PSF), Harry S. Truman Papers, Truman Library, Independence, Mo.

[10]Hornbeck, "United States and the Netherlands East Indies," p. 132.

[11]William Clayton, "The Foreign Economic Policy of the United States," *U.S. Department of State Bulletin*, 15 (November 24, 1946):590–93. According to a report issued by the President's Commission on Foreign Economic Policy in 1954: "The transition of the United States from a position of relative self-sufficiency to one of increasing dependence upon foreign sources of supply constitutes one of the striking economic changes of our time. The outbreak of World War II marked the major turning point of this change. Both from the viewpoint of our long-term economic growth and the viewpoint of our national defense, the shift of the

Such concern was particularly appropriate in the case of the Dutch East Indies, an area that Hornbeck labeled "the world's richest island empire."[12] American officials continually reminded Dutch and Indonesian representatives that the United States desired the immediate normalization of commercial relations with Indonesia;[13] and in its statement of December 17, the State Department expressed its hope that Linggadjati would lead to "the political stabilization and economic rehabilitation of the Indies." On several occasions throughout 1945 and 1946, the United States entered into negotiations with the Netherlands in an effort to conclude agreements that would ensure long-term American access to rubber and tin. Dutch officials, however, resisted what they viewed as Washington's attempt to reach trade agreements overly favorable to its interests.[14] Reflecting the deep American economic interest in the East Indies, Acting Secretary of State Dean Acheson emphasized in a cable of March 12, 1947, that the United States "considers that immediate free and unhampered trade and commerce between N.E.I. and rest of world is one of most essential steps to world rehabilitation as well as to economic rehabilitation of the N.E.I.; that it believes 'open door' policy is an essential predicate of such free and unhampered commerce."[15]

American interest in this regard was quite direct. Before World War II the East Indies had supplied the United States with several important raw materials, notably rubber, tin, copra,

---

United States from the position of a net exporter to that of a net importer is of overshadowing significance in shaping our foreign economic policies." See the President's Commission on Foreign Economic Policy, *Staff Papers Presented to the Commission* (Washington, D.C.: U.S. Government Printing Office, 1954), p. 224. On the interdependence of the world economy, see Thomas G. Paterson, *Soviet-American Confrontation: Postwar Reconstruction and the Origins of the Cold War* (Baltimore: Johns Hopkins University Press, 1973), pp. 3–8.

[12]Hornbeck, "United States and the Netherlands East Indies," pp. 124–25.

[13]See, for example, Foote to Byrnes, March 8 and October 21, 1946, in *FR*, 1946, 8:813, 849–50.

[14]Robert J. Leupold, "The United States and Indonesian Independence, 1944–1947: An American Response to Revolution," Ph.D. dissertation, University of Kentucky, 1976, pp. 140–49.

[15]Acheson to H. Webb Benton (chargé, The Hague), March 12, 1947, in *FR*, 1947, 6:905. See also Drumright to Dening, March 31, 1947, FO 371 F4687/45/62, PRO.

kapok, quinine, and palm oil, but the subsequent political unrest in the Indonesian archipelago had terminated the flow of those essential commodities, causing alarm in political and business circles.[16] Indonesia, in addition, was the largest source of petroleum in the Far East and possessed vast reserves of untapped mineral wealth. American dependence on certain Indonesian resources is strikingly revealed by a brief glance at prewar trade statistics. Before the Pacific war, the United States relied on the East Indies for approximately 32 percent of its rubber needs, 10 percent of its tin, 90 percent of its quinine, 90 percent of its kapok, 80 percent of its palm oils, and 25 percent of its tea.[17] Walter Foote wrote a brief foreword to a pamphlet published by the Netherlands Indies government in which he extravagantly spelled out the importance of these raw materials to the United States:

> Indonesia, richest jewel of the East, where nature is gentle, and lavish in giving us rubber, so that we may ride with ease; vegetable oils for hungry people; fibres for industrial use; kapok for good mattresses and other purposes; tea and coffee over which we may gossip or philosophize; coal and iron for industries; precious soap and many other valuable items, is so important to manufacturing

[16]U.S. Department of State, Interim Research and Intelligence Service, "The Economic Situation in Java and Prospective Business Policies," Research and Analysis Report no. 3288, November 2, 1945, and "Preliminary Survey of the Tin and Rubber Industries of Southeast Asia after Four Years of Japanese Occupation," Research and Analysis Report no. 3272, October 5, 1945, both in DSR; Office of Strategic Services (OSS), "The Rubber Industry of Southeast Asia: An Estimate of Present Conditions and Anticipated Capabilities," December 18, 1944, Research and Analysis Report no. 2589, DSR; U.S. Department of Commerce, Bureau of Foreign and Domestic Commerce, *Report on Netherlands Indies Rubber Industry, 1946* (Washington, D.C.: U.S. Government Printing Office, 1946); P. T. Bauer, "The Prospects of Rubber," *Pacific Affairs*, 29 (December 1947):381–90; Charles H. Morrell, "The Future of the Netherlands East Indies as a World Economic Unit," *Asiatic Review*, 42 (July 1946):262–64.

[17]OSS, "Pre-War Petroleum Statistics," Research and Analysis Report no. 1900, April 20, 1944, DSR; Netherlands Information Bureau, *Facts and Figures* (New York, 1948); U.S. Department of Commerce, Bureau of Foreign and Domestic Commerce, Industrial Reference Service, "U.S. Trade with the Netherlands Indies in 1940" and "Summary of the Foreign Trade of the United States—Calendar Year 1940" (Washington, D.C.: U.S. Government Printing Office, 1942); "Indonesia: Peace Brings Trade Rebirth," *Business Week*, May 8, 1948, pp. 117–20.

industries everywhere that greedy eyes have looked upon it with envy. . . .[18]

In an attempt to resume commercial relations with the republic, in early 1947 an American firm, the Isbrandtsen Steamship Company, concluded a contract with the Perseroan Bank, an organ of the Indonesian government. On February 5 the S.S. *Martin Behrman*, an American government-owned ship chartered to the Isbrandtsen Company, arrived at the republican port of Cheribon to pick up a cargo of rubber, sugar, and other commodities sought by the American market. The arrival of the vessel in Indonesian waters marked the first effort to develop direct trade relations between the United States and the republican-controlled areas of the East Indies. One week before the *Martin Behrman* landed, however, the Netherlands Indies government had published new trade regulations, rendering illegal the export of such commodities from republican ports. In effect, the new import-export regulations represented an embargo on nearly all of the products that the struggling republic had to seell. Intent on completing its lucrative transaction regardless of the new law, the *Martin Behrman* defied the Dutch order and proceeded to load its cargo. Dutch officials moved quickly. On March 7 they seized the cargo, placed Dutch soldiers and marines on the ship, and under a court order began to unload the cargo.[19]

There were strong protests in the United States about Dutch handling of the *Martin Behrman* incident. Joseph Curran, head of the powerful National Maritime Union, complained to Assistant Secretary Clayton that the "unfortunate" seizure recalled "the days of the Tripoli pirates."[20] Officially, the United States con-

[18]Netherlands Indies Government Information Service, *What's It About in Indonesia?* (Batavia, 1947), p. 2.

[19]"S.S. 'Martin Behrman' Incident," *U.S. Department of State Bulletin*, 16 (April 20, 1947):720; Marshall to Foote, February 4 and February 6, 1947, in *FR*, 1947, 6:896–97; *Netherlands News Letter*, April 1, 1947, pp. 15–17. For the Dutch view of the incident, see Report of Commanding Officer, HMNS Kortenaer: "Report about the *S.S. Martin Behrman* from February 6, 1947, till March 2nd," enclosed in Parke H. Brady (U.S. naval attaché, The Hague) to CNO, April 8, 1947, in Naval Attaché Reports File, Naval History Division, Washington National Records Center, Suitville, Md. (hereafter cited as WNRC).

[20]*New York Times*, March 13, 1947, p. 55.

ceded that the Netherlands government "had acted within its legal rights with respect to the action taken toward the *Martin Behrman* and its cargo."[21] Privately, the State Department was appalled by The Hague's apparent reversion to the discriminatory trade practices of the prewar years.[22] The practical effect of the Dutch regulations, noted newly appointed Secretary of State George Marshall, was to "paralyze trade with NEI, and to prolong and intensify economic disturbances already resulting from world shortages [of] commodities covered by these regulations."[23] In private conversations with Dutch officials, the State Department sought to arrange a quiet diplomatic adjustment of the *Martin Behrman* case, but the larger issues raised by the seizure deeply troubled American policy makers: the Dutch appeared determined to deprive the world of critical raw materials that were in extremely short supply. "This Government has therefore taken the position," wrote Acheson to an angry congressman, "that these measures will retard the rehabilitation of the Indies and seriously affect world political and economic stabilization, and has urged that the regulations be reconsidered."[24] Despite American efforts, the Dutch refused to rescind their import-export regulations; American trade thus continued to suffer.

The American economic interest in Indonesia encompassed more than just the desire to secure certain raw materials; Indonesia also served as a significant outlet for American investment capital. The United States ranked third, behind the

[21]"S.S. 'Martin Behrman' Incident," p. 720.

[22]Memorandum from Cumming to Hickerson, February 28, 1947, 656D.006/3-1147, DSR; Benton to Marshall, March 14, 1946, 656D.006/3-1447, DSR. *The Times* (London) charged the Dutch with "discriminatory trade policies which have paralyzed foreign trade and brought foreign commerce to a virtual standstill" (March 26, 1947, p. 4).

[23]Marshall to Benton, March 3, 1947, in *FR*, 1947, 6:899.

[24]Acheson to Representative Lawrence H. Smith, March 26, 1947, 656D.006/3-1147, DSR. See also Acheson to Benton, March 8, 1946, in *FR*, 1947, 6:900–902; Marshall to Foote, May 7, 1946, 656D.006/5-747, DSR; Southeast Asian Division, "Policy and Information Statement: Netherlands East Indies," in folder labeled "N.E.I.: Relations with U.S.," Box 12, PSA Records, DSR; Drumright to George C. Whitteridge (British Foreign Office), March 5, 1947, FO 371 F3052/45/62, PRO; U.S. Department of State, Office of Intelligence Research (OIR), Division of Research for the Far East, "Current Foreign Trade Situation in Indonesia," Situation Report—Southern Areas, no. 3480.25, February 12, 1947, DSR.

Netherlands and Great Britain, as a leading investor in the East Indies; American investments in Indonesia, moreover, were greater than those in all but one other country in the Far East.[25] Some of the United States' largest corporations had considerable capital in the rich archipelago, with the Standard-Vacuum Oil Company's investment of approximately $100 million topping the list. The State Department—keenly aware of the strategic value of this petroleum—on several occasions expressed deep concern that renewed fighting might endanger American-owned oil installations.[26] A total of thirty-one American companies owned Indonesian properties valued before the war at about $250 million, including the U.S. Rubber Company, the Goodyear Rubber Company, General Motors, and Procter & Gamble. Many other American corporations awaited only the stabilization of conditions in Indonesia before they would join the rush to exploit the vast, unexplored mineral resources of the Indies.[27]

As Acheson and other American policy makers often noted, the maintenance of open door trading principles would be essential to the full development of commercial relations between the United States and Indonesia.[28] For this reason, American officials were acutely interested in the economic philosophy of the young Indonesian government. The republic's political manifesto, which served as the foundation of its economic policy, declared that the republic would pursue a conciliatory economic program, encouraging new foreign investment and protecting all existing foreign properties. It stated that Indonesia's raw-material wealth could make a substantial contribution to international trade and productivity, while the republic, in turn,

[25]U.S. Department of Commerce, *Investment in Indonesia*, pp. 11–12.

[26]Brynes to Harriman, June 12, 1946, in *FR*, 1946, 8:826–27; Byrnes to Hornbeck, July 23, 1946, 856E.00/7-2346, DSR.

[27]Netherlands Information Bureau, *Indonesia: Facts and Figures* (New York, 1948); "Indonesia: Peace Brings Trade Rebirth," *Business Week*, May 8, 1948, pp. 118–19; "Indies Unrest: Cost in Vital Output," *U.S. News and World Report*, September 17, 1948, pp. 26–27.

[28]Acheson to Benton, March 12, 1947, in *FR*, 1947, 6:905; Marshall to Benton, May 16, 1947, in ibid., pp. 924–26; memorandum by Moffat, April 10, 1946, in folder labeled "N.E.I.: Arms–Surplus Property Disposal," Box 11, PSA Records, DSR; Acheson to Foote, August 12, 1946, 656E.1112/8-1246, DSR; Foote to Acheson, August 20, 1946, 656E.1112/8–2046, DSR.

could benefit from foreign investment in its underdeveloped economy. This moderate policy was part of the republic's larger diplomatic strategy; eager to allay suspicions about its potentially "radical" character, Indonesia sought to present itself as a responsible regime intent on safeguarding foreign investments and engaging in nondiscriminatory international commerce. In numerous speeches and interviews throughout 1946 and early 1947, Dr. A. K. Gani, the republic's minister for economic affairs, reassured all interested parties that his government wanted to attract foreign capital and would deal fairly and reasonably with all investors.[29] Republican representatives reiterated this position in several meetings with State Department officers. In one such conference in Washington, Sutan Sjahsam, the republic's special representative in commercial and economic matters in the United States, emphasized that the Indonesian Republic was eager to establish commercial and economic relations with the United States. He explained that he had found commercial interests in New York City eager to trade with the republic, but those interests had informed him that the resumption of American trade was entirely dependent on the attitude of the U.S. government.[30] The unsettled conditions in the East Indies thus continued to thwart all efforts to reestablish commercial relations between the United States and Indonesia.

Great Britain's efforts to reestablish normal commercial relations with Indonesia were also being blocked by the unsettled conditions in the islands and Dutch commercial policies. For the British, who were suffering from an acute shortage of foodstuffs, trade with the East Indies was of particular importance. The Dutch import-export laws effectively blocked any such trade; between January and March 1947, the Dutch intercepted Brit-

[29]Foote to Byrnes, October 2, 1946, in *FR*, 1946, 8:846–47; Foote to Byrnes, October 25, 1946, 856E.00/10-2546, DSR; *New York Times*, April 9, 1947, p. 14; Charles Wolf, Jr., *The Indonesian Story: The Birth, Growth, and Structure of the Indonesian Republic* (New York: John Day, 1948), pp. 77–83; John O. Sutter, *Indonesianisasi: Politics in a Changing Economy, 1940–1950,* 2 vols. (Ithaca: Cornell University Press, 1959), 1:310–12, 480.

[30]Memorandum by William S. B. Lacy (Southeast Asian Division) of a conversation with Sjahsam, April 14, 1946, in Box 3, Hickerson Files, Records of the Office of European Affairs, RG 59, DSR.

ish vessels eleven times to examine their cargoes and confiscated all produce subject to those laws. These actions infuriated British officials. The minister of food attempted to impress on the prime minister the urgency of the situation, suggesting that London strongly pressure The Hague into rescinding the regulations. Though larger diplomatic considerations led to the muting of British protests over the incidents, Britain's interest in obtaining sugar, fats, vegetable oils, and tea from the Indies remained strong and it continued to press for a full restoration of trade relations.[31]

In order to facilitate the normalization of those relations and simultaneously to find an amicable solution to a complicated colonial dispute, American and British diplomats pressed both the Dutch and the Indonesians for an early ratification of the Linggadjati agreement. The State Department's position was that the agreement represented "an equitable and working compromise, and that negotiators on both sides deserve the backing of their respective governments." This department memorandum, concurred in by both the Office of European Affairs and the Office of Far Eastern Affairs, went on to say: "A failure on either side to ratify this agreement, or a protracted delay in ratification, will lead to a deterioration in good will so severe as to render impossible the resumption of negotiations." While noting that certain sections of the agreement were extremely vague, the memorandum expressed the belief that the unsettled issues would be "worked out with mutual good will and to the satisfaction of both parties."[32]

The agreement's very vagueness, however, enabled the republic and the Netherlands to take markedly different views of Linggadjati's meaning. After the settlement was initialed on November 15, 1946, it was subjected to an endless series of questions and clarifications between the commission general

[31]Minutes from minister of food to prime minister, March 8 and April 17, 1947, in Prime Ministers' Records (PREM) 8/596, PRO; memorandum by Treasury on financial and economic policy in regard to Netherlands East Indies, April 18, 1946, in Cabinet Records (CAB) 134/283, PRO; minute from Sir Orme Sargent to Attlee, March 16, 1946, PREM 8/596, PRO; Minutes of Far East Committee, April 23, 1947, CAB 134/282, PRO.

[32]Memorandum from Vincent and Hickerson to Acheson, November 27, 1946, in *FR*, 1946, 8:853–55. See also Marshall to Foote, January 6, 1947, in *FR*, 1947 6:890.

and the Indonesian delegation; indeed, Sjahrir warned at one point that Linggadjati was in danger of being "buried under interpretive material."[33] At least two major problems delayed ratification of the pact. One was that the agreement continually referred to the need for "cooperation" between the Netherlands and the republic—cooperation in forming the U.S.I., cooperation in the joint problems of defense, economic affairs, and foreign policy—although there was no indication that mutual mistrust and enmity could be easily overcome. As long as each party remained suspicious of the other's sincerity and trustworthiness, true cooperation was impossible. The other central problem was the federal structure of the proposed U.S.I. This provision, on which the Dutch had insisted, called for a federation to consist of three semiautonomous states: the republic, East Indonesia, and Borneo. As Charles Wolf, formerly an American vice-consul in the East Indies, correctly pointed out in 1947, this provision assumed a "paper equality of areas which are not, cannot and will not be equal—economically, politically, or culturally." The area of the republic—Java and Sumatra—contained about 85 percent of the total Indonesian population, "and at least the same percentage of the educated Westernized intellectual group." Wolf added: "Before the war they accounted for between four-fifth and nine-tenths of the total export and import trade of the whole Indonesian archipelago."[34]

Unable to reconcile conflicting interpretations of the agreement, the two parties looked to its arbitration clause for a peaceful adjustment of those difficulties. With each side harboring a considerable amount of skepticism, while at the same time issuing the obligatory professions of goodwill, the Dutch and republicans ratified Linggadjati on March 25, 1947.[35] In the sober view of the British consul general in Batavia, the agreement was

[33]Quoted in David Wehl, *The Birth of Indonesia* (London: George Allen & Unwin, 1948), p. 158.

[34]Wolf, *Indonesian Story,* pp. 44–45. See also Alastair M. Taylor, *Indonesian Independence and the United Nations* (Ithaca: Cornell University Press, 1960), pp. 30–33; George McTurnan Kahin, *Nationalism and Revolution in Indonesia* (Ithaca: Cornell University Press, 1952), pp. 196–98. For a detailed analysis of the federal question, see A. Arthur Schiller, *The Formation of Federal Indonesia, 1945–1949* (The Hague: van Hoeve, 1955).

[35]Kahin, *Nationalism and Revolution,* p. 198; Wolf, *Indonesian Story,* p. 46; *New York Times,* March 26, 1947, p. 14; statement of Sjahrir, in United Nations Security Council, *Official Records (SCOR), 2d yr., 184th meeting, August 14, 1947, p. 1999.*

signed "only just in time to prevent the whole Dutch military machine being set in motion."[36] Washington promptly expressed to van Mook and Sjahrir its gratification with the signing of the Linggadjati agreement and urged its prompt implementation. On April 3 the United States officially recognized the republic's de facto jurisdiction over Java and Sumatra.[37] When pressed by The Hague for a clarification of its recognition statement, the State Department assured the Dutch that its message was drawn in consonance with the Linggadjati agreement and was in no way intended as a derogation of Dutch sovereignty over the East Indies.[38] Great Britain, Australia, India, China, and several Arab states also recognized the republic's de facto sovereignty at this time.[39]

Nevertheless, the basic issues dividing the Dutch and republicans—issues that Linggadjati attempted to skirt—persisted. "The signing of the Linggadjati agreement," explained one State Department report, "does no more than to ease tensions between the two parties slightly and make further negotiations possible. In essence both the Indonesians and the Dutch cling to their original viewpoint."[40] Whether Linggadjati would work or not, departing ambassador Hornbeck explained to President Truman, remained "problematic."[41] Talks regarding implementation of the accord made little progress during April and May, and observers noted a perceptible hardening of attitudes. The republicans objected to the Netherlands' interpretation of federalism; they charged the Dutch with attempting to set up "puppet states" in East Indonesia and Borneo which would remain under nominal Dutch control. Those actions contravened both the letter and the spirit of Linggadjati, contended the re-

[36]Gilbert MacKereth to Foreign Office, March 19, 1947, FO 371 F3788/45/62, PRO.

[37]Acheson to Foote, April 3, 1947, in *FR*, 1947, 6:912.

[38]Acheson to Herman Baruch (ambassador in Netherlands), April 18, 1947, 856E.01/4-1847, DSR; Acheson to Benton, April 9, 1947, in *FR*, 1947, 6:916; Drumright to Allen, April 9, 1947, FO 371 F5036/45/62, PRO.

[39]Taylor, *Indonesian Independence*, p. 33.

[40]U.S. Department of State, OIR, Division of Research for the Far East, "Recent Developments in the Netherlands–Indonesian Conflict," Situation Report—Southern Areas, no. 3480.28, March 26, 1947, DSR.

[41]Memorandum by Hornbeck of a conversation with Truman, March 31, 1947, in folder labeled "Letters to President Truman," Box 417, Hornbeck Papers; memorandum from Hornbeck to Truman, March 31, 1947, in ibid.

public, since the Dutch were acting unilaterally in those areas whereas the agreement had specifically called for Dutch–republican cooperation. Republican suspicions were further aroused when they discovered that high-ranking Dutch officials were clandestinely fostering a secessionist movement in West Java in an apparent attempt to weaken the republic from within. According to the republic, these Dutch actions fitted a distinct pattern: the Netherlands, it believed, was pursuing a policy of "divide and rule" in a deliberate effort to reimpose colonialism in the East Indies. In addition, the republic accused the Dutch of innumerable truce violations and vehemently objected to their import-export laws, which, even after the signing of the Linggadjati agreement, imposed a virtual embargo on all republican trade.[42]

The Hague made some equally vociferous accusations. The republic, countered the Dutch, displayed no willingness to abide by the terms of the Linggadjati pact. The chief Dutch grievance was that the republic had begun to conduct an independent foreign policy. The expansion of the Indonesian government's foreign relations—symbolized by the activities of Hadji Agus Salim, the republic's vice-minister for foreign affairs, who opened a diplomatic headquarters in Cairo and attempted to improve the republic's international standing—particularly irked Netherlands officials. The Hague believed that either the republic did not comprehend the subtle distinction between de facto and de jure recognition or it was intent on creating an international reputation for itself as an entity apart from the projected U.S.I. This action, along with repeated republican truce violations, prompted the Dutch to question the sincerity of the republic's commitment to the terms of the Linggadjati agreement. With no sign of the mutual goodwill and cooperative spirit demanded by Linggadjati, yet another deadlock seemed imminent.[43] H. L. Hirschfeld, economic adviser to Prime Minis-

[42]U.S. Department of State, OIR, Division of Research for the Far East, "Post-Linggadjati Developments in Indonesia," Situation Report—Southern Areas, no. 3480.29, April 9, 1947; Wolf, *Indonesian Story*, pp. 106–12; statement by Sjahrir, SCOR, 2d yr., 184th meeting, August 14, 1946, pp. 1999–2000.

[43]S. Pinckney Tuck (U.S. Embassy, Cairo) to Marshall, April 22, 1947, 756.83/4-2247, DSR; Hubertus J. van Mook, *The Stakes of Democracy in Southeast Asia* (New York: Norton, 1950), pp. 224–25.

ter Beel, revealed to a British diplomat on May 20 that further talks with the republic were futule because it was playing for time, which the Dutch could not afford. In addition to the expense of maintaining their military forces, he lamented, the Netherlands was "suffering a terrific financial drain in foreign exchange" because exports from the East Indies were totaling less than half its imports.[44] Some leading Dutch politicians began to demand military action.[45]

The British viewed these Indonesian developments with mounting apprehension. On May 15 George C. Whitteridge of the British Foreign Office informed American representatives that the Dutch and the Indonesians had reached a virtual stalemate. He feared that unless Beel and Jonkmann were able to exercise some moderation, Indonesia might very well turn into another Indochina. "Such a development would be disastrous," Whitteridge warned, "and particularly so to Britain which is most anxious to have peace and amity restored, and Indonesia opened to foreign trade so that Britain may obtain from Indonesia certain almost desperately needed products."[46]

At a meeting of the cabinet on May 20, Prime Minister Attlee revealed that he was increasingly disturbed by the recent reports from Indonesia. Negotiations seemed to be making little progress, he noted, and there was now some reason to suspect that the Dutch might resort to force, an action that would amount to a war of reconquest. "The political and economic consequences for us," Attlee said,

> would be so serious that we should spare no effort to dissuade the Dutch from adopting such a policy. Politically, we should be criti-

[44]Memorandum of a conversation between F. C. Everson (British Embassy, Washington) and Moffat, Schnee, and Landon, May 23, 1947, 856D.00/5-2347, DSR.

[45]John L. M. Mitcheson (British consul general, Batavia) to Foreign Office, FO 371 F373/45/62, PRO; U.S. Armed Forces, Pacific Command, Weekly Intelligence Digest, May 23, 1947, Naval Operational Archives, Naval History Divison, Washington Navy Yard; Lewis W. Douglas (ambassador to Great Britain) to Marshall, May 21, 1947, in *FR*, 1947, 6:927–28; Baruch to Marshall, May 10, 1947, in *FR*, 1947, 6:921–22.

[46]Memorandum by Drumright of a conversation with Whitteridge, May 15, 1947, 856D.00/5-1547, DSR. For a similar view regarding Britain's important economic stake in Indonesia, see Douglas to Marshall, June 11, 1947, in *FR*, 1947, 1:756–57.

> cized for having made such a situation possible by keeping British forces in the Dutch East Indies until Dutch troops could be brought in; and an armed conflict between the Dutch and the Indonesians was also bound to disturb our own relations with native populations throughout South-East Asia. Economically, a war of reconquest would delay for years the development of food exports from the Dutch East Indies which we were anxious to encourage in order to reduce our dependence on hard-currency countries.

Members of the British government, he stressed, were virtually unanimous in believing that "strong pressure" must be brought to bear on the Dutch to induce them to reach an early agreement and put aside thoughts of using force. To this end, Foreign Minister Bevin suggested that Washington be asked to act in concert with London to forestall an outbreak of hostilities in the Indies. The United States had considerable leverage with the Netherlands, he remarked, since the Dutch badly wanted dollars for rehabilitation in Indonesia.[47]

On May 21 Attlee summoned Dutch Ambassador Jonkheer E. Michiels and told him that in London's view a resort to military force in the Indies would have disastrous consequences. Any attempt to destroy the republic, Attlee argued, would plunge the Dutch into a long and exhausting military campaign with little likelihood of success; it would also alienate foreign opinion and might well bring about intervention by a third power or the United Nations. On the same day, Attlee instructed the Foreign Office to relay to the United States Britain's pessimistic appraisal of the Indonesian stalemate and to explore with Washington possible measures to cope with the crisis.[48]

The United States also began to take a more serious view of the Dutch–Indonesian impasse at this juncture. This heightened sensitivity to developments in Indonesia was due in part to the growing possibility of outright military confrontation there. Reports from the U.S. military attaché in The Hague repeatedly

[47]CAB 128/48, May 20, 1947, PRO; minute from Bevin to Attlee, May 20, 1947, FO 371 F7032/45/62, PRO.

[48]Record of prime minister's conference with Dutch ambassador, May 21, 1947, FO 371 F7092/45/62, PRO; Douglas to Marshall, May 23, 1947, 856E.00/5-2347, DSR.

stressed the possibility of a Dutch military offensive, and in a conference with members of the Army's Intelligence Division, the American naval attaché in the Netherlands reported that the Dutch had no doubt of their ability to win a quick victory in Java, and "were merely waiting for an OK from the US before starting their offensive." These reports, especially in the wake of the British troop withdrawal, deeply disturbed American officials. As a memorandum by the Army Intelligence Division pointed out, a Dutch resort to force would have disastrous consequences. It "would result in a stalemate from which the Dutch could not extricate themselves"; in addition, it would probably destroy the current moderate Indonesian leadership, bring extremists and communists into power, and lead to scorched-earth tactics that would adversely affect the economic rehabilitation of the Indies for years.[49]

The growing interest in Indonesia at this time also reflected the larger framework of American global objectives as the Cold War intensified. President Truman's containment speech of March 12, 1947, represented a landmark in postwar U.S. foreign policy, as he declared his nation's resolve to contain the spread of communism. Although carefully couched in a specific request for congressional military aid for the tottering regime in Greece and the financially pressed government of Turkey, the Truman Doctrine, as this policy came to be known, was proclaimed in unmistakably universalist language. "At the present moment in world history," the president declared,

> nearly every nation must choose between alternative ways of life. The choice is too often not a free one.
>
> One way of life is based upon the will of the majority, and is distinguished by free institutions, representative government, free elections, guarantees of individual liberty, freedom of speech and religion, and freedom from political oppression.
>
> The second way of life is based upon the will of a minority forcibly imposed upon the majority. It relies upon terror and oppression, a controlled press and radio, fixed elections, and the

[49]War Department memorandum, "The Situation in Southeast Asia as It Affects the Availability of Strategic Raw Materials," June 1947, in folder labeled "Southeast Asia, 1946–1948, U.S. Policy," Box 5, PSA Records, DSR.

> suppression of personal freedoms. I believe that it must be the policy of the United States to support free people who are resisting attempted subjugation by armed minorities or by outside pressures.[50]

With relations between Moscow and Washington progressively deteriorating, Truman believed that the alarmist rhetoric of his containment speech was needed to gain the domestic support necessary to implement his program and to prepare his nation for an expansion of American global commitments. The entire world was a battleground, he implied, between the forces of communism and the forces of the "free world." Soon after the announcement of the Truman Doctrine, American policy makers began to formulate plans to aid Europe's economic recovery. This complementary program, which became known as the Marshall Plan, sought to revitalize the economies of the Western democracies in an effort to create a bulwark against communism—especially the threat posed by the growing popularity of Communist parties in the Western European countries, which, the Truman administration believed, would exploit continued economic chaos.[51]

The American response to the growing tension in the East Indies can be understood within this larger context. Truman proclaimed that America was engaged in a worldwide struggle with an international Communist movement directed by the Soviet Union; each area of the world, and especially those that threatened to explode into armed conflict that Communists might exploit, thus took on added significance for the architects of U.S. foreign policy. Moreover, the central focus of that policy was the rehabilitation of the Western European nations, and since the economic recovery of the Netherlands so heavily depended on a return to full production in the East Indies, Washington could ill afford to ignore the continuing political disturbances in Indonesia. By mid-1947, then, the Dutch–In-

[50] *Public Papers of the Presidents: Harry S. Truman, 1947* (Washington: U.S. Government Printing Office, 1963), pp. 178–79.

[51] Walter LaFeber, *America, Russia, and the Cold War, 1945–1975* (New York: Wiley, 1976); pp. 50–63; Paterson, *Soviet-American Confrontation*, pp. 174–234; Yergin, *Shattered Peace*, pp. 274–335; Richard Freeland, *The Truman Doctrine and the Origins of McCarthyism* (New York: Knopf, 1972), pp. 70–114, 151–200.

donesian clash was being cast in a new light. Although still not an area of primary interest to the United States, Indonesia—because of its interrelationship with critical Cold War issues—was rapidly being elevated to the status of a major world problem.[52]

Reflecting this increased interest, on May 16 George C. Marshall, now secretary of state, instructed Herman Baruch, the new American ambassador to The Hague, to present an aide-mémoire to the Dutch Foreign Office detailing the American position. Marshall explained in his cable to Baruch that the United States had been giving serious consideration to developments in Southeast Asia. "Strong nationalist movements throughout [the] area are not isolated phenomena of concern to [a] few colonial powers only," he remarked. On the contrary, the outcome of such struggles "will have [a] profound effect on [the] future [of the] world," since the area is "strategically located athwart [the] Southwest Pacific and [is] of [the] greatest economic importance." Therefore, the United States had a special concern in regard to the future of Southeast Asia. Marshall expressed apprehension about the leaning of those nationalist movements toward "pan-Asiatic" or "totalitarian" philosophies; "as either trend would be contrary [to the] interests [of the] Western democracies," the United States believed that "every effort should be made [to] persuade [the] peoples [of] Southeast Asia voluntarily [to] seek association with [the] Western democratic powers." The United States was "convinced [that] such voluntary association [was] essential [to] world political and economic stability."[53]

Turning his attention specifically to Indonesia, the secretary of state noted that the American government had hoped that the

[52]That Indonesia was generally regarded as a problem in relation to the issue of European reconstruction and not within the context of a developing Afro-Asian revolt against Western domination was suggested to me in several interviews with former State Department officials: with Abbot Moffat, November 14, 1975; with Frederick Nolting (of the Division of Northern European Affairs and desk officer for the Netherlands, 1945–49), May 1, 1975; with Charlton Ogburn (of Division of Southeast Asian Affairs), May 2, 1974; with James Barco (of the Division of United Nations Affairs), May 7, 1975.

[53]Marshall to Baruch, May 16, 1947, in *FR*, 1947, 6:924.

Netherlands would work peaceably with the Indonesians to make an arrangement that would meet the "natural aspirations" of both the Indonesians and the Dutch. Accordingly, the United States learned of the Linggadjati signing with "profound pleasure." While expressing optimism that the political aspects of the agreement would be worked out, Marshall was particularly concerned about "resolving conflicting economic interests." The United States, Marshall reiterated, believed "that [the] immediate opening of trade and commerce throughout [the] NEI [on a] non-discriminatory basis" was the "first and most imperative step in stabilizing political and economic conditions and in rehabilitating [the] Indonesian economy." The State Department considered trade essential, not only as a means of strengthening the moderates in the republic, but also as an inducement to the investment of foreign capital. Marshall repeated the United States' interest in republican economic policies, noting that the State Department insisted that foreign capital must be treated "fairly and reasonably." He concluded this frank message by instructing Baruch to inform Dutch officials that the United States was willing to meet with Dutch and Indonesian representatives in an effort to aid the "economic rehabilitation of Indonesia on foundations which will strengthen [the] mutual respect and voluntary association [of the] Dutch and Indonesian peoples."[54]

As Bevin had pointed out, Washington's leverage with The Hague was considerable; heavily dependent on American aid, the Dutch could hardly ignore pressure—or friendly advice—from its principal ally. In late 1945, for example, the Export-Import Bank had authorized a $100 million loan for the Netherlands East Indies, but at the request of the State Department the agreement was not concluded because of the uncertainties of the colonial revolt. In its telegram to Baruch, the department instructed him to remind the Dutch Foreign Office that the nature of any economic and financial arrangements between the Netherlands and Indonesia would naturally be "one important factor" in determining whether the loan would ultimately be

[54]Ibid., pp. 924–26.

approved. The injection of the aid issue at this critical stage undoubtedly served as a forceful reminder to the Dutch that the United States could use the lever of economic assistance as a diplomatic weapon when it so desired.

Aware now that the United States, as well as Great Britain, would look on a military offensive with great disfavor, the Netherlands made another effort to reach a diplomatic accommodation with the republic. On May 27, 1947, the commission general presented Sjahrir with a fresh set of Dutch proposals. This new plan attempted to solve the key issue of sovereignty by calling for de jure Dutch sovereignty over Indonesia until January 1, 1949. Until that date, Indonesia would be ruled by an interim government that would be largely dominated by the Dutch, with a representative of the Dutch crown having jurisdiction over all final decisions. This interim regime was to be endowed with extensive powers; it would supervise the incorporation of the federated states into the proposed U.S.I., and would control the foreign commerce of Indonesia pending the creation of that sovereign state on January 1, 1949. The Dutch also called for the establishment of a joint police force, composed of an equal number of Dutch and Indonesian troops, which would be responsible for maintaining law and order throughout the archipelago during the transition period, even in the republican-controlled areas. The Netherlands further specified that the republic would not have the right to conduct its own foreign relations.[55]

The net effect of the May 27 proposals was to diminish significantly the position and role of the republic in the federal structure during the transition period. Moreover, the tone of the Dutch message was unmistakably aggressive; The Hague demanded a reply within two weeks.[56] Republican leaders realized that it was intended to be, as van Mook intimated to a British

[55]The Dutch proposals are repinted in Wehl, *Birth of Indonesia*, pp. 191–97.

[56]Ibid.; Wolf, *Indonesian Story*, pp. 118–20; Secretary of State's weekly summary, June 9, 1947, DSR; U.S. Department of State, OIR, Division of Research for the Far East, "Dutch-Indonesian Notes of May and June 1947," Situation Report—Southern Areas, no. 3480.33, June 16, 1947, DSR; Wehl, *Birth of Indonesia*, pp. 191–97.

diplomat, an ultimatum, and that their options were now sharply limited: they could either accept Holland's harsh terms or prepare for war.[57]

The Netherlands hoped that London and Washington would agree that the Dutch offer was essentially reasonable, and that if it were carried out it would be equitable and fair to both sides; if they did, they might then express this view to the republic and urge republican leaders to comply with the ultimatum.[58] The British government did find the Dutch proposals "to be on the whole sound and sensible" and conveyed this opinion to the State Department in an aide-mémoire dated June 4. Its communiqué reiterated Great Britain's desire for a rapid implementation of the Linggadjati agreement, stressing that Britain's economic interests demanded an early resumption of commercial relations with Indonesia. The British government, it continued, intended to approach the republic to recommend prompt acceptance of the Dutch plan, and wondered if the United States would be willing to undertake a similar approach.[59]

The State Department, while displeased that the Dutch proposals were presented in the form of an ultimatum, nevertheless believed that the May 27 offer presented a "timely and valuable opportunity [to] achieve [the] essential step forward towards attaining [the] objectives contemplated [by] Linggadjati." Following the British suggestion, Acting Secretary of State Acheson directed Consul General Foote to inform the republic that the U.S. government believed that the Dutch proposals "have been offered in good faith in [an] effort [to] implement Linggadjati," and that the "Republic would be well advised to respond promptly in [a] spirit of good faith and compromise, thus

[57]Memorandum by Schnee of a conversation with Everson, Nolting, and Landon, May 29, 1947, in *FR,* 1947, 6:933; Kahin, *Nationalism and Revolution,* pp. 206–7.

[58]Memorandum by Schnee of a conversation with Landon and Helb, May 29, 1947, in *FR,* 1947, 6:933–34; Baruch to Marshall, June 3, 1947, in ibid., p. 936; Douglas to Marshall, June 4, 1947, in ibid., pp. 938–39.

[59]Aide-mémoire from British Embassy to Department of State, June 4, 1947, in ibid., pp. 939–40; aide-mémoire from British Embassy to Netherlands Foreign Office, June 4, 1947, FO 371 F7609/45/62, PRO; Mitcheson to Foreign Office, June 7, 1947, FO 371 F7684/45/62, PRO.

demonstrating [the] sincerity [of] pledges undertaken [at] Linggadjati."[60] When Acheson informed the Dutch of the State Department's action, they expressed deep appreciation for this American assistance.[61]

Meanwhile, the Dutch demands were denounced by most major republican political and military leaders. Sjahrir understood that the Dutch were prepared to use military force, but he also realized that a complete acceptance of the humiliating Dutch offer would have been tantamount to political suicide. Consequently, he attempted to go as far as he could toward meeting the Dutch ultimatum without risking his own domestic base of support. On June 8 he assured the Dutch commission general that the republic would accept the principle of an interim government, but he attached so many qualifications and conditions to the Dutch proposals that his reply amounted to a virtual rejection of them.[62] Angered by this ploy, the Dutch found his counterproposals "unsatisfactory."[63] "One should not trust those so-and-sos one yard," van Mook confided to British Consul General Mitcheson.[64]

Alarmed by this sudden turn of events, and sensing crisis, the British Foreign Office on June 14 and again on June 16 urged the Dutch to exercise restraint and moderation in reacting to the republican counteroffer. By resorting to force, the Foreign Office warned, the Netherlands "would forfeit the good will of all."[65] Simultaneously, Britain proposed that the United States and Great Britain offer to mediate the Dutch–Indonesian dispute.[66]

[60]Acheson to Foote, June 5, 1947, in *FR*, 1947, 6:941–42; memorandum from Vincent and Matthews to Acheson, June 5, 1947, 856D.00/7-547, DSR.

[61]Memorandum by Schnee of a conversation with Loudon, von Vredenburch, Helb, Hirschfeld, Acheson, and others, June 6, 1947, in *FR*, 1947, 6:945.

[62]Kahin, *Nationalism and Revolution*, p. 207; Taylor, *Indonesian Independence*, p. 36; Wolf, *Indonesian Story*, pp. 121–22.

[63]Foote to Marshall, June 10, 1947, in *FR*, 1947, 6:946; Baruch to Marshall, June 10, 1947, in ibid., pp. 946–47; Foote to Marshall, June 13, 1947, in ibid., pp. 947–48.

[64]Mitcheson to Foreign Office, June 8, 1947, FO 371 F7777/45/62, PRO.

[65]Foreign Office to Bland, June 14, 1947, and Bevin to Bland, June 16, 1947, both in FO 371 F7584/45/62, PRO.

[66]Aide-mémoire from British Embassy to Department of State, June 16, 1947, 856E.01/6–1647, DSR; Foreign Office to Inverchapel, June 16, 1947, FO 371 F7584/45/62, PRO.

Although the proposal was endorsed by the offices of both European and Far Eastern Affairs, President Truman rejected joint mediation and instead instructed the State Department to communicate directly to both the Dutch and the republicans that the U.S. government hoped "that they will continue in their efforts peacefully to settle their differences."[67] On the following day, the State Department reminded the Dutch "that the use of military force would not be regarded favorably by this Govt, would arouse serious adverse reaction [of] US public opinion, and would be self-defeating in purpose."[68] At the same time, the State Department urged the republicans to resume negotiations immediately on the basis of the Netherlands' May 27 proposals.[69]

Realizing that the impasse was fraught with danger and mindful of British and American pressure, Sjahrir again tried to close the gap between the Dutch and republican positions. On June 20 he offered to accept the Dutch concept of the interim government, including recognition of the de jure position and special powers of the crown's representative. Although these were major concessions, the Dutch commission general remained unsatisfied and summarily broke off talks. On June 23 The Hague dispatched an aide-mémoire to the republic, again urging total compliance with its offer of May 27. Sjahrir considered his proposal of June 20 to be the republic's maximum compromise; yet, to his dismay, it was not enough for the Dutch and far too much for many of his republican supporters. When the magnitude of Sjahrir's concessions was revealed in Indonesia, most of the major political parties began to withdraw their support. His position now untenable, Sjahrir resigned on June 27.[70]

In an effort to bring the two parties back to the bargaining

[67]Memorandum by Marshall, June 16, 1947, in *FR*, 1947, 6:948; Inverchapel to Foreign Office, June 17, 1947, FO 371 F8129/45/62, PRO.

[68]Marshall to Baruch, June 17, 1947, in *FR*, 1947, 6:950.

[69]Marshall to Foote, June 17, 1947, in ibid., pp. 950–51; Marshall to Truman, June 18, 1947, President's Secretary's File, Truman Papers, Harry S. Truman Library, Independence, Mo.

[70]Kahin, *Nationalism and Revolution*, pp. 207–8; Wolf, *Indonesian Story*, pp. 122–24. See also Foote to Marshall, June 20 and June 25, 1947, both in *FR*, 1947, 6:955–58.

table, the United States transmitted a strongly worded aide-mémoire to the republic on June 28. "This Govt," it read, "has viewed with increasing alarm the danger inherent in failure to implement the Linggadjati Agreement." The United States "must necessarily be concerned with developments in Indonesia because of the importance of Indonesia as a factor in the world's stability, both economic and political." Washington urged the Indonesians to assent to the immediate formation of an interim government and to accept Dutch sovereignty during the proposed transition period. "In our reading of [the] Linggadjati Agreement," the aide-mémoire continued, "it is clear a transition period was envisaged (between now and Jan 1949) during which Neth retains sovereignty and ultimate authority in Indonesia."[71] Actually, this reading is not supported by the language of the Linggadjati pact; in fact, the idea that the Dutch would retain ultimate authority during the transition period appeared for the first time in The Hague's ultimatum of May 27. The American message led republican leaders, in the words of one historian, to "conclude that the United States, while anxious to avoid the outbreak of full-scale war in Indonesia, was backing the Dutch as against the Republic. Thus, they felt the strength of their political position vis-à-vis the Dutch weakened because of this obvious American backing of some of the most important of the Dutch demands."[72] The aide-mémore concluded with an offer of financial aid and assistance in the rehabilitation of Indonesia, after the interim regime had been set up along mutually cooperative lines. The Netherlands, not surprisingly, was extremely grateful to the United States for this timely display of support.[73]

At this point Abbot Moffat, head of the State Department's Southeast Asian Division, succinctly summarized American policy objectives in Indonesia in a memorandum of July 8, 1947. "The objective of the United States," he stated, "is to secure a

[71]Marshall to Foote, June 26, 1947, in *FR*, 1947, 6:959–60; Marshall to Baruch, June 26, 1947, in ibid., pp. 960–61; Baruch to Marshall, June 30, 1947, 856E.01/6-3047, DSR. The American aide-mémoire is reprinted in Wolf, *Indonesian Story*, pp. 180–81.

[72]Kahin, *Nationalism and Revolution*, p. 209.

[73]Baruch to Marshall, June 29, 1947, in *FR*, 1947, 6:963–66; Foote to Marshall, in ibid., p. 967; White House daily summary, July 2, 1947, DSR.

settlement of the present Indonesian situation which will meet the natural aspirations of Indonesian nationalism and, at the same time, preserve so far as possible for the Netherlands the economic strength which she derives from association with the Indies." Linggadjati, he noted, appeared to fulfill that objective, as it provided for a Dutch-Indonesian partnership. Accordingly, the United States had pressed both parties for a prompt implementation of the Linggadjati settlement for political, economic, and strategic reasons. Politically, he argued, such a solution was of great importance to the United States because Indonesia, with its seventy million people, was an integral part of Southeast Asia—a region that contained one-quarter of the world's population, and which since World War II had been successfully revolting against colonial status. The "achievement of nationalist aspirations and voluntary association with one of the Western democracies," he wrote, "would be an important factor in maintaining friendly relations between these emerging countries and the West." Otherwise, Moffat warned, Southeast Asia's opposition to Western colonialism and imperialism might lead it into "the Soviet orbit." America's economic interest in Indonesia was also evident:

> Economically a prompt and reasonable solution is of intense importance to this country because of our dependence on economic resources abounding in the area: tin, oil, rubber, palm oil, copra, kapoc, sugar, spices. Furthermore, there are important American investments in Indonesia now nonproductive which, when a solution is achieved, will rapidly be expanded. The Republican intention of improving living standards in Indonesia will also, if fulfilled, develop a potentially important market for American exports.

He added that Indonesia was strategically valuable because it "lies athwart the Southwest approach to the Pacific Ocean and offers a vital source of supplies essential to an American wartime economy."

Moffat noted that it was "especially important to the United States that a solution be achieved peacefully." A resort to force on the part of the Dutch would be politically disastrous, he cautioned, because it "would be construed as a new colonial war by one of the democracies and would probably greatly strengthen Soviet influence in the area." Such a war would also have serious economic repercussions; the republicans could destroy all major foreign holdings, and a war would also deprive the world of desperately needed resources. In addition, American intelligence sources believed the Indonesians to be far stronger and the Dutch far weaker than commonly supposed. In a military confrontation, one intelligence expert predicted, the Dutch would "find themselves completely bogged down by a war of attrition from which they could not emerge successfully."

After briefly reviewing the history of American policy toward the Indonesian upheaval, Moffat commented that only recently had Washington "injected itself actively in the negotiations." This involvement was prompted by the Dutch threat to use force. The effect of the American aide-mémoire of June 28, he speculated, had been "exceedingly beneficial," as it had strengthened the position of the Indonesian moderates. Expressing guarded optimism, Moffat remarked that the only serious issue now separating the two sides was the Dutch proposal for a joint gendarmerie; in conclusion, he expressed his firm belief that an amicable settlement could be quickly achieved.[74]

From Moffat's perspective the lone issue now in dispute may have appeared relatively minor, but for the Dutch and the Indonesians the concept of a joint gendarmerie remained a major impediment to a negotiated agreement. The American aide-mémoire had probably strengthened the republic moderates, as Moffat noted. Although Sjahrir had been ousted for his supposedly intolerable concessions to the Dutch, the blunt American message convinced many Indonesian leaders that the republic had little choice but to continue his moderate policy. Ironically, the new prime minister, Amir Sjarifuddin, made a series of major concessions that came closer to meeting The Hague's demands than anything proposed by Sjahrir. Nevertheless, a final agreement remained elusive. The Netherlands would not budge from its insistence on a joint police force, while the republic believed that it could compromise no further. With the final republican offer falling short of total compliance with

[74]Memorandum by Moffat, July 8, 1947, 856E.00/7-847, DSR.

the Dutch ultimatum, the Netherlands abruptly terminated all negotiations, and on July 20 turned to the oldest form of diplomacy—war.[75]

[75]Sjarifuddin to Dutch delegation, July 5, 1957, UN S/AC.10/19; Dutch proposals of July 15, 1947, UN S/AC.10/21; Sjarifuddin to Dutch delegation, July 16, 1947, UN S/AC.10/22, all in Records of the Good Offices Committee, Dag Hammarskjold Library, United Nations, New York (hereafter cited as GOC Records); Taylor, *Indonesian Independence*, pp. 37–38; Kahin, *Nationalism and Revolution*, pp. 211–12; Wolf, *Indonesian Story*, pp. 125–27. An American intelligence report considered the possibility that the Indonesians and Dutch might jointly request a senior American officer to command the proposed Dutch-Indonesian gendarmerie. "Because of the vital importance of the Netherlands East Indies as a source of basic resources," the report pointed out, "it is believed that such an invitation, if made, should not be lightly thrown aside." See S. J. Chamberlin, Director of Intelligence, to Chief of Staff, July 7, 1947, P&O 091 Netherlands, in Planning and Operation Division Files, Modern Military Branch, National Archives.

6

Intervention by the United Nations: July 1947–January 1948

The Dutch euphemistically termed their military assault against the Indonesian Republic a limited "police action"; in fact, the offensive that commenced at midnight, July 20, 1947, amounted to full-scale war. Armored Dutch columns with full aerial support slashed through republican territory, encountering slight resistance. With a modern army of over 100,000 disciplined troops, the Netherlands had little trouble realizing its immediate military objectives. Within two weeks the Dutch army had captured most of the chief towns and cities of West and East Java, and it had seized the main ports of West Sumatra, along with the rich agricultural and oil-producing areas of that island. Only its inability to destroy the main body of the elusive guerrilla-trained Indonesian troops marred the Dutch army's performance.[1]

The Netherlands government depicted its action as a justified and limited campaign aimed only at establishing conditions favorable to the implementation of the Linggadjati agreement. In a nationwide broadcast to the Dutch people on July 21, Beel maintained that his government had resorted to force because the republic was unable to restore order in Java and Sumatra; the republic, he claimed, simply lacked the authority to carry out the conditions necessary to maintain the truce.[2] Van Mook

[1]George McTurnan Kahin, *Nationalism and Revolution in Indonesia* (Ithaca: Cornell University Press, 1952), pp. 213–14; Charles Wolf, Jr., *The Indonesian Story* (New York: John Day, 1948), p. 132.

[2]*New York Times*, July 21, 1947, p. 3, and July 22, 1947, p. 2. See also Netherlands to Secretary-General of UN, July 22, 1947, UN S/426; statement of van

added that the Dutch government had embarked on the police action "with the utmost reluctance and regret" only after becoming convinced that "the present Government of the Republic of Indonesia is either unwilling or unable to implement both the truce agreement concluded on October 14, 1946, and the Linggadjati Agreement signed on March 25, 1947."[3]

But by turning to the persuasion of arms, the Dutch themselves were guilty of violating Linggadjati. One of that pact's provisions explicitly stated that should a dispute arise which could not be resolved by the commission general and the republican delegation, a third party would be asked to arbitrate the problem. The Dutch police action was thus a flagrant abrogation of that nation's commitment to the Linggadjati agreement.[4] If the two sides were apparently so close to an agreement, the key question is why the Dutch chose such a drastic course of action, ignoring the arbitration clause of the Linggadjati settlement and discounting American and British disapproval. Dutch officials insisted that in view of countless republican truce violations, they had reluctantly concluded that republican guarantees could no longer be trusted and that the Indonesian government had no control over its extremist adherents.

The underpinning of this argument was economic. Significantly, top business and financial circles in Amsterdam fully

---

Kleffens, in United Nations Security Council, *Official Records* (SCOR), 2d yr., 171st meeting, July 31, 1947; White House daily summary, July 24, 1947, in U.S. Department of State Records, National Archives, Washington, D.C. (hereafter cited as DSR); Parke H. Brady (naval attaché, Netherlands) to CNO, July 22, 1947, Naval Attaché Reports File, Washington National Records Center, Suitville, Md. (hereafter cited as WNRC); Netherlands Indies Government Information Service, *The Indonesian Problem, Facts and Figures: What Happened Since the End of the Pacific War* (Batavia, 1947), pp. 48–53.

[3]*New York Times*, July 21, 1947, p. 1; Baruch to Marshall, July 20, 1947, in *Foreign Relations of the United States* (Washington, D.C., 1972), 6:981–83 (hereafter volumes in this series will be cited as *FR*, followed by the year); Bernard Gage to Foreign Office, July 20, 1947, FO 371 F9744/45/62, Records of the British Foreign Office, Public Record Office, London (hereafter cited as PRO); Vinton Chapin (first secretary of embassy at The Hague) to Marshall, July 25, 1947, 856.00/7-2547, DSR.

[4]According to Article 18 of the Linggadjati agreement: "The Netherlands Government and the Government of the Republic of Indonesia shall settle by arbitration any dispute which might arise from this agreement and which cannot be solved by joint consultation . . . between those delegations or, if such agreement cannot be reached, by the President of the International Court of Justice."

endorsed the Dutch government's decision for war, insisting that they considered it essential for the protection of Dutch and Indonesian economic interests. Simon Posthuma, manager of the Netherlands Bank, explained publicly that the East Indies was essential to the Dutch economy because one-fifth of Holland's population depended on income from Indonesia. According to this viewpoint, the political disturbances in the East Indies were seriously hampering efforts to restore the Netherlands' sputtering economy to prewar production levels, and this intolerable state of affairs necessitated The Hague's resort to force.[5]

J. J. van der Velde, the Dutch commissioner for Northern Sumatra, gave a more complete explanation of the economic needs underlying the attack. His country's action, he said, had been motivated by a virtual economic crisis. Leading Dutch economists were convinced that both Holland and Indonesia were in danger of going bankrupt. The recovery of prewar prosperity in both countries was directly dependent on full restoration of prewar commercial activity. The Netherlands was suffering from an acute dollar shortage; it desperately needed machinery and equipment that could be purchased only in the United States, but did not possess sufficient products for export to build up the needed dollar balance. Indonesia possessed a wealth of products demanded by the American market, but the unsettled conditions there precluded the restoration of commercial relations with the United States. Faced with these "impossible" economic conditions, the Netherlands opted for military action, not as an act of warlike aggression, according to top Dutch economists, but under the necessity of opening Indonesia's ports and producing districts to trade.[6] The geographic targets of the police

[5]*New York Times*, July 28, 1947, p. 23; Charles Wolf, Jr., "Hornets' Nest in Indonesia," *Nation*, 165 (August 2, 1947):125; Raymond Kennedy, "Truce in Indonesia," *Far Eastern Survey*, 18 (March 24, 1948):65–67; Gilbert Burck, "Report from Indonesia," *Fortune*, July 1948, pp. 90–91; I. Chaudhry, *The Indonesian Struggle* (Lahore: Faroz, 1950), pp. 157–58.

[6]*New York Times*, August 10, 1947, IV, p. 5; minute by John Street, July 23, 1947, FO 371 F9837/45/62, PRO; Gage to Foreign Office, July 12, 1947, FO 371 F9837/62, PRO; Eric C. Belliquist, "Political and Economic Conditions in the Low Countries," *Foreign Policy Reports*, 24 (May 1, 1948):47; U.S. Department of State, Office of Intelligence Research (OIR), Division of Research for Europe, "European Reconstruction Survey: The Netherlands,"—Northern and Western Europe, no. 3793.14, April 17, 1947, DSR.

action—concentrated as they were around the ports and major production districts of the islands—bear out this explanation.

The rapidity of the Dutch advance caught the disorganized and ill-equipped Indonesian army by surprise. Unwilling to meet their formidable adversary in open battle, Indonesian forces stealthily withdrew to the interior of Java, where, according to plan, they began to organize for guerrilla warfare. Former prime minister Sjahrir declared on July 23: "We know we are involved in an unequal combat but we are fighting for our freedom and honor and our very existence. We shall fight to the last man—either we win or perish."[7] The Indonesian army, while certainly no match for Dutch mechanized columns, comprised approximately 200,000 troops, and was quite capable of waging a long guerrilla war of attrition. As American and British officials had noted on several occasions, the Indonesian terrain was ideally suited for guerrilla warfare. Moreover, the ongoing war in Indochina, where irregular Vietnamese troops were easily stalemating a modernized French army, clearly demonstrated the effectiveness of guerrilla tactics.[8]

Probably the republic's greatest weapon against the Dutch, though, was its appeal to the international community as the injured victim of an aggressive imperialist assault. As one Indonesian Foreign Ministry official noted: "By going to war the Dutch may cause hostility in world opinion which they have not reckoned."[9] On July 22, Prime Minister Sjarifuddin broadcast a statement from the Republican capital of Jogjakarta, calling for a halt to the bloodshed and appealing to the republic's friends in India, China, Europe, and the United States to intervene "quickly and effectively." The aim of the Dutch military action, he stated flatly, was the complete liquidation of the republic and the restoration of the old colonial rule "under the cover of nice words and phrases."[10]

As the Indonesian army prepared for an extended guerrilla war, the republican government turned once again to diplomacy. President Sukarno appointed Sjahrir an ambassador at large to

[7]*New York Times*, July 24, 1947, p. 3.

[8]Wolf, *Indonesian Story*, pp. 133–34; J. K. Ray, *Transfer of Power in Indonesia, 1942–1949* (Bombay: Manaktalas, 1967), p. 125.

[9]*New York Times*, July 21, 1947, p. 3.

[10]Ibid., July 23, 1947, p. 2.

plead the Indonesian case before the Security Council.[11] His first stop was New Delhi, where Prime Minister Jawaharlal Nehru expressed his outrage at the Dutch offensive and promised Indian support for the republic. After meeting with Sjahrir on July 24, Nehru gave a forceful indication of a growing self-consciousness and solidarity among the former colonial territories of Asia: "What has become of the U.N. Charter? The spirit of the new Asia will not tolerate such things. No European country, whatever it may be, has any business to set its army in Asia against the people of Asia. When it does so, Asia will not tolerate it."[12]

On July 25 Sukarno broadcast an urgent appeal to the United States, imploring its help to bring about a peaceful settlement. "Just as your American ancestors fought 170 years ago for your liberty and independence," the Indonesian president declared, "so are we Indonesians fighting for ours. Just as you then rebelled against domination by a country far across the seas, so are we." He asked Americans "to stand by the principles of justice and right for which you fought so valiantly only two years ago."[13]

International sympathy, as American officials were keenly aware, was largely on the side of the republicans. In its weekly summary of key international developments for Secretary Marshall, the State Department reported that the Dutch attack "started a wave of sympathy for the Indonesians which has swept around the world."[14] Editorial opinion in the United States also rallied around the republican cause and harshly denounced Dutch aggression. "Men were once more being killed for the sin of seeking freedom," wrote Theodore H. White in the *New Republic.* "Unless American or British 'good offices' can at the last moment persuade the Dutch to call off this war," warned the *Christian Century,* "it may quickly become one of the most horrible slaughters in all the black history of Western imperialism." The *New York Times* echoed this popular sentiment with its first anti-Dutch editorial: "This action cannot be inter-

[11]Wolf, *Indonesian Story,* pp. 135–37.
[12]*New York Times,* July 25, 1947, p. 3.
[13]Ibid.
[14]Secretary of State's weekly summary, August 18, 1947, DSR.

preted otherwise, therefore, than as an effort by the Dutch Government to impose by arms what it believed it was not going to gain by negotiation and which it did not choose to submit to arbitration." Even the *Washington Post*, which had consistently supported The Hague's policy in Indonesia, joined this indictment of the Dutch police action. It was "an unwise decision," concluded the *Post*, "especially in the light of the governing agreement, which provides for arbitration of disputes and third party mediation." United Nations intervention was now necessary, because "the Dutch have a bear by the tail, and the present mess is bound to add to the ruin in Indonesia, and thus deprive the world of access to Indonesian resources at a time when they are badly needed."[15]

Despite this popular sentiment, the American government refrained from any public criticism of the Dutch attack. In a statement released to the press on July 21, the State Department detailed its previous efforts to prevent military measures, and said it "profoundly regrets that negotiation has been discarded as the means of achieving the voluntary association between the Netherlands and Indonesian peoples contemplated by the Linggadjati Agreement."[16] While this guarded comment could be construed as an indirect criticism of the Dutch, the State Department was careful not to assess blame.

The major problem posed by the Dutch police action, from the American point of view, was that a nation hostile to the Netherlands might introduce the question at the United Nations. H. Freeman Matthews noted this danger in a memorandum he prepared for Secretary Marshall on July 24. If an unfriendly country took the initiative in the Security Council, Matthews warned, the subsequent debates over the police action would develop "in a manner prejudicial to the Netherlands and to the interests of the Western Democracies in the Far East." Consequently, he recommended that Marshall assure the Dutch ambassador that "the United States has the friendliest feelings

[15]Theorore H. White, "So the Dutch Are at War," *New Republic*, August 4, 1947, p. 8; *Christian Century*, 64 (July 30, 1947):916; *New York Times*, July 22, 1947, p. 2; *Washington Post*, July 24, 1947, p. 8.

[16]"U.S. Regrets Breakdown of Peaceful Negotiations in Indonesia," *U.S. Department of State Bulletin*, 17 (August 3, 1947):230.

toward the Netherlands and therefore desires to be helpful in the new situation which has arisen in the Indies." Matthews suggested that the secretary should ask the Dutch what action they would prefer the American government to take and whether or not they desired the United States or some other friendly power to bring up the matter at the United Nations, "thus forestalling a hostile power from doing so."[17]

Following Matthews' recommendation, Marshall broached the subject of possible United Nations involvement during a conversation with Dutch officials on that same day. In response to a direct question by John Morgan of the department's Division of Northern European Affairs, the recently appointed Dutch ambassador to the United States, Eelco van Kleffens, stated his belief that there would be no advantage in having the subject raised by one of the Western democracies. He explained that the Netherlands would simply stand on its record, as it had done previously. The ambassador was confident that it would be impossible to show that international peace was being threatened by the police action; it was, he contended, purely an internal matter. Van Kleffens confidently assured Marshall that the Dutch could accomplish their military aims quickly and fully intended to resume negotiations in the near future with "responsible" elements in Indonesia.[18]

Although nothing concrete resulted from this exchange, it was significant nonetheless as a barometer of American foreign policy priorities at that time. The United States' willingness to assist the Dutch in presenting their version of developments in Indonesia to the world leaves little room for doubt that Washington's "neutral" posture toward the Dutch–Indonesian conflict was an odd brand of neutrality indeed. Matthews' memorandum and Marshall's subsequent conversation with van Kleffens reveal an unmistakably pro-Dutch orientation. The gap between the anticolonial rhetoric of the war years and the

[17]Memorandum from Matthews to Marshall, July 24, 1947, 856D.00/7-2447, DSR.

[18]Memorandum by Morgan of a conversation with van Kleffens, Jonkheer C. Reuchlin (Dutch chargé), and Marshall, July 24, 1947, in *FR*, 1947, 6:986–87. The pro-Dutch view is also reflected in a memorandum by Lovett of a conversation with van Kleffens, Rusk, Matthews, and Morgan, August 6, 1947, in Box 3, Hickerson Files, DSR.

reality of Washington's accommodating response to what was nothing less than a colonial war of reconquest was enormous.

Washington's carefully measured response to the Dutch police action led several high-ranking British officials to speculate that, American protestations to the contrary, the United States never vigorously opposed The Hague's military offensive and may have even tacitly encouraged it. "The American attitude," observed John Street, head of the North American Division of the British Foreign Office, "confirms earlier impressions that the State Department would not be dismayed by Dutch police action and the manner in which the Dutch Govt has gone out of their way to link the US Govt with us in their grateful acknowledgement of assistance received suggests that the Dutch were aware of this American attitude."[19] Mitcheson's cables from Batavia strongly corroborated that view. "Though there was certainly no official support from America for military action," he suggested in one telegram, "nevertheless I gather that the Dutch Ambassador in Washington obtained the impression, from talks with certain officials, that they felt a good deal of sympathy with the Dutch desire for a quick settlement by force." Just before the outbreak of hostilities, Mitcheson had reported to the Foreign Office that he had learned from secret "Grade A" sources "that the Dutch Government and NEI Government have reason to believe that while United States official attitude is opposed to military action here at all costs, this line is only for public consumption and that beneath the surface the Americans fully appreciate and sympathize with van Mook's desire to cut short further discussion and to settle matters promptly by force."[20] Lord Killearn also accepted this view; he informed the Foreign Office in August that he and his staff had believed all along "that American encouragement must bear some responsibility for the outbreak of hostilities in the N.E.I."[21]

These are serious charges and they require closer examination. It is certainly true, as Foreign Office representatives repeatedly noted, that Herman Baruch and Walter Foote, the senior

[19]Minute by Street, July 25, 1947, FO 371 F10031/45/62, PRO.

[20]Mitcheson to Foreign Office, July 24, 1947, FO 371 F12126/45/62, PRO; Mitcheson to Foreign Office, June 27, 1947, FO 371 F8697/45/62, PRO.

[21]Killearn to Sargent, August 21, 1947, FO 371 F12126/45/62, PRO.

American representatives at The Hague and Batavia respectively, were inclined to accept uncritically the Dutch view of Indonesian developments. Their cables to the State Department consistently reflected that prejudice. It is also true that both men believed that police action was the only viable alternative for the Netherlands, and on several occasions they made their views known to high-ranking Dutch officials. On May 23, for instance, Foote casually told Mitcheson "that he personally felt that [the] Dutch would only waste time and money by continuing negotiations." He added that "Washington was now beginning to come around to [the] local Dutch view in this connexion." In another telegram to London the British consul reported that "Foote probably did a great deal of harm by openly favoring in private conversations the Dutch plan for military action, that he considered further negotiations a waste of time and believed American opinion would accept fairly easily a *fait accompli*." The American consul general was getting old, Mitcheson explained, "and he has lived here so long that his point of view is very similar to the old Dutch settlers." Many Dutch officials "probably assumed his remarks had some backing in Washington, even though he presented them as personal views."[22] At the Dutch capital, meanwhile, Ambassador Baruch freely admitted that he believed the Dutch would be completely justified in resorting to force. He did stress that these were strictly personal views, but it is entirely likely that the Dutch did not carefully distinguish between the personal views of the United States' principal representative in the field and the official views of the American government.[23]

Despite the attitude of Foote, Baruch, and possibly a few others, however, there is no hard evidence to suggest that the State Department actually encouraged The Hague to embark on its military assault against the Republic. On the contrary, there is every reason to suspect that the Truman administration sincerely sought to prevent such action, believing that peaceful avenues of arbitration had by no means been exhausted. Yet it

[22]Mitcheson to Foreign Office, May 23 and July 24, 1947, FO 371 F7055/45/62 and F12126/45/62, PRO; minute by Allen, July 28, 1947, FO 371 F10638/45/62, PRO.

[23]Bland to Foreign Office, July 25, 1947, FO 371 F10049/45/62, PRO.

seems equally clear that Washington was unwilling to exert substantial pressure on a friendly Western ally. Given Dutch reliance on American economic assistance, that pressure could certainly have been applied. Many State Department officers simply accepted the validity of Dutch claims that Holland's desperate financial plight afforded it no alternative but military action. That common departmental view, of which the Dutch were certainly aware, coupled with the indiscreet remarks of Foote and Baruch and Washington's well-known desire to maintain harmony within the Western alliance, probably led the Netherlands to believe that the United States would not react strongly to Dutch military action. "There is little doubt," Street insisted, "that the Dutch were aware, when they opened hostilities on the 21th July, that the Americans would confine action to polite expressions of regret."[24] That judgment appears eminently reasonable.

The initial American response to the Dutch police action is probably best understood within the context of a global geopolitical strategy that defined the rehabilitation and reintegration of Western Europe as its major goal. "The greatest danger to the security of the United States," spelled out a CIA analysis prepared in September 1947, "is the possibility of economic collapse in Western Europe and the consequent accession to power of Communist elements."[25] With Dutch cooperation essential to the success of the proposed Marshall Plan, the United States could hardly afford to alienate The Hague by denouncing its colonial policy. Significantly, a Joint Chiefs of Staff study called the Netherlands "a vital area to American national security"; according to the report, Holland ranked fifth in the world as a country of direct strategic importance to the United States.[26]

American policy makers, moreover, tended to consider the Netherlands and Indonesia as inseparable. "The interest of the United States in relation to the Netherlands East Indies," Hornbeck wrote in 1948, "cannot reasonably be separated from our

[24]Minute by Street, September 4, 1947, FO 371 F12126/45/62, PRO.

[25]Central Intelligence Agency, "Review of the World Situation as It Relates to the Security of the United States," CIA 1, September 26, 1947, President's Secretary's File, Truman Papers, Harry S. Truman Library, Independence, Mo.

[26]Report by Joint Chiefs of Staff, April 29, 1947, in *FR*, 1947, 1:741–46.

interest and concern in relation to the Netherlands in Europe."[27] Viewing Indonesia through a European prism, American officials reasoned as follows: Holland constituted an integral part of Europe; the rehabilitation of the Dutch economy was necessary for the full recovery of all of Western Europe; and the early resumption of trade between the Netherlands and Indonesia was in turn essential to Holland's revitalization. The Truman administration was quite obviously unwilling to endanger its entire European policy on account of a brash colonial military adventure, especially since crucial negotiations regarding the proposed Marshall Plan were currently taking place in Paris. Besides, Dutch officials convincingly insisted that only military measures could ensure the conditions necessary for a return to full productivity in Indonesia, a position to which American diplomats were quite sympathetic.

Concerned in large part with its own imperial interests, Great Britain took a far less accommodating view of the Dutch police action. In a telegram to the Foreign Office, Lord Killearn suggested that much more than just the Netherlands East Indies was at stake. "As one of the colonial powers the behavior of the Dutch will reflect discredit on ourselves and the French," he pointed out, "and may well prejudice such delicate matters as [the] relationship between Europe and Asia which in Malaya, in Burma and even in India is at a critical stage."[28] John Street's evaluation of the Dutch offensive was more blunt. The police action, he stated, was "basically stupid"; by resorting to open hostilities, "the Dutch in the long run (and possibly within the next few years) will lose far more . . . than by trying to be patient and limiting their demands to what an Indonesian coalition would accept." He added that the British were now "in the embarrassing position of trying to follow an uneasy compromise between our own position vis-a-vis South East Asia and our desire not to split Western Europe."[29]

Although eager to bring about a rapid halt to the hostilities,

[27]Stanley K. Hornbeck, "The United States and the Netherlands East Indies," *Annals of the American Academy of Political and Social Science*, 255 (January 1948):130–31.

[28]Killearn to Foreign Office, July 18, 1947, FO 371 F9741/45/62, PRO.

[29]Minute by Street, July 21, 1947, FO 371 F9759/45/62, PRO.

London was unwilling to accept again the role of sole mediator of the dispute. Instead, Bevin hoped that the United States would accept dual mediation responsibility with Britain to put an early end to a conflict that "may be incalculably damaging to the peace and stability of Asia and to the revival of economic prosperity in that and other parts of the world."[30] Following the foreign secretary's instructions, on July 24 Lord Inverchapel delivered to the State Department an aide-mémoire that expressed the British government's distress at the recent turn of events in the East Indies. The military assault "represented a breakdown of the constant efforts made by His Majesty's Government, with the concurrence and support of the United States Government, during the past two years to bring about a peaceful solution of the problem. It may be that militarily the Dutch will gain an initial success, but the resulting situation in South East Asia will make the position of the western powers very difficult indeed." Accordingly, Great Britain suggested that the United States join with it in inducing the Netherlands to accept some form of arbitral solution to the conflict.[31]

Washington's reply was immediate but negative. Acting Secretary Robert Lovett explained to Lord Balfour in a conference that same day that the State Department was convinced that the Dutch would never agree to another proposal for outside arbitration, as they considered the police action to be a strictly internal affair. Balfour explained the American position in a cable to the Foreign Office: "To approach the Netherlands Government with such suggestions at present time would, as State Department saw it, merely expose us to a rebuff and might possibly prejudice the prospect of whole-hearted Dutch cooperation in Paris talks." Lovett also reasoned that a direct offer to the Dutch by two friendly powers could still not prevent unfriendly powers from bringing the case before the Security Council.[32]

That fear was almost immediately realized when India suddenly threatened to bring the Indonesian conflict before the United

[30]Bevin to Inverchapel, July 23, 1947, FO 371 F10038/45/62, PRO.

[31]Aide-mémoire from British Embassy to Department of State, July 24, 1947, in *FR*, 1947, 6:987–89; Douglas to Lovett and Marshall, July 25, 1947, 856E.00/7-2547, DSR.

[32]Balfour to Foreign Office, July 24, 1947, FO 371 F10031/45/62, PRO.

Nations. In a telegram to the British Foreign Office on July 25, Nehru argued that the

> so-called police action by [the] Dutch is [a] carefully and long prepared military campaign whose real purpose is [to] inflict complete military defeat on [the] Republic and prepare [the] way for [a] political settlement entirely favorable to [the] Dutch. No one in India or anywhere in Asia will believe that if [the] Governments of [the] United Kingdom and [the] United States of America really desired [to] bring this conflict to [an] end they could not do it immediately without military intervention. Holland's economic as well as political dependence on these two countries is such that its Government could not afford [to] forfeit their good will and support by [a] refusal to end hostilities and reach [a] settlement with [the] Indonesians by peaceful means.

The Indian prime minister declared that it was time that the United States and Great Britain determined what positive action they could take to bring about an immediate end to the conflict. If neither nation were willing to become involved, "we shall have no option but to take the matter before the UN Security Council." In conclusion, Nehru warned that "the failure for whatever reason of these two great powers [to] intervene effectively in [the] cause of peace and on [the] side of people struggling for freedom cannot but create [the] most unfortunate impression in India and all Asian countries."[33]

John Carter Vincent, head of the State Department's Office of Far Eastern Affairs, alerted Secretary Marshall to the Indian threat on July 28. Unless the United States acted quickly, he pointed out, India would probably place the issue in "the most extreme form, thus inviting support from the Soviet Union and

[33]Quoted in Henry Grady (U.S. ambassador, India) to Marshall, July 26, 1947, in *FR* 1947, 6:990–91. See also Government of India to Secretary of State for India, July 18, 1947, FO 371 F10039/45/62, PRO; W. Norman Brown, *The United States and India, Pakistan, Bangladesh* (Cambridge: Harvard University Press, 1972), pp. 368–69. India would not become officially independent until August 15, 1947. For an examination of the American response to the decolonization of India, see Gary R. Hess, *America Encounters India, 1941–1947* (Baltimore: Johns Hopkins University Press, 1971); R. C. Jauhrai, *American Diplomacy and Independence for India* (Bombay: Vora, 1970); A. Guy Hope, *America and Swaraj: The U.S. Role in Indian Independence* (Washington: Public Affairs Press, 1968).

tending to divide the Security Council into a Russian-Asiatic bloc against the Anglo-American Governments and Governments of Western Europe." In such an event "it would be difficult for the United States Government to take a completely neutral and disinterested position."[34] Consequently, Vincent suggested to Lovett that it might become desirable for the Netherlands to request either American or British mediation in accordance with the United Nations Charter.[35]

The proposed action of the Indian government placed Washington in a quandary. The keynote of American policy was Western Europe; U.S. officials considered the postwar rehabilitation of that area, as envisioned by the Marshall Plan, to be essential to American interests—not only to restore a vital market for American goods, but also to arrest the danger of Communist advances in Europe. Marshall summarized this objective in a major policy address on July 14. Either the United States "must finish the task of assisting these countries to adjust themselves to the changed demands of a new age," he said, or "it would be faced with a radical alteration of its own position in the world."[36] But by concentrating on Western Europe, the United States did not intend to isolate itself from other world problems, for, as the Truman Doctrine indicated, every region of the globe was a potential area of interest in the struggle between the United States and the Soviet Union. Indonesia was particularly significant in this regard, as a report by a subcommittee of the State–Army–Navy–Air Force Coordinating Committee emphasized:

> Indonesia is one of the most important regions of Southeast Asia because of its large population, wealth, and strategic location. Indonesia is also in the forefront of the postwar nationalist struggle of Southeast Asiatic peoples that calls for a readjustment of old colonial

[34]Memorandum from Vincent to Marshall, July 28, 1947, 501.BC Indonesia/7-2847, DSR. These problems were anticipated earlier in a memorandum by S. K. C. Kooper and Joseph Scott, July 23, 1947, in folder labeled "N.E.I. 1947–1948: UNO & Other Organizations," Box 13, Records of the Office of the Philippines and Southeast Asian Affairs, DSR (hereafter cited as PSA Records).

[35]Memorandum from Vincent to Lovett, July 29, 1947, in *FR* 1947, 6:993.

[36]George Marshall, "A Program for Preservation of our National Interests and of European Civilization," address to the Governors' Conference at Salt Lake City, in *U.S. Department of State Bulletin*, 17 (July 27, 1947):184–85.

> relationships. The outcome of this struggle and the conditions surrounding it will have a profound effect on the future attitudes of Southeast Asia's peoples toward the Western democracies on the one hand and toward the USSR on the other.

The report concluded that "from a long range point of view, an Indonesian population hostile to the Western powers would make Indonesia particularly vulnerable in the event of war," whereas "a friendly and prosperous Indonesia might have great value as an arsenal in the Pacific."[37]

A major danger posed by the Dutch–Indonesian hostilities, from Washington's perspective, was that a display of official American support for the Dutch position could incur the wrath of the newly emerging areas of the world. This, again, was the classic dilemma that had been haunting the United States since the closing years of World War II: it could not risk alienating its traditional European allies by pursuing an anticolonial policy, but neither could it afford to abandon America's historical identification with the principles of self-determination and thereby forfeit the respect and support of Asian and African nationalist movements. Henry Villard, deputy director of the Office of Near Eastern and African Affairs, elucidated the problem posed by Nehru's threat to bring the Indonesian crisis before the Security Council. "Under present circumstances," he reasoned, "the U.S. might be placed in an extremely unfortunate position of opposing Indonesia and her supporters. Such a position could do immeasurable damage to American prestige in the Near, Middle and Far East."[38]

On July 30 Marshall informed Truman that the Indian government had announced its intention to raise the subject of the Dutch police action in the Security Council. Should it do so, he contended, the United States would be placed in a "difficult

[37] State–Army–Navy–Air Force Coordinating Committee (SWNCC), Subcommittee on Far Eastern Affairs, Country Report on Indonesia, July 22, 1947, SWNCC Records, DSR.

[38] Villard to Charles E. Bohlen (counselor to State Department), July 29, 1947, in *FR*, 6:994–96. See also H. Gordon Minnigesode (American consul, India) to Marshall, July 28, 1947, 856D.00/7-2847, DSR; memorandum from James K. Penfield (Office of Far Eastern Affairs) to Landon, August 22, 1947, 856E.00/8-547, DSR.

position." He spelled out the problems presented by UN involvement: "We would not be able to support the Dutch position involving the use of force nor to oppose the establishment of a United Nations committee for investigation or settlement which would be bitterly resented by the Dutch and which could be exploited by Communist propaganda." The best hope of avoiding this dilemma in the Security Council would be "for the Dutch Government to cease hostilities on its own initiative," or "for the Dutch Government to accept an offer of mediation." Marshall recommended that the president authorize him to inform The Hague that the United States would be willing to mediate the dispute, either by itself or jointly with Great Britain. If the United States pursued this course, he reasoned, when the case came up before the Security Council it would then be possible to state that methods of conciliation were already in progress, and, in accordance with the United Nations Charter, "discussion should be held in abeyance pending their outcome."[39] Truman approved Marshall's recommendation, and on July 31, 1947, Lovett telephoned van Kleffens and indicated to him that the U.S. government was disposed to be helpful to the Dutch in this delicate matter; it "would be available to offer its good offices in the hopes that it might remove from or compose the difficulties in the Security Council."[40]

British officials were piqued by Washington's failure to consult with them before making this unilateral offer. "It is further evidence," suggested Street, "of the thoroughly unhelpful attitude adopted by the Americans since the trouble began."[41] On August 1 Balfour asked a State Department official why his nation had not been informed in advance of the American offer. He was told that President Truman's absence from Washington due to his mother's death caused an unavoidable delay in the American decision, and in addition that the Dutch had made it abundantly clear that British mediation would not be proper, as two Com-

[39]Memorandum from Marshall to Truman, July 30, 1947, in *FR*, 1947, 6:997. See also memorandum by Robert McClintock (Office of Special Political Affairs) of a conversation with Herschel Johnson, July 24, 1947, in folder labeled "N.E.I. 1947–1948, UNO & and Other Organizations," Box 13, PSA Records, DSR.

[40]Memorandum by Lovett of a telephone conversation with van Kleffens, July 31, 1947, in *FR*, 1947, 6:10001–3.

[41]Minute by Street, August 1, 1947, FO 371 F10285/45/62, PRO.

monwealth countries, India and Australia, were preparing to bring the Indonesian conflict before the Security Council. On August 4 H. Freeman Matthews conceded to Balfour that the State Department had been remiss in not informing the British in advance of its mediation offer, but said it had been an "off-the-cuff" offer, prompted by Australia's decision to go before the Security Council.[42]

Foreign Office officials were unconvinced by these American rationalizations. Street characterized the U.S. offer as "a breach of good manners." Allen suggested that Washington acted "with what can only be described as bad manners and bad taste" in making its unilateral offer. If the major role in achieving a settlement fell to the Americans, he noted, all London could do was "hope they will keep us fully informed as we kept them over last two years."[43]

The suspicion that the United States was actually maneuvering to assert its own influence in Southeast Asia troubled many British diplomats. "I think there is little doubt that the American offer of mediation is *not* disinterested," wrote one Foreign Office representative.[44] The perceptions of Maberly Dening are particularly revealing in this regard. "I must admit," he wrote on August 2, "I have little faith in the American ability to use their good offices with tact and discretion." He added that "it looks as if they would bully the Indonesians to do all the Dutch want them to do. If this happens, India and Australia will expect us to resist this U.S. imperialism, and we shall find ourselves in a pretty dilemma. I am afraid I do not trust the U.S. at all in their Far Eastern policy."[45] These remarks suggest that British thinking on U.S. interests and policy in Southeast Asia had come full circle in less than two years. It is certainly ironic that Dening, who in 1945 had warned that any American involvement in the Indies "would probably be all on the side of the Indonesians," now feared that a U.S. presence in Indonesia would work almost completely to the

[42]Balfour to Foreign Office, August 1 and August 4, 1947, FO 371 F10444/45/62 and F10472/45/62, PRO.

[43]Minutes by Street, August 5, 1947, and Allen, August 2, 1947, FO 371 F10444/45/62 and F10496/45/62, PRO.

[44]Foreign Office minute, August 8, 1947, FO 371 F10706/45/62, PRO.

[45]Minute by Dening, August 2, 1947, FO 371 F10496/45/62, PRO.

benefit of the Dutch. And U.S. action in the Security Council did little to dispel these fears.

The Security Council debates on the Indonesian question opened on July 31, following requests by India and Australia.[46] "For days," the Indian representative lamented, "we have waited for someone, for anybody, to bring better counsel to the Netherlands Government; for days we have watched with horror and disappointment this senseless war by one of our own Members."[47] The Australian delegate added that further delay would not be justified. The Dutch–Indonesian conflict "is one of international concern and already has far-reaching repercussions. It affects the well-being and stability of the whole of the Southwest Pacific and South-east Asia. . . . The Council should also note that the hostilities proceeding are not merely a police action but are in fact warfare; that is, in international law, armed conflict between two States."[48]

In the subsequent debate, van Kleffens took strong exception to the view that the republic was in fact a state. "The Republic of Indonesia is not a sovereign state," he argued, "any more than the State of East Indonesia or of Borneo." Indeed, "it is a political entity to be affiliated ultimately with the other two states I have named." Van Kleffens claimed that the republic was comparable to New York State or Utah or Parahiba in Brazil, and reiterated his government's contention that the Dutch police action was strictly an internal affair of the Netherlands and not an appropriate matter for international concern.[49] Herschel V. Johnson, the

[46]UN S/477, July 30, 1947; UN S/479, July 30, 1947. For an interpretation of Indian and Australian actions within the context of their respective foreign policies, see Ross N. Berkes and Mohinder S. Bedi, *The Diplomacy of India: Indian Foreign Policy in the UN* (Stanford, Calif.: Stanford University Press, 1958), pp. 38–41, 67–69; Ravindra Varma, *Australia and Southeast Asia: The Crystallisation of a Relationship* (New Delhi: Abhinav, 1974), pp. 91–95; W. J. Hudson, "Australia and Indonesian Independence," *Journal of Southeast Asian History*, 8 (September 1967):226–39.

[47]SCOR, 2d yr., 171st meeting, July 31, 1947, p. 1621.

[48]Ibid., pp. 1622–23. See also aide-mémoire from Australian government to Commonwealth Relations Office, July 25, 1947, FO 371 F10116/45/62, PRO; memorandum by John C. Ross (U.S. Mission to UN) of a conversation with Ralph Harry (Australian delegation), July 30, 1947, in Box 81, Records of the U.S. Mission to the UN, RG 84, DSR.

[49]SCOR, 2d yr., 171st meeting, July 31, 1947, pp. 1619–20. For an examination of the complex legal technicalities involved in assessing the republic's sovereignty,

American representative, tried to avoid the question of the republic's status in international law entirely. "I do think, however," he remarked, "that the Council must take cognizance of fighting on such a scale and in such conditions that the peace of that region and ultimately of the world might be put in danger."[50]

On August 1, after two days of acrimonious discussion, the council passed a resolution calling for a cease-fire, the first order of its kind ever issued by the United Nations. The American-sponsored resolution read simply: "The Security Council, noting with concern the hostilities in progress between the armed forces of the Netherlands and the Republic of Indonesia, calls upon the parties: (a) to cease hostilities forthwith, and (b) to settle their disputes by arbitration or by other peaceful means and keep the Security County informed about the progress of the settlement."[51]

Although this American compromise proposal was considerably weaker than the Australian resolution that the United States had refused to back—which had called on the Dutch and Indonesians to cease all hostilities immediately and submit their dispute to arbitration by a third party, as provided by the Linggadjati agreement—it was hailed nevertheless as a major triumph for the United Nations. George Barrett of the *New York Times* reflected this optimistic attitude when he commented that "the United Nations had probably won its first major victory and through this victory had given the new international organization a sorely needed boost in prestige." Likewise, Johnson said that it was a milestone decision that served notice that the United Nations intended to take action wherever necessary to maintain peace.[52]

Although both the Dutch and the Indonesians promptly assured the Security Council that they would immediately comply with its cease-fire resolution, hostilities continued unabated.

---

see Ali Sastroamidjojo and Robert Delson, "The Status of the Republic of Indonesia in International Law," *Columbia Law Review*, 49 (March 1949):344–61.

[50]SCOR, 2d yr., 172nd meeting, August 1, 1947, pp. 1657–58.

[51]UN S/459. See also Alastair M. Taylor, *Indonesian Independence and the United Nations* (Ithaca: Cornell University Press, 1960), pp. 50–51; J. Foster Collins, "The United Nations and Indonesia," *International Conciliation*, March 1950, pp. 126–28.

[52]*New York Times*, August 4, 1947, p. 3; Taylor, *Indonesian Independence*, p. 51.

Each side accused the other of ignoring the resolution and defended its own military measures as purely retaliatory. The republic sent several letters to the council, requesting that an arbitration commission be set up to implement the cease-fire order and help to mediate the basic issues dividing the two parties. With conditions rapidly deteriorating—and the ineffectiveness of its resolution becoming increasingly apparent—the Security Council reopened debate on the Indonesian question on August 6.[53]

At this juncture the United States offered its good offices to the Indonesian Republic for the purpose of mediating the conflict. On August 6 Consul General Foote informed republican officials that the United States was prepared to assist the two disputants to settle their differences. The Dutch had already accepted a similar American offer on August 3; now the State Department anxiously awaited the reply of the republican government. On August 7 Indonesian leaders announced their acceptance of the American offer of good offices, but at the same time they asked the United States to use its influence to persuade the Dutch government and the Security Council that an international arbitration commission should be dispatched without delay to Indonesia. Initially puzzled by the seemingly contradictory Indonesian response, American diplomats ultimately interpreted it as a rejection of their overture in favor of UN intervention.[54] In the words of the British consul general at Batavia, the Indonesian reply amounted to a "polite refusal of American mediation."[55]

A significant shift was already occurring in Indonesian attitudes toward the United States; the republic was beginning to believe that its interests would be better served by the United Nations. Indonesian republicans, who had previously displayed vigorous pro-American sentiments, now began to suspect "that covertly the United States was partial to the Dutch and that, if it had strongly desired to, it could have stopped them from resort-

[53]UN S/469, August 5, 1947; UN S/475, August 6, 1947.

[54]Marshall to Foote, August 4, 1947, in *FR*, 1947, 6:1012–13; Foote to Marshall, August 8, 1947, in ibid., pp. 1017–18; Lovett to Foote, August 14, 1947, in ibid., pp. 1028–29; Gani to President of Security Council, August 7, 1947, UN S/477.

[55]Mitcheson to Foreign Office, August 8, 1947, FO, 371 F10791/45/62, PRO.

ing to force."[56] In the ongoing Security Council debates, the Soviet Union berated the American proposal as a devious attempt to circumvent the United Nations. Soviet delegate Andrei Gromyko charged: "The attempt of the United States, in the matter of arbitration, to force its 'good offices' on the Indonesian Government and the Indonesian people, despite the Indonesians' wish that arbitration should be handled by a commission of the Security Council, indicate a lack of respect not only for the Indonesians, who are asking the United Nations to defend their vital interests, but also for the Security Council."[57] There was a certain element of truth to the Soviet charges; American officials feared that Security Council action might prove embarrassing to the Netherlands.[58]

The republic, however, continued to seek United Nations intervention, and on August 12, over Dutch objections, the Security Council voted to invite a republican delegation to present its case before that body. On August 14 Sjahrir delivered a passionate exposition of the republic's plight. After detailing the history of the Indonesian nationalist movement and the frustrating course of Dutch–republican negotiations, he concluded with a ringing indictment of Dutch policy. "In view of these facts," Sjahrir said, "it appears that the Netherlands Government has never at any time sincerely desired a peaceful settlement with the Republic. On the other hand, all Netherlands action—political, military and economic—was nothing but preparation for aggressive action against its partner in an agreement." At the following session the former prime minister pleaded, "How can there be free negotiations when one party stands with a pistol pointed at the head of the other? We ask for direct action of the Security

[56]Kahin, *Nationalism and Revolution*, p. 214. See also U.S. Department of State, OIR, Division of Research for the Far East, "Major Developments and Trends in the Netherlands-Indonesian Conflict," Situation Report—Southern Areas, no. 3480.40, October 8, 1947, DSR; Chaudhry, *Indonesian Struggle*, p. 164.

[57]SCOR, 2d yr., 187th meeting, August 19, 1947, pp. 2060–61. See also Ruth T. McVey, *The Soviet View of the Indonesian Revolution* (Ithaca: Cornell University Modern Indonesia Project, 1957), pp. 21–23.

[58]Memorandum from Gordon Knox to Herschel Johnson and Charles P. Noyes, August 16, 1947, in folder labeled "N.E.I., 1947–1948: UNO & Other Organizations," Box 13, PSA Records, DSR; memorandum by Lovett of a conversation with van Kleffens, Rusk, Matthews, and Morgan, August 6, 1947, in Box 3, Hickerson Files, DSR.

Council because we have no faith in the honesty and good will of the Netherlands Government."[59]

During these Security Council debates, two distinct problems emerged: the maintenance of the cease-fire order and the promotion of a long-term political settlement. A solution to the first problem was of urgent importance, as Dutch military operations were continuing under the guise of mopping-up actions. On August 25 the Soviet Union proposed that a commission composed of all Security Council members be set up to supervise the cease-fire. When the French vetoed that resolution, the council then voted to accept an American proposal to establish what came to be called the Consular Commission. This commission, which in a conscious effort to exclude the Soviet Union comprised only those council members that had career consular officers in Indonesia, was instructed to submit a report on the observance of the cease-fire order to the council.[60] Then, in another effort to halt the continuing hostilities, the Security Council issued a new cease-fire order on August 26, calling on the parties "to adhere strictly" to its earlier resolution forbidding any further military activity.[61]

In an attempt to effect a long-term political agreement between the Netherlands and Indonesia, the council members proposed various resolutions aimed at establishing an arbitral body to mediate the dispute. This was the most divisive issue. The republic requested compulsory arbitration, whereas the Netherlands expressed its preference for some neutral government, such as the United States, to tender its good offices. As the Security Council split into blocs on this pivotal question, the

[59]SCOR, 2d yr., 184th meeting, August 14, 1947, pp. 2002–3, and 187th meeting, August 19, 1947, p. 2075.

[60]Ibid., 194th meeting, August 25, 1947, pp. 2197–2220; Collins, "United Nations and Indonesia," p. 129; Taylor, *Indonesian Independence*, p. 152. Philip C. Jessup explained the strategy to exclude the Soviets from the Consular Commission: "The Western powers then resorted to a device which insured the nonparticipation of the Soviet Union in the supervisory body. It was a little less obvious than saying that the commission should not be composed of the representatives of those members of the Security Council whose names, in French, did not begin with 'U,' but the result was achieved by having the commission composed of the representatives of those members of the Security Council who had career consuls in Batavia—the Soviet Union had no consul there" (*The Birth of Nations* [New York: Columbia University Press, 1974], p. 46).

[61]UN S/521, August 26, 1947.

United States again drafted an acceptable compromise proposal. Its resolution, which was adopted on August 26, brought into being what was later called the Good Offices Committee of the Security Council. This committee would be composed of three member nations; each party to the dispute would designate one country to represent its point of view, and those two nations in turn would select the third member.[62] By September 18 the composition of the committee was completed. As expected, the Netherlands named Belgium and the republic selected Australia, their principal advocates respectively in the council debates, while the United States, because of its middle-ground position in the debates and its enormous prestige as the preeminent world power, was designated to occupy the strategic third spot on the commission.[63]

Despite the two cease-fire orders by the Security Council, conditions in Indonesia continued to deteriorate. The Consular Commission, which had begun to investigate various Dutch- and republican-controlled areas in Java and Sumatra on September 3, became so alarmed at the prospect of a return to full-scale hostilities that it transmitted an urgent interim report to the council on September 22. The report stressed that the cease-fire orders had not been fully effective, as substantial fighting continued to rage throughout the archipelago. In this and a subsequent report on October 11, the Consular Commission noted that the Dutch and republicans had pursued widely divergent interpretations of the cease-fire directives. Whereas the republican government had ordered its troops to halt all hostilities and remain in their positions, the Netherlands government had instructed its army "to proceed with the restoration of law and order within the limits of the lines laid down by it." The net effect was that what the Dutch considered to be legitimate mopping-up operations, the republic regarded as a blatant effort to extend Dutch control. There was a growing possibility, the commission cautioned, that the already shaky truce would break down entirely, leading once more to all-out war. Colonel Oliver

[62]UN S/514, August 22, 1947; SCOR, 2d yr., 193rd meeting, August 22, 1947, pp. 2177–78; UN S/525, August 26, 1947; Collins, "United Nations and Indonesia," pp. 131–34.

[63]Taylor, *Indonesian Independence*, p. 55.

Dixon, the senior American military adviser to the commission, urgently informed the State Department that he believed the Dutch were attempting by military means to reestablish their control over Java.[64]

In light of the Consular Commission's findings, there was general agreement in the Security Council that the initial cease-fire resolutions had been sadly ineffective. Opinions varied sharply, however, on methods to remedy the problem. Both the Soviet Union and Poland submitted draft resolutions calling for a withdrawal of Dutch forces to the areas they had occupied before the police action of July 20. The newly named American representative to the United Nations, Warren Austin, countered that the Security Council did not possess sufficient information on the complex crisis to justify such a decision or to be certain it would not prejudice the rights, claims, or positions of the parties. Although Austin personally favored the withdrawal of Dutch troops, the State Department instructed him to oppose the Soviet-Polish motion, as it would be "clearly not acceptable to the Dutch." Accordingly, he argued that it would be far more effective to request the Good Offices Committee, then en route to Indonesia, to help the parties work out a cease-fire observance. This proposal, which was included in an American-sponsored draft resolution, was approved on November 1, one day after the defeat of two Soviet-backed proposals calling for troop withdrawals.[65]

An analysis of the various resolutions adopted demonstrates that the United States successfully manipulated the Security Council to serve its own policy objectives. American policy makers had initially sought to avoid UN intervention entirely. Intent on maintaining the support of both the European colonial pow-

[64]UN S/573, September 22, 1947; UN S/581, October 11, 1947; memorandum by Landon of a conversation with Oliver Dixon, October 13, 1947, 856E.00/10-1347, DSR. David McCallum, the U.S. naval attaché in Batavia, reached a similar conclusion. See McCallum to CNO, October 24, 1947, Naval Attaché Reports File, WNRC.

[65]UN S/575, October 3, 1947; UN S/568, October 29, 1947; memorandum from Landon to Butterworth, October 15, 1947, in folder labeled "N.E.I. 1947–1948: UNO & Other Organizations," Box 13, PSA Records, DSR; SCOR 2d yr., 213th meeting, October 22, 1947, p. 2604; UN S/588, October 27, 1947; Taylor, *Indonesian Independence*, pp. 61–62.

ers and the newly emerging areas—the term "Third World" had not yet been coined—the State Department repeatedly expressed concern that the UN debates would force Washington to clarify its position on the Dutch police action, thereby endangering its cherished "neutrality." As it turned out, these apprehensions were misplaced. Instead, the United States managed to emerge as the key nation in the Security Council debates, drafting every major resolution that was ultimately accepted. Far from relinquishing its role as a neutral in the great colonial debate, then, the United States greatly enhanced it.

Not only was the United States responsible for all compromise proposals of the council, but it also shaped them so subtly that they consistently favored the Dutch position, while appearing to be reasonable and impartial. When Australia and the Soviet Union urged the establishment of an arbitration commission, for example, the United States carefully maneuvered to defeat that proposal in favor of a Good Offices Committee. The distinction was significant: Security Council arbitration, which the republic wanted, would have been binding on both parties, and obviously detrimental to the interests of the Netherlands as the aggressor, whereas the Good Offices Committee could only counsel and advise, a procedure that the Dutch could more comfortably accept. Moreover, by carefully guarding its middle-ground position during the council debates, the United States was assured that it would be the logical—indeed, only—choice for the pivotal third position on the Good Offices Committee. In the military sphere, furthermore, the United States consistently blocked attempts to force the Dutch to withdraw their troops, much to the gratification of its European ally. American action in this regard represented a superb example of the United States' postwar use of the United Nations to suit its own purposes. By shrouding itself in the robes of the even-handed compromiser, the United States not only disguised its pro-Dutch orientation, but also managed to accomplish its earlier goal of extending good offices to help settle the dispute, and did so in a multilateral rather than a bilateral fashion.[66]

The Good Offices Committee (GOC) held its first informal

[66]A detailed account of Security Council voting on the major proposals concerning Indonesia can be found in Sydney D. Bailey, *Voting in the Security Council* (Bloomington: Indiana University Press, 1969), pp. 224–26.

meeting in Sydney, Australia, on October 20, 1947. The committee faced a nearly impossible task; although formed by the Security Council to help settle a dispute of the greatest complexity, it had not been granted power commensurate with its responsibility. On the contrary, it had only the right to make suggestions to the two parties, and even then, only when requested by both sides. Indeed, Lovett privately admitted to Balfour that the State Department did not see any way in which the committee could succeed.[67] The American representative to the GOC, Frank Porter Graham, the highly respected president of the University of North Carolina and an experienced arbitrator of labor disputes, later detailed the committee's problems:

> The committee at all times was up against such realities as: (1) not only the lack of power to act as arbitrators but also the lack of power even to mediate the dispute; and therefore, (2) the lack of power to make public its suggestions to the parties; (3) the necessity for the committee to be unanimous in order for its confidential suggestions to the parties to have some moral power; (4) the power of either one of the parties to continue to veto any suggestion of the committee even when unanimous; (5) the possibility of the political overthrow of either cabinet or the realignment of the political parties on the basis of the negotiations in the Indonesian dispute.[68]

Graham and his equally distinguished colleagues—Richard C. Kirby, who had served on the Australian Commonwealth Court of Arbitration, and Paul van Zeeland, who had formerly been both premier and foreign minister of Belgium—began exploratory negotiations with representatives of the Netherlands and the republic on their arrival in Indonesia in later October. These initial meetings quickly revealed the limitations of the GOC's role. Much to the disappointment of republican officials, Graham admitted to Prime Minister Sjarifuddin that the GOC did not have the authority to compose the dispute, only to "assist in the pacific settlement."[69] On November 9 Henri van Vreden-

[67]Inverchapel to Foreign Office, FO 371 F11910/45/62, PRO.

[68]Statement of Senator Graham on the Indonesian Situation, April 5, 1949, U.S. Congress, Senate, 81st Cong., 1st sess.,*Congressional Record*, 95:3921.

[69]Summary Record of Eighth Meeting of the Good Offices Committee, October 29, 1947, UN S/AC.10/SR.8, in Records of the Good Offices Committee, Dag Hammarskjold Library, United Nations, New York (hereafter cited as GOC Records).

burch, head of the Dutch delegation, assured the committee that the Netherlands government would accept its assistance in helping to work out a cease-fire. But, he added candidly, "discussions of a political nature should as a rule be excluded from the discussions regarding the implementation of the cease-fire resolution."[70]

The Netherlands, then, was simply unwilling to countenance effective GOC intervention; it had already accomplished most of its major military aims and would have had nothing to gain by submitting the problem to an impartial arbitration commission. As Graham later observed, "A strong obstructing Dutch factor was the underlying and not always submerged determination of some powerful economic and political interests in the Netherlands not really to use the Committee of Good Offices and to eliminate the Republic from any real part in the preparation for an organization of the promised United States of Indonesia."[71] The Dutch quite obviously believed that time was on their side; they could apply political and economic pressures to destroy the republic as a viable entity or at least to render it powerless as a significant political force in the archipelago. With such clear-cut advantages over its already severely truncated adversary, the Netherlands was perfectly content to allow a further deterioration of the republic's position—and it was certainly not interested in having a meddlesome UN organ interfere in what it continued to regard as an internal matter.[72] One Dutch diplomat admitted that his nation's strategic goal was "simply to divide [Java] into an eastern and western half."[73] As the intransigence of their position became more and more apparent, Alfred Brooks of the Australian delegation to the GOC contemptuously characterized the Dutch as "Prussians without guts."[74]

[70]Memorandum from Dutch Delegation to GOC, November 9, 1947, UC S/AC.10/50, in ibid.

[71]Statement of Graham, April 5, 1949, in *Congressional Record*, 95:3922.

[72]Francis M. Shepherd (acting British consul general, Batavia) to Foreign Office, November 28, 1947, FO 371 F16113/45/62, PRO; minute by Street, December 10, 1947, ibid.; Taylor, *Indonesian Independence*, pp. 279–81; Kahin, *Nationalism and Revolution*, pp. 223–24.

[73]U.S. Naval Attaché, Nanking, to CNO, August 21, 1947, Army-Intelligence Document File, RG 319, WNRC.

[74]Quoted in a conversation between Frank Graham and Henry Brandis (Graham's assistant on the GOC), June 9, 1962, in Southern Oral History Program, University of North Carolina, Chapel Hill, N.C.

The Dutch police action had severely crippled the republic. Nearly two-thirds of Java, including its major producing areas, as well as the major economic centers of Sumatra, were now under Dutch control. Sharply reduced in size and economic resources, the republic desperately longed for outside assistance. "Indos ardently desire action by Security Council at once," reported the American naval attaché stationed in Batavia, "for they know Dutch have power to eliminate present Indo Gov if Dutch choose to disregard world opinion and take remaining cities in Java."[75] As a result of the timely action of the Security Council, noted a republican memorandum to the GOC, "the Netherlands Government was unable to accomplish the military domination of the islands." The Dutch did succeed "in gaining control of the main economic areas before August 4th. Consequently, any delay in reaching an overall political settlement, and the implementation of the cease fire, will enable the Netherlands Government to consolidate its economic gains, and must therefore inevitably weaken the position of the Republic. . . . We feel sure," concluded the statement signed by Sjarifuddin, "that it was not the intention of the Security Council that the rights and interests of one party should be prejudiced by the acts of aggression of the other party."[76] With its position now virtually hopeless, the republican government depended on prompt and effective action by the GOC to ensure its very survival.

Hampered by its lack of real power, the GOC nonetheless worked to bring the two parties to the bargaining table. The first major problem it encountered was the selection of a neutral site for the talks. The Dutch insisted that the meetings be held somewhere in Indonesia, while the republicans announced their strong opposition to holding the sessions in Dutch-controlled territory. Joseph Scott of the American delegation, a representative of the State Department's Division of International Security Affairs, proposed the perfect compromise solution: he suggested that the meetings be held on a neutral ship provided by

[75]McCallum to CNO, August 27, 1947, in Naval Operational Archives, Washington Navy Yard.

[76]Memorandum from Republic of Indonesia to GOC, November 28, 1947, UN S/AC.10/46, GOC Records, UN Library, New York. See also Sjahrir to Killearn, September 6, 1947, FO 371 F12416/45/62, PRO; statement by Sjarifuddin to GOC, December 10, 1947, UN S/AC.10/CONF.2/SR.3, Annex II, GOC Records, UN Library.

the U.S. government and anchored in Indonesian waters. Although the State Department initially resisted this proposal, fearing that an American vessel would tend to overemphasize Washington's intervention in Indonesia, Graham insisted and his view prevailed. With this recommendation acceptable to both parties, the United States commissioned the U.S.S. *Renville* to serve as the symbolic vessel.[77]

While awaiting the arrival of the *Renville*, the GOC began to explore possible talking points between the Dutch and Indonesian delegations. Speaking before the representatives of both parties on December 7, Graham remarked that the responsibility for a settlement lay mainly with the Dutch and the Indonesians. The GOC "had brought no magic from Lake Success," he said; it possessed only "faith in the miracles of the human spirit." The American representative noted that the United Nations was organizing a political framework for the peaceful settlement of disputes corresponding to the interdependent economic framework of the modern world. It was the responsibility of the delegates to transform the area of high potential for conflict in Indonesia—whose economic resources were desperately needed in the world—into an area of high potential for peace and freedom.[78]

The following day, the first meeting was held on board the *Renville*. On the recommendation of Scott and Charlton Ogburn, a member of the State Department's Division of Southeast Asian Affairs, Graham presented the view that the two parties should adopt the Linggadjati agreement as a working basis for discussion.[79] Drafted in the form of "a proposal submitted for consideration," the American suggestion reasoned:

> Had no relationship between the parties ever been defined, the concepts of a relationship would have to be explored without prec-

[77]Shepherd to Foreign Office (reporting a conversation with Graham), November 27, 1947, FO 371 F15701/45/62, PRO; interviews with Joseph Scott, August 5, 1975, and Charlton Ogburn, May 2, 1974; Jessup, *Birth of Nations*, p. 48.

[78]Summary Record of 1st Meeting between Republican and Netherlands Delegations, December 7, 1947, UN S/AC.10/CONF.2/SR.1, GOC Records, UN Library.

[79]Memorandum from Scott to Graham, December 14, 1947, in Indonesia Files, Frank Graham Papers, University of North Carolina Library; Summary Record of 41st Meeting of GOC, December 8, 1947, UN S/AC.10/SR.41, GOC Records, UN Library.

> edent or guidance. The work of the Committee would have to begin from scratch. Fortunately this is not the case. The Linggadjati Agreement, regardless of its present status, defines the areas in which an agreement between the parties must be obtained. It provides a frame of reference. . . . Each side, it may be assumed, would be less likely to take an extreme position if called upon to define its present program in terms of a compromise concept of its relation to the other to which it has subscribed.[80]

Since neither the Dutch nor the Indonesians could present concrete proposals of their own, both agreed to accept the American recommendation. The GOC then met separately with the Netherlands and the republican delegations in several informal sessions between December 11 and December 19. The meetings proved unproductive, though, as each side steadfastly maintained its own interpretation of the Linggadjati agreement. At the final session, van Vredenburch dryly commented that any further article-by-article examination of Linggadjati would probably only discover fresh areas of disagreement.[81] At this point van Mook confided to a British official that he could see no solution other than the disintegration of the republic. He added off the record that he had no confidence in the GOC's efforts; he could not see such a man as Graham succeeding, since "he was too naive and too inexperienced in dealing with Orientals."[82]

The fragile truce also began to break down at this time. The republic charged that Dutch mopping-up operations at Rawahgede had resulted in the killing of more than 300 civilians and the wounding of 200 more.[83] "The Dutch," complained the republic in a statement released on December 14, "have agreed only to those points contained in the initial suggestions of the

[80]Proposals Submitted by the U.S. Delegation for Consideration by the Committee, December 8, 1947, UN S/AC.10/58, GOC Records, UN Library.

[81]Summary Record of 47th Meeting of GOC, December 19, 1947, UN S/AC.10/SR.47, GOC Records, UN Library; Secretary of State's weekly summary, November 24, 1947, DSR.

[82]Shepherd to Foreign Office, December 4, 1947, FO 371 F16032/45/62, PRO.

[83]Memorandum from Republican Delegation's Special Committee, December 24, 1947, S/AC.10/76, Annex I, GOC Records, UN Library. The impartial Rawahgede Observation Team of the GOC reported on January 12, 1948, that "the action taken by the Netherlands Army was deliberate and ruthless" (UN S/AC.10/85, ibid.).

Committee of Good Offices which they know would be to their advantage or would not affect them in their attempts to control, administer and economically reconstruct in their own interest the territories behind what they claim to be their forward positions."[84] The Netherlands promptly countered that it could have little faith in the outcome of political discussions because of continuing republican truce violations. The *Renville*'s commander, Captain David Tyree, summed up the new impasse in a terse message to Washington: "Cannot hope for Republic to last much longer under present circumstances."[85]

In a radio speech on December 19, Dutch Premier Beel emphasized the gravity of these developments. He declared that "further delay is not justified" in reaching an agreement, "because interests too great, too vital for the peoples of Indonesia and the Netherlands and ultimately for the whole world are at stake." He warned: "It would be most regrettable if this appeal, this last appeal were not understood."[86]

Van Zeeland underscored the seriousness of the impasse at a meeting of the GOC on December 21. If the committee failed, the Belgian delegate said, "it would mean a tremendous setback for the ideals connected with the United Nations, and a very bad situation would arise for all parties concerned: the United Nations, the Netherlands, and the Republic." He added: "To me the failure of our efforts to bring about an armistice and through it a peaceful settlement, might mean practically, in one step or in two, the end of the Republic." Van Zeeland recommended that the committee draft a conciliatory message to both parties, urging a resumption of constructive talks and a renewed effort to achieve an acceptable agreement.[87]

At this critical juncture, Graham warned the State Department of the seriousness of the Dutch–Indonesian stalemate. Lovett replied that Washington believed it appropriate for the

[84]Statement released by Republican Ministry of Information, December 14, 1947, UN S/AC.10/CONF.1/SR.7, ibid.

[85]Tyree to Commander in Chief, Pacific Fleet, December 9, 1947, Naval Operational Archives, Washington Navy Yard.

[86]Quoted in memorandum from Republican Delegation to GOC, December 21, 1947, UN S/AC.10/73, GOC Records, UN Library.

[87]Memorandum submitted by Belgian representative to GOC, December 21, 1947, UN S/AC.10/SR.49, Annex I, ibid.

GOC to take a "firm stand" with the two parties "so that substantive discussion can proceed." Unless each side evidenced a willingness to enter into negotiations with a "conciliatory spirit," he pointed out, no progress would be made. The State Department believed the time had now come for the United States to take a "strong position along these lines" in order to produce a "positive and salutary effect on other GOC members and on parties."[88]

Taking the initiative, Graham drafted a special message to the two parties, which was accepted by the full committee on December 25. The "Christmas Message," as it came to be known, began by warning the Dutch and Indonesians that a longer delay, "however supported by different or divergent argumentation," would violate the spirit of the UN resolutions. It urged the two parties again "to reconsider, immediately, the whole problem with greater realism, with reciprocal toleration, and with renewed emphasis on all the human aspects of the dispute." The message went on to detail a proposed compromise settlement, which in effect asked the republic to accept the Netherlands position on the military issues in return for a fair and peaceful determination of the political issues. The military aspect of the Christmas Message provided for a truce line to be set at the Dutch forward positions as of August 4—a cease-fire line that the republic had consistently disputed. Politically, the proposal called for the restoration of republican civil administration within three months of the signing of the political agreement, and the subsequent withdrawal of Dutch forces from all territory occupied as a result of the police action. In addition, the GOC's compromise overture suggested that free elections be held within six to twelve months to determine the future relationship between the republic and the United States of Indonesia; that the GOC would continue to assist the two parties in their efforts to implement the settlement; that each side would begin gradual troop reductions; that free economic activity would be promptly and completely restored; and that an impartial United Nations body would be appointed to observe conditions pending the eventual establishment of the U.S.I.[89]

[88]Lovett to Graham, December 19, 1947, in *FR*, 1947, 6:1084–85.
[89]UN S/AC.10/75, December 25, 1947.

Graham, a firm believer in the principle of self-determination ever since his days as a professor of American history, had increasingly come to appreciate the republic's interpretation of events and had become disillusioned with Dutch policy. He later castigated the Dutch version of the proposed federated U.S.I., for example, as really "just Dutch puppet states." Drawing an analogy with the American Revolution, he offered his personal interpretation of Dutch actions: "It would be like forming the United States of America under the Tories. Just lock George Washington up, and some of the others, and then put the Tories in charge of the several states and call it the United States of America." Moreover, he considered the republic, as he explained to Marshall, to be "the rallying center of the largest, ablest, and most dedicated single group of Indos in this struggle for independence." The present leadership of the republic, he maintained, "seems as moderate, reasonable and responsive to Western ideas of any likely to arise in [the] future."[90] Yet for all of his pro-Indonesian sentiments—and some members of the State Department unfairly accused him of serving as an advocate for the republic[91]—the Christmas Message, of which Graham was the principal author, definitely favored the Dutch position. The explanation for this seeming anomaly is actually quite simple: Graham realized that the Dutch preponderance of force was so great and the position of the republic so precarious that it would be a major accomplishment to get The Hague's consent to any agreement, no matter how favorable to Dutch interests. Consequently, he sought to achieve by the Christmas Message a settlement that, under the auspices of the United Nations, would ensure the continued survival of the Indonesian Republic.[92]

On December 30 the republic announced its reluctant acceptance of the committee's plan. "Although the most recent pro-

[90]Interview with Frank Graham, June 10, 1962, in Southern Oral History Program, University of North Carolina, p. 19; Graham to Marshall, December 31, 1947, 501.BC-Indonesia/2-3147, DSR; Graham to Marshall, December 20, 1947, in *FR*, 1947, 6:1088.

[91]Interviews with Scott, August 4, 1975; Ogburn, May 2, 1974; and James Barco, May 7, 1975.

[92]Graham to Professor Amry Vandenbosch, December 3, 1948, Graham to Harold R. Isaacs, March 10, 1948, both in Indonesia Files, Graham Papers.

posals of the Committee of Good Offices involve considerable sacrifices on the part of the Republic," remarked the republican delegation's memorandum to the GOC, "and although they are not strictly in accordance with the Republicans' own understanding of the Security Council's resolutions, the Indonesian Delegation accepts them as an integrated and balanced whole for the settlement."[93] This qualified acceptance reflected the republic's realization that the proposals represented at least an opportunity to secure the continued existence of its government.

The Dutch were even less pleased with the informal suggestions of the Christmas Message. In a memorandum addressed to the GOC on January 2, 1948, the Netherlands delegation accepted the committee's plan for a truce agreement, but took strong exception to the political principles. Agreeing only to those proposals that explicitly favored their own position, the Dutch rejected the heart of the committee's recommendations and countered with a list of twelve political proposals of their own. These Dutch counterproposals eliminated all reference to the restoration of republican civil administration and the withdrawal of troops; removed the principle guaranteeing international observation during the transition period; made no provision for representation of the republic in the interim government; and deleted any mention of the Republic of Indonesia. On January 9, the Netherlands delegation informed the committee that unless it received word of the republic's unqualified acceptance of these counterproposals within three days, it would ask The Hague for further instructions, "indicating that there was reason to believe that its Government would decide to resume their freedom of action."[94]

Graham understood the urgency of this latest crisis; he realized that the Dutch intended their message as an ultimatum, and that only timely GOC intervention could hope to prevent a return to full-scale hostilities. Earlier, the American representative had advised the State Department that he believed the com-

[93]Republican memorandum to GOC, December 30, 1947, UN S/AC.10/76, GOC Records, UN Library.

[94]UN S/AC.10/81 and UN S/AC.10/81 Rev. 1, December 2, 1947, GOC Records, UN Library.

mittee had two alternatives: either to support the Dutch plan for a U.S.I. with or without the republic's participation or to support the republic's claim to sovereignty over Java and Sumatra. In respect to ultimate sovereignty in Indonesia, Graham had insisted that there could be no compromise.[95] On December 31, Lovett in a telegram to Graham, outlined these two choices against the backdrop of overall American foreign policy objectives. "Netherlands is [a] strong proponent [of] US policy in Europe," the under secretary noted.

> Dept believes that [the] stability [of the] present Dutch Govt would be seriously undermined if Netherlands fails to retain very considerable stake in NEI, and that the political consequences of failure [of] present Dutch Govt would in all likelihood be prejudicial to US position in Western Europe. Accordingly, Dept unfavorable to any solution requiring immediate and complete withdrawal Netherlands from Indies or any important part thereof.

However, Lovett explained, the United States "has long favored self-government or independence for peoples who are qualified to accept consequent responsibilities." Therefore, the State Department was favorably disposed to a solution providing for Dutch sovereignty for a limited period "and setting date in future for independence of Indonesians, both Republican and non-Republican."

Another guide to American policy toward Indonesia was economic interest. As Lovett summarized it: "Dept desires speediest acceleration of trade between all of Indonesia and rest of world. This desire of long standing now heightened by tremendous burden imposed on US ability to supply consumer goods under Marshall Plan." Indonesia would be indispensable as a supplier of food and other commodities to meet needs defined by the European Recovery Program. "Therefore," he declared, "Dept unfavorably disposed toward any solution which [would be] likely to protract existing disorder in NEI." Lovett concluded by informing Graham that he hoped these principles would prove useful in further Dutch-Indonesian discussions.[96]

[95]Graham to Marshall, December 22, 1947, in *FR*, 1947, 6:1090–93; oral report by Henry Brandis to State Department, January 29, 1948, 856D.00/11-2948, DSR.

[96]Lovett to Graham, December 31, 1947, in *FR*, 1947, 6:1099–1101.

With the two sides now in a virtual deadlock, Graham endeavored to incorporate Lovett's principles in a new program that he intended to submit informally to both parties. The U.S. delegation believed, Graham cabled the State Department on January 6, that "if conditions set by Dutch are not modified, collapse of Republic either under Dutch military action or through internal difficulties is most likely outcome and that world reaction will be most serious, particularly for US, which holds [the] key position [on the] GOC." Accordingly, in a "last attempt [to] prevent [a] crisis" and "resolve [the] legitimate interests [of] both parties," he outlined six supplementary political principles. These additional principles provided for the republic's inclusion as one of the component states of the U.S.I.; called for the continuation of the United Nations' presence during the interim period; and assured the republic of fair representation in any interim government. On January 7, Marshall informed Graham that Washington considered this approach to be "eminently fair and manifestly practical" and noted that it "should form [the] basis of [a] settlement which will be favorably received by [the Security Council] and world opinion." On January 10, after receiving the support of the full committee, Graham transmitted the six additional political principles to both the Dutch and the republicans.[97]

Simultaneously, the State Department began to pressure the Dutch to accept the GOC's new proposals. In a meeting with representatives of the Dutch government on January 8, American diplomats urged the Netherlands "in the strongest terms" to consider and accept promptly the political principles set forth by Graham. Failure to accept Graham's proposed solution, they explained bluntly, would prevent American assistance in financing Indonesian reconstruction and would endanger Dutch participation in the European Recovery Program.[98]

The Netherlands bowed to this American pressure. "I be-

[97]Graham to Marshall, January 6, 1948, and Marshall to Graham, January 7, 1948, in *FR*, 1948, 6:62–64, 68; UN S/AC.10/84 Rev. 1, January 10, 1948, GOC Records, UN Library.

[98]Memorandum by Nolting of a conversation with Helb, Lacy, and others, 856D.00/1-848, DSR; Philip Bonsal (chargé, The Hague), to Marshall, January 12, 1948, 856E.00/1-1248, DSR; General A. R. Bolling, Acting Director of Intelligence, Department of the Army, to Chief of Staff, June 15, 1948, Planning and Operation Division Files, Modern Military Branch.

lieve," reported Philip Bonsal, American chargé at The Hague, "that at the Cabinet meeting on January 11, the matter was presented by the Prime Minister and the Foreign Minister as one whose rejection would involve the serious consequences flowing from a withdrawal of the promise of economic assistance from the United States." On that same day, the Dutch informed the GOC of their acceptance of the six additional principles.[99]

On January 12 the committee members flew to Kaliurang, a mountain resort near the republic's capital at Jogjakarta, to explain the proposed settlement to the republicans. The republic's representatives, understandably, were skeptical. Sjarifuddin remarked that the republic had been convinced that Linggadjati's meaning had been clear when it signed that ill-fated pact, only to have the Dutch pursue a unilateral interpretation, and he explained that the republic sought to avoid a repetition of that unfortunate experience. After analyzing the various aspects of the proposed settlement, Graham assured the republicans that the pact would not affect the republic's present status. "You are what you are," he told them, "and that is what you will remain." With the greatest reluctance, they decided to accept the GOC's plan. Graham's assurances that the agreement would not adversely affect their current status won the republicans over; they believed that Graham and the American government could be relied on to ensure that fair, UN-supervised plebiscites would be held in the territories overrun by the Dutch army. On January 14 the Republic of Indonesia officially accepted the committee's proposals.[100]

On January 17, 1948, the Dutch and the republicans signed the agreement on board the U.S.S. *Renville*. The Renville agreement, as it came to be known, almost surely prevented another Dutch military action, but it left many of the basic issues in

[99]Bonsal to Marshall, January 19, 1948, 856E.00/1-1948, DSR; Taylor, *Indonesian Independence*, pp. 89–90.

[100]Summary records of 60th and 61st meetings of GOC, January 12 and 13, 1948, UN/S/AC.10/SR.60, GOC Records, UN Library; Hadji A. Salim to Graham, June 19, 1948, in Indonesia Files, Graham Papers; Ide Anak Agung Gde Agung, *Twenty Years Indonesian Foreign Policy, 1945–1965* (The Hague: Mouton, 1973), pp. 38–39; Johannes Leimena, *The Dutch-Indonesian Conflict* (Jakarta, 1949), p. 7; T. B. Simatupang, *Report from Banaran: Experiences during the People's War* (Ithaca: Cornell University Modern Indonesia Project, 1972), p. 32.

dispute unresolved. As Richard Kirby, the Australian representative, commented at the signing ceremonies:

> Bold signatures on impressive documents cannot alone dispel the troubles of this archipelago. Even the limited objectives and understandings of today's agreement will be impossible of performance unless the two parties approach the problem of implementation and the political discussions which will shortly commence, in a spirit of cooperation and tolerance. More important than the words of today's documents is the spirit behind the intention of the parties.[101]

His cautionary words would prove to be prophetic.

[101]Statement by Kirby, January 17, 1948, UN S/AC.10/CONF.2/SR.4, Annex IV, GOC Records, UN Library.

7

From Negotiations to War: January–December 1948

The Renville agreement represented a humiliating defeat for the Republic of Indonesia. Not only did it significantly diminish the status of the republic from that envisioned by the Linggadjati agreement, but it also accepted the crude Dutch conquest of republican territory as a fait accompli. Prime Minister Sjarifuddin agreed to the settlement in the face of strong domestic opposition, and it quickly led to the downfall of his government. Citing their disillusionment with the intolerable concessions made to the Dutch, two of the republic's major political parties abruptly withdrew from Sjarifuddin's cabinet. His delicate coalition in a shambles, he resigned on January 23, 1948.[1]

Indonesian politicians were not alone in their dissatisfaction with the Renville settlement. The Soviet Union also castigated the pact, claiming that it had been forced on the reluctant republicans by U.S. pressure and the threat of a renewed Dutch attack. Speaking before the United Nations on February 27, Andrei Gromyko, the Soviet delegate, proclaimed his nation's utter contempt for the agreement. "It should be placed in a museum," he declared sarcastically, "as proof of how shameful a document can be produced when some of the members of the United Nations betray the interests of the Indonesian people for

[1]U.S. Department of State, Office of Intelligence Research (OIR), Division of Research for the Far East, "Analysis of the Political Principles of the Renville Agreement," Situation Report—Southern Areas, no. 3480.48, February 11, 1948, U.S. Department of State Records, National Archives, Washington, D.C. (hereafter cited as DSR); George McTurnan Kahin, *Nationalism and Revolution in Indonesia* (Ithaca: Cornell University Press, 1952), pp. 230–31.

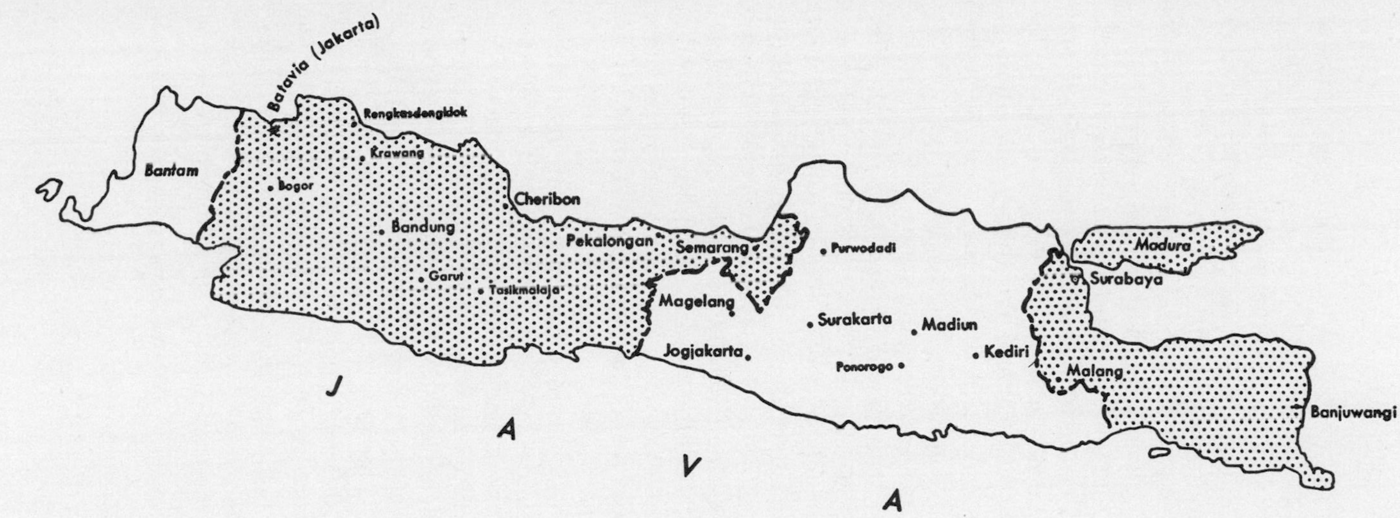

Division of Java under the Renville agreement (January 19, 1948). Unshaded areas remained under Republican control. Shaded areas were to be under Netherlands occupation. Heavy dotted lines show the Renville truce line; they approximate the previous van Mook line as last proclaimed by the Dutch.

the benefit of the colonial powers. In this connection, I cannot help recalling the words of the well-known writer and satirist Mark Twain, who said that a hen laid a normal-sized egg and cackled as though it had laid a small planet. Mark Twain was a wise man and we should remember his words now."[2]

While it is certainly true that the terms of the Renville agreement were conspicuously unfavorable to the republic, it is equally clear that the republic's options were severely limited. Unless its leaders had been willing to accept the logic of perdjuangan—full-scale guerrilla warfare against the Dutch—diplomasi remained the only viable alternative policy. And although the Renville settlement represented a dramatic setback in the republic's struggle to achieve independence, it did ensure the continued survival of the republican government. Sjarifuddin's government, moreover, had agreed to sign the pact only after Frank Graham assured its representatives at Kaliurang that the agreement would not adversely affect the republic's status. This was the Indonesians' trump card: that the United States and the United Nations, both of which had placed their prestige and power behind the agreement, would guarantee a just implementation of its terms. "Tell the American people," Sjarifuddin pleaded after the Renville signing, "that we count upon them to insure a fair plebiscite here. The plebiscite will chart the future destiny of a people."[3]

As long as the republic continued to define its options within a larger strategy of diplomasi, its leaders would be compelled to cultivate American support. The United States fully backed the Renville agreement, which had been largely drafted by Graham and cleared with the State Department. The republic could have refused to sign it only at the risk of alienating the U.S. government—a risk considered too great by nearly all republican leaders. Although Sjarifuddin was repudiated for his identification with Renville, the logic of his position was soon vindicated. On January 29 Mohammed Hatta announced the formation of a new cabinet; the new prime minister quickly revealed that his government was firmly committed to the prompt implementation of

[2]United Nations Security Council, *Official Records* (SCOR), 3d yr., 226th meeting, February 26, 1948, pp. 312, 315.
[3]*New York Times*, January 19, 1948, p. 10.

Renville, the same position for which Sjarifuddin had been ousted.[4]

For its part, the United States unequivocally supported the negotiation of the Renville settlement. A memorandum prepared for Secretary Marshall on February 10 by the directors of the three State Department offices with concurrent jurisdiction over the Dutch–Indonesian imbroglio offered the following assessment:

> The agreement reached represents an important achievement by the Security Council in a difficult and, until now, rapidly deteriorating situation. Without the Good Offices Committee, it seems highly unlikely that the parties would have succeeded in reaching a truce agreement, or any political settlement; indeed, it is not unlikely that the Republic of Indonesia would soon have been eliminated as a political factor in the Netherlands East Indies.

While recognizing that the pact was "largely favorable to the Dutch and as such represents several important compromises on the part of the Indonesian Republic," they explained that it represented the necessary first step toward a lasting settlement. They cautioned, however, that "it will be fully effective only with the maximum cooperation by both parties." Accordingly, negotiations for the permanent agreement must be entered into at once, "before any opportunity arises for exacerbation of the feelings of the parties"; they suggested that "the negotiations should be concluded as quickly as possible and agreement signed within six weeks at the most." Secretary Marshall should impress on the Dutch ambassador "the heavy responsibility already assumed by the United States in helping to settle the Indonesian dispute and the importance this Government attaches to immediate adoption of a permanent agreement." The memorandum concluded by urging Marshall to remind the Dutch that "because of their superior tactical position . . . a far greater than halfway effort by the Dutch will be required if a successful settlement is to be reached and is to endure."[5]

[4]Kahin, *Nationalism and Revolution*, pp. 231–34; Anthony J. S. Reid, *Indonesian National Revolution, 1945–50* (Hawthorn, Australia: Longman, 1974), p. 114.

[5]Memorandum from Dean Rusk (director, Office of United Nations Affairs), W. Walton Butterworth (director, Office of Far Eastern Affairs), and John D.

For all its limitations, Renville conformed perfectly with the larger policy objectives of the United States in postwar Southeast Asia. By harmonizing continued Dutch control over the Indies with a timetable for eventual native self-rule, the agreement seemed to ensure the delicate balance between European and nationalist interests that the United States had favored ever since the end of World War II. It was a compromise formula, moreover, which could be accepted with varying degrees of enthusiasm by all concerned offices within the American government; and, given the often wide divergence of opinion in Washington over the Indonesian conflict, this was in itself a remarkable accomplishment.[6]

Like the Linggadjati agreement before it, the Renville agreement was subject to widely divergent interpretations—unavoidably so, in light of the hasty manner in which the agreement had been reached. The Good Offices Committee had correctly surmised that another police action would have been undertaken had the committee not seized the initiative by presenting a compromise plan. Consequently, the GOC hurriedly drafted a conciliatory program that tended naturally to stress points of agreement while avoiding major areas of contention. This strategy—along with appropriate American pressure on both parties—resulted in a settlement whose terms were extremely vague. A successful implementation of the pact, as the February 10 State Department memorandum pointed out, thus depended on the willingness of both sides to display good faith in executing its provisions.[7]

Hickerson (director, Office of European Affairs) to George C. Marshall, February 10, 1948, in *Foreign Relations of the United States* (Washington, D.C., 1974), 6:91–94. Hereafter volumes in this series will be cited as *FR*, followed by the year.

[6]Ibid. A brief summary of U.S. interests in postwar Southeast Asia is provided in Office of Naval Intelligence, "Basic Factors in World Relations," June 1948, Post World War II Command File, Naval Operational Archives, Washington Navy Yeard.

[7]U.S. Department of State, OIR, "Draft Agreement: Comparison of Netherlands and Republican Views on Structure of USI with the Renville Agreement," April 15, 1948; "Tabular Comparison of Netherlands and Republican Views on the USI" and "Tabular Comparison of Republican and Netherlands Concepts of the Netherlands-Indonesian Union," Appendices III and V in Report no. 4679, "Dutch-Indonesian Negotiations: Major Issues and Timing," April 29, 1948, all in Indonesia Files, Graham Papers, University of North Carolina Library.

Initial indications were hopeful, as the republicans promptly demonstrated their willingness to comply with even the harshest terms of the pact. In accordance with the truce agreement, the Hatta government began the immediate withdrawal of some of the republic's finest troops from the considerable pockets of resistance they occupied behind Dutch lines. By February 26, much to the surprise of the Dutch, 35,000 republican troops had evacuated their strategic guerrilla bases within Dutch-occupied territory.[8] Colonel C. S. Meyers of the American military observer group attached to the GOC remarked with astonishment that the Dutch had not believed that there were any guerrilla forces behind their lines. "I am sure it was a considerable shock to some of our smug friends," he wrote to Graham, "to be compelled to face up to it. There were around 35,000 of them!"[9] This withdrawal represented a major concession on the part of the republic, as the bases were strategically invaluable. The Dutch, moreover, had not yet given any indication that the promised UN-sponsored plebiscites would actually be held.

On the contrary, Dutch actions in the aftermath of the Renville signing soon repeated a familiar pattern. The Netherlands delayed political discussions with the republic until mid-March; in the meantime, it unilaterally moved to form new states in the areas seized from the republic. In West Java, in Madura, and in East Sumatra, the Dutch sponsored the creation of new states that would be responsive to the interests of the Netherlands. This crude extension of their federal program to include former republican territories was actually a direct contravention of the Renville agreement, as republican officials charged and American and Australian members of the GOC privately admitted.[10] These new states did not represent a spontaneous expression of self-determination on the part of their populations, as Renville

[8]Interview with Charlton Ogburn, May 2, 1975; Kahin, *Nationalism and Revolution*, p. 234.

[9]Meyer to Graham, May 13, 1948, in Graham Papers.

[10]Kahin, *Nationalism and Revolution*, p. 235; Central Intelligence Agency, "Review of the World Situation as It Relates to the Security of the United States," CIA 3–48, February 12, 1948, President's Secretary's File (PSF), Truman Papers, Harry S. Truman Library, Independence, Mo. See also "Suggestions by the United States Delegation on a Time Table of the Steps to Be Taken toward the Creation of the USI," April 26, 1948, UN S/AC.10/115, GOC Records, UN Library, New York.

had explicitly stipulated; instead, the Dutch themselves had taken the lead in establishing these states, had not allowed GOC supervision, and had blocked the "freedom of assembly, speech, and publication" and the "uncoerced and free discussion and consideration of vital issues" that they had agreed to ensure under the Renville agreement.[11]

With great fanfare, Queen Wilhelmina had dramatically declared on February 3, 1948, that "colonialism is dead," but in light of Dutch actions in Indonesia, her statement appeared increasingly meaningless to republican officials.[12] Their suspicions of Dutch intentions increased substantially when van Mook announced the establishment of an interim federal government on March 9. This government, which was to function until the creation of the United States of Indonesia, still slated for January 1, 1949, was created independent from the Republic of Indonesia. Although the Dutch formally requested republican participation in the interim regime, this was a hollow gesture, for, as the republicans pointed out, Renville had called for joint Dutch-republican cooperation in the formation of an interim government, not unilateral action by one party. The Dutch action, charged the Indonesian Republic, was "a unilateral action proceeded to without consultation of the Republic," and was "contrary to the spirit as well as to the letter of the Renville Agreement."[13] The Dutch-created interim regime "represented no real change in the power structure of Dutch-controlled Indonesia. It was merely the old Netherlands Indies regime in new dress and was run by the personnel of the colonial regime with a few anti-Republican Indonesians included to present a better facade."[14]

On March 18, 1948, political discussions between the two parties finally resumed, once again under the mediation of the Good Offices Committee. The composition of the GOC had

[11]Kahin, *Nationalism and Revolution*, p. 235.

[12]*New York Times*, February 4, 1948, p. 1.

[13]Republican Delegation to Good Offices Committee, March 15, 1948, UN S/AC.10/121 Appendix II, Records of the Good Offices Committee, UN Library (hereafter cited as GOC Records). See also U.S. Department of State, OIR, "Developments in the Indonesian Situation for the Period February through March, 1948," April 14, 1948, in Graham Papers.

[14]Kahin, *Nationalism and Revolution*, p. 245.

changed since the Renville negotiations. The American representative, Frank Graham, had asked President Truman to replace him so that he could return to his duties as president of the University of North Carolina. Truman then named Coert duBois to serve as chief of the United States delegation. DuBois had recently retired after a long career in the Foreign Service; as a consul general in the East Indies during the 1930s he had become closely acquainted with the problems of the Indonesian archipelago, and this experience undoubtedly influenced his appointment as successor to Graham. DuBois had also developed cordial ties with Dutch political and business leaders while serving in the East Indies; the State Department, which was keenly aware of Dutch objections to Graham, wanted an American on the committee who would be more acceptable to Netherlands officials. The Belgian and Australian delegation chiefs had also departed, and they were succeeded by their respective deputies—Raymond Herremans, a minister in the Belgian diplomatic service, and Thomas K. Critchley, an officer in the Australian Department of External Affairs and an accomplished economist.[15]

The negotiations soon revealed that fundamental areas of disagreement still existed between the Dutch and the republicans. As the GOC later reported to the Security Council, the "major issues dividing the parties are the very issues which have always divided them and which the Linggadjati Agreement failed to resolve."[16] The most divisive issue was still sovereignty: the republic insisted that it could maintain its de facto authority, including its army and foreign relations, until the transfer of sovereignty to an independent federal United States of Indonesia; the Dutch categorically denied the republic's right to any such authority.[17]

Initially the American delegation to the GOC pressed the republicans to accept Dutch terms. On April 5 duBois met with

[15]Alastair M. Taylor, *Indonesian Independence and the United Nations* (Ithaca: Cornell University Press, 1960), pp. 102–3; interview with James Barco, May 7, 1975; Arnold C. Brackman, *Indonesian Communism: A History* (New York: Praeger, 1963), p. 77.

[16]UN S/848, June 21, 1948.

[17]J. Foster Collins, "The United Nations and Indonesia," *International Conciliation*, March 1950, pp. 154–57; Taylor, *Indonesian Independence*, pp. 117–20.

republican officials and candidly informed them of the American government's interpretation of the Renville agreement. Under the terms of that settlement, duBois stressed, there could be no doubt that sovereignty resided with the Dutch during the interim period; the republic, accordingly, had no right to conduct independent foreign relations. He criticized the republic's refusal to join the Dutch-created interim government and asserted that the Netherlands had thus far made the most far-reaching concessions that could be asked; any reluctance on the part of the republic to join the provisional government, he insisted, reflected an unjustifiable suspicion of Dutch intentions. When Indonesian leaders pointed out that they had been promised by Graham at Kaliurang that they could maintain their foreign representatives, duBois said he regretted that the republic had been misled. DuBois reiterated this position in another meeting with republican officials on April 8. Asked directly if he believed the Dutch could be trusted, the American representative quickly replied that the United States was "absolutely convinced" that the Dutch intended to carry out the provisions of the Renville agreement and noted that the attitude of top Dutch spokesmen had undergone a marked change in the past few months.[18]

Other members of the American delegation to the GOC were far less sanguine about Dutch intentions. Charlton Ogburn, a representative of the State Department's Division of Southeast

[18]DuBois to Marshall, April 6 and April 10, 1948, in *FR*, 1948, 6:135–36, 143–44. Arnold Brackman, who served as a correspondent in Indonesia at this time, later wrote that duBois was astonished to receive the assignment to the GOC. Because of past friendships with the Dutch, he informed the Department by letter that he could not, with a clear conscience, accept the post. DuBois believed that his pro-Dutch biases were simply too strong (Brackman, *Indonesian Communism*, p. 77). James Barco, who at that time represented the State Department's Office of United Nations Affairs on the GOC, related a similar story in an interview. Barco explained that the department selected duBois specifically because he was known to be pro-Dutch. There had been strong feelings in the department that Graham had antagonized the Dutch, and there was a general consensus, Barco pointed out, that the next American representative should be more sympathetic to The Hague's position. In an interview Charlton Ogburn also emphasized duBois's initial tendency to accept uncritically the Dutch version of events. This tendency is also evident in the records of the GOC meetings. See particularly summary record of 105th meeting of GOC, May 10, 1948, S/AC.10/SR.105, GOC Records, UN Library.

Asian Affairs, later recalled his steady disillusionment with Dutch actions:

> The one thing that came to us pretty soon and is bound to come to anybody pretty soon when he gets involved in one of these colonial conflicts is that there's no way you can slice sovereignty; there's no way you can divide sovereignty. The compromise agreements always look very good—there's going to be a division of authority and cooperation and equal participation—but when you come right down to it, one side or the other has to be the final arbiter. . . . According to the Dutch plan, no matter how they sliced it, the final say-so was going to be a Dutch say-so. . . . It became apparent to us that this was not going to work, that you could not leave the ultimate authority in Dutch hands, even temporarily, because the Dutch had no intention of relinquishing that authority now or at any conceivable time in the future. No matter what kind of native instrumentalities they worked through, they were going to retain the ultimate governing voice.[19]

After less than two months in the Indies, duBois also began to question Dutch policies. Despite his friendly personal relations with many ranking Dutch diplomats, the American representative gradually began to doubt the sincerity of their pledges. On May 10 he conveyed this disillusionment to Washington. "Like all other neutral observers," he said, the American delegation was convinced that the republic was the "only force in Indonesia of [any] real consequence apart [from the] Netherlands army." Unless the Dutch could convince the republicans of The Hague's interpretation of Renville, "settlement by force appeared inevitable"; and though duBois did not doubt the Dutch army's ability to capture the republican capital and all the main roads within ten days, it was a "foregone conclusion" that the outcome would be a duplication of the Indochina stalemate and would result in a drastic reduction of the Indonesian export potential. He reasoned that the republic was "working for [the] freedom [of] all Indonesia and represents [the] spearhead [of the] independence drive to Indonesian nationalists [in] all areas." Consequently, the Dutch were making a "serious mistake [in] dis-

[19] Interview with Ogburn, May 2, 1975.

counting these factors"; it was now crucial for them to "make every reasonable concession" to the republic.[20]

But instead of offering concessions to the republic, the Netherlands proceeded with a further expansion of its federal program. On May 1 the Dutch-controlled interim government announced a federal conference that would begin on May 27 at Bandung, a city in western Java. The Dutch sent invitations to thirteen Indonesian "states," all in nonrepublican territory. The head of the Netherlands delegation explained the Dutch action this way: "Even if the Republic contends that a federation without its participation is an impossibility, the federalists are of exactly the opposite opinion. They consider a federation without the Republic in no way an impossibility." In his opening address to the convention, van Mook reiterated this theme: "It did not seem possible to continue waiting for the moment when the Republic would join us: the problems we have to deal with are too urgent and of too great importance to all of us to postpone this conference any longer."[21]

Alarmed by this unilateral action, the republic lodged official protests with the Good Offices Committee and the United Nations Security Council. In a letter to the committee, the republican delegation charged that "the Netherlands Government is preparing to present the Republic of Indonesia with a new *fait accompli.* This is a policy which is in distinct contradiction to the Renville principles."[22] The author of that agreement, Frank Graham, added considerable weight to the republican view in a letter to Secretary of State Marshall. The Bandung Conference, Graham complained, violated both "the intent and spirit of the Renville Agreement."[23]

DuBois was equally disturbed by this arbitrary Dutch action. In a cable to the State Department on May 21, he suggested that the Dutch were speeding the formation of the U.S.I. "in order that either (1) Republic will be forced [to] enter strictly on

[20]DuBois to Marshall, May 10, 1948, in *FR,* 1948, 6:165–68.

[21]GOC, "Report to the Security Council on the Federal Conference Opened in Bandung on 27 May 1948," June 16, 1948, UN S/842, pp. 22–23; UN S/AC.10/130, Appendix II, GOC Records, UN Library.

[22]Republican Delegation to GOC, May 23, 1948, UN S/AC.10/130, Appendix I.

[23]Graham to Marshall, June 10, 1948, in Graham Papers.

Netherlands terms or (2) if Republic stays out, resultant conflict can be presented [to the] world as civil Indonesian conflict." This, duBois maintained, is "precisely what [the] French endeavored [to] accomplish [in] Indo-China." In the view of the U.S. delegation, the Dutch "have from the start never deviated from objective of transferring sovereignty to an Indonesian Government in which Republican representatives will be in minority and major role will be played by Indonesians amenable [to the] Netherlands and opposed [to the] Republic." DuBois repeated his conviction that the republic enjoyed the confidence of the Indonesian people to a "far greater extent than any other group" and that the republicans were both the most representative group in Indonesia and the most capable of governing the archipelago. If the Netherlands continued to carry out its federal program without the participation of the republicans, he cautioned, the resultant provisional federal government of the U.S.I. "will be [an] unnatural organization which only Dutch arms, if anything, can maintain." He warned the department that, regardless of Dutch intentions, a final breakdown of negotiations would be followed automatically be a "crumbling truce" and the resumption of hostilities. In conclusion, he summarized the pessimistic appraisal of the American delegation. If the republic were forced either to accept a political settlement so disadvantageous to its interests that it could not live up to the terms or to reject such a settlement completely, "we fear results will be extremely unfortunate [with] respect [to] both Netherlands and US long-run interests [in] Indonesia."[24]

A report prepared by the State Department's Office of Intelligence Research on June 2, 1948, examined the implications for the United States of the threatened breakdown of Dutch–Indonesian negotiations. Noting that the American delegation to the GOC had recently expressed apprehension about the latest Dutch actions, the memorandum emphasized the strong possibility of another armed assault against the republic. "Among the indications substantiating fears that the Netherlands is preparing to pursue such a unilateral course," it pointed out, "are the continued strengthening of Dutch armed forces, the continua-

[24]DuBois to Marshall, May 21, 1948, in *FR*, 1948, 6:180–83.

tion of the blockade against the republic, and the political offensive at Bandung aimed at an early formation of a USI government." If the Dutch succeeded in forming a provisional regime without the republic, the report cautioned, a complete breakdown of Dutch–republican negotiations could occur. "The consequences of a breakdown would be an immediate outbreak of widespread hostilities." If another military action occurred, moreover, the economic recovery of Indonesia could be drastically curtailed, as guerrilla warfare would inevitably follow. According to the report, Dutch economic recovery could also be significantly affected, as the continuing need to maintain costly armed forces in Indonesia "will continue to drain the Netherlands limited economic resources." In addition, "the present moderate Republican leadership, which seeks a peaceful settlement, would be discredited, and there would be an immeasurable increase in the appeal to the Indonesian masses of extremist and Communist propaganda."

A particularly telling issue for the United States, the memorandum contended, was the "obvious danger that the US will be identified with Netherlands policies by the South East Asia peoples and countries sympathetic to Indonesian Nationalist aspirations." It noted that "the favorable predisposition of Indonesian nationalists toward the US in 1945 and 1946 is slowly degenerating into suspicion." This development could aid the Soviet Union's drive to supplant the United States as champion of the colonial nationalist movement. "As a consequence, the USSR will have added opportunity to secure emotional and political allegiance that might otherwise accrue to the US."[25]

On June 3 duBois informed the State Department that the American delegation had concluded that a continuation of present Dutch policy toward the republic would also endanger American economic interests in the archipelago. Only a settlement satisfactory to the republic, he stressed, would work to the advantage of the United States. According to the U.S. delegation, American economic interests in Indonesia were threefold: (a) the earliest possible restoration of the islands to stability and

[25]U.S. Department of State, OIR, Division of Research for the Far East, "Implications for the U.S. of Threatened Breakdown in Indonesian Negotiations," Situation Report—Southern Areas, no. 3480.54, June 2, 1948, DSR.

full production; (b) the "maximum reasonable protection" of Holland's economic stake in Indonesia in the interest of the "sound recovery [of] Holland and western Europe"; and (c) the protection of established U.S. interests plus assurances of equality of opportunity for American investors and enterprise. The prewar Dutch policy of monopoly controls, duBois explained, had enabled the Netherlands to assert complete political control over the archipelago; a settlement favorable to the republicans would remove that control permanently and leave the "door potentially fully open for US business." Additionally, as "the chief source for capital funds," the United States would be the only nation in a position to provide adequate assistance in the reconstruction and development of Indonesia during the early years of the provisional U.S.I. Republican leaders would undoubtedly seek a counterweight to the initially predominant Dutch economic interests in the archipelago, duBois suggested, and "private American capital is only logical contender." Moreover, "US political prestige in Indonesia will soar on [the] strength [of a] political settlement satisfactory to nationalist sentiment." He noted that the restrictions on the sovereignty of the future U.S.I. which the Dutch envisaged would only harm the prospects for a Western-oriented Indonesian state and would "lead eventually to [the] complete dislodgement [of] Netherlands interests" at the very least. DuBois suggested that the Dutch delegation's approach to the sovereignty issue was "conditioned as much by fears of opening Indonesia to free competition [from] other foreign enterprises as by [the] fear of Indonesian measures against Dutch economic interests."[26]

With Dutch–republican relations rapidly deteriorating, the American and Australian delegations to the GOC began to realize that they would have to take a more active role in breaking the impasse. Consequently, the two delegations jointly drafted a compromise plan for an overall political settlement. The duBois-Critchley proposals, as they became known, attempted to solve the fundamental issue of sovereignty during the transition period. According to the plan, elections would be held

[26]DuBois to Marshall, June 3, 1948, in *FR*, 1948, 6:211–13. A similar view of the potential value of Indonesia to American business was expressed in "Indonesia: Peace Brings Trade Rebirth," *Business Week*, May 8, 1948, pp. 117–20.

throughout Indonesia for delegates to a constituent assembly, which would serve as both a provisional legislature and a constitutional convention. The election would be held by secret balloting under the close supervision of the Good Offices Committee. The Constituent Assembly would convene as soon as possible after the election and, acting as a provisional parliament, proceed to form an interim government responsible to it. The Assembly would also delineate the states to be included in the United States of Indonesia. During this period the Assembly would attain control over all internal and external affairs of the archipelago, including control of armed forces, foreign relations, trade, and currency; sovereignty and ultimate authority, however, would remain with the Netherlands. The acting government would then serve as a constitutional convention, drafting a constitution for the United States of Indonesia which would safeguard legitimate Dutch economic, military, and cultural interests. After the Dutch and Indonesians ratified the new constitution, the Netherlands would officially transfer sovereignty to the U.S.I.[27]

DuBois cabled a copy of this plan to Washington on June 5 and asked for the State Department's approval. He contrasted the realistic approach of the duBois-Critchley proposals with the unrealistic federal policy being pursued by the Dutch at the Bandung Conference. The fact was, duBois emphasized, that the "non-Republican Indonesians [were an] element [of] minor importance [in the] Indonesian situation." After nearly three years of "Netherlands promises, Netherlands military successes, Netherlands distribution of commodities, and increasing physical hardships in the Republican areas," the Dutch had "not yet succeeded [in] attracting [a] single one clearly of consequence to their side or prompting one demonstration [of] popular enthusiasm for their cause." The basic problem, he explained, was that sovereignty could not be divided; the actual government of Indonesia would have to be in the hands of either the Dutch or the Indonesians. The republic would never surrender to the Dutch the powers of self-government that it had exercised

[27]"Proposed Working Paper by the Committee of Good Offices on an Outline of a Political Settlement," enclosed in duBois to Marshall, June 5, 1948, in *FR*, 1948, 6:219–23.

for three years, duBois commented, and "we do not see why it should." If the Netherlands strategy of forming a federal Indonesian government without the republic's participation were pursued, "economic and political stability" in Indonesia would "be postponed until time when Indonesians [are] able [to] throw Dutch out of islands." There was a strong chance, duBois cautioned, "that if Netherlands [is] allowed [to] carry through its plan, Holland will prove sink without stopper so far as US economic and financial assistance [are] concerned."

The duBois-Critchley plan, however, would result in the "speedy formation" of an "orderly and by no means incompetent Indonesian Government strongly disposed [to] cooperate with Dutch and rely heavily [on] Dutch assistance." A U.S.I. formed under these conditions would be inclined to exert a "strong pro-western influence throughout Southeast Asia" and to represent a "vitally important achievement" by "giving lie to Communist propaganda throughout Far East." Time was running out, duBois warned, and the opportunity now available would not recur. Accordingly, he concluded that "unless Department can subscribe [to the] essentials [of the] US Delegation plan, on which compromise would render whole plan worthless, I believe my usefulness and that of the US Delegation here will be completely nullified."[28]

In reply, Marshall cabled duBois that the State Department wished the delegation "to continue to regard itself as free agent making such choices on spot as USDel believes will lead to agreement between parties and in accordance with larger interests of United States." Without specifically commenting on the duBois-Critchley plan—which the department, curiously, later claimed that it had not yet received—Marshall in effect authorized the American delegation to act in whatever manner it deemed appropriate to avert another outbreak of hostilities.[29]

[28]DuBois to Marshall, June 7, 1948, in ibid., pp. 226–28.

[29]Marshall to duBois, June 8, 1948, in ibid., p. 229. It is curious that the department would claim that it had not even received a copy of the duBois-Critchley proposals. DuBois enclosed a copy of the plan in a telegram he sent to the department on June 5. There had never been any problem previously with communications and it is difficult to understand why there would have been a problem at this time. The department, moreover, was still claiming that it had not received a copy of the proposals long after the contents of the American-

On June 10 the American and Australian delegations to the GOC informally submitted their compromise plan to Dutch and Indonesian officials. DuBois personally handed the draft proposal to van Mook that day. The American representative, who was a personal friend of the Dutch spokesman, later said that it was one of the most difficult things he had ever done. Van Mook quickly perused the plan without saying a word to duBois. Visibly angry, he abruptly dismissed the aging American diplomat.[30]

The American and Australian representatives were convinced that this direct approach, no matter how unpalatable to the Dutch, was the only way to preserve peace in the archipelago. In a statement released on that day, the two delegations observed that negotiations between the Dutch and the republicans appeared to have reached a standstill. In the five months since the signing of the Renville agreement, "no significant progress has been made toward a political settlement between the Kingdom of the Netherlands and the Republic of Indonesia." The failure thus far "raises the question of whether the Committee's effort can be of value unless the Committee can make a positive contribution to an agreement which it has in the past refrained from attempting." Only by "coming forward with such a suggestion now that the delegations of the parties appear unable to make further progress towards an agreement," they explained, "can be acquit ourselves of our obligation and justify

---

Australian plan had become public knowledge. It is far more likely that an interdepartmental dispute over the approach offered by duBois delayed the department's response to the American representative's overture. Several former State Department officials (Barco, Scott, Philip Jessup, Dean Rusk) assured me that such conflicts did in fact exist. For further evidence of interdepartmental conflicts over Indonesia policy, see Philip C. Jessup, *The Birth of Nations* (New York: Columbia University Press, 1974), pp. 51, 56.

[30]Interview with Charlton Ogburn, May 2, 1975. The Belgian delegation, which generally reflected the Dutch point of view, refused to go along with the American-Australian plan. DuBois and Critchley found the Belgian delegation's reservations about their plan irreconcilable and so proceeded to present the working paper without their Belgian colleagues' concurrence. See summary record of 116th meeting of GOC, June 9, 1948, S/AC.10/SR.116, GOC Records, UN Library. DuBois had repeatedly complained to Washington about the Belgian delegates' inability to depart from the Dutch view of events. See, for example, Hickerson to Alan G. Kirk (ambassador to Belgium), May 6, 1948, 501.BC Indonesia/4-2148, DSR.

the seven and a half months the Committee has spent in Indonesia endeavoring to assist the parties."[31]

The republicans almost immediately accepted the duBois-Critchley proposals as a basis for further discussion. The Dutch, on the other hand, viewed the American-Australian overture with haughty disdain, objecting to the plan on both procedural and substantive grounds.[32] Hendrik N. Boon, the chief of political affairs in the Netherlands Foreign Office, complained to the American Embassy in The Hague that duBois's action had "created havoc [in] all respects." The Dutch government believed that there was no justification for the "precipitate action" taken by the American delegation. Cooperation among members of the GOC, he added, was now impossible.[33] On June 14 the Dutch ambassador met with Under Secretary of State Lovett to explain the Dutch position. Van Kleffens, who had previously complained that duBois was "off the beam" in his negotiating efforts, reiterated his government's intention to negotiate a settlement on the basis of the Renville principles and suggested that the rash action of duBois and Critchley would now make that task more difficult.[34]

On June 16 the Netherlands abruptly broke off all negotiations with the republic, using the purported leak of the confidential duBois-Critchley proposals to an American correspondent as a pretext. In actuality, the reporter in question, Daniel Schorr of *Time*, had more likely received the contents of the American-Australian plan from Dutch officials themselves.[35] Nevertheless,

[31]DuBois and Critchley to van Mook, June 10, 1948, S/AC.10/CONF.2/BUR/W.1, GOC Records, UN Library.

[32]DuBois to Marshall, June 14, 1948, 501.BC Indonesia/6-1348, DSR; DuBois to Butterworth, June 23, 1948, 501.BC Indonesia/6-2348, DSR; van Mook to GOC, June 14, 1948, S/AC.10/136, GOC Records, UN Library.

[33]Quoted in Baruch to Marshall, June 11, 1948, in *FR*, 1948, 6:237–38.

[34]Memorandum by Lovett of a conversation with van Kleffens and Butterworth, June 14, 1948, in ibid., pp. 243–44; memorandum by Nolting of a conversation with van Kleffens, Lovett, and Lacy, 856D.00/6-548, DSR. See also White House daily summary, June 15, 1948, DSR; Baruch to Marshall, June 14, 1948, 856D.00/6-1448, DSR.

[35]Kahin, *Nationalism and Revolution*, p. 248. Daniel Schorr recalled that, as far as he knew, the Dutch were not responsible for the leak. "They did seem about ready to break off negotiations," he wrote, "and seemed to be looking for the first occasion. They had early warnings of the leak because they clearly were monitoring outgoing press cables. My recollection is that they made their first

the Dutch privately charged Coert duBois with responsibility for the leak. DuBois, in turn, categorically denied that he or any member of the American delegation was responsible, explaining to the State Department that Schorr's source "was almost certainly Dutch."[36] This curious incident illustrates the lengths to which the Netherlands was willing to go in order to avoid the consideration of substantive issues; the American members of the GOC suspected that the Dutch were simply looking for an excuse to circumvent the committee entirely. During a committee meeting on June 21, Ogburn charged that the Dutch had deliberately maneuvered the GOC into an impossible position: by "a peculiarly cowardly device" they had implied that the Americans were responsible for the controversial leak, and then, because of the leak, had begun negotiating directly with the republicans, bypassing the GOC and rending it powerless to fulfill its appointed function. "It seems to me," Frank Graham observed, that "the Dutch are up to their old 'shinanagins.' They used their old alibi of a leak to the press. . . . The controversial leak may have come from the Dutch rather than from other sources."[37]

The Dutch refusal even to discuss the duBois-Critchley proposals is particularly revealing of The Hague's policy objectives in the post-Renville period. In part, the decision to reject the proposals can be explained by domestic political considerations: a general election was scheduled for July 7 in Holland and the Indonesian question was emerging as a central issue.[38] More

---

move in the Security Council before anything had been published" (personal communication, May 20, 1976). See also Daniel Schorr, *Clearing the Air* (Boston: Houghton Mifflin, 1977), p. 4.

[36]DuBois to Marshall, June 16, 1948, in *FR*, 1948, 6:248, 250.

[37]Summary records of 123rd meeting of GOC, June 21, 1948, UN S/AC.10/SR.123, GOC Records, UN Library; Graham to Brandis, July 24, 1948, in Indonesia Files, Graham Papers.

[38]George W. Renchard (secretary of embassy, The Hague) to Marshall, July 12, 1948, 856.00/7-1248, DSR. As a result of the election, the Dutch Labor Party lost two seats in Parliament to the Catholic Party, which had charged it with pursuing too liberal a policy in Indonesia. The Catholic Party thus attained a dominant voice in the governing coalition. Shortly after the election, E. M. J. A. Sassen, a conservative member of the Catholic Party, became minister for overseas territories. Determined to pursue a "tougher" policy vis-à-vis the republic, in October Sassen replaced van Mook—who he believed was too flexible—with

important, though, the protracted delay in implementing the Renville agreement had worked to the advantage of the Dutch, and the American-Australian plan for an overall settlement contained an element of risk for The Hague which it was unwilling to accept. Its prime fear was that free elections might substantiate what it already suspected: that the republic represented the nationalist aspirations of the vast majority of the archipelago's people. Such a result would have exposed the federal program as a sham. By refusing to consider the duBois-Critchley proposals, moreover, the Dutch could retain the advantages that their preponderance of force had given them, and could proceed with their plans to shape the future of the Indonesian archipelago unilaterally.[39]

The vehement Dutch reaction to the duBois-Critchley proposals placed the United States in an extremely sensitive position. The Department of State had consistently upheld the Renville principles as the basis for a lasting settlement between the Indonesians and the Dutch. American representatives in Indonesia, however, perceived that the Dutch intended to ignore Renville while pursuing a federal policy aimed at excluding the republic from any interim regime. When duBois informed Washington that a new approach to the Dutch–Indonesian conflict was necessary, the State Department again assured him that the American delegation to the GOC should consider itself a "free agent" in making suggestions that it believed would lead to an agreement between the two parties in accordance with the larger interests of the United States. DuBois, understandably, interpreted this message to mean that the department would support any attempt he might make to resolve the continuing stalemate. When the Dutch categorically rejected the joint American-Australian working paper, duBois hoped that State Department pressure would force The Hague to reconsider the proposals.[40] Instead, department officials rebuked the American delegation for constituting itself "as an arbitral body" and re-

Louis Beel, who became high commissioner for the crown (Anthony J. S. Reid, *Indonesian National Revolution, 1945–50* [Hawthorn, Australia: Longman, 1974], p. 149; Taylor, *Indonesian Independence*, p. 137).

[39]Taylor, *Indonesian Independence*, pp. 132–36.

[40]DuBois to Marshall, June 12, 1948, in *FR*, 1948, 6:240–43.

minded it of the limited nature of "good offices."[41] In addition, at the United Nations Security Council, American Deputy Representative Philip C. Jessup argued on June 23 that the council should vote not to receive the U.S.-Australian working paper because it was evident that the whole GOC did not consider its submission desirable. This decision, Jessup explained to Dean Rusk, was "in line with our general policy of supporting the Dutch as much as we could."[42]

This negative reaction baffled the American representatives in Indonesia. After all, they regarded the compromise plan as an eminently just and practical solution to Dutch–Indonesian differences. They believed, as Andrew Roth had written in *The Nation*, that the "Australian-American draft must be considered a fair basis for discussion by anyone desiring a peaceful settlement here without prejudice to the right of democratic self-determination."[43] In a cable to Washington on July 28, Ogburn complained that the American delegation "has faced increasing difficulties in following course presumably acceptable to Department since we have had no knowledge how Department intends [to] adapt itself to emerging issues." He continued: "We have had no comment whatever from Department on US-Australian working paper. While we assume Department had rejected our analyses situation, we have no idea what or whose analyses are accepted."[44]

In reality, the work of the U.S. delegation had been sacrificed to the larger interests of American foreign policy, which at this juncture dictated solidarity with Washington's European allies. The success of the Marshall Plan was the central focus for American policy makers in mid-1948; any friction that might result from a seemingly peripheral issue such as colonial relations in Indonesia was to be studiously avoided. It was not that the State Department rejected the analysis of its representatives in the field, as Ogburn surmised; rather, the maintenance of friendly relations with the Netherlands was an overriding concern.

[41]Marshall to duBois, June 14, 1948, in ibid., pp. 245–46.

[42]SCOR, 3d yr., 226th meeting, June 23, 1948, pp. 32–34; transcript of a telephone conversation between Jessup and Rusk, July 6, 1948, in Box 81, Records of the U.S. Mission to the UN, RG 59, DSR.

[43]Andrew Roth, "American Flipflop in Indonesia," *Nation*, July 10, 1948, p. 40.

[44]Ogburn to Marshall, July 28, 1948, in *FR*, 1948, 6:293.

The success of the European Recovery Program (ERP) depended, to a large extent, on the interrelationship between the economies of Western Europe and the economies of the colonial dependencies of Southeast Asia. Acheson underscored that fact before the House Committee on Foreign Affairs during the Marshall Plan hearings. If the ERP was to succeed, he pointed out, the Western European countries would have to increase their exports substantially. "Most of them—we hope a very large part—will go to southeast Asia," he said. "Before the war, over a billion dollars of exports went to southeast Asia. Now practically none go there." The "Dutch and British and French possessions in southeast Asia," commented another administration spokesman in an appearance before the Senate Foreign Relations Committee, are "extremely important" to the success of the Marshall Plan because "they have historically been earners of dollars for the home countries." This was particularly true, he emphasized, of the Dutch East Indies and British Malaya, with their rich supplies of tin and rubber. "The estimate of allocations needed" for the ERP, he added, "is in very substantial part a judgment as to when or if those territories will be politically pacified, and if so, how soon thereafter they will be able to begin making substantial exports of petroleum products, rubber, tin, and other minerals, which could make a decisive difference in the dollar interests of the controlling European countries."[45]

It was a fundamental assumption of the Marshall Plan, then, that the European countries would resume their prewar control over the colonies of Southeast Asia. Given this expectation, for most policy makers Indonesian developments continued to be filtered through a European prism. This view unavoidably prejudiced the American stance of "neutrality." In fact, while its representatives on the GOC were trying to settle the Dutch–

[45]Testimony of Dean Acheson, January 29, 1948, in U.S. Congress, House Committee on Foreign Affairs, *Hearings: U.S. Foreign Policy for a Post-War Recovery Program*, 80th Cong., 2d sess., 1948, pt. 1, p. 739; testimony of Richard M. Bissell (secretary, Subcommittee on Economic and Financial Analysis for the President's Committee on Foreign Aid), January 12, 1948, in U.S. Congress, Senate Committee on Foreign Relations, *Hearings: European Recovery Program*, 80th Cong., 2d sess., 1948, pt. 1, p. 273. For the importance of Southeast Asia to the success of ERP, see Economic Cooperation Administration, Far East Program Division, Division of Statistics and Reports, *The Role of ECA in Southeast Asia* (Washington: U.S. Government Printing Office, 1951).

Indonesian conflict in an impartial manner, the U.S. government was allocating $506 million in ERP aid to the Netherlands, with the stipulation that $84 million was to be used for reconstruction of the Netherlands Indies. This aid, which was formally authorized in the spring of 1948, had profound implications for the Dutch–Indonesian dispute: clearly, American financial assistance would inevitably strengthen the Netherlands vis-à-vis the Indonesian Republic; and the United States, which continued to pose as an impartial mediator, distributed economic aid specifically earmarked for Indonesia through the Netherlands—an action that most republican officials believed was yet another indication that Washington's impartiality was a sham. "The practical effect of ECA [Economic Cooperation Administration] aid on the political conflict," noted a State Department intelligence report, "is to strengthen the economic, political, and military position of the Netherlands in Indonesia. . . . Reactions to ECA grants by the Dutch and by Indonesians show that this effect is clearly understood by both sides."[46]

Indeed, both Dutch and Indonesians speculated that the Marshall Plan represented a new stage in American policy toward the Indonesian conflict. The Dutch press in Holland and in the Indies suggested that the European Recovery Program indicated that the United States had reversed its previous position of withholding financial aid until a political settlement had been reached; this reversal, it suggested, was due to Washington's realization that Dutch economic recovery was closely tied to the economic recovery of Indonesia.[47] The Marshall Plan was as warmly applauded in the Netherlands as it was coldly denounced in the Republic of Indonesia. In a memorandum to the States General on February 5, Prime Minister Beel expressed his belief that "without American aid the future of Europe would be extremely dim."[48] When the first Marshall Plan ship arrived in Rotterdam on April 26, 1948, carrying 4,000 tons of wheat, an impromptu ceremony was held during which the United States

[46]U.S. Department of State, OIR, Division of Research for the Far East, "Political Implications of E.C.A. Aid to Indonesia," Situation Report—Southern Areas, no. 3480.56, October 29, 1948, and "The Role of Indonesia in the European Recovery Program," Report no. 3480.51, April 7, 1948, DSR.

[47]Cited in OIR, "Political Implications."

[48]Bonsal to Marshall, February 17, 1948, 756.00/2-1748, DSR.

was repeatedly lauded. The Netherlands Information Service took out a full-page advertisement in nearly all Dutch daily newspapers that week, hailing this first ship as "the symbol of our second liberation: liberation from black insecurity."[49] Relations between the United States and the Netherlands, despite the protracted dispute in the Indies, could not have been more friendly.

Some Asian specialists in the State Department had warned that the European Recovery Program would inevitably compromise the U.S. position in Southeast Asia. "It is apparent," wrote William S. B. Lacy of the Division of Southeast Asian Affairs in November 1947, "that the drafters of the ERP legislation deliberately avoided the basic political problem of sovereignty which besets the relationship between colonial peoples in southeast Asia and elsewhere, and their metropolitan powers." Another department officer commented that the Marshall Plan would inevitably lead to "a greater wave of criticism against the United States in Southeast Asia. . . . The fact that two of the ERP countries, France and Holland, are conducting military operations in these colonies lays U.S. open to the charge that it is assisting them in a colonial war." Similarly, in a memorandum for President Truman, the CIA noted that "to the extent that the European recovery program enhances Dutch and French capabilities in Southeast Asia, native resentment toward the United States will increase. This tendency will be exploited and intensified by Communist propaganda on the theme of U.S. 'imperialism'."[50] These objections, despite their prescience, appear to have had little impact on the upper reaches of the Truman administration, where the conviction that the economic recovery of Western Europe was the key to the myriad foreign policy problems of the United States remained virtually unchallenged.

[49]Baruch to Marshall, April 27, 1948, 840.50-Recovery/4-2748, DSR; Bonsal to Marshall, May 11, 1948, 840.50-Recovery/5-1148, DSR.

[50]Lacy to Butterworth, November 25, 1947, in folder labeled "S.E.A.: European Recovery Program," Box 4, Records of the Office of the Philippines and Southeast Asian Affairs, DSR (hereafter cited as PSA Records); Haldore Hanson to Butterworth, November 12, 1947, in ibid.; CIA, "Review of the World Situation as it Relates to the Security of the United States," CIA 2, November 14, 1947, PSF, Truman Papers.

The European orientation of American foreign policy was further reinforced by the deepening Cold War. With the Communist coup in Czechoslovakia in February 1948, American policy makers strengthened their resolve to defend Western Europe from the perceived Soviet threat. "The Communist coup in Czechoslovakia," suggested a Joint Chiefs of Staff paper, "may have been one of those events which from time to time change the course of history. . . . In the circumstances, there is no alternative but to revitalize the military potential of Western Europe, with active United States participation and assistance, as rapidly as possible."[51] Administration efforts in this regard soon began to focus on the Brussels Pact, the defense agreement signed in March by Great Britain, France, Belgium, Luxembourg, and the Netherlands, as a possible model. The speed with which the Brussels Pact was agreed upon, noted a CIA report, was "a measure of the sense of common danger pervading Western Europe."[52] President Truman applauded the treaty and the State Department and Congress subsequently began to formulate a similar treaty for Western Europe. The result would ultimately be the North Atlantic Treaty Organization (NATO). High-level meetings with European diplomats, including Dutch representatives, began in June 1948, about the same time that the duBois-Critchley proposals were being submitted to the Dutch and the republicans. Washington's reluctance to support its representatives' initiative in Indonesia may well have derived from an unwillingness to pressure a friendly ally while in the midst of delicate negotiations regarding an issue that the administration regarded as the primary objective of American diplomacy.[53]

While preoccupation with European policy dominated official circles, the argument that Dutch transgressions in Indonesia should be downplayed to avoid antagonizing the Netherlands and the Western democracies was by no means unanimously

[51]JCS 1868/13, "Military Collaboration between the United States and the Western Union Nations," July 12, 1948, P&O 146–148, 092TS, OPD Records, RG 319, Modern Military Branch.

[52]CIA, "Review of the World Situation as It Relates to the Security of the United States," CIA 4–48, April 8, 1948, PSF, Truman Papers.

[53]On these negotiations, see especially *FR*, 1948, 3:1–351.

accepted. Other, equally vital issues were involved in the Indonesia crisis, as dissenting voices in the Truman administration repeatedly advised. Major General A. R. Bolling, acting director of intelligence for the Army, noted some of these other interests. "After five months of political maneuvering," Bolling asserted, "it appears that negotiations are about to break down because the Dutch, who never bound themselves to accept GOC recommendations, have not been willing to live up to the spirit of the political principles embodied in the Renville Agreement." The general warned that the Dutch were willing to establish a U.S.I., "but only on such terms as would permit Dutch control." If negotiations collapsed, the Dutch would probably launch another police action; renewed fighting would then drive the moderate nationalists underground, "encourage extremism, and result in guerrilla fighting approaching the scale of similar fighting in Indo-China." A breakdown of talks would thus place the United States in an untenable position: "The U.S. will be accused of turning its back on native independence movements; U.S. prestige in the Far East will be irreparably damaged; and the Indonesian Republic and other sincere independence movements in Southeast Asia will turn to Russia in desperation." This outcome would be particularly unfortunate, since Indonesia was "a vital source of strategic war materials."[54]

[54]Bolling to Chief of Staff, June 15, 1948, P&O 091 Netherlands, Planning and Operation Division Files, Modern Military Branch. At this time the U.S. government also commissioned several studies to assess the strategic importance of Indonesian oil to the United States. See, for example, memorandum from Armed Services Petroleum Board to Joint Chiefs of Staff, May 18, 1948, "Availability of Petroleum and Petroleum Products in the East Indies," P&O 463.7; memorandum from General Albert C. Wedemeyer (director, Planning and Operation Division, U.S. Army) to William S. B. Lacy, "The Relation of the East Indies to the Overall Petroleum Situation," June 23, 1948, P&O 463; and memorandum from W. G. Lalbor (captain, U.S. Navy) to Armed Services Petroleum Board, "Availability of Petroleum and Petroleum Products in the East Indies," July 27, 1948, P&O 463, all in Planning and Operation Division Files, Modern Military Branch. These studies deplored the "highly uncertain political situation in the East Indies, which makes the ultimate petroleum potential of the area not readily foreseeable." According to these evaluations, East Indies oil, while not absolutely critical to the strategic and military needs of the United States, was quite valuable, and production levels were expected to increase over the next few years. Moreover, in the event of a denial of oil from the Middle East, the importance of Indonesian oil to the United States would be greatly increased. "It is incontestable," concluded one study, "that any surplus of petroleum produc-

The duBois-Critchley plan, Bolling observed, appeared to serve American interests by keeping negotiations open and by sponsoring an equitable implementation of Renville. "The success of this program," the general argued, "would establish a United States of Indonesia capable of providing a pro-western, stabilizing influence of the greatest importance over all Southeast Asia." A failure to keep negotiations open would be disastrous for United States policy:

> If the Dutch were allowed freedom of action, military operations would eventually be renewed, financed directly or indirectly with ERP funds; the U.S. would be accused of betraying the Republic of Indonesia which has followed U.S. guidance in the negotiations thus far and thereby force it to accept Russian sponsorship; and the moderate practical thinking Republican Government, the very thing the French are seeking in Indo-China, would be forced underground to carry on a relentless fight against the Dutch.[55]

Bolling's arguments found wide acceptance in certain quarters of the State Department, especially among many of the Asianists in both the Office of Far Eastern Affairs and the Office of Intelligence and Research, and among many of the internationalist-minded diplomats in the Office of United Nations Affairs. Unlike their counterparts on the European desks and in the upper levels of the State Department hierarchy, these officers, while certainly cognizant of the importance of maintaining friendly relations with the Netherlands, tended to view international developments from a broader historical perspective. Looking toward the future, they foresaw the growing political and economic importance of the underdeveloped world and argued that the United States could not afford to alienate the newly emerging areas by supporting European colonialism in

---

tions in this area, beyond minimum essential civilian needs of the area, would be a welcome addition to the U.S. military petroleum situation, and would result in economies in tankers and tanker fuel needed for potential supply of U.S. forces in the Far East."

[55]Bolling to Chief of Staff, June 15, 1948. See also Army Intelligence Division, Memorandum for the Record (by Lieutenant Colonel Milner), "Dutch–Republican Negotations in Indonesia," P&O 091 Netherlands, Planning and Operations Division Files, Modern Military Branch.

Southeast Asia or elsewhere. In a letter to Dean Rusk, which received wide circulation in the State Department, Philip Jessup offered an excellent summary of these views. The United States, he wrote, "ought to take some steps which would overcome the general impression that we are taking an old-fashioned 19th century imperialist attitude toward the emerging nationalist groups, particularly in East Asia and Southeast Asia." He explained his reasoning as follows:

> In the long run, it seems to me that one of the dominant considerations which we ought to keep in mind is the fact that looking forward ten or twenty years, we are pretty sure that there will be a very large Asiatic bloc in the United Nations. . . . It is by no means too soon in my opinion to begin to lay our lines in such a way as to establish and maintain ourselves as the particular friend of the Asiatic bloc. In my opinion, we ought to develop with them relations as close as those which we have over the years established with the Latin-American group.[56]

In the aftermath of the abortive duBois-Critchley plan, the State Department found itself in a quandary. While full support for the uncompromising Dutch position, as Bolling's memorandum suggested, would entail hazardous consequences for American foreign policy, Washington was not inclined to back a program such as that embodied in the duBois-Critchley proposals over the determined resistance of a key European ally. In an effort to find a middle ground, the department gradually began to recognize that the American delegation to the GOC would have to take the initiative in presenting an acceptable compromise settlement to the two disputants; a proposed working paper, while it "would have to be modified to meet insurmountable Dutch objections" to the duBois-Critchley plan, would be largely modeled on that program. When a combination of illness and State Department displeasure forced Coert duBois to leave Indonesia in early July, he was replaced by H. Merle Cochran, a

[56]Jessup to Rusk, July 20, 1948, in Philip Jessup Papers, Library of Congress, Washington, D.C.; memorandum from Rusk to Hickerson, Butterworth, Satterthwaite, and Paul C. Daniels (Office of Inter-American Affairs), July 27, 1948, in folder labeled "Southeast Asia, 1946–1948, U.S. Policy," Box 5, PSA Records, DSR.

career Foreign Service officer with well-known sympathies for the Netherlands. The department instructed Cochran to begin studying fresh approaches to break the Dutch–Indonesian impasse. "It seems to us," the department cabled the American Embassy in The Hague, "that Cochran should have when he departs from Batavia detailed workable proposals which in essentials this Govt could support as basis for agreed settlement."[57]

On July 12, 1948, Frederick Nolting, the acting assistant chief of the Division of Northern European Affairs, drafted a memorandum for Under Secretary of State Lovett, outlining proposed American policy toward the Indonesian struggle. The memorandum—approved by W. Walton Butterworth, director of the Office of Far Eastern Affairs; Dean Rusk, director of the Office of United Nations Affairs; and Samuel Reber, deputy director of the Office of European Affairs—noted that State Department experts had just recently completed a revision of the duBois-Critchley working paper. The revised plan, Nolting pointed out, "will undoubtedly require of the Dutch further compromise, and a certain flexibility in negotiation which is at present lacking." Nonetheless, he explained, there was no other viable course; only effective GOC action could break the current deadlock. "The ideal solution, of course, would be for the Dutch and the Republic to settle their dispute between themselves. The Dutch apparently believe that they can do this. Our representatives on the spot believe that they cannot, and that the attempt to do so will result in partition of the islands and possibly in eventual civil war."

Lovett was scheduled to meet with Dutch officials the following day, and Nolting recommended that the under secretary impress upon them the importance of resuming constructive negotiations. They should be reminded "that considering our relations with the Netherlands in connection with the Western European Union, the ERP, and other spheres in which we are partners, it is a matter of more than passing interest to us to help promote a settlement in Indonesia which will be both lasting

[57]Marshall to Baruch, June 25, 1948, in *FR*, 1948, 6:270–71; Baruch to Marshall, August 9, 1948, 123 Cochran, H. Merle, DSR.

and beneficial to the Dutch as well as the Indonesian peoples." Nolting suggested that Lovett candidly inform the Dutch that while "the Netherlands Government appears now to feel that it can reach a settlement on its own initiative, with the role of the Good Offices Committee limited to inducing the Republic to accept a new Dutch proposal," American officials had reached the conclusion "that any proposal originating with the Dutch, or with the Bandung Conference, will not gain the acceptance of the Republic."[58]

Following Nolting's recommendation, on July 13 Lovett gave van Kleffens and Blom the State Department's frank assessment of recent developments in Indonesia. "In the course of the conversation," the under secretary recorded, "I told Dr. van Kleffens that I found the present state of affairs in Indonesia very unsatisfactory since it appeared to me that little progress had been made in negotiating a final political settlement during the past several months." He added that the areas of disagreement between the two parties had appeared to increase in recent weeks, noting that the republican position had so hardened that it now seemed "highly unlikely" that the republic would accept any unilateral Dutch proposals for a final solution. "I stated my view," Lovett wrote, "that since neither party appeared to be prepared to accept a proposal offered by the other, a compromise solution could be offered only by the GOC." In regard to the Dutch federal program, Lovett informed van Kleffens and Blom that the formation of federal states in Indonesia with or without the republic was "tantamount to partition of the area"; the State Department viewed such a contingency as "highly undesirable," as it believed that "the preservation of the unity of the entire archipelago was extremely important not only to the Indonesian Republic but to the Dutch people and the rest of the world." The under secretary concluded this candid conversation by asking the Dutch representatives to consider "the probability that a final solution would require certain concessions to the realities of the situation at the expense of an ideal solution."[59]

[58]Memorandum prepared for Lovett by Nolting, July 12, 1948, in *FR*, 1948, 6:279–81.

[59]Memorandum by Lovett of a conversation with van Kleffens and Blom, July 13, 1948, in ibid., pp. 282–83.

This lively discussion evidently had the intended effect on The Hague. On July 21 Dutch officials informed Washington that "the Netherlands Prime Minister had expressed his hope that the US delegate would begin to prepare, upon his arrival at Batavia, a working paper acceptable to both sides which would provide a practical basis for a final settlement of the Netherlands–Indonesian Republican Dispute." The Hague insisted that the working paper include at least the two following principles: (1) "the preservation of Netherlands sovereignty in the interim period, and (2) a provision that the existing body of Netherlands Indies law would be administered during the interim period." Only about two months would be required to reach a final settlement, the prime minister predicted optimistically.[60] Buoyed by this softening of the Dutch position, Cochran immediately began to formulate an acceptable draft agreement.

At this point, the urgency of drafting a conciliatory plan for an overall settlement was underscored by the continuing deterioration in Dutch–republican relations.[61] Dutch officials blamed the volatile conditions on Indonesian communists, whose strength and influence within the republican government, they charged, was steadily growing. This was a familiar Dutch refrain: beginning with the Truman Doctrine speech, The Hague consistently played on the anticommunist sentiments of the American government, exaggerating the strength of communist elements within the nationalist movement in a calculated effort to cultivate Washington's support.[62] In actuality, communist strength within the republic was quite small. The Indonesian Communist Party (PKI) had only 3,000 members in the summer of 1948, and even though PKI leaders estimated they had another 60,000 supporters in the Socialist and Labor parties, communists remained a comparatively small minority within the nationalist

[60]Memorandum of a conversation by Lacy, July 21, 1948, in ibid., p. 285.

[61]For an indication of the deterioration in Dutch–republican relations, see Republican Delegation to GOC, September 9, 1948, "Report by the Delegation of the Republic of Indonesia on Recent Developments in Indonesia," UN S/AC.10/CONF.2/BUR.32, GOC Records, UN Library.

[62]See, for example, Brady to CNO, June 4, 1947, which forwarded two lengthy reports on communism in the Indies which had been prepared by the Dutch Ministry of Overseas Territories, Attaché Reports File, Washington National Records Center, Suitville, Md. (hereafter cited as WNRC).

movement.[63] Nonetheless, this minority was growing, and State Department analysts who had once scoffed at Dutch charges began to take them more seriously in mid-1948.

Reflecting on the increased American concern about Indonesian communism, Charles Reed, chief of the State Department's Division of Southeast Asian Affairs, warned that if the communists ever came to power in Indonesia, "the situation there would be comparable to that in Indochina." Reed realized that the communist factor could force a reevaluation of American policy objectives in Indonesia. "Much will depend upon the situation elsewhere," he predicted, "and the possibility that our need for strategic materials from Southeast Asia may outweigh our desire for independence of the indigenous populations of the area, if such independence is to be a pawn in the hands of militant and organized communists."[64] The new American consul general in Batavia, Charles Livengood, was similarly concerned about the appeal of Indonesian communism; he urged Secretary Marshall to announce that the Truman Doctrine applied to Indonesia, and that the United States would exert the necessary pressure to ensure its observance there.[65]

Most observers within the State Department held, conversely, that it was actually Dutch policy that was directly responsible for the increasing popularity of communism in the republic. The failure of the Dutch to comply with the terms of the Renville agreement had led to a mounting disillusionment within the republic with the policies of the Hatta government; the communists, naturally, fed on this discontent. After all, the prime minister's domestic critics reasoned, the republic had agreed to Dutch occupation of its richest areas and to the withdrawal of its finest troops from strategic guerrilla positions behind Dutch lines and had gained no perceptible advantage in return. Instead, the Dutch had proceeded to create new states and

[63]Kahin, *Nationalism and Revolution*, p. 277.

[64]Reed to Benninghoff (Office of Far Eastern Affairs), August 27, 1948, 856D.00/8-2748, DSR.

[65]Livengood to Marshall, August 2, 1948, 856E.00/8-248, DSR. In June 1948 the State Department organized a conference of U.S. officials serving in Southeast Asia to analyze the problem of communism in the area. It met at Bangkok, June 21–26. See folder labeled "S.E.A., 1948: Southeast Asia Conference," in Box 2, PSA Records, DSR.

seemed intent on forming a provisional federal government without the republic's participation. The strategy of diplomasi, as dissident republicans contended, had thus far only increased the power of the Netherlands at the expense of the republic.[66]

Leftist opposition to the Sukarno-Hatta leadership was fueled by this widespread disillusionment with the republic's diplomatic strategy, symbolized by the humiliating Renville settlement. On February 26, 1948, the major parties constituting the leftist opposition to the Hatta government had reorganized into the People's Democratic Front (Front Demokrasi Rakjat, or FDR), under the chairmanship of former prime minister Amir Sjarifuddin. The FDR's program, which was remarkably similar to that advanced by Tan Malaka in 1946, called for the repudiation of the Renville agreement, the cessation of all negotiations with the Dutch until their total withdrawal from Indonesia, and the nationalization of Dutch and other foreign properties without compensation. With considerable support from labor and the army, the FDR presented a formidable challenge to the moderate policies of the Hatta cabinet. One of the FDR's strongest weapons against Hatta and his supporters was its charge that the republican government was truckling to the United States. Sjarifuddin, who believed himself more responsible than any other republican official for signing the Renville pact, felt particularly bitter toward the United States; he was convinced that Washington had betrayed the republic by failing to ensure a fair implementation of the agreement as it had repeatedly promised.

The dramatic return of the legendary Communist leader Musso to Indonesia in early August 1948 provided the FDR with the charismatic leadership it sorely lacked. After a twelve-year absence in the Soviet Union, the man who had led the abortive Communist revolt of 1926 and founded the underground PKI in 1935 quickly moved to consolidate the leftist forces opposing the Hatta government. The PKI readily accepted Musso's leadership and the other parties within the FDR coalition soon fell in line, accepting his revolutionary program. Once again the line between the proponents of diplomasi and perdjuangan was starkly drawn.[67]

[66]Kahin, *Nationalism and Revolution*, pp. 253–56.

[67]Ibid., pp. 259–79; Reid, *Indonesian National Revolution*, pp. 129–40.

American officials were concerned that a continuation of present Dutch policy would increase this internal opposition, threatening the very survival of the moderate Hatta government and raising the specter of a Communist ascendancy within Indonesia. On August 31 the State Department informed Cochran that it agreed with his assessment that Dutch attitudes, "intentional or unintentional," appeared to be hastening the fall of the Hatta government, and it feared that the successor of that government would be "strongly Left Wing if not Communist controlled." The department urged Cochran to "take all practicable steps" to hasten the resumption of political negotiations with the republic in an effort to forestall the possibility of a Communist takeover.[68] On the following day the department informed the American representative that it agreed with his conviction that the "deteriorating situation makes [it] imperative [that a] plan for [a] political settlement be formulated and presented at [the] earliest possible moment."[69]

On September 7 Cochran transmitted the American delegation's proposed draft agreement to Washington and urged the State Department to support it. "USDel's considered opinion," Cochran said, "is that action should be quick as possible since we are convinced situation will deteriorate further unless overall political agreement reached." The State Department promptly approved the Cochran plan, and recommended that the delegation present it immediately to both parties as well as to the Australian and Belgian delegations. Expressing its deep concern about the "Communist threat to present moderate Repub regime," the State Department emphasized that the stability of the Hatta regime would best be ensured through the acceptance by both parties of a "just and practical settlement" of the Dutch–republican dispute. Accordingly, Marshall instructed the American Embassy in The Hague to inform the Dutch Foreign Office that the United States supported the proposals of the American delegation and attached the greatest importance to bolstering the Hatta government at this juncture "in order [to] prevent further swing toward Communism within Republic." The

[68]Marshall to Cochran, August 31, 1948, in *FR*, 1948, 6:312. See also memorandum from Barco to Rusk, September 3, 1948, in ibid., pp. 318–22; White House daily summary, September 1, 1948, DSR.

[69]Marshall to Cochran, September 1, 1948, in *FR*, 1948, 6:314.

secretary noted that without question Netherlands officials in Batavia could "deftly contribute to strengthening Hatta's position and should do so promptly as possible in order [to] prevent further deterioration."[70]

Cochran submitted his proposals for an overall settlement to the two parties on September 10 in the form of a confidential note. The Cochran plan was similar to the duBois-Critchley proposals, although it made several significant concessions to the Dutch point of view. Like the American-Australian working paper, it provided for an elected federal representative assembly that would serve as both an interim government and a constitutional convention. In order to appease Dutch objections to that earlier draft agreement, the Cochran plan strengthened the federal character of the U.S.I., ensuring against republican domination of the government. In addition, the power of the Netherlands representative was increased measurably; he retained the right to veto any proposed legislation.[71]

Still The Hague remained unsatisfied.[72] On September 17, the newly appointed Netherlands foreign minister, Dirk U. Stikker, traveled to Washington in an effort to explain his government's position to American policy makers. "The problem of negotiation alone versus the use of force in the Indonesian problem," he later recalled, "was still not decided. And before making up my own mind, I determined personally to find out the thinking of the American Government on Indonesia—which I understood to be decisive for the scope of action available to us. It was essential, in my view, to have clear indications of whether or not there was any flexibility in the American position."[73]

[70]Cochran to Marshall, September 7, 1948; Marshall to Cochran, September 8 and September 9, 1948; Marshall to Baruch, September 9, 1948, all in ibid., pp. 322–29. See also memorandum from Milner to General Cortlandt V. Schuyler, "Conference on Status of Dutch–Indonesian Negotiations," attended by Milner (of Planning and Operation Division), Lacy, Lieutenant Colonel Dixon (of Army Intelligence Division), and Captain Nathaniel M. Martin (of P&O), September 22, 1948, P&O Netherlands, Planning and Operation Division Files, Modern Military Branch.

[71]"Draft Agreement for Overall Political Settlement," September 10, 1948, UN S/AC.10/184, GOC Records, UN Library. See also Taylor, *Indonesian Independence*, pp. 142–43; Collins, "United Nations and Indonesia," pp. 161–62.

[72]Cochran to Marshall, September 11 and September 13, 1948, in *FR*, 1948, 6:333–34, 336–37.

[73]Dirk U. Stikker, *Men of Responsibility: A Memoir* (New York: Harper & Row, 1966), p. 109.

In a meeting with Marshall, Stikker conveyed his government's view that some of the provisions of the Cochran plan were unacceptable. He pointed out, moreover, that his government had been surprised by the procedure followed in the submisssion of the proposals, as they had been presented without any prior consultation with Dutch officials. Marshall remarked that for his part he was "very impressed by the fact that for the first time all the elements of the American Government concerned with this problem both in the Netherlands Indies and here were unanimous in regarding the proposals as fair and in their conviction that it was of the utmost importance to act promptly."[74] In another conversation, Under Secretary Lovett told Stikker that the State Department was determined "that the growing Communist strength in Indonesia be contained and, if possible, eliminated." It was the "grave and immediate" Communist threat that most alarmed American policy makers. Lovett explained: "I said that it appeared to us that Indonesian nationalism must be accommodated in a just and practical way as a condition precedent to dealing with Communism in that area and for these very reasons, Mr. Cochran had offered his plan in the most expeditious way possible in the belief that its acceptance by both parties would strengthen Mr. Hatta and his government sufficiently to enable him successfully to liquidate Communists within the Republic." Lovett concluded the discussion by expressing the American government's hope that the Dutch would accept the Cochran plan "with its essentials unchanged as soon as possible."[75]

Just before Stikker's visit, the Army Intelligence Division had informed the State Department that it enthusiastically supported the Cochran plan, as it had the duBois-Critchley proposals earlier. On September 14 S. J. Chamberlin, director of intelligence for the Army, wrote that "since the Republic, even according to Dutch admissions, has wide popular support, the

[74]Memorandum by Marshall of a conversation with Stikker, van Kleffens, and Blom, September 17, 1948, in *FR*, 1948, 6:343–45.

[75]Memorandum by Lovett of a conversation with Stikker, van Kleffens, and Blom, September 17, 1948, in ibid., pp. 345–47. Lovett was urged to take this position in a memorandum from Hickerson, Butterworth, and Rusk, September 15, 1948, 856D.00/9-1548, DSR. For Stikker's version of these conversations, see *Men of Responsibility*, pp. 116–17. See also Jessup, *Birth of Nations*, pp. 60–61.

Dutch must be persuaded to adopt a liberal policy toward the Republic if they expect to form a USI with the wide base of popular support necessary for its survival." The nationalist movement was in danger of passing into Communist hands, and such an eventuality would adversely affect the United States' economic and strategic interests in Indonesia. Reflecting on the American stake in the archipelago, Chamberlin noted, "Indonesia is an important source for the U.S. of strategic war materials—tin, rubber, petroleum, quinine, and kapok. It is in the interest of the U.S. that all possible steps be taken to establish political stability in Indonesia so that economic rehabilitation can proceed, and these strategic materials become available to U.S. when needed." Summarizing the Intelligence Division's reasons for supporting the Cochran plan, he explained:

> If this plan succeeds the ID feels that in the long run, the best interests of the Dutch will be protected; the danger of widespread guerrilla warfare will be averted; the moral position of the U.S. regarding nationalist movements will be upheld; the Communist menace can be met by joint Dutch-Republic opposition; and economic stability, with its promise of availability of war materials of strategic interests to the U.S. can be restored.

The Army Intelligence Division, accordingly, urged the State Department "to exert pressure" to have the Dutch and republicans accept the Cochran plan.[76]

The issue of communism in Indonesia suddenly came to a head in late September 1948. At Madiun, a city in eastern Java, Indonesian Communists boldly launched a revolt against the Hatta government. Attempting to capitalize on an unmistakable leftward drift within the Indonesian republic—a drift that had been fueled by the increasing disillusionment with Renville and the apparently disastrous and unwarranted faith of republican leaders in the United States' pledges to support the agreement—the PKI made its bid for power.[77] "If govt can quell this upris-

[76]Chamberlin to General Wedemeyer, September 14, 1948, P&O 092, Planning and Operation Division Files, Modern Military Branch.

[77]Some authors have argued that the Communist revolt in Indonesia in September, coupled with Communist revolts in Burma in March of the same year and in Malaya in June, took place under orders from Moscow. According to

ing," Consul General Livengood cabled Washington, "it will be in much stronger position internally and for negotiations; if it can not, it will either disintegrate or require immediate assistance from outside." Cochran met with Hatta on September 10 and similarly informed the prime minister that, although he regretted the Madiun revolt, "crisis gives Republican Government opportunity [to] show its determination [to] suppress Communism."[78]

Hatta used the opportunity masterfully. Acting swiftly and decisively, the republican government moved to suppress the Madiun insurgents. The attempted coup proved to be premature; the Communists had foolishly overestimated their strength. By October the abortive revolt had been crushed, and once again Hatta and the republican moderates were in firm control of the nationalist movement.[79]

The prompt action of the republic in suppressing the Communist rebellion at Madiun impressed American officials. The State Department could no longer question the staunch anti-communism of the republican regime; and with the continuing stalemate in Indochina and the spectacular successes of Mao

---

this theory, the Soviet Union decided on a more aggressive policy in Southeast Asia, proclaimed the policy at a Communist youth conference in Calcutta in February 1948, and then instructed the respective Communist parties in Southeast Asia to foment rebellions in the very near future. Although direct evidence of such a conspiracy is lacking, the theory nonetheless has its adherents. See, for example, Justus M. van der Kroef, *The Communist Party of Indonesia: Its History, Program, and Tactics* (Vancouver: University of British Columbia Press, 1965), pp. 35–36; Brackman, *Indonesian Communism*, pp. 91–92; Louis Fischer, *The Story of Indonesia* (New York: Harper & Row, 1959), pp. 112–13; Jeanne S. Mintz, *Mohammed, Marx, and Marhaen: The Roots of Indonesian Socialism* (New York: Praeger, 1965), pp. 92–93. Ruth T. McVey analyzed this thesis and dismissed it in her *Calcutta Conference and the Southeast Asian Uprisings* (Ithaca: Cornell University Modern Indonesia Project, 1958). As a result of an investigation of all available sources, she concluded that there was little reason to suspect that the Calcutta Conference led to the Madiun revolt; instead, the rebellion grew out of domestic conditions within Indonesia.

[78]Livengood to Marshall, September 20, 1948, and Cochran to Marshall, September 20, 1948, in *FR*, 1948, 6:356–57.

[79]The most detailed examination of the Madiun revolt can be found in Kahin, *Nationalism and Revolution*, pp. 256–303. See also Virginia Thompson and Richard Adloff, "The Communist Revolt in Java," *Far Eastern Survey*, 17 (November 17, 1948):257–60; Reid, *Indonesian National Revolution*, pp. 134–47; George McTurnan Kahin, "The Crisis and Its Aftermath," *Far Eastern Survey*, 17 (November 17, 1948):261–64.

Tse-tung's Communists against the Koumintang in China, the rapid dénouement of the Madiun affair took on added significance. Washington increasingly came to view the Indonesian Republic as a bulwark against communism in Southeast Asia. The republic, noted Lovett approvingly, was the "only govt in Far East to have met and crushed an all-out Communist offensive."[80] Significantly, shortly after the Madiun rebellion the CIA dispatched its first regular agent to the republican capital of Jogjakarta in an effort to provide covert assistance to the republic's anticommunist leadership.[81] Considered against this backdrop, the intransigence of the Dutch was becoming more and more intolerable.

On September 17 the republican delegation voted to accept the Cochran Plan. The Netherlands delayed its reply until October 14, a full month after the plan had been presented. While accepting it as a basis for discussion, the Dutch delegation had "objections of such a serious nature" to some of Cochran's proposals that they attached a series of amendments so sweeping that they amounted to a substitution of Dutch counterproposals.[82] "The provisions which the Netherlands

[80]Lovett to Certain Diplomatic and Consular Officers Abroad, December 31, 1948, in *FR*, 1948, 6:618–20. See also Butterworth to Lovett, September 21, 1948, in folder labeled "SEA, Secretary's Press Conference," Box 2, PSA Records, DSR. Several former State Department officials (Jessup, Barco, Nolting, Rusk) emphasized to me the importance of the Madiun affair in favorably affecting the American government's perception of the Indonesian Republic. See also Acheson to Louis B. Wehle (former chief, Foreign Economic Administration, Netherlands), March 15, 1949, in Box 75, Wehle Papers, Franklin D. Roosevelt Library, Hyde Park; John F. Cady, "America's Postwar Role in Southeast Asia," in Kan Kyo Kim, ed., *Essays on Modern Politics and History Written in Honor of Harold M. Vinacke* (Athens: Ohio University Press, 1969), p. 59; Fischer, *Story of Indonesia*, p. 114; Reid, *Indonesian National Revolution*, p. 146; Brackman, *Indonesian Communism*, p. 107.

[81]I thank George McT. Kahin for bringing this point to my attention. See his essay "The United States and the Anticolonial Revolutions in Southeast Asia, 1945–50," in Yonosuke Nagai and Akira Iriye, eds., *The Origins of the Cold War in Asia* (New York: Columbia University Press, 1977), pp. 350, 360. The person in question, Arthur Campbell, is mentioned briefly in *FR*, 1948, 6:372–74, but is not identified as a CIA agent.

[82]Republican Delegation to Cochran, September 20, 1948, UN S/AC.10/186, GOC Records, UN Library; Netherlands Delegation to U.S. Delegation, October 14, 1948, UN S/AC.10/185, ibid. See also UN S/AC.10/198 and UN S/AC.10/CONF.2/BUR/W.3, ibid. For a detailed examination of the Dutch counterproposals, see Taylor, *Indonesian Independence*, pp. 146–53.

wishes to eliminate are of course the heart of the US plan," lamented Harding Bancroft of the State Department's Office of United Nations Affairs. "The amendments required by the Netherlands Government would in fact leave no US plan at all."[83] Hatta complained to Cochran that the "Dutch do not actually want to come to an agreement that is not in line with their preconceived design." He added: "The amendments proposed by [the] Dutch radically alter [the] contents and purport of [the] Cochran plan and moreover flagrantly contradict the Renville principles."[84]

Even H. Merle Cochran, who admitted that "no one could have come to Batavia with [a] more friendly attitude toward [the] Netherlands than I did," began to doubt the sincerity of Dutch pledges. Like Graham and duBois before him, Cochran gradually came to question whether the Netherlands had any intention of reaching an accommodation with the Indonesian Republic. On November 1 he informed the State Department that he believed a crisis was now inevitable unless the Netherlands delegation "revealed better faith in resuming negotiations." Speaking with T. Elink Schuurman of the Dutch delegation two days later, the American representative remarked that progress toward a settlement "had been slow principally because of [the] adamant position taken by [the] Netherlands Delegations."[85] Cochran expressed this increasing disillusionment in a telegram to Washington on November 6. Noting that the State Department was understandably reluctant to put "improper pressure" on The Hague, he nonetheless urged the department to consider exerting direct influence if conditions failed to improve:

> We have responsibility not to put US funds into Netherlands colonial enterprise involving suppression militarily of truly nationalistic aspirations. Furthermore I am convinced moral suasion or mere threat sanctions by military would be less effective than simple

[83]Bancroft to Barco, October 14, 1948, 501.BC Indonesia/10-1548. See also Secretary of State's weekly summary, October 11, 1948, DSR.

[84]Hatta to Cochran, October 21, 1948, reprinted in Cochran to Marshall, October 23, 1948, in *FR*, 1948, 6:431.

[85]Cochran to Marshall, November 6, November 1, and November 4, 1948, in ibid., pp. 467, 448, 455.

> procedure US Government telling Netherlands Government at high level that no more financial aid of any sort will be forthcoming if police action taken against Republic and as long as Netherlands fails consummate settlement through GOC permitting Republic enter USI honorably and peacefully.[86]

But Cochran had not yet given up all hope that the Dutch and Indonesians could reach an agreement; he suggested that the "greatest possibility of achieving [a] settlement" rested with the direct talks between Hatta and Stikker which had commenced on November 4.[87]

The Netherlands government had decided on direct talks with the republic's prime minister in a determined effort to block GOC participation in the negotiations. Cochran and the State Department, although initially appalled by this tactic, gradually came to appreciate Stikker's honesty and ability and even began to express guarded optimism about the chances for a successful agreement.[88] At first this optimism appeared justified, as Hatta offered major concessions to the Dutch position on such critical issues as the nature of the interim government, the powers of the Dutch representative during the transition period, and the right of Holland to retain sovereignty during that period. Only minor details appeared unresolved, and a hopeful Stikker flew to The Hague in late November for further instructions from his government.[89]

When the foreign minister returned to Indonesia to renew the discussions with Hatta, however, there was a marked change in the atmosphere. Accompanied now by E. J. M. A. Sassen, the minister for overseas territories, and a group of parliamentary advisers, Stikker and the Dutch delegation took a harder line. Accusing the republic of a mounting number of truce violations, the Dutch now insisted on a stricter observance of the cease-fire.

[86]Cochran to Marshall, November 6, 1948, in ibid., p. 467. See also Cochran to Marshall, October 29, 1948, in ibid., p. 441; Butterworth to Lovett, November 12, 1948, 501.BC Indonesia/11-1148, DSR.

[87]Cochran to Marshall, November 11, 1948, in *FR*, 1948, 6:482.

[88]See, for example, Lovett to Baruch, November 10, 1948, and Lovett to Cochran, November 10, 1948, both in ibid., pp. 478, 479.

[89]Stikker, *Men of Responsibility*, pp. 122–29; Taylor, *Indonesian Independence*, pp. 154–55.

On this and other points, the negotiations quickly stalled.[90] Baruch reported from Holland that if the talks failed, the use of force by the Dutch would be inevitable. On December 5, 1948, with the two parties again stalemated, the Dutch delegation once more departed for the Netherlands. Explaining this abrupt action to Cochran, the Dutch delegation asserted ominously: "Under the circumstances, the Netherlands Government is forced to draw the unavoidable conclusion that it is absolutely impossible to reach agreement with the Republican Government."[91]

On December 5 Cochran reported to Washington that "there is now [a] definite breakdown of direct talks." There was no indication "of any present disposition on [the] part of [the] Netherlands to negotiate either within GOC or in any other way." Believing that a second police action might now be imminent, Cochran urged the State Department to help bring the Dutch back to the bargaining table. "If representations are to succeed," he emphasized, "they must be strong."[92]

Following Cochran's advice, the State Department transmitted an aide-mémoire to the Netherlands government on December 7. Expressing disappointment with the suspension of the Stikker–Hatta talks, the department said that the "United States Government is convinced that a resumption of bona fide negotiations is imperative." The aide-mémoire reiterated the American belief that "the preponderant desire of the Indonesian people to govern themselves finds its chief expression in the Republic of Indonesia, which must be considered not as a geographical concept but as a political force." Mohammed Hatta, who acted "with skill and fortitude against a Communist revolt," had recently "given persuasive evidence of his desire to cooperate in a reasonable solution of the political differences between the Netherlands and the Republic," but his "moderate and concilia-

[90]Stikker, *Men of Responsibility*, pp. 129–37; Taylor, *Indonesian Independence*, pp. 158–59. See also "Report to the GOC from the Republican Delegation on the Informal Conversations between Hatta and the Dutch," December 7, 1948, UN S/AC.10/213, GOC Records, UN Library.

[91]Baruch to Marshall, December 2, 1948, 856D.00/12-248, DSR; Dutch Delegation to Cochran, December 5, 1948, in Special Report by the GOC to the Security Council, UN S/1129, Appendix III.

[92]Cochran to Marshall, December 5, 1948, in *FR*, 1948, 6:523–26.

tory policy" would be endangered by any arbitrary Dutch action. Washington warned that a resort to military measures, even if followed by initial successes, was likely to lead to protracted guerrilla warfare. "Such an outcome could seriously deplete the resources of the Netherlands and tend to nullify the effect of appropriations made to the Netherlands and Indonesia under the Economic Cooperation Administration." Although the United States did not raise the possibility of a suspension of Marshall Plan funds if the Dutch embarked on a second police action—as an earlier draft of this message had done—that option was nonetheless implicit. This frank statement of the American government's views, the aide-mémoire concluded, was intended "only to give the Netherlands Government the benefit of its perspective so that the Netherlands Government will embark upon no course of action which, while undertaken with the most unexceptionable motives, could result in weakening the newly emerging Western European structure to the lasting disadvantage of the component nations."[93]

Dutch authorities deeply resented this pointed American message. Members of the Netherlands Foreign Office reacted to the aide-mémoire with "pained and angry surprise"; A. H. J. Lovink remarked that it was "very plain speaking" and he "understood fully what it meant." Likewise, the Dutch cabinet was "unanimously bitter" about Washington's intervention; Stikker later wrote that "the United States did not understand that this type of action always has the opposite effect from what is intended." On December 10 the Netherlands replied with an equally blunt aide-mémoire of its own. "The Netherlands Government is convinced," this message asserted, "that the conclusion and views contained in the United States *aide-memoire* are based on an insufficient understanding of the circumstances which have led to the present situation."[94]

Top-ranking State Department officers alerted Lovett that The

[93]Aide-mémoire from Department of State to Netherlands Embassy, December 7, 1948, in ibid., pp. 531–35.

[94]Quoted in Lloyd V. Steer (chargé, The Hague) to Marshall, December 7, 1948, in ibid., p. 530; Stikker, *Men of Responsibility*, pp. 138–39; aide-mémoire from Netherlands Embassy to Department of State, December 9, 1948, in *FR*, 1948, 6:545.

Hague's aide-mémoire "strongly foreshadows the possibility of an outbreak of hostilities in Indonesia." Realizing this, Prime Minister Hatta hastily drafted a letter to the Dutch delegation on December 13 in which he attempted to satisfy earlier Dutch objections to the republican position. Washington applauded Hatta's efforts as providing a "reasonable basis [for the] resumption [of] negotiations" and reflecting the "conciliatory attitude [of the] Repub Govt." Reed called it the most conciliatory statement ever made by a top-ranking official of the republic. Nonetheless, the Netherlands flatly rejected the prime minister's overture, and on December 17 presented him with an ultimatum that, as Cochran summarized it, called "for surrender to the position" of The Hague "on every material point."[95] The Dutch maintained that this was "truly the last possible move from the Netherlands side" and gave the republic only one day to reply.[96]

Cochran angrily criticized this crude and arrogant approach. After detailing all his efforts to help the two parties to reach an agreement, he informed the Dutch: "I cannot, however, consistently with my obligations as a member of the Committee of Good Offices, press Dr. Hatta to reply summarily on the conditions imposed by your telegram because it calls for a nonnegotiated blanket assent which would preclude the possibility of bona fide negotiations, rather than effect their resumption."[97] Equally shocked by the preemptive Dutch action, W. Walton Butterworth instructed the American Embassy in The Hague to remind the Netherlands Foreign Office "of the great urgency of

[95]Memorandum prepared for Lovett by Hickerson, Butterworth, and William Sanders (acting chief, Office of United Nations Affairs), December 13, 1948, in ibid., p. 550; Hatta to Dutch Delegation, December 13, 1948, in Special Report, UN S/1129 and Corr. 1; Lovett to Cochran, December 14, 1948, in *FR*, 1948, 6:558–59; Lovett to American Embassy, Belgium, December 15, 1948, UN S/AC.10/220, GOC Records, UN Library; Reed to Butterworth, December 15, 1948, 856D.00/12-1548, DSR; Dutch Delegation to Hatta, December 17, 1948, in Supplementary Report of the GOC to the Security Council, UN S/1129 and Corr. 1; Cochran to Dutch Delegation, December 17, 1948, UN S/AC.10/220, GOC Records, UN Library.

[96]Quoted in White House daily summary, December 17, 1948, DSR.

[97]Cochran to Dutch Delegation, December 17, 1948, UN S/AC.10/220, GOC Records, UN Library. For Cochran's report to the GOC in the days before the second policy action, see Summary Record of the 169th Meeting of the GOC, December 24, 1948, S/AC.10/SR.169, ibid.

the situation and of the great importance that the Department attached to a peaceful settlement of the Indonesian problem." Butterworth remarked that "it seemed incredible to the Department that the Netherlands would resort to police action."[98] But the drift toward war was now irreversible; Dutch officials had already made the "incredible"—and fateful—decision. On December 19, 1948, they suddenly launched their second police action against the Republic of Indonesia.

[98]Memorandum by Butterworth of a telephone conversation with Steere, December 18, 1948, in *FR*, 1948, 6:571–72.

8

The Road to Independence: December 1948—December 1949

The main objective of the new Dutch military campaign was to capture the city of Jogjakarta, the seat of the republican government. The assault began in the early hours of December 19, 1948, as Dutch bombers strafed the nearby airport. The attack caught Indonesian leaders by surprise. Although the possibility of another police action had been seriously considered, Prime Minister Hatta and other nationalist leaders firmly believed that the Dutch would not strike until the opportunity for constructive negotiations had been exhausted; it was unlikely, they reasoned, that The Hague would risk insulting the United States by resorting to armed action while Cochran was still cajoling the Dutch to resume negotiations. As Hatta and a top military adviser had concluded only hours before the attack: "Unquestionably the Dutch could attack; but wouldn't this mean that they had gone mad?"[1]

The element of surprise thus combined with the overwhelming superiority of Dutch troops and weaponry to ensure the early success of the police action. By mid-afternoon of December 19 the Dutch army not only had seized Jogjakarta, but had captured Sukarno, Hatta, and half of the republican cabinet as well. The victory appeared complete: the city and the leaders that had come to symbolize the Indonesian nationalist movement were now in the hands of the Dutch military. Unprepared for the well-planned Dutch onslaught and ill equipped to fight a con-

[1]T. B. Simatupang, *Report from Banaran: Experiences during the People's War* (Ithaca: Cornell University Modern Indonesia Project, 1972), p. 17.

ventional war, Indonesian troops offered only slight resistance; they quickly fled the occupied city, regrouped in the countryside, and began to prepare for a prolonged guerrilla struggle.[2]

During the next week, the Dutch military machine overran nearly all of the major republican-held cities in Java and Sumatra. By the end of December, Dutch control of the republic's principal cities and towns was virtually complete. Intent on presenting the world with a fait accompli, Netherlands officials reported that the Dutch army had encountered little or no resistance from the Indonesian population; their troops, they claimed, had been greeted as liberators. In order to guarantee that their version of the offensive was widely reported, the Dutch imposed strict censorship on all outgoing news stories and refused to allow outside observation by either the Good Offices Committee or the military observer group attached to it. The demise of the Republic of Indonesia, The Hague hoped, would be both swift and complete. The Dutch realized that their second police action was a calculated gamble. Its success hinged on two factors: the quick suppression of all republican resistance and the willingness of the international community to accept the Dutch offensive as a fait accompli. On both counts, Dutch hopes would be profoundly shattered.[3]

The Netherlands had expected to be criticized for its unilateral abrogation of a UN-sponsored agreement, but it was unprepared for the floodtide of condemnation that greeted the police action. The most virulent reaction came from the newly independent nations. Nehru charged that the Dutch action was "contrary to the principles of the United Nations charter." Speaking before the Indian National Congress on December 19,

[2]Anthony J. S. Reid, *Indonesian National Revolution, 1945–50* (Hawthorn, Australia: Longman, 1974), pp. 151–52; George McTurnan Kahin, *Nationalism and Revolution in Indonesia* (Ithaca: Cornell University Press, 1952), pp. 337–38; Bernhard Dahm, *History of Indonesia in the Twentieth Century* (New York: Praeger, 1971), p. 137. For an Indonesian military leader's firsthand account of the fall of Jogjakarta, see Simatupang, *Report from Banaran*, pp. 17–27.

[3]Kahin, *Nationalism and Revolution*, pp. 338–39. Cochran informed the State Department of the Dutch censorship of news stories. There was "little likelihood," he cabled Washington, "of firsthand information reaching outside world as to actual situation in Repub." See Cochran to Lovett, December 21, 1948, in *Foreign Relations of the United States* (Washington, D.C., 1974), 6:594. Hereafter volumes in this series will be cited as *FR*, followed by the year.

the prime minister declared: "No one can prevent the tide of independence in Asiatic countries. Our foreign policy is that no foreign power should rule over any Asiatic country. A reaction to the Dutch action will be heard soon all over Asiatic countries, and we will have to consider our course of action in the circumstances."[4]

The following day the Arab League expressed outrage at the Dutch military offensive and pledged support for the Indonesian Republic in the United Nations Security Council. On December 22 the government of Ceylon announced that its harbor and airfield facilities could no longer be used for ships and aircraft carrying troops or war materials intended for use against the Indonesians; Pakistan and India quickly made similar pronouncements. In Australia, maritime workers banned the transport of all war-related materials to Indonesia and urged fellow dockworkers around the world to impose boycotts of their own. On December 24 the Philippines expressed "dismay and grave fears" in regard to The Hague's resort to armed force. Burmese students in Rangoon and Indian students in Bombay demonstrated against the Dutch attack, while in Karachi, angry Pakistanis marched against the Dutch Embassy.[5]

The United States government was equally dismayed by the latest Dutch transgressions. On learning of the Dutch decision for war, Robert Lovett immediately cabled Philip Jessup, the acting United States representative at the United Nations, that "it will be necessary for [the] SC to meet in emergency session to deal with what may prove to be a grave threat to internatl peace and security." Later the same day, W. Walton Butterworth remarked to Helb of the Dutch Embassy that "the Netherlands as a responsible member of the Atlantic community had done itself a grave disservice and in doing so had done one to the Christian nations." He intimated that "very unhappy times were in store for many." On the next day, December 19, Helb told William S. B. Lacy of the State Department's Division of Southeast Asian

[4]*New York Times*, December 20, 1948, pp. 1, 14.

[5]Ibid., December 21 and December 24, 1948; League of Arab States to Security Council, December 21, 1948, UN S/1128; *Times* (London), December 23, December 24, and December 28, 1948; Loy W. Henderson (ambassador in India) to Marshall, December 22, 1948, 856D.00/12-2248, DSR.

Affairs that his government had learned of the United States' intention to bring the issue of the police action before the Security Council and was concerned about the effect that the development might have on Dutch public opinion. Lacy reminded the Dutch diplomat of the American government's "unalterable opposition to [the] police action" and explained that Washington "could hardly fail to respond to the obvious moral pressures which had resulted from the Dutch resort to force."[6]

The State Department quickly determined that the United Nations, which had already assumed direct responsibility for helping to settle the Dutch–Indonesian dispute, would be the proper forum to express its opposition to the Dutch police action. But the department believed that although the United States should formally go on record as condemning the police action, it should act in concert with other nations. As Lovett told Jessup, "We do not desire US [to] assume a position of outstanding and solitary leadership in dealing with this case." President Truman reinforced this position in a conversation with Acting Secretary of State Lovett on December 20. He said that the United States should label the Dutch police action as an act of aggression, but should be careful to "avoid taking any action in the Security Council which would involve us subsequently, in consequence, in adopting positions which we would be unable to maintain, either through the defection of our allies or because of the inadequacy of our own facilities."[7] American action in the Security Council, then, was to be critical but limited. The White House and the State Department were clearly upset by the Dutch action and sought to denounce it in the Security Council; they did not, however, wish to endanger otherwise friendly relations with the Netherlands over the question of Indonesia, nor were they willing to sponsor direct sanctions of any kind against the Dutch.

On December 21 Paul Hoffman, administrator of the Euro-

[6]Lovett to Jessup, December 18, 1948, in *FR*, 1948, 6:577–78; Philip C. Jessup, *The Birth of Nations* (New York: Columbia University Press, 1974), p. 71; memorandum by Butterworth of a conversation with Helb, December 18, 1948, in *FR*, 1948, 6:578–79; memorandum by Lacy of a conversation with Helb, December 19, 1948, in ibid., pp. 583–84.

[7]Lovett to Jessup, December 19, 1948, in ibid., p. 585; memorandum by Lovett of a conversation with Truman, in ibid., pp. 587–88.

pean Cooperation Administration, announced that his agency, with the concurrence of the State Department, had suspended further Marshall Plan aid to Indonesia pending clarification of current developments.[8] In a memorandum to Hoffman, Lovett explained that the department's decision was based exclusively on economic criteria. Recent developments in Indonesia "lead us to the conclusion that, at least in certain parts of Indonesia, economic and political conditions over the next few months are likely to be so unsettled as to make it very uncertain that the investment of funds in that area will achieve the purpose intended under the ECA program."[9] This announcement was largely symbolic, however, since only $14 million of the $68 million allocated to Indonesia was directly affected; the remainder had already been distributed. Moreover, $298 million had been allocated directly to the Netherlands under the European Recovery Program, and that substantial sum remained unaffected by the ECA's decision.[10]

It is not surprising, then, that U.S. aid to the Netherlands became a controversial subject in the aftermath of the Dutch attack. Sumitro Djojohadikusomo, acting head of the Indonesian delegation to the United Nations, charged that American financial assistance was so crucial to Holland that The Hague had been able to allocate its own funds at the rate of $1 million a day toward the support of an army of 130,000 in Indonesia. Sumitro elucidated this point in a memorandum to Secretary of State Marshall:

[8] *New York Times*, December 23, 1948, p. 1; interview with Harry Kahn, Jr. (chief, Netherlands desk, ECA), January 9, 1953, in Harry Price Oral History Interviews, Truman Library, Independence, Mo.; statement of Dr. Alan Valentine (chief, ECA Mission to Netherlands), February 11, 1949, U.S. Congress, House Committee on Foreign Affairs, *Extension of European Recovery Program: Hearings*, 81st Cong., 1st sess., pt. 1, pp. 260–73; statement of Valentine, February 14, 1949, U.S. Congress, Senate Foreign Relations Committee, *Extension of European Recovery Program: Hearings*, 81st Cong., 1st sess., pp. 313–30.

[9] Memorandum from Lovett to Hoffman, December 20, 1948(?), and Hoffman to van Kleffens, December 22, 1948, both in folder labeled "ECA Operation in Indonesia," Box 11, Records of the Office of Philippines and Southeast Asian Affairs (hereafter cited as PSA Records), U.S. Department of State Records, National Archives, Washington, D.C. (hereafter cited as DSR).

[10] *New York Times*, December 22, 1948, p. 1; "U.S. Business and Indonesia," *Business Week*, January 8, 1949, p. 101; Blair Bolles, "Indonesia Raises Knotty Colonial Issues for U.S.," *Foreign Policy Bulletin*, 28 (December 31, 1948):1.

> In view of the fact that the present Dutch military campaign is an act of war in Indonesia, a threat to peace and stability in Southeast Asia, and dangerously impairing the implementation of the European Recovery Program, furthermore, in view of the fact that the Netherlands are diverting E.R.P. dollars for the purpose of waging a colonial war against freedom-loving people, we respectfully but urgently request the United States Government to discontinue rendering American dollars to the Netherlands under the European Recovery Program or otherwise.[11]

A front-page story in the *New York Times* revealed on December 22 that, according to American officials, this aid had enabled the Netherlands "to send supplies and equipment to Indonesia that otherwise might have been impossible." And ERP dollars were not the sole source of American aid to the Dutch. "Beside $298 million in Marshall Plan aid for the Netherlands and $61 million for Indonesia, the Dutch, since the war, have received Export-Import Bank credits of $300 million, credits for the purchase of U.S. war surplus supplies totaling $130 million, and $190 million worth of civilian supplies as military relief."[12]

The implication was obvious: the United States, through its financial assistance to the Netherlands, was indirectly supporting a colonial war. That fact belied any official protestations against Dutch belligerency. According to George Kahin, an American graduate student studying in Indonesia at the time, most Indonesians believed, understandably, that the Dutch would have been unable to launch their second police action had it not been for the considerable economic assistance provided by the Marshall Plan. The more knowledgeable Indonesians insisted most adamantly, Kahin wrote, "that the subsidizing of the Netherlands home economy under the Marshall Plan allowed the Dutch to divert a major portion of the wealth of that economy to the reconquest of Indonesia. This was a financial outlay, they insisted, which could not possibly have been made

[11]Sumitro to Marshall, December 19, 1948, 501.BC Indonesia/12-1948, DSR. Sumitro's statement was reprinted in *New York Times*, December 21, 1948, p. 7. See also memorandum by Lovett of a conversation with Sumitro, December 20, 1948, in *FR*, 1948, 6:590–92.

[12]*New York Times*, December 22, 1948, p. 1.

had not Marshall funds replaced this drain on the home economy."[13]

Some opponents of Dutch policy, accordingly, joined with Sumitro in urging Washington to cut off all Marshall Plan aid to the Netherlands. John W. Burton, the Australian foreign secretary, stated that either American or British pressure could have prevented the police action, and he could not understand Washington's reluctance to use ERP as a diplomatic weapon. Officials in Burma were similarly convinced that Marshall Plan aid made the Dutch offensive possible, and urged the United States to reconsider its economic assistance to Holland.[14] On December 20 the government of India transmitted a sharply worded aide-mémoire to the State Department which reflected this critical point of view. The message complained that ERP assistance was being used by the Dutch and the French to oppose national freedom in Southeast Asia and maintain colonial domination. "Intense popular feelings roused against the Netherlands Government in Indonesia and elsewhere as well as the French Government in Indo-China," the memorandum warned, "have thus a tendency to become hostile to concept of Western Union and Marshall Aid Plan."[15]

Within the United States, outspoken critics of the police action similarly recommended the curtailment of all American financial assistance to the Dutch. Writing on behalf of the six million members of the Congress of Industrial Organizations on December 23, President Philip Murray suggested this action to the Secretary of State:

> At a time when the world is striving desperately to find a road to peace, we feel that the action of the Netherlands government in

[13]Kahin, *Nationalism and Revolution*, pp. 402–3. Sumitro later commented that Asian intellectuals were unshakably convinced that American economic interests made both Dutch military actions acceptable to the United States. Asians were convinced that in every case the United States would place the interests of Europeans above the interests of Asians (memorandum by Charlton Ogburn of a conversation with Sumitro, May 19, 1949, 501.BC Indonesia/5-1949, DSR).

[14]Andrew B. Foster (chargé, Australia) to Marshall, December 20, 1948, 856D.00/12-1748, DSR; J. R. Andrus (chargé, Burma) to Marshall, December 22, 1948, 856D.00/12-2248, DSR.

[15]Aide-mémoire from Government of India to Department of State, December 20, 1948, 856D.00/12-1748, DSR.

> suddenly and wantonly attacking the people of Indonesia conforms neither to the morality of our civilization nor to the practical political needs of the people of western Europe and the United States. We feel that insofar as American aid is now available to the Netherlands government, it is being used for purposes inconsistent with the original intent and objectives of the European Recovery Program.[16]

Walter White, secretary of the National Association for the Advancement of Colored People, also called for the suspension of all Marshall Plan aid to the Netherlands;[17] and on December 28 former vice-president Henry Wallace demanded that the United States immediately cease all ERP aid to the Dutch and place an embargo on all armament shipments to Holland.[18] *The Nation* added a word of caution, noting that "the direct use of E.R.P. as a political club could provide a dangerous precedent," but suggested, nonetheless, that "the State Department ought to address a solemn message to the Netherlands Government that its improper use of American aid is endangering the whole future of E.R.P. and could lead to a refusal by Congress to provide further supplies for Holland."[19]

Throughout the United States, the public outcry against Dutch aggession was intense. On December 23 Senator George Malone of Nebraska declared at a press conference that "without the money we gave the Dutch under the Marshall Plan they could not do what they are doing in Indonesia." Senator Margaret Chase Smith of Maine expressed grave concern that Dutch belligerency in Indonesia threatened the very structure of world peace embodied in the United Nations. Speaking on January 4, she warned: "The potency of the U.N. is threatened by renewed

[16]Murray to Lovett, reprinted in *U.S. Department of State Bulletin*, 19 (January 16, 1948):82.

[17]Quoted in *New York Times*, December 24, 1948, p. 2. For analyses of the black community's reaction to colonialism and American foreign policy, see James L. Roark, "American Black Leaders: The Response to Colonialism and the Cold War, 1943–1953," *African Historical Studies*, 4 (1971):253–70; Mark Solomon, "Black Critics of Colonialism and the Cold War," in Thomas G. Paterson, ed., *Cold War Critics: Alternatives to American Foreign Policy in the Truman Years* (Chicago: Quadrangle Books, 1971), pp. 205–39.

[18]*New York Times*, December 28, 1948, p. 14.

[19]*Nation*, January 1, 1949, p. 4.

fighting in the Dutch-Indonesian war. Holland has defied the U.N. by starting what it calls 'police action.' People have been killed by the use of arms. If the U.N. fails to stop this war, then its own future is threatened." Popular radio commentator Walter Winchell stated flatly over the American Broadcasting Corporation network that "the terribly stupid blunder of the Dutch over Indonesia is worth twenty-five divisions to the communists."[20]

Business and editorial opinion also reacted sharply. *Business Week*, reflecting a view common within a large segment of the business community, lamented that "U.S. business will have to wait a little longer to see where it stands in the fabulous Indonesian market." Matthew Fox, a prominent businessman whose American-Indonesian Corporation had lined up several prospective deals with the republican government, similarly bemoaned the absence of stability in the archipelago, complaining that the Dutch police action had once again impeded the restoration of American trade with Indonesia. The press was equally vociferous in its condemnation of Dutch aggression. The staid *Christian Science Monitor* harshly denounced The Hague's militancy, while the *New York Times* emphasized that the police action would deal a "hard blow" to both the United Nations and Western prestige in the East, and the *Chicago Tribune* angrily suggested that Queen Juliana and top Dutch officials deserved to be hanged for their indefensible actions.[21]

Domestic and international criticism of the Dutch military action placed the United States in an extremely delicate position. American policy makers sought to place the blame for the current hostilities squarely on Dutch shoulders, yet to avoid a rupture with its European ally. Dean Rusk brilliantly summarized these dilemmas in a cable to Jessup on December 23. The director of the State Department's Office of United Nations Affairs observed that Dutch action in Indonesia brought into "sharp conflict" several important United States national interests:

[20]*New York Times*, December 23, 1948, p. 3, and January 4, 1949, p. 3; Louis Fischer, *The Story of Indonesia* (New York: Harper & Row, 1959), p. 120.

[21]"U.S. Business and Indonesia," pp. 101–2; *New York Times*, December 23, 1948, p. 18 (see also ibid., December 26, 1948, sec. IV, p. 6; ibid., December 31, 1948, p. 14); *Christian Science Monitor*, January 3, 1948, p. 8; *New York Times*, December 30, 1948, p. 29; *Chicago Tribune*, December 30, 1948, p. 12.

> On the one hand we are deeply interested in political and economic stability [in the] Western European countries and [the] solidarity [of] Western Europe as [a] whole. On the other hand we have [a] long established policy favoring [the] rapid development [of] non-self-governing people toward self-govt and independence and estab[lishment] in so-called colonial areas of govts based on [the] consent and agreement [of the] peoples concerned.

The United States opposed Dutch action in Indonesia because it encouraged the "spread of Communism in Southern Asia" and dealt a "serious blow" to the development of moderate nationalism in that area. Dutch handling of the Indonesia crisis, moreover, placed United States cooperation with Western Europe in jeopardy on such matters as the European Recovery Program and the Atlantic Pact, and endangered the United Nations system for the maintenance of world peace. "We have no desire," Rusk emphasized, "to condone or wink at Dutch action [in] Indonesia."

Although the State Department "agrees unequivocally that Neth[erlands] is at fault in resuming military action," Rusk quickly added, "that in itself does not decide what we do about a country which is at fault in such situations." As a permanent member of the Security Council, the United States should support all UN actions aimed at maintaining the peace. This did not mean, however, that Washington should assume those responsibilities alone: "US cannot accept [the] role [of] world policeman either in military or political sense if other permanent members refuse to join in SC action." Reminding Jessup that the American government had "no intention [of] bringing about [a] general break with [the] Dutch over [the] Indonesian question," Rusk spelled out the paradoxes inherent in a strongly anti-Dutch stance:

> For us to insist upon full compliance with highest standard of conduct as price of our association with other govts and peoples would lead us quickly into position of not too splendid isolation. On that basis we might have already broken with Russia (Berlin, Korea, etc.), Albania (Greece), Yugoslavia (Greece), Bulgaria (Greece), France (Indo-China), and UK (Palestine), Arab States (Palestine), India (Kashmir and Hyderabad), Pakistan (Kashmir),

> South Africa and so on down the list. In same way others might have in fact broken with us.

Instead, he argued, "we must pursue our basic objectives under whatever conditions we find, shaping such conditions to extent we can." Such flexibility was necessary, he reasoned, if the United States was to avoid putting itself "in such a position that any wrong committed anywhere in world and left unpunished constitutes diplomatic defeat and humiliation for US."

Consequently, Rusk went on, the United States should properly label and condemn Dutch aggression in Indonesia, acting in concert with other nations; but at the same time, Washington "did not intend to propose or support sanctions against the Netherlands in Europe." Rusk thus ruled out the possibility of using Marshall Plan aid as a bargaining lever against the Dutch. The United States was equally reluctant to "espouse" the Indonesian case before the Security Council. As he explained American *realpolitik* to Jessup: "We are pursuing our own interests and policies, as they appear both outside and inside framework UN. Today pursuit of our policy may make us critical of Dutch; tomorrow pursuit of same policy in different circumstances may make us equally critical of Indonesians."[22]

An Army Intelligence Division memorandum, also distributed on December 23, generally concurred with Rusk's assessment of American interests vis-à-vis the Dutch–Indonesian dispute. "The initiation of sanctions of any kind against the Netherlands Government," it warned, "would be counter to the military interests of the U.S." Reflecting on the active role the United States government had already taken in the Indonesian crisis, the memorandum noted that the "State Department has exerted pressure on the Dutch by a strong *Aide Memoire* and oral representations, to the extent consistent with dealings with a friendly nation and without placing undue strain on Western Union relationships." Further pressure on the Dutch—in the form of jointly sponsored Security Council resolutions critical of the police action, but short of sanctions—were now appropriate, and

[22]Rusk to Jessup, December 23, 1948, in *FR*, 1948, 6:597–600.

would not drive the Dutch out of the Western Union. The position paper reasoned:

> It is not believed that the Dutch would withdraw from Western Union over the issue, as they would have no place to go except into the Soviet camp. However, the U.S. might lose prestige throughout the Far East, if we do not adequately support legitimate independence movements. The U.S. State Department has further considered that a settlement with the present moderate Republican leaders would preclude Communist domination of the independence movement.

The long-term military interest of the United States, according to the Army Intelligence Division, required "the development of a friendly Indonesia, the release of Dutch troops there engaged, and their return to Europe." The establishment of a "friendly Indonesia" would best serve American economic and strategic needs in Southeast Asia:

> A politically and economically stable Indonesia would be valuable to the U.S. in order that an important source of strategic raw materials (oil, tin and rubber) may be made available to this country, and in order to curtail the influx of Communism into Indonesia. If a final peaceful political settlement is achieved it is expected that Indonesian economic levels will be raised, trade restored, and Soviet penetration there offset and curtailed.

A settlement could best be accomplished "by a peaceful and equitable implementation of the principles of the Renville Agreement and by facilitating the economic reconstruction of the Indies"—essentially, the position of the State Department.[23]

In accordance with State Department directives, Acting Ambassador Philip Jessup called for an emergency session of the UN Security Council to discuss the Indonesian crisis. Speaking before the hastily convened assembly on December 22, he sharply denounced the Dutch police action, declaring that his government "fails to find any justification for renewal of military operations in Indonesia." He continued: "It is our considered

[23]Maddocks to Wedemeyer, December 23, 1948, P&O 091 Netherlands, Planning and Operations Division Files, Modern Military Branch, National Archives.

view that the renewed outbreak of hostilities in Indonesia may prove to be a grave threat to international peace."[24] Accordingly, he offered a draft resolution, jointly sponsored by Colombia and Syria, which called for an immediate cease-fire and withdrawal of troops, and instructed the Good Offices Committee to assess blame for the outbreak of hostilities. After much heated discussion, the Security Council adopted the cease-fire resolution on December 24, along with an Australian-sponsored amendment requesting the immediate release of the republican leaders. The council rejected the important withdrawal clause, however, along with the clause instructing the GOC to assess blame for the onset of the new conflict.[25]

Initially, Washington was pleased by the mildness of the UN response. Lovett informed Sir Oliver Franks, the British ambassador to the United States, that "it was our hope that reasonable and moderate measures taken immediately would reduce pressure upon us to take more extreme measures ultimately, measures such as sanctions." He later instructed the American Embassy in The Hague to inform Foreign Secretary Stikker that the State Department considered it essential for the Netherlands to comply immediately with the Security Council directive; "otherwise," he warned, "Netherlands action could have most serious effect upon solidarity Western Europe and upon US public opinion with respect to cooperation with Western Europe."[26] Prompt compliance with the cease-fire resolution was thus crucial in the opinion of State Department analysts in order to forestall criticism of the council's limited measures.

That criticism had been both pointed and immediate. As the Indonesian delegation to the United Nations bitterly noted, the resolution was "meaningless and completely inadequate," as it permitted the Dutch to continue "mopping-up operations" in

[24]United Nations Security Council, *Official Records* (SCOR), 3d yr., 389th meeting, December 22, 1948, pp. 42–49.

[25]Alastair M. Taylor, *Indonesian Independence and the United Nations* (Ithaca: Cornell University Press, 1960), pp. 172–73; J. Foster Collins, "The United Nations and Indonesia," *International Conciliation*, March 1950, pp. 169–71; UN S/1150.

[26]Memorandum by Lovett of a conversation with Franks, December 24, 1948, in *FR*, 1948, 6:602; Lovett to American Embassy, United Kingdom, December 24, 1948, in ibid., p. 603.

the recently occupied territory.[27] Still, several days after the Security Council had issued its cease-fire order, the Netherlands had not yet taken any positive steps toward fulfilling its provisions.[28] This failure angered Jessup, who advised the State Department that a follow-up resolution would be necessary. He cabled Lovett that the Netherlands reaction to the United Nations resolution was "not satisfactory to us or other members of SC"; there would be mounting pressure, the American representative predicted, "for something to at least save the face of the SC in case of continued Dutch noncompliance."[29] Increasingly dismayed by this continuing Dutch intransigence—brought into sharp focus by Dutch delegate J. H. van Royen's arrogant declaration that it was not yet possible for the Netherlands government even to make a statement[30]—the United States and other Security Council members recognized the need for further action. Consequently, on December 28 the council adopted two new resolutions—proposed by China and Colombia respectively and supported by the United States—which called on the Dutch to free all republican leaders immediately and requested the Consular Commission to make "a complete report on the situation in the Republic of Indonesia, covering in such report the observance of the cease-fire orders and the conditions prevailing in areas under military occupation or from which armed forces now in occupation may be withdrawn."[31]

An analysis of the Security Council resolutions of December 24 and December 28, 1948, is quite revealing of the limited nature of the American response to the second Dutch police action. The United Nations directives had requested the Dutch to

[27]Press statement by Dr. D. Sumitro, acting head, Republican Delegation to United Nations, in *New York Times*, December 25, 1948, p. 6. In an editorial, the *Times* argued that the United Nations cease-fire resolution was so mild that it was almost a "Christmas present" to the Dutch (ibid., December 26, 1948, sec. IV, p. 6).

[28]Collins, "United Nations and Indonesia," p. 171; Kahin, *Nationalism and Revolution*, p. 341. The GOC reported to the Council on December 26 that the Dutch army continued to advance into Republican territory despite the cease-fire resolution (report of GOC to Security Council, UN S/1156).

[29]Jessup to Lovett, December 27 and December 28, 1948, in *FR*, 1948, 6:607–8, 611–12. See also Jessup, *Birth of Nations*, p. 81.

[30]SCOR, 3d yr., 393d meeting, December 27, 1948, pp. 2–3.

[31]UN S/1162, December 28, 1948; UN S/1165, December 28, 1948.

cease all hostilities in Indonesia, but had not demanded that the Netherlands military forces withdraw to the positions held before the offensive, nor had the resolutions attempted to assess blame for the inception of the current military measures. To Indonesian republicans, these omissions represented a betrayal of their cause by the United States as well as the United Nations. Short of admonishments, it appeared to them that the Security Council would do nothing to restrain Dutch aggression; and republican leaders believed that the American government was all too willing to sacrifice Indonesian interests to the priority of Western European solidarity.[32] In reality, the UN measures conformed neatly with the American policy goals outlined by Rusk. The United States, while eager to place itself on record as opposing the Dutch police action, was equally intent on maintaining friendly relations with The Hague and avoiding the implementation of sanctions against the Netherlands in Europe. From that perspective, the limited action taken by the Security Council was ideal: while firmly aligning itself with the newly emerging nations that were harshly critical of the Dutch, Washington carefully sidestepped the problems inherent in placing too much pressure on The Hague. In short, the United States contented itself with half-measures. Entangled once again in a vexing colonial dilemma, the American government thus attempted to steer a middle course, hoping that it could avoid alienating either party to the dispute.

But events were rapidly rendering this middle course untenable, and State Department authorities soon began a reevaluation of American policy toward Indonesia. On December 31 Acting Secretary of State Lovett sent a telegram to American diplomatic and consular officers abroad outlining department policy vis-à-vis the Indonesian crisis. Washington was "profoundly concerned by Dutch action, manner in which action taken and complications arising therefrom," he said. "By taking action for which moral justifications difficult [to] find, Dutch have unquestionably hurt Western cause throughout Asia." The police action, Lovett lamented, had "undone much of postwar efforts of US diplomacy southern Asia." The objectives of

[32]Kahin, *Nationalism and Revolution*, pp. 343–44.

that policy had been twofold: "(1) prevention [of] division [of the] world on lines Asia vs. West, and (2) winning confidence and support of political movements through which aspirations and convictions [of] Asiatic peoples expressed." By attacking the "moderate" republican government of Sukarno and Hatta—a regime that was the "only govt in Far East to have met and crushed an all-out Communist offensive"—the Netherlands "may have destroyed last bridge between West and Indo nationalists and have given Communists everywhere weapon of unanswerable mass appeal." He was particularly concerned that the Dutch would be unable to attain their military objectives in Indonesia and instead would get bogged down in an interminable guerrilla war. Independent estimates of military conditions foresaw that the Dutch army in Indonesia might find itself in a position analogous to the French army in Indochina, "where ruinous inconclusive war now entering third year with result Communists in firm control nationalist movement." There was nothing the United States could do at present, Lovett pointed out, except "fix responsibility on Dutch and make own position clear for sake US standing in Asia." Foreshadowing a more active American intervention, he stressed that the United States must seek to "keep issues clear since in future [it] may be required [to] take measures unpleasant to Neth."[33]

In another background cable, sent to most major U.S. diplomatic missions abroad on January 5, 1949, the State Department further explained U.S. policy toward the Indonesian conflict. Although Washington ran some risk "in relying upon any nationalist movement in Southeast Asia to adopt a pro-Western orientation and to hold a firm anti-Communist front, it cannot be assumed that every nationalist movement in SEA has a communist complexion." The department summarized recent U.S. decisions as follows:

> In the course of the past few months, the Department had come to believe that the Sukarno-Hatta Government might well constitute the last bridge between the West and the Indonesian nationalists. Rather than scrap this bridge in the probably futile hope that 9

[33]Lovett to Certain Diplomatic and Consular Officers Abroad, December 31, 1948, in *FR*, 1948, 6:618–20.

> million Dutch would be able indefinitely to control 75 million Indonesians against the will of effective elements, wisdom had appeared to require that on the basis of a calculation of the obvious risks, the United States should endeavor to persuade the Netherlands to offer such concessions to the nationalist movement as would have made possible an agreement.[34]

The most effective leverage that the United States could bring to bear on the Netherlands, of course, was the suspension of all Marshall Plan aid. This was the course recommended by many critics of Dutch policy, both in the United States and overseas, but such action was categorically rejected by leading State Department and ECA officials. As Butterworth explained to Sir Benegal Rama Rau, the Indian ambassador to the United Nations, "A resort to unilateral punishment of Holland by cancellation of ECA would establish a dangerous precedent of attempting to achieve solutions to world problems by direct individual nation approach and of employing economic aid to achieve political goals." During the same conversation, Rusk added that such an approach "could only result in the ultimate destruction of the UN, the support of which is the corner stone of both Indian and American foreign policy"; and Joseph C. Satterthwaite, director of the department's Office of Near Eastern and African Affairs, commented that use of the ECA program in the manner suggested by the Indian government would be tantamount to "economic imperialism."[35] The respected political commentator Arthur Krock reflected official thinking when he offered the following assessment of the problem in the *New York Times*:

> The halt of recovery funds to Indonesia actually slows the whole Marshall Plan project, since they operate in the interest of the

[34]Lovett to Certain Diplomatic and Consular Officers Abroad, January 5, 1949, 890.00/1-549, DSR.

[35]Memorandum by J. S. Sparks (assistant chief, Division of South Asian Affairs) of a conversation with Rau, Butterworth, Satterthwaite, and Rusk, January 3, 1949, in *FR*, 1949, 7, pt. 1:123–25. ECA officials concurred with this judgment. See interview with Kahn, Harry Price Oral History Interviews; statement by Valentine, February 11, 1949, in House Committee on Foreign Affairs, *Extension of ERP: Hearings*, pp. 260–73; statement by Valentine, Senate Foreign Relations Committee, *Extension of ERP: Hearings*, pp. 313–30.

> European economy. And if Holland were eliminated as a recipient the surrounding Marshall Plan structure would be shaken as by an earthquake, and with it our security policy. . . . The delicate fabric of Western security against Russian communism, woven with such difficulty and still far from complete, could readily be shattered by an American attempt to isolate Holland unless it completely recedes from its present action.[36]

Although Washington remained reluctant to threaten the Dutch with its ultimate weapon, the suspension of all ECA payments, American policy makers increasingly began to realize, as Lovett's telegram of December 31 indicated, that in the future the United States "may be required to take measures unpleasant to Neth." Several developments at this juncture began to push the State Department in the direction of a more active policy. One was the decision by the Indian government, announced by Nehru on January 2, to convene immediately a conference of Asian nations in New Delhi for the purpose of condemning Dutch actions in Indonesia. This announcement deeply disturbed American officials; they were already apprehensive that the Dutch offensive might intensify simmering tensions between Asia and the West, fueled by the colonial issue, and feared that a conference in New Delhi might raise the specter of a world bitterly divided on that emotional question. At a time when the United States was determined to present as solid a front against the Soviet Union as possible, such a development was dangerously unwelcome. George F. Kennan, director of the State Department's Policy Planning Staff, informed Loy W. Henderson, the U.S. ambassador in India, that the department was "deeply concerned over [the] longrange implications [of the] present Indonesian situation as we see it aggravating polarization between [the] Atlantic community and Asia."[37] Henderson

[36] *New York Times*, December 26, 1948, sec. IV, p. 3.

[37] Kennan to Henderson, January 4, 1949, 890.00/1-448, DSR. See also Fred W. Riggs, "U.S. Firm on Indonesia as Asians Meet in New Delhi," *Foreign Policy Bulletin*, 28 (January 21, 1949):2–3; Cochran to Lovett, January 3, 1949, in *FR*, 1949, 7, pt. 1:119; Lovett to Embassy in Philippines, January 11, 1949, in ibid., p. 141; Ton That Thien, *India and Southeast Asia, 1947–1960* (Geneva: Libraire Droz, 1967), pp. 99–102; Norman Brown, *The United States and India, Pakistan, Bangladesh* (Cambridge: Harvard University Press, 1972), p. 369.

similarly warned that a growth of "Pan-Asianism" would be "extremely dangerous" to the United States, a view generally echoed in Washington.[38] But the Department of State also fully realized that any attempt to block the gathering would only further alienate the nations of Asia. Accordingly, a policy of strict noninterference was adopted, with most concerned officers expressing the hope that the convocation would not move in a radical, anti-Western direction.[39]

At the same time, the American dilemma was exacerbated by the continuing refusal of the Dutch to abide by the Security Council's directives. As Cochran informed the department on January 4, "There has been no Netherlands compliance even by verbal formula and reasonable compliance with resolution no longer possible."[40] Dutch defiance of the United Nations placed the United States in an extremely awkward position: not only did it weaken a major American policy objective, which, in Butterworth's words, was " to place itself in the best possible light with the Asiatic and Islamic countries whose sympathy with the Indonesian Republic is great,"[41] but The Hague's blatant disregard for the United Nations also called into question the viability of that organization, thus threatening what Rusk called a "cornerstone" of postwar American foreign policy.

Cochran's cables to Washington, which consistently castigated Dutch actions, also argued that only strong measures against the Netherlands could lead to a just settlement in Indonesia. He informed Lovett on January 3 that as a result of the police action, he no longer had an "appropriate role" to play as the American representative on the Good Offices Committee. In fact, Cochran pointed out reluctantly, the committee had been rendered so ineffective by the Dutch assault that it might as well be dissolved; only prompt and effective action by Washington could justify his continued presence in Indonesia. He implored the State Department to take the following steps:

[38]Henderson to Lovett, January 6, 1949, 890.00/1-549, DSR.

[39]Lovett to Henderson, January 5, 1949, 890.00/1-149, DSR; Satterthwaite and Butterworth to Lovett, January 6, 1949, in folder labeled "New Delhi Conference—Nehru," Box 2, PSA Records, DSR.

[40]Cochran to Lovett, January 4, 1949, in *FR*, 1949, 7, pt. 1:126.

[41]Memorandum from Butterworth to Charles E. Bohlen (counseler, Department of State), January 7, 1949, in ibid., p. 136.

> US clearly and publicly disassociate itself from present Netherlands policy. This requires definite unequivocal statement by us made either individually or in SC that in our view Netherlands is aggressor. This is to be followed or accompanied by public notice that further ECA aid both to Netherlands and Indonesia is suspended until fair and reasonable settlement of Indonesian question has actually been achieved.

Recognizing the reluctance of American policy makers to use ECA assistance as a "political weapon," Cochran offered his personal view: "Should we not be equally conscientious and solicitous to see that funds given under [the] guise [of] economic recovery are not used to conduct what is generally viewed as war of aggression against a people seeking promised freedom?"[42]

Gradually the State Department began to accept the compelling logic for taking a stronger stand against Dutch transgressions. On January 6 Rusk informed Jessup of this changing attitude and instructed him to cover the following points in his next Security Council speech: that the United States "can find no adequate justification for the military action taken by the Netherlands"; that the continuation of the military action after the resolution of December 24 "is an act of defiance of that resolution on the part of the Netherlands"; that the Indonesian problem cannot be solved by force; and that the United States believes that a just settlement between the Netherlands and Indonesia can be reached only "if all elements of coercion and duress are removed" and if negotiations are conducted "on the basis of the free and democratic procedures as reflected in the principles set forth in the Linggadjati and Renville agreements."[43] On the same day, Butterworth noted that the State Department had directed Jessup to speak before the Security Council "to the end that the United States fully and finally dissociate itself from Netherlands police action, place the blame for the rupture of negotiations squarely on the Netherlands, and

[42]Cochran to Lovett, January 3, 1949, in ibid., pp. 119–21. See also Cochran to Lovett, January 4, 1949, in ibid., pp. 126–28.

[43]Lovett to Jessup, January 6, 1949, in ibid., pp. 131–32. See also Jessup, *Birth of Nations*, pp. 83–84.

compel the Netherlands to state in practical and definite terms its plans for a solution of the Indonesian problem."[44]

Lovett revealed this firmer policy in a meeting with Dutch officials on January 11. Speaking with van Kleffens and Helb, the acting secretary underscored American displeasure with recent Dutch actions:

> I replied that the Indonesian problem had been blown up, as a result of Dutch military action, to a point where it was extremely difficult to handle. I said that public and Congressional opinion might force us in a direction which would be extremely adverse to the interests both of the Netherlands and of the United States, including jeopardizing ECA aid to Holland and the North Atlantic Security Pact. . . . I replied that we had to face the political reality of an extremely adverse reaction to the Dutch attack and that what the Dutch have stated as their intentions in Indonesia was not sufficient to take the heat out of the situation. . . . I mentioned particularly the serious possibilities inherent in the Asian conference called by Nehru.

Lovett reminded the Dutch representatives that the United States was "greatly disturbed" by developments since the Dutch military offensive; it believed now "that the situation was one in which almost anything could happen."[45]

Philip Jessup's speech before the UN Security Council on January 11 signaled this shift of emphasis in American policy; for the first time, the United States condemned outright the Netherlands police action and subsequent flouting of the Security Council's cease-fire resolution. "The United States Government," he declared, "can find no adequate justification for the military action taken by the Netherlands in Indonesia." The continuance of the Dutch military measures after the resolution of December 24 "was an act of defiance on the part of the Netherlands authorities," Jessup stated flatly. "No excuses offered by the Dutch Government can conceal the fact that they have failed to comply with the Security Council demands, both

[44]Memorandum from Butterworth to Bohlen, January 7, 1949, in *FR*, 1949, 7:1, 136.

[45]Memorandum by Lovett of a conversation with van Kleffens and Helb, January 11, 1949, in ibid., pp. 139–41.

in refusing to cease-fire immediately and in refusing to release the political prisoners immediately." Criticizing the Dutch for their continuing "mopping-up operations," the American representative commented sarcastically: "I am sure that the Security Council has no intention of approving action consolidating military victories which themselves were gained as a result of open defiance of an order of the Council." Jessup ended his biting speech by cataloguing the "history of non-cooperation on the part of the Netherlands in the work of the Good Offices Committee in Indonesia" and suggesting that bona fide negotiations be resumed promptly on the basis of the ill-fated Cochran plan.[46]

Still desiring to act in concert with other powers—as Lovett instructed Jessup, "we did not with to carry the banner and make ourselves solely responsible for whatever action was taken"—the United States sought support for a new Security Council resolution that was circulated as a "working paper" on January 14.[47] A revised version of the resolution, jointly sponsored by Cuba, China, and Norway and backed by the United States, was officially submitted to the council on January 21. The Dutch vigorously objected to the new proposal. Van Royen charged that it would put the Netherlands "under the guardianship of the United Nations"; the Dutch people, he stormed, "have not guided the development of Indonesia for three hundred and fifty years to surrender their responsibility at the last minute before the final consummation of that development: the achievement of Statehood for Indonesia."[48] Added Stikker, in a speech to the Foreign Press Association at The Hague: "I can foresee only chaos if the resolution is allowed to stand as it is now before the Security Council, chaos in Indonesia and subsequently chaos in the Netherlands—and all this because of a lack of confidence, a lack of faith in the spiritual forces and values of the West, a basic mistrust of our proclaimed intentions, of our most formal pledges."[49]

[46]SCOR, 4th yr., 398th meeting, January 11, 1949, pp. 2–10.

[47]Memorandum by Rusk of a conversation with Jessup, January 18, 1949, in *FR*, 1949, 7, pt. 1:168; Jessup to Lovett, January 12, 1949, in ibid., pp. 144–46.

[48]SCOR, 4th yr., 406th meeting, January 28, 1949, pp. 18–19.

[49]*New York Times*, January 22, 1948, p. 7.

Despite the Dutch objections, the council unanimously adopted the resolution on January 28. The new directive was considerably stronger than any previous resolution: it called on the Netherlands to cease all hostilities at once, to release the republican political prisoners "immediately and unconditionally," and to resume negotiations with the republic on the basis of the principles enunciated in the Linggadjati and Renville agreements. It suggested, furthermore, that an interim government be established by March 15, 1949, that elections for a constituent assembly be completed by October 1 of that year, and that a transfer of sovereignty to the United States of Indonesia take place no later than July 1, 1950. The resolution also reconstituted the Good Offices Committee as the United Nations Commission for Indonesia and expanded its powers: it was now "authorized to make recommendations" to the two parties or to the Security Council and was permitted to make decisions on the basis of agreement between two of its three representatives.[50] At last, it seemed that the United States and the United Nations had taken decisive action.

How effective the new resolution would be, however, remained problematical. A story that appeared in the *New York Times* on February 3 proved to be quite embarrassing to Washington. It cited reliable State Department sources who had intimated that the United States would give the Dutch a "reasonable time" to work out a solution between themselves and the Indonesians. "The provisions of last week's Security Council resolution," the story pointed out, "will not be applied at this time."[51] This report was officially denied by administration spokesmen, who indignantly insisted that "we only agreed not to press [the] Dutch too fast or too hard in Batavia, in order [to] give reasonable time for psychological and political adjustment necessary to carry out provisions SC res."[52] Jessup reiterated this point in a telegram to Rusk. Noting the flap caused at

[50]UN S/1234. The revisions from the original draft are explained in Jessup to Lovett, January 17, 1949, in *FR*, 1949, 7, pt. 1:163–66. See also Jessup, *Birth of Nations*, pp. 84–88.

[51]*New York Times*, February 3, 1949, p. 11. See also Jessup, *Birth of Nations*, pp. 88–89.

[52]Acheson to Baruch, February 3, 1949, in *FR*, 1949, 7, pt. 1:204.

the United Nations by the controversial *New York Times* story, he said: "We are taking line that Dutch should have reasonable time but that time must be used to arrange compliance with SC resolution and not circumvention of it."[53]

Personally, Jessup believed that the firm American stand in the Security Council had "secured important advantage in terms of relations with Asiatic and Near Eastern states." The solid American backing of the January 28 resolution, moreover, had strengthened the United Nations and the general United States policy of support for the United Nations, in his opinion. "On the other hand," he cautioned, "any weakening of our position in support of action taken by SC would be highly injurious to UN, to our position in SC and to our relations with other delegations."[54]

A report prepared for President Truman by the CIA on January 19 closely analyzed the important interlocking security interests of the United States which were "simultaneously affected" by the Dutch police action and their subsequent refusal to comply with Security Council directives. The objective of the Dutch police action, the report asserted, "was to reduce a complex political and economic deadlock to an older and simpler pattern of colonial control." According to the report, however, Dutch aggression in the Indies had far-reaching implications for American foreign policy. "If Indonesia had its own private 'iron curtain'," the CIA suggested, "long-term US security interest might not be involved. But Indonesia does not exist in a vacuum and basic US security interests are not simple and limited. US security rests on the strategic consequences of related events in China, India, Southeast Asia, and the offshore islands; and what happens in Indonesia both affects and is influenced by these events." The report analyzed the interrelationship between developments in Indonesia and overall U.S. policy objectives as follows:

> US security also rests on the outcome of already well-established social trends in Asia generally, and on the judgments and preferences of the Asiatic masses. It also depends on the final character

[53]Jessup to Rusk, February 4, 1949, in ibid., p. 206.
[54]Ibid., pp. 205–6.

> of the relation between Western European states and their colonial territories, in the capacity of the United Nations to reduce and dispose of the tensions that arise in connection with these relations, and on the maintenance of the economic programs which are being developed in ECA in collaboration with Western European states.
>
> Each of these aspects of US security is affected to a greater or less degree by Dutch action in Indonesia. The balance in which they have been precariously held has now been knocked over by a blunt instrument. Regardless of the momentary stability that "police action" may impose, it is considered likely that this action will ultimately release more dangerous social and political forces than those it has brought under control.

According to the CIA estimate, the immediate damage of the Dutch police action came in three areas. The first was the colonial problem, which had nagged Washington since the close of World War II. "The essence of this problem since 1945," the report noted, "has been how to satisfy the nationalist aspirations of colonial peoples while at the same time maintaining the economic and political stability of European colonial powers." While the problem remained unsolved before the Dutch offensive, it was "at least kept from developing to the point where a critical US decision would be required." The Dutch police action, however, "has pushed the US close to this critical point. US security interests in Europe and the Far East are in danger of appearing as mutually exclusive, when, in fact, the power position of the US vis-a-vis the USSR requires that they be pursued concurrently."

The other areas in which the Dutch offensive affected basic American security interests were in its impact on the political stabilization of the Far East and in its impact on U.S. economic programs. By threatening to prolong the nationalist struggle in Indonesia, the Dutch might inadvertently allow the Communists to join in the nationalist movement and manipulate it to their own advantage. "The Dutch 'police action,'" the report suggested, "provides ample material for a prolonged Communist propaganda campaign and the greater part of this material will seem irrefutable when presented in the context of Asiatic nationalism versus Western imperialism." The CIA cautioned that the primary target of a Communist propaganda drive would be the colonial powers of Western Europe, "with the US subject to probable identification as an imperialistic fellow-traveler." Finally, the CIA estimated that the Dutch attack had an important economic dimension. The interest of the United States in maintaining the availability of Indonesian commodities for the U.S. economy, for the European Recovery Program, and as a source of dollar credits for the Netherlands government would be seriously impeded. "It only remains to point out that Dutch 'action' has cut the US position to the bone by touching on nearly all basic US security interests simultaneously. Furthermore, this has occurred at a moment of dubious balance, when possible gains in Western Europe have to be measured against possible losses in the Far East."[55]

These interlocking security interests, so clearly depicted in this report, would continue to be cut to the bone as long as the Dutch dragged their feet in complying with the resolutions of the Security Council, especially the one of January 28, a fact that was becoming increasingly recognized in Congress. On February 7 Senator Owen Brewster of Maine introduced a resolution, signed by nine other Republican senators, which called for the suspension of all ECA and other financial aid to the Netherlands until it stopped its military measures against the republic. "It is a well-settled rule," the Maine legislator noted wryly, "that he who pays the piper is entitled to call the tune." Speaking before the Senate on February 7, Brewster termed the Dutch police action murderous, "a crushing sneak attack like Japan's on Pearl Harbor, like Nazi Germany's on Holland itself." Dutch business had shut American business out of the lucrative Indonesian market, yet American ECA money was indirectly financing the Dutch colonial adventure. "If the Dutch have $4,000,000,000 in assets in Indonesia and are shutting out American business," Brewster snapped, "why are we financing the Dutch at a rate of $500,000 a year?" Applauding the moderate character of the republicans, "who have consistently fought all radical tendencies and within the past year have suppressed by force of

[55]Central Intelligence Agency, "Review of the World Situation as It Relates to the Security of the United States," CIA 1-49, January 19, 1949, President's Secretary's File, Truman Papers, Harry S. Truman Library, Independence, Mo.

arms a small Communist uprising," he asked rhetorically: "Do we intend to support nineteenth-century Dutch-British-French imperialism in Asia which will create a climate for the growth of communism? Or do we intend to support the moderate republican nationalists throughout Asia?"[56]

The Brewster resolution particularly worried Truman administration officials, since it was offered as an amendment to the bill extending the European Cooperation Program and threatened to delay passage of that important measure. In the face of this congressional pressure, Washington intensified its efforts to secure Dutch acceptance of the Security Council's January 28 directive. To accomplish that objective, and to dispel any lingering doubts about the American government's position, the State Department sent Cochran to the Netherlands to talk with leading Dutch officials. On February 7 the senior American diplomat met with the three major architects of Dutch foreign policy: Foreign Minister Dirk Stikker, Minister for Overseas Territories E. J. M. A. Sassen, and Prime Minister Willem Drees. Speaking frankly, Cochran expressed "great disappointment" with the course of events that had led to the police action and stressed the United States' desire to help its "old friend and ally" to extricate itself from its "difficult situation." He reported to Washington: "I spared no details in picturing how bad their predicament was and how much worse it might become unless Netherlands Government implemented SC resolution." Cochran emphasized that while the United States backed the United Nations directive, it was not an American measure but represented the consolidation of ideas contributed by several nations; moreover, Washington was under mounting pressure from Congress and the American public to take far stronger steps, such as suspending all ECA payments to the Netherlands. Despite this "keen criticism" within the United States, Cochran assured the Dutch leaders, the State Department was making "great efforts" to protect its ally. Nevertheless, "non-

[56]*Congressional Record*, February 7, 1949, U.S. Congress, Senate, 81st Cong., 1st sess., 95:831; statements by Owen Brewster, February 14, 1949, U.S. Congress, Senate Foreign Relations Committee, *Extension of European Recovery Program: Hearings*, p. 477, and February 7, 1949, Senate, 81st Cong., 1st sess., *Congressional Record*, 95:831, 834.

compliance by Netherlands now with SC Resolution would give press and Congress added reason for attack and for suggesting cutting off all funds." Insisting that he was "speaking entirely personally and not briging any threat from my Department that ECA would be stopped," Cochran pointed out that "whatever might be attitude of Department of State such danger would be risked if behavior of Netherlands is such as to warrant SC calling it before its tribunal again on handling of Indonesian question."

The Dutch policy makers were notably distressed by Cochran's blunt appraisal of their "predicament." Stikker stressed the political difficulties involved for the present Dutch coalition government in accepting the detailed Security Council resolution; Drees added that the resolution interfered with Dutch sovereignty in Indonesia in political, military, and economic areas. Cochran countered that they were exaggerating the complications of the resolution; the United States recognized The Hague's difficulties and was "anxious [to] help Netherlands get out of difficulty but can only succeed if Netherlands Government accepts and implements SC Resolution." Sassen then argued that his government had embarked on the offensive in an effort to combat communism and to preserve the rights of Western peoples in the Far East. But the police measures, Cochran snapped, had had exactly the opposite effect. In the first place, "it had upset truly conservative Republican Government which with own leaders and resources had successfully put down Communist uprising few weeks earlier and had demonstrated to world its faith in democracy." Second, "it had set off resentment in all of Asia with resultant New Delhi conference." The conference, which has unanimously voted to condemn the Dutch assault on the republic, set a dangerous precedent: it gave an "incentive to first actual steps toward constituting Asiatic bloc which may conceivably develop further and establish line of demarkation if not opposition to Western groups."[57]

The fundamental problem revealed by these frank discussions and by the UN debates was that, despite all Dutch claims to the contrary, Holland's objectives in Indonesia were inherently in-

[57]Cochran to Lovett, February 9, 1949, in *FR*, 1949, 7:1, 216–19.

compatible with the resolutions of the Security Council. By this time the United States, along with the nations of the Security Council, had become convinced that the Republic of Indonesia represented the nationalist aspirations of the vast majority of the archipelago's people, and that it was a mature, responsible regime that was prepared faithfully to execute the full responsibilities of self-government. The Netherlands, beginning well before the second police action, sought to eliminate the Indonesian Republic as a viable political force. In its place the Dutch intended to create a fragmented and impotent federal structure—the proposed U.S.I.—which would exercise only nominal sovereignty while remaining loyal to The Hague and allowing the Dutch to maintain de facto control over the East Indies. Dutch delegate van Royen's statements during the Security Council debates are particularly revealing in this regard. He condemned the "irresponsible and extremist" elements who had controlled the republic and accused them of relying on Communist elements for support. Because of republican "terrorism," he argued, the Netherlands government had found it necessary to exercise its sovereignty in order "to purge the Republic by armed force." On another occasion the Dutch representative stated flatly that all republican authority had collapsed and was "no longer existent."[58] In Indonesia, another prominent Dutch diplomat conveyed this view to republican officials in a remarkably blunt conversation. As a member of the republican government reported the meeting to the GOC: "He told us that the Dutch Government no longer recognized the Republic as a political organization with a territory of her own and accordingly no longer recognized our position."[59]

While Cochran was pressuring The Hague to reconsider its policy, that policy was being steadily undermined by persistent Indonesian guerrilla activity, which, as Stikker admitted privately to Cochran, was reaching "serious" proportions.[60] As noted

[58]SCOR, 4th yr., 388th meeting, December 22, 1948, pp. 2–3; 397th meeting, January 7, 1949, p. 7; and 400th meeting, January 14, 1949, p. 28. See also Taylor, *Indonesian Independence*, pp. 179–84.

[59]Republican Delegation to GOC, January 24, 1949, S/AC.10/250/Add.2, GOC Records, UN Library.

[60]Cochran to Lovett, February 9, 1949, in *FR*, 1949, 7:1, 214; Dirk Stikker, *Men of Responsibility: A Memoir* (New York: Harper & Row, 1966), p. 144.

earlier, the Dutch had counted on presenting the world with a fait accompli; they had hoped to crush republican resistance swiftly, thereby silencing all opposition to their federal program. But as the Netherlands had seriously miscalculated the wave of international condemnation that had greeted their offensive, so too did they seriously underestimate the groundswell of popular resistance to their police action within Indonesia. By the middle of January, Dutch officials were admitting privately that Indonesian guerrilla activity had set back economic progress in the islands anywhere from six months to two years.[61] According to George Kahin, who was one of the few American civilians in the archipelago at this time, "both Republican military resistance and civilian noncooperation developed a magnitude and intensity that was stunning to them." By late January, he noted, Dutch troops in Indonesia "were actually more on the defensive than on the offensive."[62]

The remarkable resurgence of Indonesian guerrilla activity, coupled with stinging international denunciation of the police action, compelled Dutch officials to reevaluate their policy. American displeasure with The Hague's intransigence was particularly instrumental in prompting this reconsideration of policy. Dutch policy makers were well aware of the overwhelming importance of ERP assistance to the postwar recovery of their nation. It was "not a question of whether you were in favor of it," Stikker later recalled, "because it was absolutely a must—you couldn't do without it."[63] He conceded this point in a major

[61]CIA Information Reports, Military Intelligence Service (MIS) nos. 522110 and 522937, Army-Intelligence Document File, Washington National Records Center, Suitville, Md. (hereafter cited as WNRC).

[62]Kahin, *Nationalism and Revolution*, p. 391. See also *Newsweek*, March 21, 1949, pp. 44–45; Nugroho Notosusanto, *Some Effects of the Guerrilla on Armed Forces and Society in Indonesia, 1948–1949* (Canberra: Department of Defence and Security, Centre for Armed Forces History, 1974); Dorothy Woodman, *The Republic of Indonesia* (New York: Philosophical Library, 1955), pp. 249–52; J. K. Ray, *The Transfer of Power in Indonesia* (Bombay: Manaktales, 1967), William Henderson, *Pacific Settlement of Disputes* (New York: Woodrow Wilson Foundation, 1954), pp. 52–53; Reid, *Indonesian National Revolution*, pp. 153–57. A fascinating inside account of the guerrilla warfare can be found in Simatupang, *Report from Banaran*. Simatupang was a colonel in the Indonesian army.

[63]Interview with Dirk Stikker, April 23, 1964, European Recovery Program Interviews, Truman Library, pp. 1, 4. See also interview with E. H. van der Beugel (director, ERP Division, Dutch Foreign Affairs Ministry), June 1, 1964, in

speech before the Dutch Second Chamber on February 4. Cooperation with the United States in regard to the Marshall Plan and NATO, the foreign minister declared realistically, had become a cornerstone of Dutch and Western European foreign policy, and although Netherlands policy should never be determined solely by Washington's wishes, it was foolish in his view for The Hague to ignore American advice.[64] A cabinet crisis ensued, with Beel, now high commissioner for the crown in Indonesia, recommending a more flexible position, and Sassen, the minister for overseas territories, refusing to bow to American pressure. Beel's more realistic assessment of Holland's dilemma prevailed, and Sassen, who had advocated total noncompliance with the Security Council resolution of January 28, resigned on February 11. The path toward a compromise settlement now appeared open.[65]

During the next two weeks the Dutch government unveiled the details of a compromise proposal that was officially announced on February 26. In presenting the new Dutch plan, Beel emphasized that the Netherlands government was in full agreement with the *aims* of the Security Council resolution of January 28; it only suggested different *means* to attain the same objectives. The Beel plan offered an accelerated timetable for a transfer of sovereignty to the United States of Indonesia. A round-table conference would be held at The Hague on March 12, 1949, "to discuss the conditions for and the ways along

---

ibid., pp. 3, 5; interview with Dr. Van den Brink (minister for economic affairs), November 24, 1952, in Harry Price Oral History Interviews, p. 1, Truman Library.

[64]Quoted in Taylor, *Indonesian Independence*, p. 197. S. I. P. van Campen has argued that the Netherlands' signing of the Brussels Pact in March 1948 represented a reorientation in that country's foreign policy; to a certain extent, it then became part of a greater whole—Western Europe. After the Brussels Pact, the Dutch defined their ultimate interest in terms of Western European security. Since Dutch officials fully realized that the security of Western Europe was dependent on the power of the United States, they were particularly vulnerable to American pressure. European security thus superseded the need to hang on to Indonesia; and American displeasure with Dutch colonial policies brought the issue to a head. See S. I. P. van Campen, *The Quest for Security: Some Aspects of Netherlands Foreign Policy, 1945–1950* (The Hague: Martinius Nijhoff, 1958), pp. 80–88, 145–47.

[65]Stikker, *Men of Responsibility*, pp. 146–47; Taylor, *Indonesian Independence*, pp. 197–99.

which the earliest possible transfer of sovereignty" could be accomplished. All Indonesian groups, including the republicans, would be invited to attend the conference, along with the United Nations Commission for Indonesia. An interim federal government would then be established by May 1, with the final transfer of sovereignty to be completed by July 1—a full year ahead of the date proposed by the Security Council directive. Contrary to the provisions of that directive, however, the Netherlands contended that it would be impossible to restore the republican government to Jogjakarta before the conference, and, as Beel made clear, The Hague intended to go ahead with the conference with or without the republic's representatives.[66]

Washington viewed the latest Dutch overture with a great deal of skepticism. On first learning of the Beel plan, Butterworth expressed his misgivings in a conversation with Hubert A. Graves, counselor at the British Embassy. "It appeared," Butterworth pointed out, "that the Indonesians were to have little choice in the matter and that the transfer of sovereignty was to be made contingent upon certain agreements and upon Dutch terms." He emphasized, moreover, that "unless and until the Dutch took steps to carry out at least the initial requirements of the Security Council resolution," it would be difficult to enter into negotiations of a serious and binding character; "and without these there appeared to be little chance of it ever becoming operative."[67] In a discussion with British officials, Secretary of State Acheson similarly criticized the Beel plan, stressing that there appeared to be little hope of its adoption "until initial conditions of SC res were put into force." He did not believe that the Dutch offer could work until all republican political prisoners were released, so that they could negotiate with both the Dutch and the federalists without the stigma of negotiating under duress, which would unavoidably be the case if they remained, even nominally, in Dutch custody. "Under best of

[66]Netherlands to Security Council, UN S/1274; Beel to UNCI, February 26, 1949, S/AC.10/271, and memorandum from Beel, February 27, 1948, S/AC.10/271/Add.1, both in UNCI Records, UN Library; Acheson to Cochran, February 16, 1949, in *FR*, 1949, 7, pt. 1:233–35.

[67]Memorandum by Butterworth of a conversation with Graves, February 11, 1949, in *FR*, 1949, 7, pt. 1:225.

circumstances," Acheson complained, "'Beel Plan' means conditional transfer sovereignty in indefinite future whereas SC Res fixes definite date for transfer sovereignty."[68]

Dean Rusk, now assistant secretary of state for United Nations affairs, informed van Kleffens and Helb of these American reservations on February 26. The restoration of republican authority at Jogjakarta, he asserted, seemed to be a sine qua non for a just settlement and for compliance with the Security Council order. Rusk warned the Dutch representatives that the U.S. government anticipated another Dutch–republican impasse on this major point.[69]

Meanwhile, other factors were influencing Washington to take a stronger stand against the continuing Dutch defiance of the United Nations. The overwhelmingly negative response to the Beel plan within Indonesia underlined for American policy makers the bankruptcy of the Dutch position. Not only did the republican leadership, as many observers expected, refuse the Dutch invitation for a round-table conference, but the heads of the Dutch-created federal states in Indonesia rejected the Dutch offer as well. The desertion of the federalists—the backbone of the Netherlands policy in Indonesia—was a crushing blow to Dutch plans: their federal strategy had required the solid support of prominent nonrepublican Indonesians, and now that backing had dissipated, leaving the Dutch standing embarrassingly alone. "The pro-Republican attitude of the Federalists," reported the U.S. Naval attaché in Batavia, "was a rude blow to the original Dutch intention of disregarding the Republic and its leaders in forming the Interim Government." Even the federalists, he said, "consider Sukarno and Hatta to be the real nationalist leaders."[70]

The federalists' defection had undoubtedly been spurred by the mounting successes of the republican guerrillas. Throughout Java and Sumatra, the Dutch increasingly found themselves on the defensive, pressed by remarkably effective native troops.

[68]Acheson to Cochran, February 17, 1949, in ibid., p. 234. See also White House daily summary, February 17, 1949, DSR.

[69]Rusk to Cochran, February 26, 1949, in *FR*, 1949, 7, pt. 1:265–66.

[70]F. G. Dierman (naval attaché, Batavia) to CNO, January 22, 1949, Naval Attaché Reports File, WNRC; Kahin, *Nationalism and Revolution*, p. 408.

This reversal in the fortunes of the Dutch army impressed the federalist leaders; they reasoned realistically that any attempt to shape the future of the archipelago without the republic's participation would be both ill conceived and self-defeating.[71]

The State Department was equally impressed by the vigor of the republican resistance. In a conversation with Helb on March 9, Charles Reed and Charlton Ogburn observed that the paramount question in the Indonesian conflict now was whether or not the Netherlands had the military potential to establish law and order throughout Indonesia unilaterally. They maintained flatly that the Dutch were doomed to fail. By way of comparison, the American diplomats pointed to analogous conflicts raging in Indochina and Malaya. The Dutch military force in Indonesia was about the same as that of the French in Indochina, and the Dutch had a much larger territory to police; in Malaya, moreover, the British were having great difficulty trying to pacify a guerrilla force of only 3,000 to 5,000 men. Reed and Ogburn noted that three months after the inception of the police action, guerrilla activity continued unabated. In the opinion of American intelligence experts, the Netherlands would never be able to accomplish the economic rehabilitation of Indonesia; instead, they would be "bled to death" in the course of a long campaign.[72]

These developments, along with increasing criticism by congressional opponents of the Truman administration's Indonesia policy, created a crisis atmosphere in Washington. American policy makers now faced a vexing dilemma: they had already

[71]Kahin, *Nationalism and Revolution*, pp. 408–13.

[72]Memorandum by Ogburn of a conversation with Reed and Helb, March 9, 1949, 501.BC Indonesia/3-949, DSR. See also Livengood to Acheson, February 25, 1949, 856D.00/2-2549, DSR. In his memoirs, Stikker made an interesting contrast between the conflict in Indonesia and that in Malaya: "It took the United Kingdom years to achieve complete pacification in Malaya several years later. World opinion was not against them, their communications by air and sea with London were open, there were no embargoes on delivery of weapons and, finally, the territory was relatively much smaller than the three thousand islands of Indonesia, where, generally speaking, the vast majority of the population sympathized with the rebels. Small wonder, therefore, that in such completely different circumstances, our forces could not have similar success" (*Men of Responsibility*, p. 144).

placed substantial pressure on The Hague with little apparent effect; short of directly threatening Holland with a suspension of all financial assistance—a course still considered anathema in official circles—there seemed little more that Washington could do to change Dutch policy. Yet the U.S. government could not avoid the embarrassing fact that its Marshall Plan aid to the Netherlands in 1948 was almost identical to the amount of money spent by the Dutch government to sustain its military effort against the Indonesian Republic. This painful detail gained wide currency among State Department critics after the *New York Times* made it public in January.[73] Continuing American economic assistance to the Netherlands certainly seemed to belie Jessup's anti-Dutch rhetoric in the Security Council. As former vice-president Henry Wallace charged, "Marshall Plan aid has been used to maintain [Europe's] colonial system by force of arms."[74]

The strong congressional reaction to Dutch aggression in Indonesia, symbolized by the Brewster amendment, exacerbated the administration's problem. Stormy debate took place on Capitol Hill in March 1949 as both houses of Congress met to consider the proposed extension of the Marshall Plan program—and the Brewster amendment. Addressing the Senate on March 29, Senator George Aiken of Vermont drew a connection between the Indonesian crisis and the proposed Atlantic Pact. "What good would the Atlantic Pact be in promoting the safety and security of the United States," he asked, "if by winking at the Dutch actions in Indonesia we force a billion Orientals to look elsewhere for friendship and even trade?"[75] After again condemning the Dutch for their failure to maintain an open door policy toward American capital and exports, Brewster returned to the crux of the issue—America's indirect subsidy of the Dutch colonial war:

[73]*New York Times*, January 12, 1949, p. 6. See also Kahin, *Nationalism and Revolution*, p. 403.

[74]Statement by Henry A. Wallace, February 23, 1949, U.S. Congress, House Foreign Affairs Committee, *Extension of European Recovery Program: Hearings*, p. 583.

[75]Statement by Senator George Aiken, March 29, 1949, U.S. Congress, Senate, 81st Cong., 1st sess., *Congressional Record*, 95:3387.

> I think there is no question that we are actually supporting an army of 150,000 Dutch in Indonesia to suppress the Republic of Indonesia which we claim is entitled to its freedom and independence. It costs $1,000,000 a day, or approximately $350,000,000 a year. That is approximately the amount we have turned over to the Dutch during the period since the war. We have turned over to the Dutch approximately $700,000,000, close to $1,000,000,000. The $700,000,000 we have supplied has made it possible for the Dutch to maintain their forces in Indonesia carrying on a war which we say is an utterly unjust and illegal one, in defiance of the Security Council.[76]

Senator Wayne Morse of Oregon wholeheartedly concurred with his colleague's observations. "I do not see how we can escape the conclusion," Morse commented, "that to whatever extent we have been helpful to the Dutch economy under the Marshall Plan, we necessarily thereby have been helpful to the Dutch Government in carrying out its violations of what I consider to be one of the most basic principles of our pledges under the United Nations Charter, the pledge that we would seek at least to protect the interests of people in the world who sought to make a fight for freedom as we believe in freedom."[77]

Although this senatorial opposition reflected a pervasive hostility on the part of the American public to Dutch aggression in Indonesia, it is certainly worth noting that The Hague was not without its supporters in the United States. Newspapers as geographically distant as the *Worcester* (Massachusetts) *Gazette*, the *Steubenville* (Ohio) *Herald Star*, the *Birmingham* (Alabama) *News*, and the *San Diego Tribune-Sun* applauded the Dutch for taking a forthright stand against communism in Indonesia and simultaneously criticized the State Department for backing anti-Dutch resolutions in the Security Council. The *St. Louis Globe Democrat* accused the United States of "indirectly" aiding communism in Indonesia "and offending a western Europe government" whose support was crucial for the success of the European Recovery Program. "There are growing indications," observed the *New Orleans Times-Picayune*, "that the Indonesian

[76]Statement by Owen Brewster in ibid., p. 3386.
[77]Statement by Senator Wayne Morse, April 6, 1949, in ibid., pp. 4877–878.

struggle is not a simple colonial revolution, but rather has been made part and parcel of the Politburo's master plan for world domination." Dutch intervention in the East Indies, declared commentator H. V. Kaltenborn over the National Broadcasting Corporation network, "is the only thing that could make it possible for a non-communist republican regime to take effective control of Java and Sumatra." Constantine Brown, a columnist for the *Washington Evening Star,* added that the Dutch were "determined to do what some of the greater powers have been too timid to undertake, that is to eliminate the Moscow-trained subversives who aim eventually to control the East-Indies, which contain rich sources of strategic materials."[78]

Common to these Dutch supporters was a respect for the strategic natural resources of the Indonesian archipelago and a corresponding fear that the Soviet Union might eventually control them. Commentator Carroll Alcott reflected this belief in a radio address over station WINS in New York City: "If the Dutch can set up a non-Communist federation in the East Indies they'll be doing all of us a service in the long run. . . . The Far East is the greatest reservoir of raw strategic materials and manpower in the world. In the hands of the Communists and Russia those resources, organized against the West, in all probability could prove a more decisive blow against the West than a Communist-organized Europe."[79]

Louis B. Wehle, former head of the Foreign Economic Administration in the Netherlands and a tireless defender of Dutch colonial policy, concurred. In a letter to Senator Arthur Vandenberg on February 15, he warned abut the potential dangers of Communist encroachments in Indonesia: "If Russia could make a coup in Java and Sumatra and islands to the south, and maintain airfields and submarine bases there (with native oil, coal, bauxite, rubber, food-stuffs and labor), she might seal her off from participation in action in the Pacific, where the U.S. would

[78]*Worcester* (Massachusetts) *Gazette,* December 21, 1948; *Steubenville* (Ohio) *Herald Star,* December 22, 1949; *Birmingham* (Alabama) *News,* December 22, 1948; *San Diego Tribune-Sun,* December 22, 1948; *St. Louis Globe Democrat,* December 23, 1948; *New Orleans Times-Picayune,* January 7, 1949; *Washington Evening-Star,* December 28, 1948; all cited in *Holland Was Right in Indonesia* (New York: Netherlands Information Bureau, 1949), pp. 6–9, 23–24, 33, 49.

[79]Quoted in ibid., January 6, 1949, p. 52.

have to battle mostly alone to keep Russia out of the Philippines and then Alaska." Wehle expressed the belief on another occasion that "the Indies would be Soviet Russia's most precious strategic weapon for dominating the Pacific."[80]

Harry D. Gideonse, president of Brooklyn College, developed this theme further in a speech before the Chicago Council on Foreign Relations. Emphasizing the economic importance of Indonesia in world commerce, he declared: "We musn't forget that a very large part of the world's and Western Europe's rubber, palm oil, tin, tea and tobacco come from Indonesia, and that the restoration of the flow of raw materials, not to speak of the markets that you can find there in return, depends on conditions of sufficient security on the islands to warrant new capital investments." The success of the Marshall Plan, moreover, required "that there be some kind of restored order, some kind of restored productivity in those areas of the world economy from which Western Europe has drawn part of the dollar exchange with which it can continue to buy its goods from the United States." Sumner Welles and Stanley Hornbeck, both now retired from State Department service, informed Gideonse that they enthusiastically supported his viewpoint. He developed this position further at a later speech at Rutgers University. "We cannot afford to ignore the fact," he remarked, "that America's prewar exports to Europe were partially paid by American imports from Europe's dependencies in Southeast Asia and Africa. These are not merely 'colonial' problems. They are problems affecting the base of world trade as a whole."[81]

American businessmen were also deeply concerned with the possibility that Communists might take over the Indonesian

[80]Wehle to Vandenberg, February 15, 1949, Box 75, and Wehle, "Would U.N. Policy Give Indonesia Over to Soviet Rule?", unpublished article, March 17, 1949, Box 54, both in Louis B. Wehle Papers, Franklin D. Roosevelt Library, Hyde Park, N.Y.

[81]Harry D. Gideonse, *American Policy in Indonesia* (Brooklyn, 1949), pp. 9–10; Hornbeck to Wehle, February 23, 1949; Welles to Gideonse, June 10, 1949; and speech by Gideonse to 19th Annual Labor Institute at Rutgers University, June 13, 1949, all in Box 75, Wehle Papers. For a more extreme statement of this pro-Dutch point of view—and concern for the "communist" character of the republic—see speech by Colonel John V. Grombach (chief of liaison between War Department and State Department, 1942–46), April 3, 1949, in Box 92, H. Alexander Smith Papers, Princeton University Library.

nationalist movement. In a conversation with State Department representatives, H. L. Riddle of the Goodyear Tire and Rubber Company questioned the dependability of "our little brown brothers in Indonesia." Since Indonesia was probably "the key to the whole Far East," he feared that all of East Asia would be lost to the West if the United States could not keep Communists from controlling Indonesia.[82] Officials of the Standard-Vacuum Oil Company sounded similar warnings in several communications with the State Department. In a detailed memorandum Standard asserted:

> Of all the countries in the Far East, Indonesia is one of the most important, if not the most important, from the standpoint of natural resources. Its strategic location and its resources make Indonesia an attractive target for the communists. If Indonesia should come under communist influence, then Indo-China, Siam, Malaya and the Philippines will be subjected to communistic pressure from China on the North and Indonesia on the South. Under such pressure, it will be difficult to prevent these countries from falling under communist domination.[83]

Although most American policy makers disagreed with this kind of analysis, they too had a deep appreciation for Indonesia's strategic importance and were equally apprehensive about the threat of Communist advances in Southeast Asia. This concern was expressed in an in-depth reevaluation of United States policy toward Southeast Asia which the State Department prepared for the National Security Council on March 29, 1949. "It is now clear," the report pointed out, "that SEA as a region has become the target of a coordinated offensive plainly directed by the Kremlin." It stated flatly: "There can be little doubt that the Kremlin seeks ultimate control over SEA as a pawn in the struggle between the Soviet World and the Free World." Here the

[82]Memorandum by Ogburn of a conversation with H. L. Riddle (Assistant comptroller, Goodyear Tire and Rubber Company), April 4, 1949, 856D.00/4-449, DSR.

[83]Memorandum of Standard-Vacuum Oil Company to Department of State in Respect of Indonesia, enclosed in Philo W. Parker (chairman of board, Stanvac) to Jessup, September 31, 1949, 856D.00/9-1346, DSR. See also L. W. Elliott (president, Stanvac) to Acheson, August 11, 1949, 856D.00/8-1149, DSR.

assessment of NSC-51, as the document was called, diverged fundamentally from the views of those sympathetic to the Netherlands. Noting the necessity of developing "an effective counterforce to communism" in the region, the report emphasized that it was "essential that relations between SEA and the Atlantic Community be rationalized." The "heart of the problem" lay with the irrational and self-defeating policies being pursued by the Dutch and the French in Southeast Asia. "Nineteenth century imperialism is no antidote to communism in revolutionary colonial areas. It is rather an ideal culture for the breeding of the communist virus. The satisfaction of militant nationalism is the first essential requirement for resistance to Stalinism." The State Department found the Netherlands and France guilty of continuing colonial policies that were:

> (1) anti-historical in direction; (2) an economic drain on and political liability for us; (3) a vain and insupportable extravagance for the Dutch and the French; (4) a drag on the economic and military revitalization of Western Europe; (5) the greatest single immediate factor contributing to the expansion of communism in SEA; (6) the principal obstacle to the development of an effective counter-force to communism in the Far East; (7) the major cause of white-colored polarization; and (8) doomed to ultimate failure.

Contrary to the claims of the Dutch and their supporters, the State Department found the Republic of Indonesia to represent the "most virile expression" of nationalism in the archipelago. "The principal leaders of the Republic were, notwithstanding their long revolutionary ordeals, essentially men of moderation. Their anti-Stalinism was dramatically proved, while they were subjected to a Dutch blockade, by the unexcelled skill with which they liquidated the communist revolt led by the Kremlin agent Muso." The Dutch "are now and in the long run the disruptive element in the Indonesian scene." The American people "have no inclination to underwrite this Dutch imperialism" with ERP aid. "And, finally, even if we thus subsidized the Dutch and if they 'pacified' Indonesia, the so-called solution would be temporary—historical forces can be dammed-up for a time but sooner or later they burst their bounds with redoubled havoc." Accordingly, NSC-51 reasoned that American interests lay in "the creation of a sovereign Indonesian state which will satisfy the fundamental demands of militant nationalism in the archipelago." To accomplish that goal, "the earliest feasible cessation of hostilities and transfer of authority from the Dutch to the Indonesians is imperative, and will probably require additional pressure on the Dutch."[84]

The view contained in NSC-51, which by now commanded widespread support throughout the government, was reinforced by the continuing failure of the Dutch to move in any meaningful way toward a truly independent Indonesia. This continued intransigence, which by March 1949 was threatening to disrupt not only appropriations for ECA but the Atlantic Pact as well, forced yet another high-level reevaluation of U.S. policy. Finally, the State Department began to recognize, as many of its critics had long suggested, that only strong and firm pressure on The Hague by Washington, including the threat to discontinue all economic assistance, could lead to a reversal of its present Indonesian policy.

While many factors led the State Department to accept reluctantly this line of action, one appears to be crucial: that as a result of Dutch actions in Indonesia and stubborn noncompliance with UN resolutions, the very survival of the centerpiece of U.S. foreign policy, the European Recovery Program and the Atlantic Pact, was being directly threatened. The Brewster amendment, by linking developments in Indonesia with congressional action on pending European economic and defense programs, truly put the State Department in a bind. The department clearly saw that the Brewster amendment, and the general congressional opposition to administration policies in Indonesia which it symbolized, could easily lead to the defeat in Congress of ERP appropriations and the Military Assistance Program (MAP), a key component of NATO.[85] The possible defeat of MAP on account of Dutch actions in Indonesia was quite simply un-

[84]"U.S. Policy toward Southeast Asia, a Report to the National Security Council by the Secretary of State," March 29, 1949 (NSC-51), P&O 092 Asia, Planning and Operations Division Files, Modern Military Branch. NSC-51 was approved by the president on July 1, 1949.

[85]Acheson to Douglas and Harriman, March 4, 1949, in *FR*, 1949, 4:163; summaries of daily meetings with secretary, March 3 and March 15, 1949, in Box 1, Records of the Executive Secretariat, RG 59, DSR.

acceptable to the overall foreign policy priorities of the Truman administration. Accordingly, the State Department lobbied its case on Capitol Hill throughout March, only to find that the Indonesian stalemate was hanging ominously over the legislative future of the administration's European policy.[86]

Washington's European allies, especially the British, considered the Brewster amendment a serious threat to the future of the Western European defense program. If congressional displeasure with some aspect of one Western European country's foreign policy could cause the United States to refuse to sell arms to that country, then the defense of the whole continent could be endangered. As Foreign Minister Bevin explained to Acheson during a conference in Washington, this possibility raised a fundamental question: would the United States refuse arms to a country involved in a conflict of which it disapproved? The Indonesian case could establish an extremely dangerous precedent, he suggested, indicating that the United States could let an emotional public wave sweep it along to the detriment of a European army dependent on American arms. Acheson, who acknowledged that the Indonesian situation was "a cloud on the horizon," was clearly uncomfortable with Bevin's pointed questions.[87]

When Stikker met with Acheson in Washington on March 31 to discuss the future signing of the Atlantic Pact, the secretary of state decided to use the occasion to underscore American dissatisfaction with recent developments and to impress on the Dutch foreign minister the urgent need to break through the current impasse in Dutch–republican relations. Speaking candidly, Acheson described the adverse reaction of the American people and Congress to the Dutch police action. The "deep-

[86]Ernest A. Gross (acting assistant secretary of state) to Tom Connally (chairman, Senate Foreign Relations Committee), February 25, 1949, in S-833 folder, Box 1, Records of the Senate Committee on Foreign Relations, RG 46, National Archives; "Indonesia," position paper prepared by State Department for Senate Committee on Foreign Relations, undated, in S-833 folder, Box 4, ibid.; Ogburn to Rusk, March 24, 1949, in folder labeled "ECA Operations in Indonesia, 1948–1951," Box 11, PSA Records, DSR; summary of daily meeting with secretary, March 30, 1949, Box 1, Records of the Executive Secretariat, DSR.

[87]Transcript of proceedings, North Atlantic Pact discussions, April 2, 1949, Records of the Washington Exploratory Talks on Security, 1948–49, RG 353, DSR.

rooted conviction on the part of our people" that the "Dutch were wrong" and "guilty of aggression," the secretary said, "has now led to a situation which gravely jeopardizes the continuation of ECA assistance to the Netherlands." Noting the support in Congress for the Brewster amendment, he pointed out that "the basic cause for its growing support—namely, the failure of the Netherlands to reach an equitable settlement with the Indonesians—must be promptly removed." The Military Assistance Program was also endangered by congressional opposition to Dutch colonial policy. Acheson said frankly that in the absence of a settlement in Indonesia there was "no chance whatever of the Congress authorizing funds for military supplies to the Netherlands." In concluding this "forceful presentation" of the American position, the secretary told Stikker that the United States must receive "prompt tangible evidence" of the Netherlands' willingness to negotiate a just settlement with the republic; it was not just a matter of principle, Acheson observed, but a "question of hard political facts."[88]

Behind Acheson's careful words lay a threat: if the Dutch government did not immediately enter into meaningful negotiations with republican representatives, Washington would have to consider withdrawing all economic assistance to The Hague. Dutch officials understood all too well the seriousness of that warning. Since they were heavily dependent on American financial and military support, an outright rupture with the United States over the Indonesian question would have been disastrous to Holland. "Nothing made any impression upon the Dutch," one American diplomat later wrote, "until the United States made it quite clear that no Marshall Plan aid would be forthcoming until the Dutch settled with the Indonesians." In his well-chosen words: "Money talked."[89] Acheson was equally blunt on this point in his memoirs. "Withholding help and exhorting the ally or its opponent," he observed, "can be effective

[88]Memorandum by Acheson of a conversation with Stikker and van Kleffens, March 31, 1949, in *FR*, 1949, 4:258–61. See also Acheson to Cochran, April 2, 1949, in *FR*, 1949, 7, pt. 1:355–57; Acheson to Cochran, April 2, 1949, in ibid., p. 357.

[89]Howard Palfrey Jones, *Indonesia: The Possible Dream* (New York: Harcourt Brace Jovanovich), pp. 111–12.

only when the ally can do nothing without help, as was the case in Indonesia."[90]

Although in retrospect it seems clear that the conversation between Acheson and Stikker on March 31 led to a major shift in Dutch policy, it was by no means clear to American officials at the time. Indeed, they feared that the Dutch and Indonesians might once again repeat the all too familiar pattern of previous negotiations: the presentation and subsequent consideration of fairly detailed working papers, followed by the submission of counterproposals, and finally stalemate, with the Dutch proceeding with their federal strategy and the republicans appealing to the United Nations to uphold their claims. In order to avoid the repetition of that pattern, the United States kept steady pressure on the Dutch. Acheson met with Stikker again on two occasions after their March 31 meeting. On April 2 he "forcibly" expressed to the Dutch foreign minister the American hope that the Dutch "would now really set about settling this situation." He emphasized the importance of sending van Royen to Batavia "with broad instructions to do whatever was necessary to settle [the] Indonesian affair without being circumscribed with detailed or picayune conditions."[91] On April 5 he spoke with Stikker again in New York. Following Cochran's recommendations, Acheson stressed that the restoration of the republican government in Jogjakarta was essential if the Dutch were to reach a binding agreement with the republic. He also argued that Dutch troops must be withdrawn from the city and its immediate environs and that republican police must be permitted to supplement available civil police in order to maintain

[90]Dean Acheson, *Present at the Creation: My Years in the State Department* (New York: Norton, 1969), pp. 341, 857. See also Stikker, *Men of Responsibility*, pp. 145–46. The British Foreign Office also recognized the importance of American pressure. Foreign Secretary Ernest Bevin informed the State Department that he was gratefully appreciative of Acheson's intervention with Stikker, which he said had contributed so materially to the successful settlement between the Dutch and the republicans (cited in Butterworth to Acheson, May 12, 1949, 856D.00/5-1249, DSR).

[91]Rusk to Cochran, April 7, 1949, in *FR*, 1949, 7, pt. 1:362. After his meeting with Stikker on April 2, Acheson informed his top advisers that as a result of these conversations "he was very hopeful that the Dutch would really go to work and try to settle this situation" (summary of daily meeting with secretary, April 4, 1949, in Box 1, Records of the Executive Secretariat, DSR).

public order and safeguard republican officials. At the end of their conversation, Stikker indicated his agreement that the Indonesian conflict had to be settled, as "it was adversely affecting almost every important problem in Europe."[92]

On April 14 negotiations between the Dutch and the republicans reopened in Batavia, under the auspices of the United Nations Commission for Indonesia. It quickly became apparent that the key issue, as Acheson had emphasized to Stikker, would be the terms under which the republican government would be returned to Jogjakarta. The republican delegation, led by Mohammed Rum, insisted that the restoration of the republic must precede a cease-fire, while the Dutch delegation, under the chairmanship of J. H. van Royen, argued for the opposite sequence. Only the forceful intervention of Cochran prevented yet another impasse. Convinced that the Dutch at this point were sincerly committed to an independent Indonesia, the American representative urged the republic to yield on several crucial points. He drafted a compromise formula, largely based on the Dutch proposals, which Sukarno, Hatta, and the majority of the republican leaders reluctantly accepted on May 6. Significantly, Mohammed Natsir, a key member of the republican delegation and a major nationalist leader who would emerge within a year as prime minister of Indonesia, resigned in protest. On May 7 the Cochran-sponsored preliminary agreement was formally accepted by the Dutch and republican delegations.

The Rum–van Royen agreement, as it was called, represented a series of major concessions on the part of the Indonesian Republic. As a condition for the restoration of the republican government in Jogjakarta, Sukarno and Hatta gave their "personal assurances" that they would urge the republic to issue a cease-

[92]Rusk to Cochran, April 7, 1949, in *FR*, 1949, 7, pt. 1:362–64; Cochran to Rusk, April 3, 1949, in ibid., pp. 359–61. Acheson also discussed the Indonesian crisis with Bevin on April 4. "With respect to Indonesia," Acheson noted, "I recognized the situation could go to pieces. The Dutch had stupidly delayed many obvious decisions. I had urged the earliest dispatch of van Roijen to that area and had assured the Dutch that Cochran will work with them. The main thing is to get the Dutch and the Republicans talking together" (memorandum by Acheson of a conversation with Bevin and others, April 4, 1949, in *FR*, 1949, 6:51–54). See Kahin, *Nationalism and Revolution*, pp. 416–19, for an interesting analysis of the Indonesian interpretation of the Acheson-Stikker talks.

fire order, to cooperate in the restoration of peace and the maintenance of law and order, and to participate in a round-table conference at The Hague "with a view to accelerating the unconditional transfer of real and complete sovereignty to the United States of Indonesia." While the agreement called for the full restoration of republican authority in the residency of Jogjakarta, it did not call for Dutch withdrawal from any of the other areas of the republic overrun during the second police action, nor did it even mention the long-promised plebiscites in those former areas of the republic that the Dutch had seized during the first police action. In effect, the agreement legitimized Dutch conquest of those areas. Even more disappointing for the republicans, the Rum–van Royen agreement stipulated that only one-third of the representation in the proposed provisional assembly of the U.S.I. could be republican; the republic would thus be only one of fifteen states—albeit much the largest and most important—within the future U.S.I., a major victory for The Hague's vaunted federal program and a crushing setback to advocates of a unitary state.[93]

To many nationalists, the Rum–van Royen agreement represented yet another betrayal of the Indonesian revolution by civilian republican officials. This feeling was probably strongest within, although by no means confined to, the Indonesian armed forces. Convinced that it was the strength of the Indonesian resistance that had brought the Dutch back to the Batavia negotiations, republican military leaders reasoned that their hard-won gains on the battlefield had been surrendered at the conference table. "It was generally believed among educated Republicans," wrote George Kahin, "that the Roem–Van Royen Agreement had been engineered through strong American pressure on the Republican leaders."[94] In their eyes, the republi-

[93]Cochran to Acheson, April 28, 1949, in *FR*, 1949, 7, pt. 1:391–93; Cochran to Acheson, in ibid., pp. 409–10; summary record of 5th meeting of UNCI, May 7, 1949, S/AC.10/CONF.3/sr.5, UNCI Records, UN Library; Kahin, *Nationalism and Revolution*, p. 423; Taylor, *Indonesian Independence*, pp. 213–17.

[94]Kahin, *Nationalism and Revolution*, p. 426. See also Simatupang, *Report from Banaran*, pp. 99–112; John R. W. Smail, Introduction to ibid., pp. 1–6; Ali Sastroadmidjojo, *Milestones on My Journey*, ed. C. L. M. Penders (St. Lucia: University of Queensland Press, 1977), pp. 193–96; Reid, *Indonesian National Revolution*, p. 160.

can leadership was seriously discredited for once again capitulating to the Dutch and the Americans.

For their part, the republican leaders believed that the Rum–van Royen agreement was just another pragmatic compromise that brought them significantly closer to their ultimate goal: a truly independent Indonesia. Some of these leaders had feared that if they rejected the Cochran-sponsored settlement, the United States might withdraw its support. If they agreed to it, Cochran had promised them, the United States would "stand behind" the transfer of sovereignty; he had also hinted that Indonesia could then expect substantial American economic assistance in the postindependence period. In short, the adherents of diplomasi once again triumphed over the adherents of perdjuangan.[95]

By the summer of 1949 it appeared that the republic's diplomatic strategy was finally bearing fruit. On July 6, a day that is still commemorated in Indonesia, Sukarno and Hatta triumphantly returned to Jogjakarta. The ensuing celebrations, Cochran cabled Washington, were both "dignified and impressive."[96] The following day, General Sudirman, the widely respected and influential leader of the republic's armed forces and the one man who could have refused to accept the negotiated settlement and led the army back to a final struggle against the Dutch, left his guerrilla base to meet with Sukarno and Hatta in Jogjakarta. In a dramatic and highly symbolic meeting, Sudirman in effect subordinated his forces to the civilian leadership of the republic, confirming a relationship that would endure for more than a decade. On July 19 a series of conferences began in Java between representatives of the republic and representatives of the federal states (now known as the Federal Consultative Assembly, or BFO). The two delegations reached major compromises under which the federal states were ensured a strong role within the future U.S.I. and agreed, in turn, to support the republic's demand for a complete and unconditional transfer of sovereignty at the upcoming round-table conference. On August 1 the Netherlands and the republic finally agreed to a cease-

[95]Kahin, *Nationalism and Revolution*, pp. 421–26; Ali Sastroadmidjojo, *Milestones*, p. 495.

[96]Cochran to Acheson, July 7, 1949, in *FR*, 1949, 7, pt. 1:455.

fire, which was to go into effect on August 11 in Java and on August 15 in Sumatra. Shortly thereafter, the republican and BFO delegations departed for The Hague, where the round-table conference was to open on August 23.[97]

Officials in Washington, who were following these developments closely, were extremely pleased and hopeful. On the eve of the round-table conference's opening session, the State Department informed Cochran that since most of the remaining substantive issues were of concern only to the Dutch and Indonesian delegations, it would be best for the United Nations Commission for Indonesia (UNCFI) to let the parties work out an agreement between themselves. At the same time, since the United States was "vitally interested in the outcome of the controversy and the settlement reached at The Hague," Cochran and the UNCFI should stand ready to aid the two parties by presenting solutions to any problems that might arise. "The primary result of the Conference should be the establishment of a genuinely independent Indonesian state." Washington's interest lay in the stability of Southeast Asia and the development of "friendly, peace-loving and economically sound governments" there; it was equally important "that the adjustment in Indonesia be accomplished in a fashion which will not vitiate the Netherlands' position as a leading democratic nation." The fear of future Communist advances in Asia was beginning to dominate all other factors in the policy equation. "Unless an amicable settlement, allowing room for the peaceful adjustment of nationalist aspirations, is accomplished by the parties," the State Department reminded Cochran, "Southeast Asia and Indonesia will be more susceptible to Communist expansion. This hazard would constitute a major source of trouble for the U.S. and the free world."[98]

Despite the department's hopes, at least three major issues threatened to break up the conference completely. On all three of these issues—the Netherlands-Indonesian Union, the debt

[97]Smail, Introduction to Simatupang, *Report from Banaran*, pp. 3–6; Kahin, *Nationalism and Revolution*, pp. 427–31; Taylor, *Indonesian Independence*, pp. 222–26; Ide Anak Agung Gde Agung, *Twenty Years Indonesian Foreign Policy, 1945–1965* (The Hague: Mouton, 1975), p. 67.

[98]Acheson to Cochran, August 23, 1949, in *FR*, 1949, 7, pt. 1:474–78. See also memorandum for Acheson, May 11, 1949, in folder labeled "Documents Relating to the Development of US Policy," Box 12, PSA Records, DSR.

question, and West Irian (West New Guinea)—Cochran's timely and forceful intervention was crucial and almost certainly saved the conference from dissolution. The question of the proposed Netherlands-Indonesian Union arose first. T. B. Simatupang, a member of the republican delegation, aptly summarized the central dispute: "Already at the beginning of the conference, the Union had become a matter that could no longer be rejected. There remained only the question of its substance and form. We wanted a very loose Union, in the nature of a free cooperative relationship without any general, permanent organization. The Dutch were anxious to create a tight Union, providing for broad cooperation and a large permanent apparatus."[99] Although the union would consist of two sovereign and independent nations, according to the Dutch plan, the head of the federation was to be the queen of Holland, who would be not just a figurehead, as in the case of the British sovereign via-à-vis the Commonwealth, but the "head of a united nation" with considerable powers. To the republican and BFO delegations, this Dutch concept was merely "a cloak for their intention to continue their colonial rule of Indonesia."[100]

After nearly a month of debate on the issue, the Dutch and Indonesian delegations reached a deadlock. They then asked Cochran to help resolve the dispute, not as a member of the UNCFI but as a private individual—an unmistakable testament to his standing with both sides. "His authority and influence were so great," recalled one member of the republican delegation, "that agreement on all matters was achieved that same day." By synthesizing the two conflicting positions, Cochran offered the following wording as a compromise: "The Head of the Union symbolizes and personifies the voluntary and lasting cooperation between the Union Partners." His compromise proved acceptable to all three delegations; it soothed Indonesian fears that the Dutch were trying to restrict their sovereignty and offered the Netherlands the important symbolism of a permanent union headed by the queen.[101]

[99]Simatupang, *Report from Banaran*, p. 174.

[100]Sastroamidjojo, *Milestones*, p. 201.

[101]Ibid., pp. 201–3; Cochran to Acheson, September 19, 1949, in *FR*, 1949, 7, pt. 1:494–97; Cochran to Acheson, September 23, 1949, in ibid., pp. 497–98; Taylor, *Indonesian Independence*, pp. 229–32.

The intricate debt question proved even more divisive. Initially the Dutch demanded that Indonesia assume the total debt of the Netherlands East Indies, amounting to 6.1 billion guilders (approximately $1.73 billion): overseas debts of 3.1 billion guilders and internal debts of 3 billion guilders. The Indonesian delegates countered that while they were willing to assume all debts incurred before the Dutch surrender to the Japanese in March 1942, of the debts incurred after that date they would take over only those that resulted in direct benefits to the Indonesian people. Particularly odious to the Indonesians was the concept that after independence they would be responsible for all debts incurred by the Dutch army in its attempts to suppress them. According to the Indonesian delegations' calculations, the Netherlands actually owed Indonesia 540,000 guilders, a position the Dutch labeled "fantastic." On this seemingly intractable issue negotiations stalled.[102]

At this critical juncture Cochran once again seized the initiative and offered to mediate the debt problem personally. Initially the republican delegates resisted his offer. Fearing that American interest in strengthening the Dutch economy would lead Cochran to recommend a settlement unfavorable to their interests, they pressed for the full UNCFI to act as arbitrator. But both Indonesian delegations ultimately accepted Cochran's mediation offer; they were pleased by his fair settlement of the Netherlands-Indonesian Union issue and did not want to jeopardize their standing in Washington by an outright rejection of the American representative's overture.[103] Consequently, at a "top secret meeting" with members of the Dutch and Indonesian delegations in Cochran's quarters, he read them a proposed compromise settlement that he admitted "probably would not please either delegation." He was right. Cochran's compromise solution, which called for Indonesia to assume Dutch debts totaling 4.3 billion guilders (approximately $1.3 billion) was still far too high for the Indonesians. The Dutch were equally upset; in fact, the Dutch ambassador promptly registered his government's displeasure to Deputy Under Secretary of State Rusk in

[102]Taylor, *Indonesian Independence*, pp. 239–44; Sastroamidjojo, *Milestones*, pp. 203–4; Kahin, *Nationalism and Revolution*, pp. 438–40.
[103]Kahin, *Nationalism and Revolution*, pp. 441–43.

Washington, suggesting that the Dutch cabinet might be forced to resign over the issue.[104]

But Cochran was firm—and persistent. In a cable to Rusk he explained that his effort to reach a settlement was designed to make the Indonesians realize that they could not completely wipe out debts arising from the police actions and other causes that did not benefit the Indonesian people, and at the same time to impress on the Dutch that it was in their own interests to conclude a financial settlement with Indonesia that did not impair its sovereignty and would "be politically acceptable and so fair as to afford USI [a] reasonable chance to succeed." Unless the Netherlands was soon willing to accept a "realistic arrangement" on the debt question, the conference would be "hopelessly deadlocked"; and if the conference did break down, he warned, military activities could well resume in Indonesia. Sovereignty would probably pass to the Indonesians by January 1, whatever the results of the round-table conference. Accordingly, Cochran suggested, if the Dutch truly desired to have sovereignty transferred within the Netherlands-Indonesian Union, they "should treat [the] Indonesians as partners and not seek [to] tie them up like bad debtors and deprive them [of] support essential to live."[105]

Cochran's views eventually prevailed. At a climactic meeting on October 24, the Dutch and Indonesian delegations accepted the compromise plan, which Cochran insisted was "fair and technically sound."[106] Neither side was pleased with the compromise; indeed, one republican delegate later suggested that it was only "pressure tactics" by Cochran that led the Dutch and Indonesian delegations to accept his plan.[107] The debt settlement, moreover, papered over serious differences between the Dutch and the Indonesians which would haunt relations between the two countries after independence. Nevertheless, by preventing a dissolution of the conference, Cochran's intervention accomplished its chief goal.

[104]Cochran to Acheson, October 8, 1949, in *FR*, 1949, 7, pt. 1:505–9; Acting Secretary of State James Webb to Cochran, October 8, 1949, in ibid., pp. 511–12.
[105]Cochran to Rusk, in ibid., pp. 512–15.
[106]Cochran to Acheson, October 23, 1949, in ibid., pp. 546–47.
[107]Ali Sastroamidjojo, *Milestones*, p. 205.

The one remaining barrier to a successful conclusion of the round-table conference—the future status of West Irian—proved to be the most difficult of all to resolve. Long before the conference convened, the Dutch and the Indonesians had articulated their widely divergent views on West Irian. The Indonesians, pointing to the fact that the island had traditionally been part of the Netherlands East Indies, insisted that it must be part of any independent Indonesian state; they pointed out that the Linggadjati and Renville agreements had stipulated that sovereignty was to be transferred over the entire territory of the Dutch East Indies. The Dutch, advancing a combination of religious, economic, ethnological, and sociological arguments, claimed that West New Guinea (as they called it) had no essential ties with the other areas of Indonesia and was so underdeveloped that it should retain a special relationship with the Netherlands.

The issue was an extremely emotional one. To the Dutch, the retention of West Irian would probably certify their continuing role as a Pacific power. To a nation of nine million people, on the verge of surrendering control over a vast archipelago with a population estimated at approximately 80 million, such psychological factors cannot be underestimated. Many Dutch leaders feared that the loss of Indonesia would reduce the Netherlands to the status of "a Denmark." To the Indonesians, however, continued Dutch rule in West Irian would be an insult. "We could not accept the idea," recalled one republican delegate, "that one portion of our homeland would be separate from it, even if only temporarily."[108] On October 29 the Dutch and Indonesian delegations reached a predictable deadlock on this question. Once again it seemed that the conference might end in failure.[109]

Cochran informed the State Department that unless a compromise solution to the West Irian problem were found quickly, the conference would surely break down. On October 31 he

[108]Simatupang, *Report from Banaran*, p. 180.

[109]Taylor, *Indonesian Independence*, pp. 235–39. On the background of the West Irian dispute, see especially Robert C. Bone, Jr., *The Dynamics of the Western New Guinea (Irian Barat) Problem* (Ithaca: Cornell University Modern Indonesia Project, 1958); Arend Lijphart, *The Trauma of Decolonization: The Dutch and West New Guinea* (New Haven: Yale University Press, 1966).

drafted and submitted for consideration to both parties a proposal that called for the Netherlands to maintain control of West Irian, with the stipulation that within a year after the transfer of sovereignty the future status of the island would be determined through negotiations between the Netherlands and Indonesia.[110] Cochran, who had earlier assured Dutch officials privately that he supported their claims to West Irian, urged Indonesian representatives to accept his recommendation. He pleaded with them not to let the round-table conference collapse over this issue. "I pictured great results Indonesians were achieving and future ahead," he cabled Washington. "I said [I] could make no promise what decision on New Guinea might be year from now but felt they should go home with success now gained and depend on later negotiations for determination New Guinea."[111] The BFO delegation, which took an even more staunchly nationalistic view on West Irian than the republican delegation, accepted Cochran's compromise only with the greatest reluctance. Unwilling to accept responsibility for a breakdown of the conference, however, both Indonesian delegations conceded to Cochran's compromise formula. His timely intervention had once again staved off defeat. Once again, however, serious problems were postponed rather than resolved. On returning to Batavia, one BFO delegate commented prophetically that "by the exclusion of Irian Barat from the transfer of sovereignty, in fact, the projected Dutch-Indonesian Union is a stillborn child."[112]

The round-table conference closed on November 2. Although it left some major nagging problems—the Dutch-Indonesian Union, the debt settlement, and West Irian—the conference achieved its overarching goal. The deliberations at The Hague had paved the way for a complete and unconditional transfer of sovereignty to an independent Indonesian state. The transfer was formalized at joint ceremonies in Amsterdam and Djakarta on December 27, 1949. Finally, Indonesia became a sovereign, independent nation.

[110]Cochran to Acheson, October 30, 1949, in *FR*, 1949, 7, pt. 1:550–54; Cochran to Acheson, October 31, 1949, in ibid., pp. 554–58.

[111]Cochran to Acheson, October 31, 1949, in ibid., pp. 554–55.

[112]Anak Agung, *Twenty Years Indonesian Foreign Policy*, p. 70.

9

The United States and Indonesian Independence

Unquestionably, the United States played a major role in helping the Indonesians to secure independence from the Dutch. American support was a sine qua non for the continuance of The Hague's presence in the archipelago; once that support was withdrawn, the Dutch position became untenable. To infer, however, that American policy toward the Indonesian revolution was motivated by a historic opposition to colonialism would grossly misrepresent the American record in the East Indies during the immediate postwar years. On the contrary, throughout the four bitter years of Dutch–republican conflict, American authorities continually sided with the Netherlands, believing that the support of a European ally was more dependable and more useful than that of a group of untested Asian nationalists. Only after the second Dutch police action did American policy makers begin to shift their allegiance. And even then Washington moved haltingly and often reluctantly, motivated not by some altruistic attachment to the hallowed principles of self-determination, but by more tangible factors: the weight of domestic and international opinion, concern for the viability of the United Nations, and the strength of a vigorous Indonesian guerrilla movement that thwarted all Dutch efforts to pacify the islands and exposed The Hague's policy as an abject failure. It was only then, when the Dutch themselves appeared to be the greatest threat to stability and order in Indonesia, and in the process endangered appropriations for the Marshall Plan and the passage of the Atlantic Pact, that the United States placed its power and prestige behind the republican nationalists.

Despite the avowed principles of the Atlantic Charter and the Charter of the United Nations, then, and despite the repeated pronouncements of Roosevelt and administration spokesmen throughout World War II, the United States never pursued an anticolonial policy toward the Netherlands East Indies. American attachment to the principles of self-determination remained rhetorical; such sentiments were never translated into substantive policy. The retreat from these anticolonial statements began at least as early as 1944 and can best be explained by the confluence of several developments.

First, postwar planning anticipated the need for close cooperation with the European nations, the major imperial powers. Active encouragement of native self-rule would have interjected a potentially inflammatory issue into American-European relations, thereby threatening this fundamental American policy consideration. Winston Churchill, the unofficial spokesman for the imperial powers, expressed his unalterable opposition to American meddling in colonial affairs on several occasions, and American leaders, mindful of the need for harmonious postwar relations, chose not to press the issue. In addition, the War and Navy departments, intent on securing American bases in the Pacific, overrode all State Department proposals for a comprehensive international trusteeship program.

Finally, and most significant, American authorities never equated the principles of anticolonialism and self-determination with support for the early and dramatic independence of all colonized peoples. On the contrary, American policy makers unanimously clung to the view that the dependent areas of the world would be prepared to act as responsible members of the global family of nations only after an appropriate period of preparation under the guidance of their respective European mother countries. American sponsorship of independence for the Philippines was constantly pointed to as an appropriate precedent. Native self-government for most other dependencies was a distant goal, in the view of American officials, not an immediate prospect. The American devotion to self-determination, then, was sharply limited; Washington favored gradual, evolutionary changes in what it believed to be a hopelessly outdated imperial system. It certainly did not favor or anticipate revolutionary upheaval.

This is not to deny, however, that American policy makers were motivated by a sincere desire to reform the colonial structure. Indeed, traditional American ideals in this regard neatly dovetailed with tangible material interests. U.S. leaders viewed the European imperial order as an anachronism that not only thwarted legitimate native aspirations for ultimate self-rule but also denied American business equal access to the rich markets and raw materials of the underdeveloped areas of the world. Convinced that such barriers to free trade were injurious not only to American commercial interests but to international peace and stability as well, officials in Washington eagerly sought to transform what they considered to be the most objectionable aspects of traditional colonialism.

Woodrow Wilson pursued similar objectives in the period immediately following World War I. An ardent internationalist and firm believer in free trade, Wilson also tried to liberalize the prevailing colonial structure by eliminating all obstacles to the natural flow of international commerce. At the Versailles Peace Conference he struggled to have these principles incorporated in the proposed League of Nations mandate system. In Wilson's view, such a program would extend liberal American values and institutions to backward peoples while at the same time opening up hitherto closed areas of the globe to American commerce. Wilson's approach, while visionary, was essentially a gradual, evolutionary one. He did not envision a radical transformation or restructuring of the imperial system; rather, he favored a slow reform of that system under the progressive guidance of the League of Nations. Most significant, Wilson never questioned the hierarchic relationship between the advanced, industrial nations and the underdeveloped world. While strenuously objecting to the more exploitive aspects of European imperialism, he never challenged the assumption that Western hegemony was essential to world stability and order. Indeed, he consistently argued the need for continued Western control and guidance over the backward areas of the globe. In short, his vision was of a more progressive, less exploitive imperialism; his squabble with the European powers was over the form of their dominance rather than its substance.[1]

[1]N. Gordon Levin, *Woodrow Wilson and World Politics* (New York: Oxford University Press, 1968), pp. 236–37, 246–51.

There is a remarkable degree of continuity between the Wilson administration and the Roosevelt administration on the colonial question. Both presidents viewed traditional imperialism as atavistic; both fervently believed that American economic interests could best be served by a liberalization of the prevailing colonial structure. Both were convinced that the peaceful penetration of American commerce, ideas, and institutions into the underdeveloped world would be a boon not only to the narrow economic interests of the United States, but also to the material and spiritual progress of the colonized peoples—and to the larger goal of global peace and stability. Like Wilson, Roosevelt was dedicated to the principles of self-determination but defined it very narrowly. Both men believed that colonial self-rule was inevitable, but that it was a development for the future, not the present. Both believed that liberalization of the colonial system should be carried out under Western dominance. In short, both Wilson and Roosevelt were convinced that traditional imperialism was outdated and in need of reform, but they complained more about the form of the imperial system than about its substance. And, perhaps most important of all, they viewed the threat of revolutionary upheaval as an even greater danger than imperialism to the interests of the United States and the world community.

During the Roosevelt administration, staunch opposition from the European powers blocked the development of a comprehensive plan to deal with the colonial problem. Since administration officials considered harmonious relations with Western Europe to be an overriding policy objective, anticolonialist sentiment was sharply tempered, although never completely abandoned. U.S. policy makers continued to cling to the notion that they could use their nation's enormous power and prestige to effect a liberalization of the imperialist order. While notably short on specifics, this strategy envisioned gently nudging the European allies into accepting the inevitability of native self-rule and beginning to develop, accordingly, concrete plans to prepare native elites for that ultimate responsibility. The example of the Philippines was often heralded as an appropriate model for the European mother countries to emulate.

American policy toward the Netherlands East Indies can be understood within this larger context. Toward the end of the war, American diplomats had repeatedly reassured Dutch officials that the United States did not question their right to reassert sovereignty over the Indonesian archipelago. At the same time, those diplomats hoped that Dutch imperialism could be liberalized so as to eliminate its most exclusionary and exploitive features. The need to cooperate with The Hague in postwar Europe, however, effectively blunted this reforming zeal and prevented the State Department from translating such vague sentiments into substantive policy. The emergence of a broad-based nationalist movement in Indonesia, capped by the proclamation of the Republic of Indonesia on August 17, 1945, further complicated the American dilemma. Unwilling to countenance support for an untested and inexperienced nationalist regime, especially one under the fiery leadership of a Japanese collaborator such as Sukarno, Washington gravitated more and more toward the Dutch position. After all, American officials had advocated the reform of the imperialist system, not its destruction; they had pressed for gradual, evolutionary changes, not abrupt, revolutionary ones. Washington had always assumed that European influence and control, while limited, would and should continue in the underdeveloped world. By challenging the reassertion of Western hegemony, Asian nationalists were thus threatening the very foundation of American plans for a new order in the Far East.

Given the perspective of 1945, it is difficult to imagine the United States pursuing a different policy. The Dutch were trusted allies who had ruled the East Indies for over three hundred years. While the United States had traditionally objected to the excesses of the imperialist system, it also recognized and applauded the stability and order that the colonial powers had brought to the underdeveloped world. Faced with a choice between a native government of revolutionary nationalists and a return to Dutch control over the archipelago, the United States not surprisingly chose to support the Netherlands.

Nevertheless, the United States could not completely disavow its identification with the cause of the colonized peoples of the world. To do so would have been inconsistent with traditional American beliefs and would have contradicted proclamations made throughout the war; active support for the reimposition of imperial rule, moreover, would have seriously damaged American prestige in the underdeveloped world. The United States sought to sidestep this dilemma by maintaining a position of public neutrality and strict noninvolvement toward all colonial disputes. The resulting policy was distorted and contradictory: while declaring its strict impartiality toward the growing rift between the Dutch and the Indonesians, Washington consistently bolstered the position of its European ally. As Stanley Hornbeck astutely observed, "We in effect attempted to support neither side and yet favored one and hoped not unduly to offend the other."[2]

An early indication of this attitude was revealed in the American government's stance toward the question of lend-lease supplies. Washington continued to supply surplus property credits and lend-lease equipment to British and Dutch troops in Indonesia long after it had proclaimed its neutrality toward the Dutch–Indonesian dispute, and even though it was well aware that the material was being used to suppress Indonesian nationalists. After Sukarno delivered several strongly worded protests to the White House in October and November 1945, the Truman administration ordered the removal of all American insignia from the equipment; the equipment itself continued to be freely supplied.

Official American sympathy for the Dutch position was most strikingly revealed by the form that Washington's neutrality took. By recognizing the Netherlands' right to rule Indonesia as the "territorial sovereign," as it did in its policy statement of December 19, 1945, the United States in effect denied the Indonesian Republic's quest for status as an equal party to the dispute. This was a severe blow to the young nationalist regime, which had hoped that America's repeated wartime pronouncements in favor of self-determination for all peoples might be translated into an aggressive anti-imperialist program. Although the American message was couched in the niceties of international law, its intent was unmistakable: the United States would not challenge the right of the Dutch to reestablish their

[2]Stanley K. Hornbeck, "The United States and the Netherlands East Indies," *Annals of the American Academy of Political and Social Science*, 255 (January 1948):132–33.

imperial control over the islands. American diplomats might try to nudge the Dutch gently into pursuing a more liberal approach to the colonial issue—one that would perhaps grant certain concessions to Indonesian nationalism—but the republic could expect no significant moral or material aid from Washington. When Sukarno appealed to the United States to assume the role of an impartial arbitrator, his request was summarily rejected, since, as Secretary of State James Byrnes explained, such a request could be honored only if it came from the "territorial sovereign." Indonesian leaders quickly learned that American neutrality had a distinctly nonneutral flavor.

By the end of 1945, then, the United States was pursuing a policy that represented a virtual repudiation of the anticolonial ideals expressed in the Atlantic Charter and the Charter of the United Nations. Rather than challenge the reimposition of the Dutch colonial structure, the Truman administration consciously acquiesced in it. The dominant viewpoint within the State Department and throughout the government was that the need for Western solidarity obviated any secondary interest in mounting a crusade to reform European colonialism.

At first Washington sought to achieve this objective by remaining neutral and uninvolved, but this was hardly a viable policy option for the world's leading power. As one National Security Council study so aptly put it, "Evasion of major international issues is a real possibility for Costa Rica; for the U.S. it is an illusion. Our silence is as loud as our words."[3] In addition, Indonesia was simply too strategically and economically valuable for the United States to remain a passive observer, especially when the dispute threatened to escalate into all-out warfare. Gradually, then, the United States began to exert its considerable influence on the Dutch and the republicans, first through unilateral pressure and later through the United Nations. Officially the United States position toward the Dutch–Indonesian struggle remained one of nominal neutrality, and American participation on the Good Offices Committee helped to bolster Washington's image as an impartial and even-handed mediator.

[3]"U.S. Policy toward Southeast Asia" (NSC-51), March 29, 1949, Modern Military Branch, National Archives.

In actuality, though, American actions consistently violated this surface neutrality. American policies and statements at the United Nations and mediation efforts on the GOC repeatedly worked to the advantage of the Dutch, as most interested observers quickly realized. When Marshall Plan aid began to flow to the Netherlands in 1948, moreover, the United States was placed in the anomalous position of serving on a United Nations commission as a nominally impartial arbitrator when in fact its financial assistance was at least indirectly making Holland's aggressive policy financially feasible. In short, Washington was helping to settle a dispute it was actually financing.

Its pro-Dutch orientation remained dominant until the early months of 1949. The rehabilitation and reintegration of Western Europe and the corresponding desire to present a solid front against the Soviet Union led the United States to support The Hague's position in Indonesia. American support was not uncritical, of course; Washington strongly advised the Dutch against resorting to military force before both police actions and continually urged the Netherlands to reach an equitable settlement with the Indonesian nationalists. It was pressure from Washington, in fact, that led the Netherlands reluctantly to accept the Renville settlement. But the United States never pushed the Dutch too far; it was extremely careful to maintain friendly relations with its European ally. The success of the Truman Doctrine, the European Recovery Program, and NATO necessitated the steadfast support of the European nations, including, of course, the Netherlands. The intensification of the Cold War during these years underscored this need. American officials, moreover, viewed Indonesia as an adjunct to the metropolitan country; it would contribute to the economic health of the Netherlands, which in turn would contribute to the economic health of Western Europe. The Marshall Plan, consequently, assumed that the European imperial powers would resume their former positions in Southeast Asia. As Lovett reminded Graham in January 1948:

> Netherlands is [a] strong proponent [of] US policy in Europe. Dept believes that [the] stability [of the] present Dutch Govt would be seriously undermined if Netherlands fails to retain very consider-

> able stake in NEI, and that [the] political consequences of failure [of] present Dutch Govt would in all likelihood be prejudicial to US position in Western Europe. Accordingly, Dept unfavorable to any solution requiring immediate and complete withdrawal Netherlands from Indies or any important part thereof.[4]

In the wake of the second Dutch police action, American policy changed drastically. The nearly universal denunciation of The Hague's militancy by the international community merged with similar sentiment in the American public and Congress to bring the issue to a head. Events within Indonesia, moreover, exposed Dutch policy as hopelessly flawed: republican guerrilla troops fought the Dutch army to a standstill, while the Dutch-sponsored Indonesian federalist leaders summarily abandoned the Netherlands. NSC-51 then helped to crystallize long-run American objectives in Southeast Asia, pointing out that "nineteenth century imperialism," as practiced by the Dutch, was simply "no antidote to communism in the revolutionary colonial areas." Dutch efforts to pacify the archipelago, the report added, were doomed to failure and were an economic drain on the United States and the European Recovery Program. Given the fact that the republic was "moderate" in character and had already demonstrated its staunch opposition to communism, NSC-51 recommended that the United States unequivocally support independence for Indonesia; it was a gamble, surely, but at that juncture it seemed the only viable policy. "The sympathetic encouragement of Asiatic nationalism is bound to be a rough passage," the report concluded,

> but it is the only channel lying between polarization and Stalinization. It is only by following this difficult course that we can hope to facilitate—in collaboration with like-minded nations—the development of an effective counter-force to communism in the Far East leading eventually to the emergence of SEA as an integral part of the free world, contributing spontaneously and fully to our welfare and security.[5]

[4]Lovett to Graham, December 31, 1947, in *Foreign Relations of the United States* (Washington, D.C., 1972), 6:1099–1100.

[5]"U.S. Policy toward Southeast Asia."

It was primarily European rather than Asian considerations, however, that proved to be the prime factor in the American decision to pressure the Dutch into granting independence to the Indonesians. As a result of Dutch intransigence in Indonesia, Congress placed substantial pressure on the Truman administration to move in that direction by threatening to cut off funds to the European Recovery Program and to hold up passage of the Atlantic Pact. Those programs, which lay at the heart of the administration's Cold War strategy, were far too important to be jeopardized by a colonial war in Indonesia—a conflict that to most senior American policy makers was an annoying sideshow.

Given the thrust of American foreign relations in the postwar period, perhaps the chief significance of this American support for Indonesian independence lies in its singularity. Admittedly, American support came rather late—only after the Dutch had twice violated internationally sanctioned agreements—but the salient fact is that it did come; the United States did align itself with a national liberation movement against a friendly European imperial power. Significantly, at the same time that the United States was applauding the transfer of sovereignty to native nationalists in Indonesia, it was opposing a similar struggle for independence in nearby Indochina, and was already considering plans to underwrite the French colonial war in that embattled land.

There are of course some extremely significant differences between the Indonesia and Indochina cases. Unlike the Indonesian independence movement, the Vietnamese nationalist movement was led from its very inception by Communists. Captive of a Cold War ideology that viewed all local Communists as part of a monolithic Communist movement directed by Moscow, American policy makers never seriously considered support for Ho Chi Minh and his followers. In Indonesia the elusive "third force" of moderate nationalism that Washington sought to create in Indochina already existed; it had proved its mettle, moreover, by suppressing the PKI during the ill-fated Madiun rebellion. As early as 1945, Indonesia's nationalist leaders recognized that their bid for independence could best be ensured through cooperation with the West; accordingly, they consistently tried to present an image of a responsible, moderate regime interested in Western assistance and intent on protecting foreign investment.

Another key difference between the decolonization struggles in Indonesia and Indochina was that the Indonesian conflict was internationalized after the first police action. United Nations involvement made it virtually impossible for the Dutch to present the world with a fait accompli. And the United States, which sincerely hoped that the United Nations would not suffer the fate of the League of Nations, viewed the Indonesian case as an early test of that body's viability. France could use its Security Council veto to block any United Nations consideration of its colonial difficulties. Vietnam's international support, in addition, was always much weaker than Indonesia's. India and Australia consistently placed their prestige on the side of the young republic, and as a predominantly Muslim land Indonesia had vigorous support among the emerging Muslim nations of Asia, Africa, and the Middle East. Eager to maintain its leverage and prestige with those newly emerging areas, Washington had to weigh that factor in its policy deliberations. In contrast, U.S. policy toward Indochina could be formulated without concern for strong outside pressure.

A final factor affecting American policy toward the two colonial struggles was the relative power and internal stability of France and the Netherlands. While Dutch support for the Marshall Plan and the Atlantic Pact was always deemed extremely important by American policy makers, all agreed that French support was absolutely crucial. Without French support, the Truman administration's European policy would have collapsed; and to endanger such support by meddling in French colonial affairs would have been the height of diplomatic folly in the view of senior administration policy makers. The French Communist Party, moreover, would surely have gained great political capital from any "imperialist" intervention by Washington, a fact that was clearly recognized by American officials. In addition, the stability of France itself during the late 1940s was a constant source of concern for American diplomats; any outside pressure by the United States on an issue as sensitive as colonial policy in Indochina would have placed great strain on the

French government and possibly led to Communist participation in the cabinet. Dutch postwar governments, on the other hand, were seen as largely reliable and relatively stable, and Communist strength within Holland was negligible.[6]

The important and dramatic differences between Washington's response to postwar nationalism in Indonesia and Indochina should not obscure some equally significant similarities. Although the United States eventually supported the Indonesian Republic and played a major role in persuading the Dutch to withdraw from their prized colony, the support came only very slowly and reluctantly. Moreover, it was tied less to a deep understanding of the transforming dynamic of Asian nationalism than to global geopolitical considerations stemming from America's Cold War struggle with the Soviet Union. Indeed, the tumultuous nature of the postindependence relationship between Washington and Djakarta amply attests to the fact that American understanding of Indonesian nationalism remained quite limited and shallow.

The inability of American policy makers to come to grips with Indonesian nationalism points to a larger failure of American policy in Asia during the postwar period. While the tragic intervention in Indochina and the attempted isolation of China for over two decades are more obvious manifestations of this general failure, the case of Indonesia is equally reflective. Washington's ill-conceived attempts to align Indonesia with the West through a mutual security agreement and then through a Pacific defense pact, its insensitivity to the emotional appeal of the West Irian issue, its exaggerated concern for Dutch interests in Indonesia, its serious miscalculation of the internal and external Communist threat, its misunderstanding of Sukarno's appeal to the Indonesian people, its callousness toward Indonesian "neutralist" sensibilities, and finally, its outright intervention in Indonesia's civil war of 1958—all are symptomatic of a deeper

[6]For a comparison of American policy toward Indonesia and Indochina during these years, see Evelyn Colbert, "The Road Not Taken: Decolonization and Independence in Indonesia and Indochina," *Foreign Affairs*, 51 (April 1973): 608–28. On American policy toward Indochina, see Gary R. Hess, "The First American Commitment in Indochina: The Acceptance of the 'Bao Dai Solution,' 1950," *Diplomatic History*, 4 (Fall 1978):331–50.

problem: the failure of American officials to comprehend that nationalism, not communism, was the most dynamic force in Indonesia and throughout Asia during the second half of the twentieth century. Indeed, American policy toward Indonesia and much of the Third World during the postwar era has been characterized by a pervasive reluctance to accept Third World countries on their own terms. The United States has instead consistently subordinated the interests and concerns of developing countries and the importance of local and regional developments to a larger geopolitical strategy that has generally filtered all events through the prism of American–Soviet relations. As in Indonesia during the 1940s, Third World countries have more often than not been viewed by American officials as little more than pawns in the global struggle between Washington and Moscow.

Epilogue: The United States and Indonesia, 1949–65

As Indonesia moved into the postindependence period, diplomatic relations with Washington appeared to be based on a firm foundation. Grateful for American support during the latter phase of their independence struggle, Indonesian leaders were on the whole quite favorably disposed toward the United States. This tendency was reinforced by their need for American military and economic assistance as well as by their generally vehement antipathy toward communism. To be sure, Indonesia, like India and Burma, was determined to pursue an independent or neutral foreign policy in an effort to avoid being drawn into the orbit of either of the two major power blocs. Nonetheless, to most informed observers it was clear that Djakarta would move closer and closer to Washington. President Sukarno aptly explained his nation's position during a conversation with Cochran. "He referred to America as the mother," the newly appointed ambassador noted, "and the new young Asiatic countries as grown sons who looked to their mother with affection and understanding but who did not wish her to interfere with the running of their own lives."[1]

American policy makers were careful not to interfere with the most important internal movement within the new nation: the

[1]Memorandum by Jessup of a conversation with Cochran and Sukarno, February 3, 1950, in *Foreign Relations of the United States* (Washington, D.C., 1976), 6:976. Hereafter volumes in this series will be cited as *FR*, followed by the year.

effort to destroy the Dutch-sponsored federal system. Convinced that their revolution would not be complete until the unitary state proclaimed in August 1945 had been established, many Indonesian nationalists, almost immediately after independence, began to agitate against the alien-imposed federal structure. One by one, the federal states voted to dissolve themselves and join the republic. Within eight months the movement was complete; on August 17, 1950, a unitary Republic of Indonesia was proclaimed. In the face of strong protests by the Dutch government, Cochran urged Washington to view this development with patience and understanding. He and other American officials agreed that the young nation's internal structure was far less important to the United States than its international orientation.[2]

Indeed, the United States was hopeful that Indonesia would soon realize that its true national interests lay in alignment with the West. American officials, keenly aware of the archipelago's strategic and economic value in any future conflict with the Soviet Union, believed that strong pro-Western leadership in Indonesia would have a salutary effect on the other states of Southeast Asia. On January 9, 1950, Secretary of State Acheson spelled out these concerns in a memorandum for President Truman. "Because of the dynamic character of [Indonesia's] Nationalist movement," he wrote, "because of its great wealth and because it is the second largest Moslem country in the world, its political orientation has [a] profound effect upon the political orientation of the rest of Asia." With the Communist threat to the Asian mainland increasing, "the importance of keeping Indonesia in the anti-Communist camp is of greater and greater importance. The loss of Indonesia to the Communists would deprive the United States of an area of the highest political, economic and strategic importance."[3]

For these reasons, the United States quickly moved to shore up the new government by providing it with desperately

[2]Cochran to Acheson, April 3, 1950, in ibid., 1000–1005. On the unitary movement, see George McTurnan Kahin, *Nationalism and Revolution in Indonesia* (Ithaca: Cornell University Press, 1952), pp. 446–69.

[3]Memorandum from Acheson to Truman, January 9, 1950, in *FR*, 1950, 6:964–66.

needed economic, technical, and military assistance. On January 9 Truman approved the provision of $5 million in military aid to the Indonesian constabulary in order to help maintain Indonesia's internal security "against communist encroachment." The following month the Export-Import Bank announced that it had agreed to lend Indonesia $100 million to finance the purchase of capital goods in the United States for the reconstruction of its economy. In April a mission headed by R. Allen Griffin arrived in Indonesia to survey the new nation's needs for technical assistance under the Point IV program. Later in the year the United States dispatched a military survey mission to Indonesia to review Djakarta's defense needs.[4]

Despite these hopeful beginnings, underlying problems continued to plague United States–Indonesian relations. Indeed, many of the problems of the postindependence years closely resembled those that plagued American relations with the Indonesian Republic during the years of revolutionary struggle against the Dutch. The inability of the United States to appreciate the depth of Indonesian nationalism, the tendency to view all local and regional developments within the context of a global geopolitical strategy aimed at containing communism and the Soviet Union, the gross exaggeration of the Communist threat to Indonesia, both internal and external, and the effort to balance Indonesian interests with Dutch interests—all were critical elements affecting American policy toward Indonesia throughout the 1950s and early 1960s.

The outbreak of the Korean War in June 1950 had a great impact on United States–Indonesian relations. As the fighting in Korea continued, American officials became more than ever convinced that there could be no compromise with communism, and that there could be no room for neutrality in the worldwide struggle between the United States and the Soviet Union. The Department of State informed Cochran in July 1950 that Indonesia simply had to choose between the Soviet Union and the "free world," a theme that it emphasized continually. In early 1951 American officials even sounded out Indonesian leaders on the possibility of entering into a Pacific defense pact with the United

[4]Ibid., pp. 914ff.

States and the other noncommunist nations of Asia.[5] But these efforts, no matter how well intentioned from Washington's perspective, were anathema to a young government struggling to maintain its independence of action. To Indonesian officials, Washington's thinly disguised efforts to align Djakarta with the West struck at the very heart of the republic's nationalist ideology. In October 1950 Indonesia informed the United States that it could not accept any military assistance under the Mutual Defense Assistance Program, as such acceptance of aid would tend to be interpreted by the Communist countries as "having taken sides."[6] Although some American officials were reasonably sensitive to Indonesia's interest in maintaining an independent foreign policy, most U.S. diplomats viewed Indonesians as hopelessly naive to the Soviet threat. The Chinese move into Korea was part of an "overall Soviet plan to control Asia," Cochran patiently explained to Sukarno on one occasion, and a resolute defense against communism on the continent of Asia was "vital if Indonesia itself [was] to be spared."[7]

America's failure to appreciate the depth of Indonesian nationalist sentiment in the immediate postindependence years is well illustrated by two cases: the abortive Cochran-Subardjo agreement of January 1952 and the continuing Dutch–Indonesian struggle over the future disposition of West Irian. Between December 1951 and February 1952 the United States tried unsuccessfully to conclude an economic and military assistance agreement with Indonesia under the terms of the Mutual Security Act of 1951. Pleased with the strong pro-American, anticommunist orientation of Prime Minister Sukiman and Foreign Minister Subardjo, and buoyed by Indonesia's support for the Japanese peace treaty, the State Department believed that Indonesia was finally ready to align itself unequivocally with the West. Cochran and the State Department hoped to accomplish this objective, at least in part, through a mutual security pact. Their timing, however, could not have been worse. Many of Indone-

[5]Acheson to Cochran, July 26, 1950, in ibid., p. 1040; Cochran to William J. Sebald (political adviser to General MacArthur), January 31, 1951, *FR*, 1951, 6, pt. 1:142–43; Cochran to Acheson, February 3, 1951, in ibid., pp. 145–47.

[6]Cochran to Acheson, October 10, 1950, in *FR*, 1950, 6:1078–80.

[7]Cochran to Acheson, December 8, 1950, in ibid., p. 1098.

sia's major political figures, already uncomfortable with Sukiman's pro-Western foreign policy, interpreted the proposed Cochran-Subardjo agreement as a direct threat to Indonesia's vaunted independent foreign policy; although their complaints were probably far more symbolic than substantive, they were convinced that the agreement violated fundamental nationalist values. As a result of this ill-timed American initiative, the Sukiman cabinet fell in February 1952. This incident would serve as a forceful reminder to future Indonesian cabinets of the risks inherent in identifying themselves too closely with Washington.[8]

The inability of American officials to understand Indonesia's virtual obsession with West Irian proved to be an even more serious obstacle to the development of a close relationship between Washington and Djakarta during this period. According to the terms of the round-table agreement, the Dutch and the Indonesians were to hold discussions within a year after the transfer of sovereignty to determine the future disposition of the area. Those discussions quickly bogged down, however, as the Dutch showed no inclination to relinquish control over West Irian. Sukarno saw the continuing Dutch presence there as an insult to his nation and held that the Indonesian revolution would not be complete until West Irian became part of the Indonesian state, a view that was endorsed by nearly all major Indonesian leaders. The Dutch were equally emotional on the West Irian issue; they continued to cling to this one remaining vestige of their colonial empire in Southeast Asia, probably more for psychological reasons than for economic and political ones. Once again the United States found itself in the middle, with both sides actively courting its support. Eager to establish a close relationship with Djakarta and yet unwilling to offend a loyal NATO ally on such an emotionally charged issue, Washington opted for a position of strict neutrality. Many times Sukarno implored American leaders to support Indonesia's claim to West Irian, insisting that only one word from Washington was needed to bring Indonesia closer to the United States, but to no avail. The dispute, which was not settled until 1962, remained

[8] *FR*, 1951, 6, pt. 1:729ff.; Herbert Feith, *The Decline of Constitutional Democracy in Indonesia* (Ithaca: Cornell University Press, 1962), pp. 198–207.

one of the most important issues dividing the United States and Indonesia during the 1950s.[9]

Serious differences between Washington and Djakarta over West Irian and other matters grew steadily throughout the 1950s. One of the prime reasons for this growing estrangement was the Eisenhower administration's intolerance of Indonesia's self-styled "active and independent" foreign policy. Indonesia's neutralism directly clashed with Secretary of State John Foster Dulles' strategy of forming regional defense pacts as a means of solidifying the pro-American, anticommunist forces around the globe. Indonesia opposed the formation of the Southeast Asia Treaty Organization (SEATO) in 1954; and, almost as a countermove, President Sukarno and Prime Minister Ali Sastroamidjojo assembled a conference of the Afro-Asian nations at Bandung the following year. Coming at the height of the Cold War, the Bandung initiative was viewed with extreme displeasure in Washington; much as the New Delhi Conference did six years earlier, the Bandung Conference raised the specter of an Afro-Asian bloc of nonaligned nations. From Dulles' perspective, this was indeed a dangerous development. For him there was no room for neutrality in the global struggle against communism; by advocating neutralism, he was convinced, such Third World leaders as Sukarno were just dupes of Moscow. In a celebrated speech in 1956, Dulles sanctimoniously labeled neutralism "immoral," a remark that infuriated Indonesians.[10]

Another major cause of strain during these years was Sukarno's increasing reliance on Soviet aid and his tolerance of the Indonesian Communist Party, whose strength and influence in-

[9]See, for example, Cochran to Acheson, March 23, 1950, in *FR*, 1950, 6:989–90; Cochran to Acheson, October 26, 1950, in ibid., p. 1091; note, in *FR*, 1951, 6, pt. 1:746. On the importance of the West New Guinea issue in United States–Indonesian relations, see especially the works by former American ambassadors in Indonesia Howard P. Jones and John M. Allison: Allison, *Ambassador from the Prairie or Allison Wonderland* (Boston: Houghton Mifflin, 1973), pp. 297–344; Jones, *Indonesia: The Possible Dream* (New York: Harcourt Brace Jovanovich, 1971), pp. 174–82.

[10]*U.S. Department of State Bulletin*, 34 (June 18, 1956):999; ibid., 35 (July 23, 1956):147; Ali Sastroamidjojo, *Milestones on My Journey*, ed. C. L. M. Penders (St. Lucia: University of Queensland Press, 1977), pp. 236–37, 280; Ide Anak Agung Gde Agung, *Twenty Years Indonesian Foreign Policy, 1945–1965* (The Hague: Mouton, 1973), p. 375.

creased exponentially during the 1950s. Dwight D. Eisenhower invited Sukarno to visit Washington in mid-1956 in an effort both to stem Indonesia's seeming move toward the left and to establish a closer relationship with the man who once again was beginning to dominate Indonesian politics. Initially American officials viewed the trip as a rousing success, but when Sukarno followed his American visit with long stops in Moscow and Peking, their enthusiasm receded. Shortly thereafter Sukarno announced his plan to establish a system of "guided democracy" in Indonesia, a plan that Dulles later equated with Communist-style dictatorship. At the same time, the continuing electoral successes of the PKI exacerbated American uncertainty about Indonesia's future orientation.[11]

By mid-1956 American policy toward Indonesia was dominated by one overarching concern: to prevent a Communist takeover of Indonesia. But by reducing complicated Indonesian internal developments to a simple Cold War formula, American policy makers almost totally misread the dramatic events that were shaking Indonesian society to its very roots. When a long-simmering regionalist rebellion led to outright civil war in early 1958, the United States foolishly chose to give covert support to the dissidents in Sumatra and Sulawesi in the apparent hope that the rebels in the outer islands would serve as an effective counter to the Communists, whose stronghold was on the main island of Java. As a result of this ill-conceived intervention, the United States not only got caught supporting the losing side but managed to alienate nationalists of all political hues with what was generally seen as a heavy-handed neo-colonial adventure. The capture of Allan Pope, a CIA pilot who was flying bomber missions for the rebels, along with the capture of large caches of American weapons in rebel territory, exposed the American role.[12] "The general opinion in Indonesia," recalled former In-

[11]Jones, *Indonesia*, pp. 233–35; Anak Agung, *Twenty Years Indonesian Foreign Policy*, pp. 369–70. On the growth and strength of the Indonesian Communist Party, see especially Donald Hindley, *The Communist Party of Indonesia, 1951–1963* (Berkeley: University of California Press, 1964); Rex Mortimer, *Indonesian Communism under Sukarno: Ideology and Politics, 1959–1965* (Ithaca: Cornell University Press, 1974).

[12]Although a full account of the CIA's role during the so-called Colonels' Revolt of 1958 has never been revealed, numerous memoirs and secondary

donesian foreign minister Anak Agung, "was unanimous that the CIA had a hand in the rebellion"; this suspicion "was to linger on for a long time and was the main cause of further deterioration in Indonesia–US relations, despite the effort of the US government to bring some improvement."[13]

In the aftermath of its disastrous intervention in Indonesia's civil war, the Eisenhower administration tried desperately, and with some limited success, to repair its relations with Djakarta. Following the advice of newly appointed ambassador Howard P. Jones, Washington initiated a program of military assistance to the Indonesian armed forces in mid-1958. The rationale for the program was that the Indonesian military was strongly anticommunist and, partly as a result of its impressive victory during the rebellion, had emerged as a rival center of power. The United States hoped that it could bolster the position of the military as a counterforce to Sukarno and the PKI; the orientation of the all-important Indonesian Army, headed by the influential and vigorously anticommunist major general A. H. Nasution, was a key to this strategy. Jones predicted that an eventual clash between the army and the PKI was virtually inevitable.[14]

This new policy direction, while infinitely more farsighted than the previous one, met with little immediate success. West Irian remained a major stumbling block, as the United States refused to depart from its neutral position, which amounted to nothing less than support for the status quo—that is, continued Dutch control. American support for the Indonesian military, moreover, was cautiously limited. When Nasution visited Washington in October 1960, American officials informed him

---

accounts allude to the operation; see especially David Wise and Thomas B. Ross, *The Invisible Government* (New York: Random House, 1964), pp. 136–46; Roger Hilsman, *To Move a Nation: The Politics of Foreign Policy in the Administration of John F. Kennedy* (New York: Delta, 1967), pp. 363, 369; Ray Cline, *Secrets, Spies, and Scholars* (Washington: Acropolis, 1966), pp. 181–83; Arthur M. Schlesinger, Jr., *Robert Kennedy and his Times* (Boston: Houghton Mifflin, 1978), pp. 490–92; Anak Agung, *Twenty Years Indonesian Foreign Policy*, pp. 380–81; Joseph Burkholder Smith, *Portrait of a Cold Warrior* (New York: Putnam, 1976), pp. 225–48.

[13]Anak Agung, *Twenty Years Indonesian Policy*, pp. 380–81.

[14]Jones, *Indonesia*, pp. 147–56.

that they could simply not meet his considerable arms requests. The Soviets were more generous. In January 1961 he traveled to Moscow and signed a major arms agreement with the Soviet Union, a development that deeply disturbed American officials. They feared that the Indonesians might use this new Soviet equipment, as Sukarno had repeatedly warned, in an effort to liberate West Irian from Dutch rule.[15]

The seemingly intractable West Irian dispute as well as the general deterioration in United States–Indonesian relations were among the numerous foreign policy problems inherited by President John F. Kennedy. Surrounded by advisers who were sympathetic to the aspirations of Asian and African nationalists, Kennedy promised that his administration would pursue new directions in its relations with the Third World. One area of particular concern was Indonesia, where an outright clash between Indonesian and Dutch troops over West Irian appeared increasingly likely. Convinced that such a clash would seriously affect American interests in Southeast Asia, and equally certain that the decade-old West Irian dispute was only increasing the appeal of the PKI within Indonesia, the Kennedy administration rejected the long-held American position of neutrality; Indonesian sovereignty, it believed, was not only inevitable but in the long-term interest of the United States. In February 1962 the president dispatched his brother, Attorney General Robert F. Kennedy, to Indonesia and the Netherlands for discussions with officials of both countries. As a result of his trip, both parties agreed once again to try negotiations. A month later the talks opened in Middleburg, Virginia, outside Washington, with veteran American diplomat Ellsworth Bunker acting as mediator. On August 15, 1962, an agreement was finally reached: Indonesia would acquire administrative control over West Irian by May 1, 1963, with a plebiscite to be conducted no later than 1969, under United Nations supervision, to let the 700,000 native Papuans choose between continued Indonesian rule and independence.[16]

[15]Ibid., pp. 189–90; Hilsman, *To Move a Nation*, p. 372; Guy J. Pauker, "General Nasution's Mission to Moscow," *Asian Survey*, 1 (March 1961):13–22.

[16]Hilsman, *To Move a Nation*, pp. 361–80; Schlesinger, *Robert Kennedy and His Times*, pp. 613–16; Jones, *Indonesia*, pp. 202–14. For a detailed analysis of the

That American diplomatic support for Indonesia's claim to West Irian did not usher in a new era of friendly relations between the two countries was a keen disappointment to the Kennedy administration. Roger Hilsman, assistant secretary of state for Far Eastern affairs during the Kennedy years, suggested that the initiative simply came too late to bear much fruit. The PKI and the Soviet aid programs were far too entrenched by 1962. A complicated triangular relationship between Sukarno, the army, and the Indonesian Communist Party, moreover, was well developed by that time, and Sukarno probably believed that he could turn away from the PKI only at his peril. He considered the party's support essential in order to balance the powerful army; the PKI, in addition, was a key source of domestic support for Sukarno's "guided democracy."[17]

Kennedy had hoped that after the West Irian settlement the United States could move forward with desperately needed economic assistance and financial stabilization programs in Indonesia, but those hopes were quickly dashed as the mercurial Sukarno turned his attention to another external issue: the creation of Malaysia. Sukarno's violent opposition to the British-sponsored Federation of Malaysia, consisting of Malaya, Singapore, and the British crown colonies of North Borneo, effectively thwarted the proposed American aid program to Indonesia. As his "crush Malaysia" campaign intensified throughout 1963, relations between Washington and Djakarta steadily deteriorated. Just before his fateful trip to Dallas, President Kennedy had approved a recommendation that he visit Indonesia in an effort to turn Sukarno away from his confrontation policy and toward peaceful cooperation with the West; an assassin's bullet, however, destroyed the initiative.[18]

Kennedy administration's policy toward Indonesia, see Frederick P. Bunnell, "The Kennedy Initiatives in Indonesia, 1962–1963," Ph. D. dissertation, Cornell University, 1969.

[17]Hilsman, *To Move a Nation*, pp. 400–402; Anak Agung, *Twenty Years Indonesian Foreign Policy*, pp. 397–400. On the triangular relationship of Sukarno, the army, and the PKI, see Herbert Feith, "Dynamics of Guided Democracy," in Ruth T. McVey, ed., *Indonesia* (New Haven: Human Relations Area Files, 1963), pp. 309–409.

[18]Jones, *Indonesia*, pp. 262–98; Hilsman, *To Move a Nation*, pp. 382–407. For a detailed account of Indonesia's dispute with Malaysia, see J. A. C. Mackie,

Under the new president, Lyndon B. Johnson, American–Indonesian relations reached their lowest ebb. Abandoning the previous administration's policy, the Johnson administration offered its unequivocal support for Malaysia in its war of words with Indonesia. In July 1964 Johnson met with Malaysian Prime Minister Tunku Abdul Rahman and in a joint communiqué pledged American military support for the new Malaysian Federation. The American Congress, moreover, aroused by Sukarno's confrontation with Malaysia and his increasingly anti-American tone, voted to suspend all American aid to Indonesia. Sukarno's reaction was predictable. On March 25, 1964, in the presence of Ambassador Howard P. Jones, he delivered a passionate speech in which he told the United States to "go to hell with your aid." During his Independence Day speech on August 17 of that year he delivered another ringing diatribe against the United States, once again telling America to "go to hell." Anti-American demonstrations erupted throughout Indonesia in 1964; in Djakarta and Surabaya, angry mobs attacked U.S. Information Service libraries. The United States subsequently withdrew its Peace Corps program from Indonesia. Sukarno stepped up his rhetorical assaults on the United States; in 1965 he even withdrew Indonesia from the United Nations. The downward spiral in U.S.–Indonesian relations appeared to have no end, certainly not while Sukarno remained in power.[19]

A new era in U.S.–Indonesian relations opened in 1965, when the army crushed an attempted coup led by elements of the Indonesian Communist Party. Although Sukarno's precise role during the so-called Gestapu was ambiguous, the attempted coup seriously discredited him. Under the firm leadership of General Suharto, the army gradually began to strip the aging revolutionary hero of his power. American officials watched with undisguised glee as their former nemesis was replaced by staunch anticommunist Suharto and the army-sponsored slaughter of hundreds of thousands of leftists was carried to its

---

Konfrontasi: The Indonesia-Malaysia Dispute, 1963–1966 (London: Oxford University Press, 1974).

[19]Hilsman, *To Move a Nation*, pp. 407–9; Jones, *Indonesia*, pp. 301–29, 342–51; Anak Agung, *Twenty Years Indonesian Foreign Policy*, pp. 400–406.

bloody conclusion. To the Johnson administration, engaged in a steadily escalating conflict against communism in Vietnam, the ruthless purge of communists in Indonesia was an unmixed blessing. Washington, moreover, quickly discovered that the new rulers in Djakarta shared its passion for economic development and regional stability. Out of the chaos and destruction, a new relationship between the two nations was forged.

Bibliography of Archive Collections

Dag Hammarskjold Library, United Nations, New York
  Records of the Good Offices Committee, 1947–49
  Records of the United Nations Commission for Indonesia, 1949
Hoover Institution on War, Revolution, and Peace, Stanford, California
  Stanley K. Hornbeck Papers
Library of Congress, Washington, D.C.
  Philip C. Jessup Papers
  William D. Leahy Diary
Douglas MacArthur Memorial Archives, Norfolk, Virginia
  Douglas MacArthur Papers
National Archives, Washington, D.C.
  Records of the Department of State
  Modern Military Records
  Records of the Senate Foreign Relations Committee
Princeton University Library, Princeton, New Jersey
  H. Alexander Smith Papers
  Bernard Baruch Papers
Public Record Office, London
  Records of the British Foreign Office
  Cabinet Records
  Prime Ministers' Records
Franklin D. Roosevelt Library
  Franklin D. Roosevelt Papers
  Louis B. Wehle Papers
Harry S. Truman Library, Independence, Missouri
  European Recovery Program Interviews
  Harry Price Oral History Interviews
  Harry S. Truman Papers

University of North Carolina Library, Chapel Hill, North Carolina
Frank P. Graham Papers
Southern Oral History Collection
Washington National Records Center, Suitland, Maryland
Army Intelligence Document File
Records of the Foreign Economic Administration
Southeast Asia Command War Diaries
Washington Navy Yard, Washington, D.C.
Naval Operational Archives
Yale University Library, New Haven, Connecticut
Henry L. Stimson Diary

INDEX

Colonialism and Cold War

Designed by Richard E. Rosenbaum.
Composed by Eastern Graphics
in 10 point Linotron 202 Palatino, 2 points leaded,
with display lines in Palatino.
Printed offset by Thomson/Shore, Inc. on
Warren's Number 66 Antique Offset, 50 pound basis.
Bound by John H. Dekker & Sons, Inc.
in Joanna book cloth
and stamped in Kurz-Hastings foil.

Library of Congress Cataloging in Publication Data

McMahon, Robert J., 1949–
Colonialism and cold war.

Bibliography: p.
Includes index.
1. United States—Foreign relations—Indonesia. 2. Indonesia—Foreign relations—United States. 3. Indonesia—Politics and government—1942–1949. 4. United States—Foreign relations—1945–1953. I. Title.
E183.8.I5M35 327.730598 81-66648
ISBN 0-8014-1388-5 AACR2

ST. JOHN FISHER COLLEGE LIBRARY
E183.8.I5 M35
McMahon, Robert J., 010101 000
Colonialism and cold war : The
0 1219 0066713 4